Letters in Exile

Letters in Exile

Transnational Journeys of a Harlem Renaissance Writer

CLAUDE MCKAY

Edited by

BROOKS E. HEFNER

and

GARY EDWARD HOLCOMB

Yale UNIVERSITY PRESS/NEW HAVEN & LONDON

Published with assistance from the Kingsley Trust Association Publication Fund established by the Scroll and Key Society of Yale College and with assistance from the Mary Cady Tew Memorial Fund.

Designed by Mary Valencia
Set in Adobe Garamond Pro type by Westchester Publishing Services.
Printed in the United States of America.

Library of Congress Control Number: 2024950359
ISBN 978-0-300-27647-3 (hardcover)

A catalogue record for this book is available from the British Library.

Authorized Representative in the EU: Easy Access System Europe, Mustamäe tee 50, 10621 Tallinn, Estonia, gpsr.requests@easproject.com

10 9 8 7 6 5 4 3 2 1

He had grown accustomed to a vagabond way of life and love.
And it was hard for him to wrench himself away from that.

—*Romance in Marseille* (ca. 1933, published 2020)

Do you of the exile dream?

—"The Spanish Needle" (1920)

CONTENTS

A NOTE ON THE TEXT

Curiously paralleling the author's wide-ranging existence, Claude McKay's letters are scattered over two dozen archives across the globe, from Houston to Moscow, from Ontario to Atlanta, and from New Haven to Martinique. This edition, covering McKay's correspondence from 1916 through his early 1934 return to the United States, draws on twenty-eight different archival collections, most of them in the papers of McKay's many correspondents. The provenance of each letter is indicated after the document with an abbreviation keyed to the list in "Abbreviations for the Archival Locations of McKay's Correspondence." It's clear from the work of Wayne F. Cooper that many McKay letters from this period were kept in private collections; as we have been unable to access these (beyond transcriptions produced by Cooper for *The Passion of Claude McKay*), our collection focuses on those in publicly accessible archives. We have not included every bit of correspondence from this period; such a collection would be significantly larger. In making editorial decisions, we cut letters that duplicated information, letters of a purely transactional nature (IOUs, simple requests for advances or loans), and business correspondence for the *Liberator* (soliciting or responding to manuscript submissions).

In transcribing the letters, we have provided three-letter conventions to identify the letter's typography, format, and closing. For example, a piece of correspondence marked "TLS" would be a typed letter signed by McKay, while "APS" would mean a handwritten postcard signed by McKay.

A = autograph (handwritten)	L = letter	S = signed
T = typed	G = telegram	U = unsigned
	P = postcard	

McKay and his agent, William A. Bradley, often corresponded through Paris's pneumatic post system, though these exchanges were mostly transactional. Only one appears here, identified as a telegram, with a parenthetical note. In addition, we have attempted to identify the location from which McKay composed each bit of correspondence, allowing the reader to track McKay's movements across Europe and North Africa. Pinpointing McKay's exact location can be difficult at times. McKay generally received his mail through the offices of the British tourism company Thomas Cook & Son, and often used Cook offices in different cities for his return address, especially when making short trips away from a larger home base. When not using a Cook office to receive mail, McKay often had his correspondents write him "poste restante," or general delivery, and retrieved his mail (sometimes with difficulty) at the post office. We have not indicated these details in our indication of his location, though McKay does occasionally mention them in the text of his letters. When McKay used letterhead—indicating his residence in a particular hotel or his appropriation of paper from a particular establishment—we have noted this as well.

McKay's access to a typewriter was sporadic and dependent on his financial situation, and the quality of his handwriting could vary wildly. When he was without a typewriter and was writing to authority figures, he could be detailed and produce elegant and readable handwritten correspondence. More often, however, he was rushed, sick, emotional, or undernourished. In these cases, his handwriting could become a scrawl. In a 1 August 1927 letter to Harold Jackman, he admits as much in a slangy metaphor: "I hope you scan my fist all right. It's not so good since I started to typewrite." We have made every effort to decipher McKay's writing, but in some cases, we were unable to determine with any confidence individual words in his handwritten correspondence. These indecipherable spots have been indicated in brackets.

We have sought to remain as true to McKay's informal prose as possible, while trying not to create a distracting experience for the reader. As a result, we have retained McKay's curious and inconsistent misspellings, punctuation, and capitalization in this edition. For example, McKay used several different abbreviations for manuscript (ms, m.s., ms.); these appear here as they did in his writing. Educated in the British colonial system, McKay used single quotation marks (or inverted commas) to offset titles and quotations—especially in his earlier letters—but seemed to prefer double quotations after spending more time in the United States; we found that these choices interestingly reflected McKay's complex experience and kept the inconsistencies.

McKay also indicated titles of books and other publications—from novels and books like *Home to Harlem* and *The New Negro* to publications like the *Crisis* or the *Liberator*—in several different ways: he most commonly put titles in quotation marks, but he occasionally underlined them, and sometimes did no more than capitalize the title with no additional punctuation. At times McKay used French spellings (especially for place-names like Tanger, Alger, and Japon), and other times he used British spellings (words like "sceptical" or Marseilles), though he was not always consistent in either case. Given his international experience and his multilingual existence, we retained his inconsistency but did not mark these non-American English spellings with "[*sic*]." In general, McKay's facility with languages other than English was weak, though he regularly tried to introduce terms in French, Spanish, and Arabic, often in error. In a 7 May 1933 letter to Schomburg, for example, he proudly states, "I have picked up a few words of your beautiful native language and so if ever we do meet I shall be able to ask como usted?" Because his errors are unusual, interesting, and difficult to address in a consistent fashion, we have retained them. The same is true of diacritical marks in these languages and other punctuation in general. For errors and issues that we regarded as confusing, we have attempted to clarify with as little intrusion as possible.

McKay's correspondence also features additional stylistic tics that can be surprisingly consistent. This includes a fascinating approach to compound words, in which McKay routinely splits words normally combined (for example, any way, every thing, some one, worth while) and combines words generally split (for example, allright, anymore, everytime). These have not been marked with "[*sic*]." We also did not include "[*sic*]" with respect to the spelling of the name of Max Eastman's wife, Eliena, which McKay consistently struggled with in his letters. Other inconsistencies in the spelling of proper names (for example, Du Bois/DuBois/Dubois and Countee/Countée/Counteé) have also been preserved. In addition, we avoided noting when McKay ended a question with a period rather than a question mark. Otherwise, we have preserved errors and noted them with "[*sic*]," because they may shed light on McKay's state (harried, hungry, desperate, or distracted) while composing the letters. In cases where McKay's use of the typewriter has produced obvious typographical errors (running words together, erroneously inserting a space, transposing letters, or misstriking a key), we have silently corrected these.

The included "Glossary of Names" lists McKay's correspondents in bold with relevant information, including their importance with respect to points

McKay is making. The glossary also lists the many names he mentions, also with germane facts. Typically, we have reserved glossary entries for individuals mentioned more than once, or individuals with special significance in McKay's correspondence. In the case of passing references in the text, we have included footnotes identifying names and other information needed to understand the context for McKay's remarks; these names mentioned in passing do not appear in the glossary.

The reader should occasionally expect to encounter letters with demeaning language about women and people of diverse national and ethnic identities. While he spent a good deal of his life in solidarity with oppressed groups, McKay was not immune to some of the more pervasive and troubling prejudices of his era. When met with personal and professional affronts—a betrayal of confidence or a bad review—McKay could resort to antisemitic or misogynistic slurs. And, curiously, although he could be frank about his own queer sexuality, he occasionally resorted to derogatory language (in English, Spanish, and French) to characterize those whom he saw as not conforming to generally conventional presentations of masculinity or femininity. Part of what makes McKay's correspondence so thought-provoking is his lively and uncensored communication—he rarely shied away from presenting strong opinions, even if those included broad and unfair cultural generalities. This means that he could self-consciously meditate on the value of obscene expressions but also deploy them in ways that reflect both conscious and unconscious biases. A complete picture of McKay unquestionably must take into account his full complexity.

ABBREVIATIONS FOR THE ARCHIVAL LOCATIONS OF MCKAY'S CORRESPONDENCE

AASP Arturo Alfonso Schomburg Papers, Schomburg Center for Research in Black Culture, New York Public Library

ALP Alain Locke Papers, Moorland-Spingarn Research Center, Howard University, Washington, D.C.

CCP Countée Cullen Papers, Amistad Research Center, Tulane University, New Orleans

CKOF C. K. Ogden Fonds, Archives and Research Collections, McMaster University, Hamilton, Ontario

CMCA Claude McKay Collection, Additions, Schomburg Center for Research in Black Culture, New York Public Library

CMLM Claude McKay Letters and Manuscripts, Schomburg Center for Research in Black Culture, New York Public Library

CMP Claude McKay Papers, Beinecke Rare Book and Manuscript Library, Yale University, New Haven

HBC Harper & Brothers (and Successors) Correspondence, 1923–1954, Franklin D. Roosevelt Presidential Library and Museum, Hyde Park, New York

HCBA Henri Cartier-Bresson Archive, Fondation Henri Cartier-Bresson, Paris

HHHP Hubert H. Harrison Papers, Rare Book and Manuscript Library, Columbia University, New York

HLMP H. L. Mencken Papers, Manuscripts and Archives Division, New York Public Library

JESPH Joel Elias Spingarn Papers, Moorland-Spingarn Research Center, Howard University, Washington, D.C.

JESPN	Joel E. Spingarn Papers, Manuscripts and Archives Division, New York Public Library
JFP	Joseph Freeman Papers, Hoover Institution Library and Archives, Stanford University, California
JHP	Josephine Herbst Papers, Beinecke Rare Book and Manuscript Library, Yale University, New Haven
JTP	Jean Toomer Papers, Beinecke Rare Book and Manuscript Library, Yale University, New Haven
JWJP	James Weldon Johnson and Grace Nail Johnson Papers, Beinecke Rare Book and Manuscript Library, Yale University, New Haven
LBP	Louise Bryant Papers, Manuscripts and Archives, Yale University, New Haven
LHP	Langston Hughes Papers, Beinecke Rare Book and Manuscript Library, Yale University, New Haven
MEP	Max Eastman Papers, Lilly Library, Indiana University, Bloomington
NAACPR	National Association for the Advancement of Colored People Records, Library of Congress, Washington, D.C.
NCC	Nancy Cunard Collection, Harry Ransom Center, University of Texas, Austin
NIA	*The Negroes in America,* edited by Alan L. McLeod and translated by Robert J. Winter (Port Washington, N.Y.: Kennikat Press, 1979)
PCM	*The Passion of Claude McKay: Selected Poetry and Prose, 1912–1948,* edited by Wayne F. Cooper (New York: Schocken, 1973)
PN	Papiers Nardal, Archives Territoriales de Martinique, Collectivité Territoriale de Martinique
RGALI	Russian State Archive of Literature and Art, Moscow
WABLAR	William A. Bradley Literary Agency Records, Harry Ransom Center, University of Texas, Austin
WEBDP	W. E. B. Du Bois Papers, Special Collections and University Archives, University of Massachusetts Amherst Libraries
WSBP	William Stanley Braithwaite Papers, Houghton Library, Harvard University, Cambridge, Mass.

Letters in Exile

Introduction

Black modernist author Claude McKay's letters in exile, composed between 1916 and 1934, capture the Harlem Renaissance's emergence and heyday followed by, as the Great Depression took its toll, the New Negro vogue's decline. While his work became a critical flashpoint of the Black cultural awakening, McKay was absent from Harlem during its most vibrant years, traveling and writing from across the Soviet Union, Europe, and North Africa. Fortunately for the contemporary reader, the émigré writer was an avid letter writer, creating an abundant archive of his ongoing dialogue with the world. McKay produced not only most of his published work but also his most significant correspondence while sojourning in—to name but a few of the cultural capitals he memorialized in verse—London, Berlin, Moscow, Paris, Marseille, Barcelona, and Tangier. McKay relied on the international mail to report on the progress of his literary projects, analyze the social and political order of the world, explore the culture of his present location, critique the work of his contemporaries, flirt with those he was fond of, reproach those who roused his ire, and gossip with and about friends, acquaintances, and adversaries. And, when the funds for his travels dwindled, to implore his correspondents for assistance.

The list of luminaries with whom McKay corresponded, and with whom he was most candid, includes American socialist intellectual Max Eastman, bohemian leftist Louise Bryant, proletarian novelist Josephine Herbst, New Negro bard Langston Hughes, poet and diplomat James Weldon Johnson, literary agent William A. Bradley, and bibliophile Arturo Alfonso Schomburg. He also carried on periodic dialogues with critic and tastemaker H. L. Mencken, editor and publisher Eugene Saxton, British heiress and activist Nancy Cunard, benefactor Charlotte Osgood Mason, and progressive scholar Joel E. Spingarn.

Along with Hughes, Johnson, and Schomburg, McKay's most notable Black correspondents of the 1920s and 1930s included Pan-Africanist philosopher W. E. B. Du Bois, Pan-African leader Marcus Garvey, Harlem Renaissance "philosophical midwife"[1] Alain Locke, literary modernist Jean Toomer, literary critic William Stanley Braithwaite, sociologist Charles S. Johnson, NAACP activist Walter White, journalist James Ivy, and poet Countee Cullen's stylish educator companion, Harold Jackman. The letters denote McKay's acquaintance with such Harlem Renaissance figures as Jessie Fauset, Richard B. Moore, Eric Walrond, and *Fire!!* generation figures Wallace Thurman and Gwendolyn Bennett. They also show his affiliation with Manhattan bohemians and Paris expatriate artists and writers like Sinclair Lewis, Carl Van Vechten, Berenice Abbott, Frank Harris, and Edna St. Vincent Millay. As he traveled, McKay thirsted for an exchange of ideas and experiences with the intellectuals and artists he could not see in person, and so he wrote letters with frequency and hunger. His letters from exile stand, in conversation with his creative yield, among the most significant testimonies to Black transnationalism, queer culture, leftist thought, and Black modernist literary culture that we have today.

Indeed, as momentous as McKay's poetry and fiction are, it's tempting to see his letters as the most important piece of his literary legacy. His pioneering biographer, Wayne F. Cooper, noted as much in a landmark 1973 collection of the Harlem Renaissance author's work: "Of all McKay's unpublished material, his letters are by far the most important, from both a literary and historical point of view. He was an excellent letter writer, and necessity forced him to write many. A complete edition of his letters should someday reveal one of the great stories in Negro American literary history."[2] At the very least, McKay's letters in exile are an essential companion to his most revolutionary writings, from the groundbreaking poetry he produced after he left Jamaica through his trailblazing novels and short fiction and into his extraordinary memoirs and journalism. McKay's correspondence displays the arc of the author's evolving aesthetic, from his meditations on classicism versus modernism and his restless need to move forward to his denunciation of the idea, despite the radical fury of some of his sonnets, that Negro art must serve social objectives.

Over fifty years after Cooper made his assertion, McKay's correspondence is finally in print. In many respects, McKay was far ahead of his time. His frank and tender depictions of queer sexuality are a case in point, contributing to the rejection of his early 1930s manuscript *Romance in Marseille* (which appeared posthumously in 2020). McKay's 1929 novel *Banjo* depicted and theorized Black diasporic spaces twenty years before the phrase "African diaspora" entered the critical discourse. His interest in the intersections of race and leftist politics anticipate debates of the 1930s, the 1960s, and the 2000s. And his more radical poetry echoes across the history of white supremacist violence in the United States, from his own time to ours. His famous sonnet "If We Must Die" (1919) was quoted in Shaka King's 2021 *Judas and the Black Messiah,* a Black Lives Matter–era film about the 1969 murder of Black Panthers organizer Fred Hampton. It is no surprise that his work has been rediscovered, and two of his previously unpublished novel manuscripts have been made available, alongside several biographies.[3] We find ourselves now in a McKay moment, in which the Black transnational author's intersectional experience and literature have received new life—perhaps a moment, too, when McKay's pioneering aesthetic can be more fully appreciated because we have finally caught up to his vision.

Claude McKay's Exile Years

In a 7 December 1929 letter to Max Eastman, probably written in Madrid, McKay expresses his disappointment that, through a series of mix-ups, he's missed a Paris reunion with his old friend. McKay writes, "From knowledge + experience you know so much, I am sure a talk with you would have done me lots and lots of good. I'll have to wait until I come 'home' next year." McKay repeats this tentative term, enclosed in quotation marks, again in the same letter, employing it again in several 1933 letters to Eastman posted from Tangier. Tired of political persecution and surveillance in what he called the "international wasps' nest" of Tangier, McKay wrote on 20 October 1933, "I feel better all over with the idea of <u>a voyage</u> and <u>going</u> '<u>home</u>.'" By "home," McKay meant America, that is, New York, and even more specifically, Harlem. Still, his use of quotation marks accentuates the haziness of the idea to him as well as its centrality to his thinking. This was the peripatetic author, after all, of *Home to Harlem* (1928) and *A Long Way from Home* (1937), his travel book/memoir written several years after he had been forced to return from Europe to Harlem.

As our title signifies, this collection frames McKay's correspondence, 1916 to 1934, on the theme of exile. McKay states repeatedly that being an outsider to national and cultural ideologies played a key role in his vision of creating a revolutionary Black art. We have limited our focus to McKay's exile period letters, in other words, not only because these years frame the Harlem Renaissance's onset to sunset but also because the Black author generated his most revolutionary writing while inhabiting the state of exile—to use the term he titled for himself, residing and writing "a long way from home."

McKay first referred to himself as an "exile" at the beginning of the New Negro movement, several years after his departure from Jamaica. Addressing a native Jamaican plant, the deracinated West Indian speaker of "The Spanish Needle" (1920) queries, "Do you of the exile dream?" Initially published in 1920 in the *Cambridge Magazine,* while McKay was living in England, and later included in *Spring in New Hampshire* (1920) and *Harlem Shadows* (1922), "The Spanish Needle" is a testament to McKay's rootlessness and status as a Jamaican exile in the United States and England. His sonnet "The Tropics in New York" (1920), following the same publishing steps (*Cambridge Magazine* and the two poetry collections), is another example of a post-Jamaica poem that reinforces the author's feelings of exile. As the West Indian migrant stands before a Manhattan shop window teeming with the bounties of the Caribbean islands, "A wave of longing through my body swept, / And hungry for the old, familiar ways / I turned aside and bowed my head and wept."[4]

McKay resumed the exile theme a decade later, at the waning of the Harlem Renaissance, toward the end of his long period of dwelling in Europe and North Africa. The reader of his letters should note the title of his 1928 novel, *Home to Harlem.* He could not have imagined on launching his sojourn in the Soviet Union and residences in Western Europe and North Africa that he was embarking on over a decade of open-ended exile. When he first considered returning to the United States in 1928, his thoughts were far from that of homecoming. For practical and professional reasons, McKay felt it was important to be closer to U.S. publishing centers for the promotion of *Banjo,* and he also wanted to conduct research for a potential book set in New York and Washington (14 May 1928). By the end of 1928, while living in Morocco, however, McKay dreaded the idea of returning to the United States, writing "I don't know if I'll be able to stand coming back" (9 November 1928), though he had promised Harper's he would do so to promote his second novel.

Western imperialist ideologies and nationalist politics, however, conspired to chart another route for the author. Because his activities in the Soviet Union had branded him a dangerous radical, U.S. immigration authorities prevented McKay from traveling to the United States in 1929. These activities, in turn, landed him in trouble with the British authorities in Tangier, who, after almost certainly stealing his original passport in 1932, reissued him a passport in late 1932 or early 1933 that prevented him from returning to his native Jamaica. By 1933, struggling with poor health and finances and feeling persecuted by the colonial authorities in Morocco, McKay began to describe a return to New York as a "homecoming." The scare quotes convey how fraught McKay saw his own disposition vis-à-vis the idea of claiming and returning to a home. Prohibited from returning to what he would eventually recall nostalgically as *My Green Hills of Jamaica* (1979), New York was the closest thing to a home that McKay could contemplate. The chronology of his 1937 memoir, *A Long Way from Home,* published several years after his return to Harlem, concludes with this arrival in New York—at the same moment when this collection of his correspondence ends.

In a very real sense, McKay spent most of his life as an exile, and most of his life, searching for what "home" meant to him. Born in Jamaica in 1889, most of the details about McKay's first twenty-five years come from his own recollections, published as memoirs many years later. Our collection of his correspondence begins with some of the earliest letters accessible in archives, letters representing his initial exile from his Jamaican home. These come from the period following McKay's arrival in the United States, where he first began to study agriculture, but soon found himself swept up in the literary and political scene in New York in the mid-1910s. After arriving in the United States and settling in the Northeast, and having already published two books of poetry in Jamaican patois in 1912, McKay was determined to make his mark on the American literary scene and began soliciting advice from leading literary figures like Joel E. Spingarn and William Stanley Braithwaite. Despite periodically expressing interest in it, McKay would never be able to return to Jamaica, making this early period the first stage of his own exile.

In 1919 McKay left New York for London, where he worked as a journalist for Sylvia Pankhurst's splinter socialist newspaper, *The Workers' Dreadnought.* In London, with the help of linguist and philosopher C. K. Ogden, he also produced his first poetry collection since leaving Jamaica, *Spring in New Hampshire and Other Poems,* a collection that included several now widely known poems like "The Tropics in New York" and featured an introduction by the British aesthetic theorist I. A. Richards, later regarded as a doyen of the New Criticism. In the early 1920s, McKay returned to the United States, serving briefly as coeditor with Mike Gold of the Greenwich Village left-wing periodical the *Liberator,* and published his next book of poems, an expanded version of the London-printed collection, the much-praised *Harlem Shadows,* with an introduction by *Liberator* cofounder and lifelong correspondent Max

Eastman. As well as his most famous work, "If We Must Die," the collection included such notable sonnets as "America" and "On a Primitive Canoe."

In 1922 McKay returned to Europe, attending the Fourth Congress of the Third Communist International in Moscow and, at the invitation of People's Commissar of Military and Naval Affairs Leon Trotsky, remained in Russia for several months. Following his time in the Soviet Union, two of his books would be published, both printed in 1923. Released in Russian translation, the original English manuscripts now lost (later back-translated, so to speak, into English), *Negri v Amerike* (*The Negroes in America*) is a study of African American culture from an internationalist perspective and, though also unknown to the world until the 1970s, the slim volume *Sudom lincha* (*Trial by Lynching*) marks his first collection of short fiction. This trip to the Soviet Union would ultimately begin the second, much longer phase of McKay's exile.

After McKay's sojourn in Russia, he lingered for a few months in Weimar Berlin, having his mail forwarded through expressionist artist George Grosz and enjoying the alternative cabaret life, followed by a lengthy residence as an expatriate in Lost Generation–period France. During the mid-1920s, while living in France on a grant, he produced his first attempt at a novel, *Color Scheme,* which his publisher rejected, afraid that the U.S. government might ban it for obscenity, due to transgressive representations of sexuality. Discouraged by this turn of events, McKay apparently burned the sole copy of the novel manuscript, and all that is known about the text may be found in the author's correspondence. Three years later, he published the first U.S. bestseller by a Black author, the novel *Home to Harlem,* followed by something of a sequel, the Marseille-set *Banjo.*

A short visit to Morocco in the late 1920s inspired McKay to return to the North African French colony with the idea of relocating there semi-permanently, and from 1929 to 1933 he lived mostly in Tangier and wrote three more books. The short story collection *Gingertown* (1932) focused on Pan-African characters struggling to locate themselves between the polarities of tradition and modernity within the African diaspora. The compilation met with another commercially disappointing outcome for both the author and American publisher. The Jamaica-set *Banana Bottom* (1933), a narrative with a Black female protagonist who struggles to retain her heritage under the pressures of colonialism, was the last novel released in McKay's lifetime, and was also a financial failure. While in Tangier, he also completed a novel-length manuscript about a small subculture of diaspora émigrés—a severely disabled West African protagonist, an assortment of queer characters, a collection of male and female sex workers, and a Black communist labor organizer—ultimately titled *Romance in Marseille*. The failure of *Romance in Marseille* to reach print at the height of the Great Depression played a significant role in McKay's decision to return to the United States in 1934. He could no longer financially, artistically, and mentally sustain remaining abroad and so was forced to return "home" to America, the country that had targeted him as a subversive and attempted to muzzle his art.

In addition to his struggles with publishing, McKay had endured a decade of health issues and intermittent poverty by the time he returned from Europe. While living in Paris in 1923, he was diagnosed with syphilis. This experience served as the basis for the cycle of poems he called "The Clinic," most of which remained unpublished until after his death, and it seemed to inspire frequent representations of illness and disability in his fiction writing.[5] But it also led to a cascading series of health issues and treatments that plagued McKay for the rest of his life, from a 1924 "paralytic stroke" to regular bouts with vertigo and "head troubles" to a brain and spinal tap in 1930. His health troubles were amplified by his financial struggles, which only briefly abated following the success of *Home to Harlem*. Throughout his time abroad, he took a variety of low-paying jobs, but also routinely asked friends and acquaintances for financial support. Many of these correspondents appeared to break off communication after years of receiving what McKay called his "begging letters."[6] By 1933 the combination of publishing disappointments, health issues, financial distress, and the increasing feeling of political persecution from foreign authorities—including a British prohibition on ever returning to Jamaica—meant McKay was eager to end his exile and return to the United States. His 1934 "homecoming"—a term he used in a 27 January 1933 letter to Max Eastman—marks the end of one of Black modernism's most extraordinary journeys.

McKay the Black Transnationalist

McKay's letters reveal not only, as Cooper claimed, "one of the great stories in Negro American literary history"; they also represent a chronicle of Black Internationalism that is unique in its representation of Black life in New York, across Europe, and in North Africa. *Banjo* and *Romance in Marseille* both feature fictionalized versions of the port city of Marseille, a city teeming with working-class Pan-African life and a meeting point for Black characters from both sides of what Paul Gilroy called the "Black Atlantic."[7] McKay's work has been celebrated more recently for its complex and dynamic representation of the Black diaspora. But McKay's Black Internationalism takes him not just to the docks of Marseille or the streets of Paris; it sees him move across Europe, representing Black Americans in the Soviet Union, encountering Expressionists in Berlin, exploring Catalan and Castilian Spanish culture, and settling for a time in Tangier. In some respects, McKay's movements resemble that of the Lost Generation of American writers—or even the later Beat writers so enamored of North Africa. But as McKay lacked the kind of financial support they enjoyed and the privilege of their whiteness, his restless travels reveal another kind of international experience.

As the 7 December 1929 letter to Max Eastman demonstrates, the letters raise further, fascinating questions about the Jamaican émigré, Harlem Renaissance, Black transnational author's view of "home" and sense of his own identity in the midst of his restless wandering. That is, is it correct simply to identify McKay as a Jamaican immigrant who never returned to his native land? Or is the Harlem Renaissance author more accurately characterized as an African American writer, as he is typically catalogued in archives and library collections? Is he, as he seems to suggest himself, a figure who may be less determined in terms of fixed notions of national identity? McKay entered the U.S. literary scene when these questions were paramount. Radical socialist Randolph Bourne's groundbreaking theory of hemispheric identity, "Trans-National America," published in the same year that we begin this collection, 1916, provides a useful context for McKay's disposition with respect to nationalism and national identity. Bourne posed that early twentieth-century American identity must be understood as determined through the connection between human subjects and their "spiritual country," that is, *culture.*[8] McKay's connection to Bourne is more than a casual one. His first publications in the United States—the sonnets "Invocation" and "The Harlem Dancer"—appeared with Bourne's essay "Twilight of the Idols" in the October 1917 issue of the literary journal *The Seven Arts,* which would cease publication with this issue due to Bourne's uncompromising antiwar essays. McKay's literary development and his correspondence reinforces his role as a crucial Black transnational artist, reckoning with the psychological and somatic trauma and unresolved historical and pathological consequences of enslavement, racism, and colonialism.

McKay's many temporary homes and his fascination with foreign, transnational spaces have inspired others to claim him as a representative figure. Stimulated by the influence of the Négritude movement during the

1930s, French publishers issued translations of McKay's three novels, first *Banjo* and then *Home to Harlem* and *Banana Bottom*.[9] McKay's popularity with French reading culture is exemplified by Négritude artists Aimé Césaire, Léon Damas, and Léopold Sédar Senghor all claiming to have committed entire passages of *Banjo* to memory.[10] Moreover, while French literary culture took some notice of Harlem Renaissance figures like Alain Locke and Langston Hughes, McKay was the first twentieth-century Black author associated with the United States to be widely celebrated in France, anticipating the Rive Gauche postwar flights and arrivals of Richard Wright, Chester Himes, and James Baldwin. Recent translations of the circa 1941 *Amiable with Big Teeth* (2017) and the circa 1933 *Romance in Marseille* (2020) demonstrate continued interest in McKay in France.

Decades ago, such scholars as Michel Fabre and Tyler Stovall traced McKay's French bona fides.[11] The French claim to McKay is reasonable, not only because the Jamaican author spent the most transformative years of the Harlem Renaissance living in France but also because, as the letters show, McKay considered himself a Francophile, his worldview shaped significantly by French culture. Although New Negro notables like Cullen, Hughes, and Locke also claimed Paris as a kind of home away from Harlem, considering he authored two Pan-Africanist novels set in Marseille, McKay may be identified as the foremost Anglophone Black transnational literary artist of the interwar modernist phase. He may be a better representative of Gilroy's theory of the Black Atlantic than even French-esteemed expatriates Baldwin, Himes, and Wright, in that he not only dwelled in Black diaspora France and settled in the French "international zone" of Tangier, but that he also began as a "colonial" in then-British Jamaica. That is, it is easy to forget that at least during his initial phase in the United States, McKay was almost as much *l'étranger*, to cite Camus, to North America as he was in Europe and North Africa.

As well as in Jamaica, where he continues to be revered as a national bard, a Claude McKay of other nations persists. Although he resided in London for a relatively brief phase, McKay published his first post-Jamaican poetry collection in England. In the United Kingdom, McKay is deemed an Anglophone Caribbean author, as he played a role in launching a modern Afro-British literary history that is traceable to postcolonial writers like George Lamming, Derek Walcott, and Zadie Smith. A Black Russian Claude McKay? Trotsky, Grigory Zinoviev, Nikolai Bukharin, and other leaders of the Bolshevik Revolution fêted the Third Comintern party-crasher, while Soviet publishers, apparently seeing McKay as a key figure of an emergent Black internationalist, radical vanguard, translated and released two of his books.[12] McKay's place in Spanish literary history is illustrated by the Popular Front period translation of *Home to Harlem,* rendered into Castilian in 1931 as *Cock-tail negro.*[13] McKay saw Josephine Baker perform in Barcelona, and he developed a deep appreciation for Spanish music and dance, all while describing life in Spain before the rise of Franco.[14] McKay's correspondence, moreover, establishes that several decades before Wright portrayed "pagan" Spain as a mélange of African and European influences, McKay was observing the presence of Moorish Africa in Barcelona and Madrid.

After several years moving around Europe, McKay spent the final years of his exile in Morocco, most of them in the international city of Tangier. At times he dreamt of traveling further south to sub-Saharan West Africa (the home of Lafala, the protagonist of *Romance in Marseille*), but McKay soon found the Maghreb not only to represent the "real" melting-pot of the African continent, but also to resemble his memories of his Jamaican home. "I need to settle down and no place has satisfied me since I left home as much as Morocco," he wrote to Max Eastman on 1 December 1930. "There are many things in the life of the natives, their customs and superstitions, reminiscent of Jamaica." The strong sense of connection McKay felt to Morocco doubtless influenced the composition of both *Romance in Marseille,* charting an uneasy and tragic union between the Arab Maghreb and West Africa, and *Banana Bottom,* McKay's paean to Jamaica. McKay never made it further south than Morocco, but he did settle down in a native house about a mile east of Tangier's city center, and he adopted local dress, integrating himself in the community, in part, to evade the authorities. He had good reason to: McKay was evidently such an influential figure among the adherents of the anti-imperialist Trans-Saharan Arab Renaissance that, as the letters also exhibit, the French authorities conspired with the Tangier British consulate to hound him from colonized North Africa.[15] In the winter of 1933–34, McKay's transnational wanderings finally took him back across the Black Atlantic to the United States, where he would remain for the rest of his life.

McKay the Artist

By the summer of 1926, Claude McKay had been abroad in Europe for four long years. Back in the United States, debates about African American representation were raging in the journals of the Harlem Renaissance, especially in the wake of *Nigger Heaven* (1926), the controversially titled novel about Harlem nightlife published by white author and Harlem Renaissance patron Carl Van Vechten. Du Bois, George Schuyler, and others published essays debating the responsibilities of Black artists to avoid potential stereotypes and promote positive, typically middle-class images of African Americans.[16] Young writers like Hughes and Thurman meanwhile advocated for artistic liberty and championed jazz and working-class Black culture as a repository for Black creativity.[17] When it was possible, McKay kept up with the debates in these journals, but the émigré author's theoretical statements about Black art almost never appeared as part of the public discourse. Instead, during the peak of the Harlem Renaissance and McKay's most productive years, they appeared in letters to friends, adversaries, and those in between.

McKay's affable correspondence with Renaissance midwife Alain Locke took a turn south when the Howard University academic took it upon himself to blue-pencil the poet's finely honed verse. While guest editing the historic 1925 "Harlem, Mecca of the New Negro" special issue of the popular magazine *Survey Graphic,* Locke was apparently anxious that the title of McKay's "The White House" would offend white readers. Without the poet's consent, Locke reprinted the sonnet in the special number as "White Houses." Later that year, when Locke expanded the content of the issue, editing the historic anthology *The New Negro,* he repeated the offense. In a state of high dudgeon, McKay wrote Locke on 1 August 1926:

> The whole symbolical import of my poem is lost under the title you have chosen to give it + allowed to remain after I had called your attention to it. If you understand how an artist feels about the word that he chooses above other words, . . . then you will understand how I feel about "The White House." I do hope you will set this matter right in future editions of your book.

Future editions of *The New Negro* sustained the solecism, and McKay encountered similar editorial pressures in his other work. These battles, too, are chronicled in his correspondence with figures like Eugene Saxton, an editor at Harper's who sought to make changes to *Banjo* that McKay vehemently rejected.

While McKay was committed to absolute integrity as an artist, he also was dedicated to writing fiction in the modern mood of raw realism. In a letter from the summer of 1925, he described his novel manuscript *Color Scheme* in frank terms to Black archivist Arturo Alfonso Schomburg: "For it is not a 'moral' book. I make my Negro characters yarn and backbite and fuck like people the world over" (late June 1925). Though McKay failed to publish this novel and unfortunately destroyed the manuscript, *Home to Harlem* is in much the same vein and shocked many readers upon its publication. McKay defended his artistic approach to James Weldon Johnson in a 30 April 1928 letter: "In writing 'Home To Harlem' I have not deviated in any way from my intellectual and artistic ideas of life. . . . We must leave the real appreciation of what we are doing to the emancipated Negro intelligentsia of the future, while we are sardonically aware now that only the intelligentsia of the 'superior race' is developed enough to afford artistic truth."

We know from McKay's letters that *Home to Harlem* started as a short story that he began expanding into novel form after engaging William A. Bradley, the Paris-based literary agent who represented James Joyce, Gertrude Stein, and eventually Richard Wright. McKay's letters to Bradley show him trying out new ideas, shaping and reshaping *Banjo* and the posthumously published *Romance in Marseille.* Discussing one character during the drafting of *Banjo,* McKay writes to Bradley, "But by holding Ray back I think I give just enough of the modern touch of sophistication to the writing and achieve a kind of objective-subjective fusion—a mosaic that puzzles and yet intrigues and holds the reader" (3 June 1928). Comments like these—there are many—document McKay's process as a novelist and show how he staged and conceptualized his most celebrated fiction, and how he thought about the reception of his work, among both Black and white readers.

Several years after McKay had laid into Alain Locke, white British heiress and activist Nancy Cunard, at work on an anthology of Black writing titled *Negro,* solicited McKay for prose material. During the early 1930s, McKay dispatched a dozen genial letters to Cunard, including inviting her to stay with his elder brother U. Theo while visiting Jamaica. The pleasantness ended, however, when Cunard plunged into revising the author's work without his approval and refused to offer pay for the contribution. Writing from Tangier in 1933, McKay's tone turns to rage, and in letters to friends, McKay bitterly regrets his former trust in the heiress. Corresponding with Schomburg (15 June 1933), he discusses abruptly withdrawing from *Negro:* "Personally I think Miss Cunard a very unreliable person and lacking intellectual purpose and balance."

Along with charting McKay's creative process, including his contentious relationship with editors and the New Negro Renaissance (which he described as "a hopeless mess" to white patron Charlotte Osgood Mason), McKay's letters also tantalize with abandoned, discarded, and unrealized projects. In addition to the well-known disaster of the circa 1925 novel project *Color Scheme,* McKay also describes in detail other unrealized projects, including a circa 1926 passing novel titled "Black Belt" and a project taken up near the end of his exile in 1933 about a "Smart Set" of African Americans living it up in 1920s Paris. Nothing apparently survives of these novels, aside from his descriptions in letters to his friends. However, letters like these show McKay trying out ideas, giving advice (sometimes unsolicited) to younger writers like Hughes, describing his own rationale in shifting from poetry to prose, and generally charting his creative evolution over the most productive period of his artistic life.

McKay the Leftist

When McKay defended *Home to Harlem* in his letter to James Weldon Johnson, he described the book as a "real proletarian novel," demonstrating that his thoughts about art were intricately intertwined with his politics (30 April 1928). While he later moved away from communist principles, during this time he conceived of himself as leftist, though the terms were never entirely clear. His trip to the Soviet Union caused him many difficulties and contributed to his long exile in Europe—he was trailed by the British secret service and found difficulty securing a visa to re-enter the United States after being labeled a subversive (having published "If We Must Die" in 1919 did not help things on that account). The FBI amassed a file on McKay, showing that agents regarded him as a threat to U.S. hegemony.[18]

McKay's primary political interlocutor was Max Eastman, a poet and essayist who also served as an editor on the *Liberator.* Eastman, too, drifted to the political right in the 1930s, but he published extensively on both modern literature and Marxism in the 1920s and early 1930s. Although McKay regarded Eastman as among his closest allies, in April 1923 he posted a long, blistering letter that takes Eastman to task for his clumsy understanding of the relationship of political revolution to race politics and for the white editor's misrepresentation of McKay's role on and exit from the *Liberator:* "I never once thought you grasped fully the class significance of national and racial problems, and little instances indexed for me your attitude on the race problem. It was never hostile, always friendly, but never by a long stretch revolutionary" (3 April 1923). McKay could be brutal in his vitriol, but he still managed to maintain a friendship with Eastman that lasted throughout the 1930s. When Eastman published his Modern Library edition of Marx's *Capital* in 1932, McKay congratulated him, the letter reflecting the Black émigré's evolving thoughts on Marxism: "I think now you might make it possible for the eclectic intellectual, the Voltarian type, to accept Marx as a great social scientist and teacher without the dogma and the infallibility. . . . Marx will certainly have to take his place in history alongside other social thinkers and stand above them by his actual achievement" (18 June 1932). McKay's initial revolutionary commitments of his *Liberator* days had softened by the early 1930s, as he worried about Marx's ideas serving as a new kind of religion for revolutionary thinkers.

McKay also wrote positively of his 1922–23 experience in the Soviet Union. After heading west at the conclusion of his visit, he wrote to the skeptical, anticommunist critic H. L. Mencken, "Before I went into Russia I thought there was a rigid literary censorship there, but no such thing exists. I have seen an Anarchist paper selling in the streets of Moscow, criticizing the communists in the most scathing language. I have heard Zinowiew read long passages of lies from a white Russian paper printed in Berlin to a great proletarian crowd in Petrograd. And I have seen copies of Russian counter-revolutionary papers published in Germany lying carelessly about in two homes that I visited in Petrograd" (17 July 1923). As scholars like Kate Baldwin and James Smethurst have charted, McKay's firsthand accounts of the early days of the Soviet experiment serve as valuable documentation of the connection between Black intellectuals and the USSR.[19] They also demonstrate the lasting connections between Black cultural production and leftist politics. For example, McKay's correspondence shows a passing acquaintance with Paul Robeson and Eslanda Goode Robeson, whom he met in Nice in November 1925, as the Robesons were beginning their own political movement to the left. By 1934, around the time McKay was returning to the United States—and becoming disillusioned with Soviet communism—Robeson traveled to Russia for the first time, the beginning of his decades as a pro-Soviet activist and foremost target of state surveillance.

McKay discussed politics widely but carefully, for example, urging the leftist Nancy Cunard in a 20 August 1932 letter to avoid political talk if she managed to meet the Martinican writer Paulette Nardal. And with many of his closest political comrades his discussion ranged far beyond the political. With John Reed's widow, Louise Bryant, who was in the Soviet Union at the same time as McKay, he carried on a long correspondence about his creative work, regularly soliciting her advice (and asking for money). McKay also supported Bryant through her own struggles with alcoholism and her relationships, but some evidence suggests he harbored a long unrequited infatuation with her, particularly when he waxed poetic in a 1929 letter about dancing with her at a *Liberator* ball over a decade earlier.

McKay's Queer Black Correspondence

Ernest Hemingway referred to the Lost Generation expatriate experience of the 1920s as a "Moveable Feast," and, though at times McKay faced challenging, even desperate circumstances, his own experiences show him delighting in all sorts of pleasures. Most illuminating in his letters is McKay's discussion of his own sexuality. While most McKay scholarship done before Cooper's illuminating 1987 biography did not show much interest in his divergent sexuality, since the late 1980s scholars have written about the queer imagery in McKay's writing, particularly the complex representation of homosociality bordering on homosexual desire in the novels *Home to Harlem* and *Banjo.*[20] In his own time, McKay's portrayals of open sexuality led to criticism and contretemps. The posthumously published *Romance in Marseille* depicts a fluid sexuality and unabashedly queer couples in positive terms—something that contributed to its rejection by publishers in the early 1930s. While some McKay scholars have struggled with the relationship between McKay's sexuality and his work, McKay does not shy away from these discussions in his letters.

In one of the most astonishing—and frankly funny—letters in this collection, he writes to Louise Bryant of a July 1929 party given by his agent for the touring group of the Broadway production *Blackbirds of 1928.* McKay recounts being at the Paris studio of young, out expat Canadian couple John Glassco and Graeme Taylor after a night of revelry. When he suggests to the late-night carousers a "bi-sexual party," he relates to Bryant that "our mutual friend, . . . Gwen" was offended. He reports the insulted comrade snapping, "You know, Claude, you have a reputation for being a homo," followed by his incisive retort: "Sure . . . , I sleep with all the boys, but only the aristocratic ones, and so it's hard to prove anything on me." McKay concludes the anecdote with the following fascinating literary criticism: "We went up to Cagnes from Nice—4 boys and some Lesbian girls from St. Paul and had a wild time in Harriet's studio. For my part I have never been with nor at any time liked the he-men crowd who like to 'swing on fairies.' See Hemingway's book" (1 August 1929).

This passage is stunning for its referential breadth, from the cast of the *Blackbirds,* to painter and sculptor Gwen Le Gallienne (rumored to be Bryant's lover around this time), to prominent gay Canadian expatriate couple Taylor and Glassco, to a direct reference to the homophobic Jake Barnes, narrator of Hemingway's *The Sun Also Rises*—who wants to "swing on" a group of gay men he encounters in a Paris bar—to the reference to Ma Rainey's queer blues anthem "Prove It on Me Blues," released in September 1928. Further evidence of McKay's presence in queer Paris appears in "Buffy" Glassco's 1970 *Memoirs of Montparnasse,* which refers to McKay, one of the memoirist's many lovers, with the queer code name "Jack Relief."

The letters document McKay's treatment for syphilis in Paris, his brief stint as an actor in southern France, his carousing in the bars in Paris and Marseille (contributing to his bad health), and his sexual and romantic dalliances in North Africa. McKay's letters, however, weren't always as wild as the aforementioned 1 August 1929 dispatch to Bryant, and things slowed down for him a bit as his long time in Europe and North Africa dragged on. When he was visited by friend and admirer Anita Thompson (and her Dutch boyfriend, artist Kristians Tonny) in Tangier in the summer of 1931, McKay wrote to his agent, "I couldn't help but put her out of my little house, because I had no desire to have her and Tonny together and to go in for those Montparnasse 'partous' [*sic*] and such things that I left behind me long ago" (14 July 1931). ("*Partouse*" is French slang for group sex.) McKay's frank discussion of his fluid relationships is quite compelling and helps to document how sexuality—and especially forms of queer sexuality—are central to his literary work.

Indeed, passages like these contextualize the frank representations of sexuality in McKay's fiction and poetry. As well as McKay's correspondence, his poetry expresses gay love, his fiction brims with queer content, and his memoirs speak directly about his homosexuality. Up against such oppressive ideological apparatuses as the Comstock laws that forbid the publication and circulation of "obscene" material, queer Harlem Renaissance writers like Cullen, Hughes, and Thurman were compelled to be chary about exposing their private lives. Baring one's sexual penchant could lead to criminal prosecution, compulsory mental health treatments, and the devastation of reputation. Under such conditions, McKay was unusually candid.

McKay's comment to Schomburg about having his "Negro characters . . . fuck like people the world over" (late June 1925) illustrates the frankness with which McKay talked about all varieties of sexuality in his life and in his creative work. From early Jamaican love poems addressed to "Bennie" and clearly queer-coded poems from his London travels like "To O. E. A." to the challenges to heteronormativity found in *Home to Harlem* and *Banjo* to the normalization of queer characters in *Romance in Marseille,* McKay's work during this period features a sexual openness and fluidity that shares much with the epistolary documentation of his own life. In his memoir, praising the French approach to sexuality over American puritanism, he notes that "sex was never much of a problem to me," and this plays out all over the letters.[21] On 4 December 1924, he wrote to Walter White of sexually permissive Montparnasse: "I'm living over in Montmartre—away from the Anglo-American raw rendezvous in Montparnasse, which I detest. But I go over there once in a while as it is the only place where one can pick up interesting people." And his travels in revolutionary Russia and Weimar-era Berlin offered no shortage of opportunities for the sexually liberated Jamaican writer. Indeed, he returned to Berlin in 1930—staying in a hotel near the Theater am Schiffbauerdamm—to seek treatment for his syphilis, since the medical specialists there had such a strong reputation for handling the condition.

During his time in Spain, McKay observed with fascination the romantic and sexual practices he observed there. In the letters, he writes rapturously of Spanish culture, where (as he wrote to Bradley on 5 July 1929), "Sex dominates everything." McKay's characterization of the sensuousness of Spanish life is by no means unusual, but his detailed and varied description of life there—to correspondents as different as Bradley, James Weldon Johnson, Bryant, Nardal, Charlotte Osgood Mason, and James Ivy—indicates that it held a deep fascination for him. He contrasted the frank sensuality of Spain with his experiences in France, which he found much colder and more artificial. While he gives little detail on his own queer sexual experiences in religiously restrictive Spain, in that same letter to Bradley he mentions in passing some familiarity with the "'maricones' in the bordels."

Unquestionably, a major reason he moved further south to Morocco was his discovery of the queer subculture there. An example of McKay's references to the Tangier queer enclave is a 15 June 1933 letter to Schomburg describing the flush times brought about by the success of *Home to Harlem* and enjoying the company of "seraphs and cherubs" while visiting the French-controlled city in 1928. Starting with Oscar Wilde, Tangier was the queer destination for many Western writers. In fact, McKay's residence in Tangier preceded those of Jean Genet, William S. Burroughs, Allen Ginsberg, and Paul Bowles. He knew Bowles well enough to accuse him of creating difficulties with the local authorities, which would play a role in prompting McKay's departure from Morocco.[22]

This collection ends, just as McKay's *A Long Way from Home* does, with a "Hail and Farewell to Morocco," the title of the penultimate chapter to McKay's memoir. His fond goodbye to such sites as Casablanca, Fez, Tetuán, and Tangier concludes a historic account of restless relocating and sojourning, rendezvous with the legendary and lowly, literary triumphs and professional setbacks, set between moments of raw exuberance and periods of suffering and penury. It also concludes McKay's most prolific creative period. The bulk of poetry and fiction he produced after his return "home" to the United States would remain unpublished until after his death. And while he still kept up considerable correspondence after his return, the content of the letters that survive generally shifted away from detailed musings on politics, art, and sexuality (topics he could now discuss in person with friends) and included far more instances of McKay discussing the health problems and financial struggles that plagued him until his death in 1948.

Characterized by frustration and disillusionment, McKay's post-Morocco years in Harlem were sadly eventful enough. This included, during a period when he was unable to support himself by writing, working for a few months in an alcoholic rehab center in Chester, New York.[23] A salient point of concluding the memoir—and this collection—with his self-mapped exile is that the author's revolutionary art dissipated when he returned home to Harlem. He did return to writing poetry in 1934, resulting in "The Cities" verse, his generally rhapsodic homages to cherished urban sites (with a few dark studies of locations not so loved). In yet another professional defeat, however, the corpus, less impressive when placed alongside his earlier poetry, failed to find a publisher. Tellingly, the only place where McKay could publish any of the "Cities" poems was in *A Long Way from Home,* including "Tetuán," one of his homoerotic Morocco poems.[24] Both his chronicles of life abroad and his poetry devoted to past *flânerie* reinforce that his post-exilic years were spent in reliving his uprooted past.

The book that stands out among McKay's disappointments and setbacks during the post-exile years is his 1937 travel book/memoir, *A Long Way from Home,* unquestionably among his crucial writings. Three years after returning from his time abroad, McKay saw his years of exile as the narrative frame for his reputation as a pioneering Black artist. Rather than starting with his first two decades in Jamaica, the 1937 text's chronology, like this collection, opens with the author's "American Beginning" years in New York. It then turns to his time in London and interval back in Harlem, and then maps his return to Europe and subsequent sojourns in Russia, France, and Spain, ending with the author's "Hail and Farewell to Morocco." Whether *A Long Way from Home* may have approximated the success of *Home to Harlem* is impossible to know, as McKay's new publisher, Lee Furman, went out of business not long after the book was published. The autobiography received encouraging reviews, but the collapse of the publisher killed the possibility of a marketing push.[25]

After the appearance of *A Long Way from Home,* McKay published *Harlem: Negro Metropolis* (1940), a work of journalism that recorded his growing disillusionment with the effects of international leftism on the African American population. He also worked on two longer works of fiction that he was unsuccessful in his attempts to publish. The unfinished *Harlem Glory: A Fragment of Aframerican Life* (published posthumously in 1990) is an ironically titled fiction about a weary Black protagonist who returns to New York from abroad and encounters a distressingly altered Harlem of internal Black antagonism. *Amiable with Big Teeth: A Novel of the Love Affair between the Communists and the Poor Black Sheep of Harlem* (published posthumously in 2017) is an anticommunist satire that documents the rapid shift away from international leftism in the early 1940s while also highlighting the threat of fascism and international concern around the invasion of Ethiopia. In the mid-1940s he also was drawn to Catholicism, and the poetry he wrote in the final years of his life exhibit these new political and religious commitments. This includes the ambitious if also uneven collection of fifty-three sonnets he called "The Cycle" and several other, later poems. McKay himself mourned the loss of his old poetic facility.[26] Only a few of these appeared in print during his life, most of them in the leftist newspaper the *Catholic Worker.* He began another memoir, going back even further than his first to his youth in Jamaica. When, after many years of ill health, he died in Chicago in 1948 of myocardial infarction at the age of fifty-seven, he left the slim volume *My Green Hills of Jamaica* (1979) also unfinished.

Letters in Exile is not merely a complement or annotation to McKay's most revolutionary writings. These letters of wanderlust and thirst for an enduring literary reputation collectively narrate the arc of McKay's heyday as a pioneering writer, a period that displays a Black artist paving the way for writers as diverse as James Baldwin, Ousmane Sembène, Ishmael Reed, Jamaica Kincaid, Zadie Smith, and Clarence Major. This collection articulates the ambitions of an artist who strove to radically transform the literature of modernity, to wrest the colonized word from first-world imperialism and its enablers: capitalism, heterosexism, and ableism. The publication of these letters expands and deepens our understanding of the Harlem Renaissance and the history of Black transnationalism, literary modernism, queer and disability writing, and the intersections between these critical and political perspectives. It also reveals McKay as the pioneering Black modernist figure he truly was.

1. See Jeffrey C. Stewart, *The New Negro: The Life of Alain Locke* (New York: Oxford University Press, 2018), 335.

2. Wayne F. Cooper, *The Passion of Claude McKay: Selected Poetry and Prose, 1912–1948* (New York: Schocken, 1973), 351. Cooper also published the definitive biography: *Claude McKay, Rebel Sojourner in the Harlem Renaissance* (New York: Schocken, 1987).

3. Winston James has published two biographical studies, *A Fierce Hatred of Injustice: Claude McKay's Jamaica and His Poetry of Rebellion* (London: Verso, 2001), and *Claude McKay, The Making of a Black Bolshevik* (New York: Columbia University Press, 2022). Ernest Mitchell's biography of McKay is forthcoming with Yale University Press.

4. *Liberator,* May 1920, 48.

5. See Maxwell's note on "The Clinic" poems in Claude McKay, *Complete Poems,* ed. William J. Maxwell (Urbana: University of Illinois Press, 2004), 338–39.

6. Cooper, *Rebel Sojourner,* 426.

7. Paul Gilroy, *The Black Atlantic: Modernity and Double Consciousness* (Cambridge, Mass.: Harvard University Press, 1993).

8. Randolph S. Bourne, "Trans-National America," *Atlantic Monthly,* July 1916, 87–88, 90, 97.

9. See, for example, Brent Hayes Edwards, *The Practice of Diaspora: Literature, Translation, and the Rise of Black Internationalism* (Cambridge, Mass.: Harvard University Press, 2003).

10. Cooper, *Rebel Sojourner,* 259.

11. See Michel Fabre, *From Harlem to Paris: Black American Writers in France, 1840–1980* (Urbana: University of Illinois Press, 1990); Tyler Stovall, *Paris Noir, African Americans in the City of Light* (Boston: Houghton Mifflin, 1996).

12. See Kate Baldwin, *Beyond the Color Line and the Iron Curtain: Reading Encounters between Black and Red, 1922–1963* (Durham, N.C.: Duke University Press, 2002).

13. See Gayle Rogers, *Incomparable Empires: Modernism and the Translation of Spanish and American Literature* (New York: Columbia University Press, 2016).

14. For other African American responses to Spain during and after the rise of Franco, see Robert Reid-Pharr, *Archives of Flesh: African America, Spain, and Post-Humanist Critique* (New York: New York University Press, 2016).

15. See Gary Edward Holcomb, *Claude McKay, Code Name Sasha: Queer Black Marxism and the Harlem Renaissance* (Gainesville: University Press of Florida, 2007), 62–65.

16. W. E. B. Du Bois, "Criteria of Negro Art," *Crisis,* October 1926, 296; George S. Schuyler, "The Negro-Art Hokum," *Nation,* 16 June 1926, 662–63.

17. Langston Hughes, "The Negro Artist and the Racial Mountain," *Nation,* 23 June 23 1926, 692–93.

18. See William J. Maxwell, *F. B. Eyes: How J. Edgar Hoover's Ghostreaders Framed African American Literature* (Princeton, N.J.: Princeton University Press, 2016), 225–31.

19. Starting in the late 1980s, scholars invested in recovering the history of the "Old Left" reassessed McKay's role in interwar-period internationalist politics. See Baldwin,

Beyond the Color Line; Barbara Foley, *Spectres of 1919: Class and Nation in the Making of the New Negro* (Urbana: University of Illinois Press, 2003); William J. Maxwell, *New Negro, Old Left: African-American Writing and Communism between the Wars* (New York: Columbia University Press, 1999); James Smethurst, *The New Red Negro: The Literary Left and African American Poetry, 1930–1946* (New York: Oxford University Press, 1999); Alan M. Wald, *Exiles from a Future Time: The Forging of the Mid-Twentieth-Century Literary Left* (Chapel Hill: University of North Carolina Press, 2002).

20. See, for example, the following: Holcomb, *Code Name Sasha;* A. B. Christa Schwarz, "Claude McKay: '*enfant terrible* of the Negro Renaissance,'" in *Gay Voices of the Harlem Renaissance* (Bloomington: Indiana University Press, 2003), 88–119; and, most recently, Aaron Lecklider, *Love's Next Meeting: The Forgotten History of Homosexuality and the Left in American Culture* (Oakland: University of California Press, 2021), 97–100.

21. Claude McKay, *A Long Way from Home,* ed. Gene Andrew Jarrett (1937; repr., Rutgers University Press, 2007), 188.

22. See Holcomb, *Code Name Sasha,* 66.

23. See Gene Andrew Jarrett, "Chronology," in McKay, *Long Way from Home,* xiv.

24. The other three poems in *A Long Way from Home* are "Moscow" (124–25), "Petrograd: May Day, 1923" (172–73), and "Barcelona" (249–50).

25. Cooper, *Rebel Sojourner,* 338.

26. See McKay, *Complete Poems,* 367–68.

Ж

Correspondence

To William Stanley Braithwaite

11 January 1916

Hanover, New Hampshire

Dear Sir,

Knowing how valuable your time must be, it is with much hesitation that I write; but may I, an entire stranger, submit a specimen of my work to you for your opinion +, if possible, your help?

I do not write because I am overanxious to win recognition + appreciation, but I have often thought that, if my gift is genuine, I should strive for that which might enable me to do yet better work than I can at present.

When I was in New York I sent a sonnet on the race problem to a prominent newspaper Editor who answered that he would like to print it + asked for more of my work. I sent him other verses but there was no other on the race question +, after a while they were returned with no explanation. I would not let myself believe that it was on that account why they were sent back, but recently I sent some verses to a popular magazine. The Editor wrote that they appreciated the poems + "would like to publish some part [?] of the work of my race" but not just that sort. Of the verses there was only one quatrain that contained anything about 'race.' This has set me wondering whether True Art is not beyond nation or race—if one's mind can be limited to one's race + its problems when Art is as sublime as He who gave it to man.

But I must apologize for this letter + hope you will pardon its length[.]

I am
Dear Sir
Yours Sincerely
Rhonda Hope[1]

[Enclosed: "In Memoriam: Booker T. Washington," "To the White Fiends," "Remorse," "My Ethiopian Maid," "My Werther Days."]

WSBP ALS

1. McKay used a pseudonym in his early correspondence with Braithwaite, though he never used this name in print. As William J. Maxwell notes, this may be "an allusion to the given name of his infant daughter, Rhue Hope McKay." See Claude McKay, *Complete Poems,* ed. William J. Maxwell (Urbana: University of Chicago Press, 2004), 303.

To William Stanley Braithwaite

15 February 1916

Hanover, New Hampshire

Dear Sir:

I thank you very much for your kind letter.

As a rule the race problem does not inspire me very much to poetic efforts. Of the many things I have written very few are of racial themes, but sometimes my emotions are stirred by something above the ordinary, I feel the urge to write + the thought will not down.

I have been reading your 'Anthology' for the last two years, + it has been a source of great help to me.[1]

At present I am making fair copies of the poems I have written for the last four years with the intention of submitting them to some publisher.

But I hardly know the right course of procedure here. I have heard that there are legitimate literary brokers, beside the fake self-advertised ones, who knowing certain publishers, works they require + the condition of the literary market, will submit one's work to them for a fair remuneration if accepted. But I have no knowledge of any. Perhaps you could advise me as to this; also whether the poems bearing on racial themes should be eliminated.

It is impossible for me to say how much I thank you, what hope + cheer your letter has given me—yet this is all I can say.

Yours Gratefully
Rhonda Hope

WSBP ALS

1. Braithwaite published an annual *Anthology of Magazine Verse and Year Book of American Poetry* beginning in 1914.

To Joel E. Spingarn

[1916?]

New York City

Dear Sir

Although a perfect stranger to you may I ask you to look through these twelve short poems sent herewith and, if possible, kindly give your opinion of them? May I also say that my chief object in writing is to find out if it is possible for you to obtain a reading of them by any approachable publishers and, if possible, a publication?

I have written numerous short pieces, also a long poem—a West Indian love story—which I am now making a copy of. It was written four years ago when I first came here, but I have added to and revised it since.

I was loath to make this individual appeal, but having, times and again, failed of breaking through the usual channels I thought that if I were fortunate enough to enlist the sympathy of an interested, known and distinguished person I might be, perhaps, more successful. A friend who has read most of them thinks that my failure to publish is due to the personal and pessimistic note. I should like to write in a happier vein but glad moods cannot stir me to write.

I have tried to bring my poems up to the best standard after the first outburst, and I do wish they could be judged only on their merit—as literature. I am prompted to say this because some time ago a well-known critic, in answer to a letter of mine, advised me not to send out poems on race topics because they would be judged, unfairly, by a double standard. Of course, my poems on the race question are comparatively few but I write on any subject when I feel deeply moved to and I should hate to suppress anything that I feel seriously about.

And now I must apologize first, for writing at all and second, for sending so many poems at one time to one whom I presume is busy; but I thought it would be better to send a fair and representative sample.

I could not refrain from adding three quatrains, thus uncharitably bringing them up to fifteen—quite a formidable number for even a leisured person.

Thanking you in advance,
I am
Dear Sir
Yours faithfully
Claude McKay

P.S. Not knowing your address I take the liberty of sending this through the <u>Crisis</u>.

C.McK

JESPH ALS

To Joel E. Spingarn

9 January 1917

New York City

Dear Sir:

I thank you very much indeed for your kindness in the matter of the verses.

Mr [James] Oppenheim returned them about a week ago and asked me to go down to see him. I went last Saturday and we talked for a little while.

I gathered from the gist of his talk that, though he apparently liked the spirit of some of the poems, he did not like the form in which they were cast. I tried to show him that, so far, I was nourished or, to be correct, nourished myself on the old forms; but I am afraid I failed to let him be understood, for I am a very poor talker. I much more prefer to listen. I think the free forms are very subtle. I have tried to use them and, in most cases, failed lamentably. On the other hand the sonnet I find admirable for a moment's thought. I am prone to be diffuse + repetitive and rhyme and metre help to check these faults. Indeed I often find myself thinking in rhymes.

I do not think that the attitude of the whites toward writers of other races is quite correct. The whites are always searching for that racial quality which may depend solely on the environment and training of the writer of his individual talent, emotions and depth of feeling. What appeals to me most in literature is quite independent of race + nationality—the human feeling that transcends racial boundaries. In essence I think all great writers resemble each other. The notice of Sarjini [*sic*] Naidu's poems in The New Republic seemed so unsympathetic, even unfair.[1] I read it with deep interest because it is the attitude of so many whites in general towards the work of the non-white people. If the form is denied us why not the words also?

Mr Oppenheim asked me if I had read [Vachel] Lindsay's Congo. I told him frankly that I did not care very much for it. Although it is pretty with its "coal-black maidens with pearls in their hair" + "Hip bones beating in a tin pan group." But it all seems to be on the surface, when the rich sub-soil is underneath fairly begging to be dug into. I find no real sympathy + deep feeling in it as I find in Wordsworth's sonnet on Toussaint L'ouverture. With Toussaint's name left out it would be a fitting tribute to any great soul that had been cruelly wronged. I daresay Mr Lindsay revels in the picturesque + bizarre, but however wonderful + real his picture of Legree may be I hardly think his Booker Washington poems can be liked by those who loved the man.[2] In the same way, perhaps, if I were a devout Christian + a Salvationist I should dislike his General [William] Booth poem + [George Bernard] Shaw's Major Barbara in spite of their artistic + moral value.

I suppose white writers cannot easily get on the inside of black people. But I don't think it is hard if there is enough sympathy + strength of will. Mrs [Harriet Beecher] Stowe understood + Whitman also. Many think that Negro art should be 'ragtimy'—wild + barbaric. But it is a false conception for the Negro is extremely sensitive to form + rhythm if not to colour. He all but reverences the conventions.

I am afraid I have written too much.

I left some other work of mine with Mr Oppenheim at his request—the long poem mentioned in my first letter included—+ he hopes to have me down to see him again.

Again thanking you
Gratefully yours
Claude McKay

JESPN ALS

1. Sarojini Naidu's collection *The Golden Threshold* was reviewed under the title "Another Hindoo Poet" in the *New Republic,* 30 December 1916, 247–48.

2. Vachel Lindsay's "Booker Washington Trilogy" appeared in the June 1916 issue of *Poetry: A Magazine of Verse.* Its first section ("A Negro Sermon—Simon Legree") imagines the villainous overseer of Harriet Beecher Stowe's *Uncle Tom's Cabin* in hell.

To Joel E. Spingarn

18 June 1917

New York City

Dear Sir

I hope you will overlook my not thanking you before for your letter and kind advice of Jan. 11, but I thought I'd wait as I hadn't anything much to say.

The war having reached America I know you are busy doing your bit while I, maybe a "slacker" or a "shirker," am all wrapt up in my little ideas and thoughts. The great things that are happening don't stir me as they should, I am puzzled to know why.

But perhaps you will find time to read a long narrative poem and six sonnets which I enclose, and I should be very grateful if you will give me your opinion of them.

Although the <u>Seven Arts</u> accepted two of my sonnets I don't think it cares much for my work. I read it, such articles as I can, and note the trend of its policy. Evidently it rates form higher than content and is rather intolerant of the literary traditions of the past. It is not hard for me to see that it is entirely out of sympathy with my method of presenting my few ideas and thoughts of life.

A couple months ago Mr [James] Oppenheim asked me to send him some of my latest work which I did, sending him what I considered my best lyrics—much better than the mere picture-poem which he thought was my best and which loses much of its strength by my having had to change the last lines to meet his taste.

In his reply he said: "None of these pleases us as much as the poems we accepted. Like all of your work there is much melody, there are passages of real loveliness—but the poetry is unequal." This I don[']t understand for the last sentence seems very high praise. I could not ask more of any critic. The verses, according to him, possessed the qualities of melody and loveliness which are two of the chief things I look for in poetry, a third + the most important to me being thought, and to say the poetry was unequal seemed vague and irrelevant for some of the finest poems I've read I found unequal in places, the same lofty level not being maintained throughout. However I am always glad and eager for criticism for it is such an incentive to better work.

I found your new little book in the library which I read with great interest.[1]

I am now making a fair copy of a prose sketch I wrote recently that I intend trying on one or two of the more conservative magazines. I am somewhat bewildered by the great mass of literary criticisms and controversies of these times and I often have to stop working to take stock of myself and ask: Am I on the right track? Am I moving forward or have I fallen behind. But I find myself in a quandary, for no answer is forthcoming.

Again thanking you
Yours Sincerely
Claude McKay.

JESPN ALS

1. Joel E. Spingarn, *Creative Criticism: Essays on the Unity of Genius and Taste* (New York: Holt, 1917).

To Max Eastman

28 July 1919

New York City

Dear Max

I suppose I am privileged to call you that now. Whenever you long for a weekend of mishaps you may ask me up again. I enjoyed nearly everything immensely especially the storm, though I grew afraid, and I am glad I met Joe. He is very lovable.

I was glad to see how you live—so unaffectedly free—no striving to be like the masses like some radicals, but just yourself. I <u>love</u> your life—more than your poetry, more than your personality. This is my attitude to all artists. It may be unhealthy—but life fascinates me in its passions. It may survive when everything else is dead or fused into it. I reverence all those spirits who in their little + best way are helping the life-force to attain its wonderful and beautiful consummation. It would have done your heart good to hear that chauffeur speak of your splendid + beautiful life. I don't think he knows of your art but your life has impressed him + I think he understands more than many of us who receive impressions through the intellect.

I shan't forget your kindness in paying so much attention to my poetry when you were so busy with your own work—Thanks. I shall make fair copies of about fifty or even less of the short pieces + try them on Knopf. If he won[']t take them I shall go back to the Cornhill firm which promises to come to better terms. But I won't have [William Stanley] Braithwaite's name in it.

Please convince George of my warmest regards + tell him I shall look him up as soon as I get my bearings.

With warmest feelings
Sincerely
Claude.

MEP ALS

To Marcus Garvey

17 December 1919

London, England

Dear Mr Garvey

I am sending you some news matter + an editorial from the Daily Herald of the 15th inst. which might interest you.

I think it is a splendid thing to have the representative organ of British Labour denouncing so strongly Imperial abomination and endorsing the self-determination of Britain's subject peoples. As I have said before in your paper, radical Negroes should be more interested in the white radical movements. They are supporting our cause, at least in principle. To me they are the great destructive forces within, while the subject races are fighting without. I don't mean that we should accept them unreservedly + put one cause into their hands. No: They are fighting their own battle + so are we; but at present we meet on common ground against the common enemy. We have a great wall to batter down + while we are working on one side we should hail those who are working on the other. We need have no fear if, as a race, we have ability to safeguard our own peculiar rights.

It is amusing, but very pathetic, to see Negroes under British rule wasting valuable money sending deputations + petitions to the officials of the

Imperial capitalists in Downing Street. For, after all, what are we but poor black devils whom our exploiters put a little lower down in the scale of human life than their poor white devils. And if, in spite of the fact that they have robbed us for centuries, they have been unable to make existence for their masses worth-while, can we reasonably expect improvement of our conditions at their hands?

Surely, if we must appeal to the whites, it would be better for us to let the thinking white workers of the British Isles know of the real conditions obtaining among England's subject races.

Yours for an awakened Negro race
Claude McKay

HHHP ALS

To C. K. Ogden

25 February 1920

London, England

Dear Mr Ogden

Thanks for your letter. I could meet you on any day that is convenient for you, at any hour. I was doing some work for Miss [Sylvia] Pankhurst whilst she was on the Continent but she is back again and I am quite free. You might let me know where you would prefer to see me. I live with a German family in a hideous little gutter street near the Angel + although I don't mind—I rather like it—you mightn't care to come! I sometimes go to the Socialist Club, 28 East Road, which is opened from 12–12, but it also is quite a sordid palace + there are no conveniences for private talk. But, if you don't object, any of the two would do for me.

About the m.s. I've never had any comment on it from a literary point of view since I put the verses together. Watts + Co + some young men I met at the club, who said they were connected with publishing houses, talked about it from the purely commercial side.[1] I shouldn't mind cutting out such things that a saner + more cautious judgment than mine thought should best be left out.

You wonder why I am over here. Well, it is like this. Last August I was introduced to a Dutchman who had travelled in the East studying the people + getting data for a book he is writing. He employed me to help him do research work on the Negro at the New York Library + I was glad to do it as it was a happy change from the factory life. We worked together until October when he got a letter from a relative in Holland asking him to come over for she was very ill. He suggested that I should go along and I agreed, for I have a mania for wandering and wanted to see Europe, especially England. So I took my poems along + he arranged and typed them for me. When we reached the Hague we found that the woman was more frightened than ill + so we decided to go to London and finish our work at the British Museum. But I soon felt that I couldn't work in close harmony with him. He would be nice, but possessed little tricks of manner, more pronounced in his own country, which exasperated me. I am rather strange, I think—too sensitive and rash, indeed, for a man of colour. I told him how I felt + threw up the job. It was an unwise thing to do, but he was quite generous. He gave me my fare back to America + £50 to bring out the verses if I could. Not bad, so far. I'm not stranded and I am thinking seriously of working my way to Africa before I return to America!

Although weak, I must also do my part to keep my poor people awake and discontented. I hope that wherever they are they won't act foolishly and let themselves be mowed down and bombed by the military. As a race we can work + wait, for Time is on our side + undeveloped energy. Perhaps ten years hence the white peoples will realize what the war has done to this civilization. When I read of Churchill, [Gustav] Noske + [Ferdinand] Foch still trying to raise great armies I can only smile bitterly + wonder if the European nations are determined to destroy the little that is left of them[.]

Sincerely yours
Claude McKay

CKOF ALS

1. Watts & Co. was a freethinking British publishing house associated with the Rationalist Press Association. Founded in 1864 by two secularists, at this time it was run by Charles Albert Watts, Jr.

To C. K. Ogden

26 March 1920

London, England

Dear Mr Ogden

I am really sorry if I caused you any embarrassment but it was so odd that that man should butt into our talk like that. He knocked me clean off my balance. I was merely telling Miss [Daphne] Olivier that my holding an I.W.W.[1] card might prevent me from getting back into the states. I could understand anyone intruding at the Socialist Club—but at the 1917!—it quite beats me. I am nervous about nice society for I don't know when I might inadvertently say or do things that may offend others.

I had thought of Sir Sydney Olivier and the Museum permit sometime ago but I was shy of troubling him. There is a funny incident about him and myself. Mr [Walter] Jekyll wanted the book of dialect verses dedicated to him, for he was known in Jamaica as a literary governor + that would help the sale. But there was a political rhyme in it, called "De Gubnor's Salary," attacking the amount and calling for a reduction. We thought that for a small + poor island like Jamaica a governor could do quite well on about 100 + travelling expenses, instead of 5000, if the lavish entertainments were cut out. Then I mentioned that in the days of King Rum and Sugar when swagger dukes + lords were sent out to govern it was a different matter from now when we only got second-rate civil servants and military misfits. It was a cheeky thing for a policeman to do but I didn't care then. The Inspector General saw it + said that I should write of my own salary of 2/4 a day + I told him I should, + Sir Sydney wrote back asking that the verse should be left out + explaining why he thought that 5000 was barely enough for a governor. It was only about five years before that he was Colonial Secretary at 800. Well we cut it out for the dedication, but somehow the Daily Gleaner got hold of it and a few days before Sir Sydney's last term expired it was published with a footnote explaining why it had been held back. I was in America then, but I heard that the local sheets knifed him for it +, as he was unduly sensitive to criticism, I suppose he was quite put out.

Mr Jekyll is a very fine type of Englishman, the sort that I think you admire. He's a scholar + he lives quietly with his books + music never bothering about local or foreign affairs although he hates everything that is dishonourable.

The only thing I never liked in him was his always saying that England + the Empire were going to the dogs because his clan had abdicated the right to rule in favour of unscrupulous middle class politicians. Being a mere peasant boy then I was very sensitive of sneering remarks relative to birth and place. But he was extremely nice to me. I met him when I was 18, leaving my trade + writing in the dialect. And he showed me a new world in literature. He translated poems + passages from the German + romance writers and some of the ancients for me. And he told me what was best in English literature + sent me many books. He wouldn't let me study poetic form for he thought I should do better in writing in any rhythm that came to me naturally. But when I went away to America I studied poetry to become modern + began writing sonnets + blank verse + he said I was spoiling myself. He is a member of the R.P.A.[2] because he thinks it is the only live organization fighting superstition. But it is about 30 years since he left England. All that he writes he gives to the association free to keep it along. I don't know if you can imagine what it meant for an ignorant boy just thirsting for knowledge to meet with a man like that. And he was so simple + honest; he never tried to patronise me. Once I called him my patron + he resented it + said I should call him paĉjo.[3] His relatives here were so good to me, also. Mrs [Pamela Jekyll] McKenna sold many copies of the book in her set and Lady Herbert sent me warm underwear during my first year in America. And I think they got Percy Grainger to set one of my songs to music. I am not quite sure about it. They were published by Augener. But, of course, I drifted away from them after a while. They always said they would welcome me whenever I came to England, but that was before I became Bolshevik, + when I asked about Mrs McKenna I learnt that her husband was a big bank director. That just froze me, for I came here under such peculiar conditions I thought that if I tried to see them they would think I was presuming on them because of their relative's interest in me. Besides they might have forgotten me quite.

Hoping you will very soon be better.

Yours sincerely
Claude McKay.

CKOF ALS

1. Industrial Workers of the World, founded in 1905, an influential, radical, international labor union with ties to socialism and anarchism.

2. The Rationalist Press Association, a London-based organization of freethinkers founded in 1885 to support the publication of anti-religious matter.

3. "Paĉjo" is Esperanto for "father" or "daddy."

To C. K. Ogden

2 April 1920

London, England

Dear Mr Ogden

I'm very sorry that I missed you on Thursday because I never got your letter until late in the evening. I should have liked so much to be in the Egyptian room with you. Wednesday I was there with a woman who had lived in Egypt but she was very stupid and dull. Whenever you can afford a little time I should be so glad to do the picture galleries with you. I really want to appreciate + discriminate between good + bad art just for my own benefit. I have again been looking at what I consider some fair ones at the Guildhall. I wonder if there are any nice books, not too heavy, that I could get at?

I am glad that you are coming around again. Now I feel relieved about the "extreme left" fellow. I thought it was rather embarrassing for you + Miss [Daphne] Olivier; for myself I didn't care. For I am always coming up against his type and worse—in America + also here, so I'm used to it. My colour alone makes me so conspicuous; I must reconcile myself to such things. I shouldn't mind if such encounters were only amusing + tiresome, but at times they are positively dangerous. Were it not for some white friends I should have been badly mauled in Limehouse a fortnight ago + last Monday I was the chief actor in a near tragedy at the Old N Tube Station. I was walking home from the Socialist Club with a young Serbian + just as we said goodbye a drunken South African soldier (discharged) came up to me and asked whether I came from Basutoland or some other place. I answered no + tried to pass but he held me up, got hold of my tie, + was rather threatening. Of course I know what the average S.A. white thinks of the blacks + what was evidently working in his soldier brain so I thought quickly + sent him sprawling to the street. Instantly a little mob gathered around me, but some friends of mine from the club came along + two policemen who perceived what was happening + drove them off. Had there been no help they couldn't have reached me though I would have dived into the Tube immediately after hitting out. One must always be on one's guard. Since then, until to-night, I have been sleeping with a friend over West, so the incident is really the cause of my missing your letter + an interesting afternoon with you. So soon as I can find a suitable place I will move back to the west side for it's a little safer there. The grown-ups are more sensible + the children are not so disgustingly provocative + bad-mannered.

[George Bernard] Shaw has sent me a nice recommendation + I think everything will be all right in a day or two. Thanks.

Yours very sincerely
Claude McKay.

CKOF ALS

To C. K. Ogden

17 August 1920

London, England

Dear Mr Ogden

About that bill, if you have no real objection I should simply like a typed account for £75 at least showing that 40 has been paid. [Eugen] Boissvain [*sic*] advanced the first 50 + said he would give me the balance when I could assure him definitely that the book[1] was coming out. He is vain + wanted to have the credit of paying for the publication. But after I sent him the magazine + told him what we were going to publish, he was somehow displeased for our leaving out the socialist stuff and he now wants to back out. I am not going to let him if I can. I want to vet it with him nicely + show him how reliable his word is—just like the others in New York. In his last letter he was very odd—asking about the printer-publisher + whether the work was really being done. I've sent him the other set of proofs + I should like the bill if you don't mind. It's little enough to get out of and be done with him considering all the worry + trouble he has stupidly cost me.

Now about the book. The Printers showed me a dark brown cover with the title black letters + black border on a reddish label. I didn't like the border + one man said they had thought of working the label in the cover instead of having it pasted on. But as you suggest I do think the first thin cover is finer.

I think we should give as many complimentary copies as possible, don't you? And as for ads. etc. I should prefer to leave that to your judgment + the publisher's. I think [Walter] Fuller gave me a letter to some member of Allen + Unwin's[2] but I never sent it in. I don[']t think it would be advisable now! I have other letters to a few people like Lansbury[3] that I might send with an announcement of the book when it is ready. But I don['']t want the radical Press to trash the book until the artistic circles have pronounced on it.

I also send five poems which you might choose the necessary one from and which I prefer in order as they are numbered and named here:—(1) Rioting Roses,[4] (2) Bacchanal, (3) The Harlem Dancer, (4) Harlem Shadows and (5) Africa Enslaved. I don't think you have seen the first one, which I give first place, before, although it was written in America. I just came across it recently.

Yours sincerely Claude McKay.

CKOF ALS

1. *Spring in New Hampshire,* published in London by Grant Richards later in 1920.
2. A British publishing company founded in 1911.
3. George Lansbury (1859–1940), socialist reformer and editor of the *Daily Herald.*
4. No poem by this title survives. McKay's handwriting is difficult to make out in this case.

To C. K. Ogden

9 October 1920

London, England

Dear Mr Ogden:

I should have written before but I have been kept so frightfully busy by Sylvia Pankhurst since she came back. She has been experiencing all sorts of domestic and business difficulties, due to her own erratic nature, + all the routine work of getting out her paper falls upon me in consequence.

My first letter referring to the book came from my friend in Holland and he is very, very pleased—although he regrets the exclusion of his double sex sonnets! Being a powerfully sexed person who is ashamed of his passion he has sentimental ideas about that sort of stuff. But he is pleased with the printing + the general look of the book. Charmed with the photograph, although he prefers the New York one that you saw. But there he is wrong again for the one in the book is more forceful + vital. The American thing is "soft." His adjective to express his delight is "dainty." I tell you all this as he it was that made the printing possible.

Likewise I must thank you for all the unselfish interest and the trouble you have taken in making the selection and choosing the style of the volume even when fearful of delay[.] I was often impatient and troublesome. The more I read the preface, the more I like it—so quiet and dignified + impersonal it is—quite in keeping with the whole tenor of the verses. How I came to think that an introduction by [George Bernard] Shaw or any well known man would have spoilt the effect—the simple detached way in which it is published—too loud for such a little thing. I cannot think of a successful literary man, conscious that he was introducing an unknown writer, writing in just the way that Mr [I. A.] Richards has written.

I have another favour to ask of you. I should like about 6 copies of the Press notices for my near friends + relatives. I received a great shock yesterday. After 2 letters intimating that he was going to publish the poems—not to mention his written promise made to me before I left New York last year—Knopf wrote to say yesterday that he cannot publish for me as it won't pay him. Not a word about or from Max [Eastman] who was making the arrangements! I don't know if they have quarrelled. He only says I must designate another publisher + he will hand the material over to him. I am writing to him + Max right away. And do you think I should mention it to Grant Richards? It is already stated that Knopf would publish—

Yours truly
Claude McKay

CKOF ALS

To C. K. Ogden

25 November [1920]

London, England

Dear Mr Ogden

I did not get your letter until Tuesday night. The club does not open now until 6 pm. They also nearly went bankrupt being unable to realise on money that they have lent to member[s] on account of the general unemployment.

Thanks for the letter which is just the thing needed. I am sending you another signed copy. You might tell Mr [I. A.] Richards how appreciative I am of his preface. I sent a copy to Sydney Olivier but he never even acknowledged it! Before I leave I shall send one to [George Bernard] Shaw.

I wish the Times Supplement or Athenaeum would give me a review. It would help immensely in America. No I am not living at the Club but I go by every day. I hope I shall see you again before going. Perhaps at the Museum. We've never been in the Abyssinian Room together where there are a few curious Christian paintings. I shall be here for a fortnight more at least.

I'm having the funniest experiences. Haven't left 438 yet + not wanting the authorities to know with whom I was connected—as they would get my record + send it to America thus, perhaps, preventing my landing, I gave them my old Islington address at the Passport office + asked Harry[1] to tell his people for me. Unfortunately he didn't + after obtaining the visa, enquiries were made about me at the Islington address + they were told that I had left there. I am now seeking a room from someone not connected with the "Movement" where I may stay a couple of weeks. As soon as I get it I shall devise some excuse for the Passport gentleman—

Yours
Claude McKay

CKOF ALS

1. Likely Harry Pollitt (1890–1960), a British communist politician who contributed to the *Worker's Dreadnought.*

To C. K. Ogden

31 January 1921

New York City

Dear Mr Ogden

I arrived here on the 16th after an uncomfortable voyage. I was happy to see New York again, the sun shines, the sky is invariably a brilliant blue + the air is splendid. Although it is much colder than London there is something exhilarating in the atmosphere. I received the telegraph order on the boat a day after sailing + had much difficulty in cashing it, but finally got it through after giving the purser your name + address. It turned the trick—it was £3—thanks.

I have met the Eastmans since I came back + Max has been especially kind. He looks older, lazier, + his hair is more silver grey but he is still a very fine type of man—rather handsome + devoid of mannerisms. There is some trouble over the Liberator[.] I haven't seen [Walter] Fuller, but I think he is an associate editor on the Freeman—you may have seen it—so Crystal [Eastman] says. I saw the baby[,] a beautiful boy with charming manners. They want me to have dinner with them but I am so shy of domestic bliss!

Max was not able to do much with the poems. The publishers praise the quality but feel sorry that the quantity is not enough for the curious American taste. I am going to add about the same amount to it + try to beef it up to standard, with such pieces as you thought might go in. [Joel E.] Spingarn's firm might handle it. I haven't approached Knopf again. Underlying their objections is the fact that they seem to resent my publishing first in England. But I feel that if I gained nothing by my first visit but meeting with you, that was enough. When I think of all the poor stuff that I should have piled into an American edition. Here I had had critics but none that told me why, how, where this or that was wrong + showed me my real forte. Without dogmatism or any direct method you have shown me the key in which I should do my best work. It has been a great experience for I now feel that I have a sound standard for artistic endeavor. I want to subscribe to the Cambridge but I don't know to what address I shall have it sent yet. You might let me know how I stand with you—whether I shall owe you + Grant Richards anything or not. I mightn't be able to get the firm to take over those copies to be sent just now, but I think they will stand me in good stead yet.

I am not sure if I may not be sent back to England on special business in a few weeks. If I am sent I might use your name on my passport—as returning to arrange about my book + if you were asked I shall be grateful if you will say you're cognisant of it—if you should be approached officially—for I shall be passing through to the Continent + should not like my progress to be impeded. It isn't red matter so you needn't be afraid. All depends on negotiations that are being carried on now of a purely business nature. Maybe it would be best not to write until you hear from me again. I have not yet seen anything worth while to tell you of.

Sincerely
Claude McKay

CKOF ALS

To C. K. Ogden

10 March [1921]

New York City

[On Letterhead: *The Liberator*]

My dear Ogden

I've never addressed you thus before, but your latest nice, warm letter makes me feel towards you as I do to Max [Eastman] and a few other persons.

I received the books about 4 weeks ago. Thanks. I thought of having them rebound + sold here, but a publishing house has decided to bring out an entirely new edition of my poems. And most of the poems by which my reputation was made here, it insists, must go in. I may decide to keep the copies I have + those you may send over for sale at some distant date at a fancy price! Unless I'm forced to sell now. At present there is not pressing economic necessity. I am working and a few friends are helping me.

Perhaps you had better find out if [Francis Riddell] Henderson hasn't made a mistake! We asked the printer to send him 200 copies which he had agreed to take. I, myself, sent over a dozen persons there to buy—if there is an error the printer can set it right.

I was glad to have the Cambridge. I sent Crystal [Eastman] her copy as she does not come to the office very often. [Walter] Fuller I've also met twice + promised to go to his office to talk things over with him but I cannot find time. I am lazy besides being a little hard pushed on the magazine. I shall soon go, however, + tell you all about it in a future letter. He laughed so much when I took him to task for not writing to you + says he may write after our talk! Clare Sheridan[1] dines with them on the 12th.—I like the magazine. I have read the "Sense of Beauty" twice + shall always need it as a sort of art dictionary to set right ideas I want to express. There is an American audience, however small, for your stuff—the trouble is to get at it. I have been trying to make use of Max, but he is so lazy. I have aroused his interest, however, + you may hear from him. Once he sees you as he should + understands it will be possible for you to link up[.] Although you don't seem to want to. I would suggest you send copies, marking the articles that are of especial interest to Current Opinion—50 West 47th St, New York[,] The Literary Editor—Boston

Transcript, Boston, Mass. The Dial, 152 West 13th st, The Evening Post Literary Review 20 Vesey st—New York.

I shall help edit the May number of the Liberator + the thought recently came to me that you or [James] Wood might contribute a short article, about the length of the "Hymn Before Battle" in the first Cambridge Quarterly or a page of the Liberator matter, about Current Art in England. Over here they have the craziest + most confused ideas about men like Roger Fry, Nevinson, Wyndham Lewis + others who are able propagandists.[2] It would be such fun if you or Wood or both together would put them in their places + mention the few that are really accomplishing something in England + whether any are under the influence of your beloved Cezanne. It would be great if you would come out boldly + say that he is a Master or the Master since—? I note that you hint at it in the current issue. I don't think you could leave out Johns + [Jacob] Epstein[3] is worshipped by the East side Jews over here who are devourers of the Liberator. Please consider it + if you are willing let me have it for my number. We go to Press by the 8th of April but if I am sure it is coming I could keep space open until the 15th.

I am glad you could see + understand Max as you did. He is just what you say he is—a cultured man. There is more between you both I told him than there is between me + either of you. I am primitive, restless impatient with a flair for beautiful things that I love to see as rare flowers among weeds. But I'm afraid I'm perversely intolerant of civilised culture. There is something in me that would laugh to see even the things that I love most destroyed.

The new paper isn't much. It is got up by Art Young a brilliant cartoonist but empty of literary comprehension[.] Someday I shall send you a copy. I shall always be on the lookout for anything of interest. There is nothing yet at present.

I haven't seen [Frank] Harris yet although I have a nice letter from him—a month old—to answer. It isn't so much my communist friends as the publishers that I find a danger at the present time. If I had a name, it would be easy for me to publish just what I like but the publishers also need sensational things to make money. I have a fairly decent firm, however, Harcourt Brace + Co—[Joel E.] Spingarn—the booster of Croce is the literary advisor. He's got good taste but bad judgment + he is a Jew and propagandist. For the last reasons he might see or try to see more racial feelings than poetry in my work. Even the Westminster Gazette went too much on the propaganda stuff for there were only a few of such verses in comparison to the rest.

With the election of Harding as President the American state machine has definitely done away with the tradition of a strong president. This fact has been overlooked both here + abroad but it is quite clear to me. Harding is another stamp like King George + the Cabinet of big business will control. [Charles Evans] Hughes[4] will be a sort of premier like Lloyd George. He is Welsh + a very able man—the ablest in the Cabinet + keen on legal justice. Under his guidance America will take a hand in foreign affairs + I'm afraid it will be an imperial hand. The republicans have no sympathy with "democratic" (USA) ideology.

I should like to say more [?] but I'm being taken off to see the Independent Show—I shall write often—thanks ever so much—

Sincerely Yours
Claude McKay—

We might arrange for you to keep 100 or two of S. in New Hampshire—Don['']t know yet or how the proposition might strike you.

CKOF ALS

1. Clare Sheridan (1885–1970), left-wing British sculptor and writer who had traveled to the USSR in 1920 and recently arrived in New York.

2. Roger Fry (1866–1934) was an English painter, Christopher R. W. Nevinson (1889–1946) was an English painter, and Wyndham Lewis (1882–1957) was a British writer and painter. All were associated with the development of the arts around World War I.

3. McKay likely means Augustus John (1878–1961), a Welsh Post-Impressionist painter lauded by modernists like Virginia Woolf. Jacob Epstein (1880–1959) was an American-born modernist sculptor who became a nationalized British citizen in 1910.

4. Charles Evans Hughes (1862–1948) served as secretary of state under President Warren Harding and later as chief justice of the U.S. Supreme Court.

To Joseph Freeman

19 March 1921

New York City

[On Letterhead: *The Liberator*]

Dear Mr. Freeman:

Your letter has been sent on to Floyd Dell. We are keeping "Awe" and "These Days" for the Liberator.

Perhaps while you are in London you will keep your eyes open for the magazine and if anything of revolutionary interest should occur in Communist circles or in the world of Labour you might send in a letter on it. Your name need not be mentioned.

If you ever want to meet some real proletarians in London who have no regular passport to intellectualism, I know of a club in City Road where you could drop in. It's a real den for revolutionary working folk, quite rough but once in a while one meets "artists" and "intellectuals" there. I think, too, that Mr. [C. K.] Ogden, the Editor of the Cambridge Magazine[,] would be glad to meet you and see some of your verses.

Yours sincerely,
Claude McKay

JFP TLS

To C. K. Ogden

2 October 1921

New York City

[On Letterhead: *The Liberator*]

Dear Ogden: I cannot even apologise for never writing. My first two months on the magazine brought me letters from my friends everywhere. Those I answered and since then it seems I could never find time to sit down quietly to do a decent letter. Max [Eastman], Floyd [Dell] and Bob Minor went away and all the routine correspondence work of the Liberator is mine.

I am always wondering about you and the Cambridge[.] Has another number been published yet? I don't know how much I am indebted to you. Anyhow, I am in a better position to pay now than when I was in London and I should like to settle accounts. The book on the Congo was received—thanks. Please let me know the cost. Max is now reading it in view of writing the preface to my poems. I have to mention the book here for I sent a picture card of the village acknowledging it + only last week the janitor found it with other letters behind the telephone box. I should like to know if Grant Richards had any sort of a sale. I have had great trouble getting it placed over here—a chief objection is the size. [Alfred A.] Knopf wouldn't even consider it although he was so eager before I went to Europe. Harcourt, Brace + Co wanted to make a book of the hate (racial) poems (something like [W. E. B.] DuBois's Darkwater if you have seen it, if you have not I shall send you a copy) but I objected. Max has been lazing over the preface—but his book is finished + now he has time to do it. He may then take it to his publishers, Scribner[']s. I shall send you a first copy of Max's book as soon as it is off the Press. It is about Humor and very good indeed. A whole chapter is given up to Charlie Chaplin. I am glad I came in contact so closely with Max. He is a strange personality—highly intellectualised and strikingly yet not unbeautifully self-centered. You couldn't say he takes a lively interest in life and things. Yet he will read and interest himself in anything that you specially call his attention to. He goes to poetry and scientific books of his own accord. There is nothing dilettante about him. He is athletic and likes to accomplish feats. But he gives himself to things in a strangely detached and impersonal way. He gives the impression, as I told him, of a Greek statue, and my remark did not displease him.

There is nothing of note happening over here. You get all the nonsense over the cables. Were Main Street + Mooncalf published in London?[1] They are hailed here as beginning the real American school of fiction[.] The books of one Sherwood Anderson are put alongside of them—but many keen-minded people disagree. Some think they are as dreary + dull as Western prairies. I haven't read any. English books like Queen Victoria seem to stir the public more. New York went crazy over the play of that Austrian playwright—Lilliom [*sic*].[2] There is an awful lot of unemployment here and conditions are rather depressing. Things are really not as bad as in London, however—There are no marches + not so many crippled soldiers begging, but Americans like to make their virtues and vices spectacular.

I have been very much with Walter [Fuller] and I think he is rather unhappy. He is very nice though, "typically" English + all absorbed in his work on the Freeman. Crystal [Eastman] keeps him in a state of excitement, I think. She is so terribly unsettled always going from one place to the other in a state of high tension and now she is about to become a mother again! These radicals are so inconsistent, bless me. Walter would like to go back to England, but Crystal thinks there is no place for her there.

I myself want to return as soon as I can induce some stupid sentimental bourgeois to give me some more money. But I must also get my book published first. I want you to see the very first proofs of them so you might offer me some suggestions. Nobody likes my London photograph. They say it is devoid of "charm" which is my chief asset. But four of the Liberator artists have taken a try at me without being able to get anything. [Boardman] Robinson did a painting and makes me look a big contemptuous African chief.—There are some interesting African works of art in the Museum of Natural history here. There is a little chair with lovers clasped together carved on it exquisitely beautiful.

Max is not interested in an international entente of the arts. He is strangely individualistic. He is interested in a Revolutionary expression of art in a general way, but does not go beyond that—Please remember me to [James] Wood—

Yours sincerely
Claude McKay

CKOF ALS

1. Sinclair Lewis's *Main Street* (1920) and Floyd Dell's *Moon-Calf* (1920).

2. Hungarian playwright Ferenc Molnár's *Liliom* (1909) was staged on Broadway in 1921.

To C. K. Ogden

24 December 1921

New York City

[On Letterhead: *The Liberator*]

Dear Ogden: Thanks for your card.

Hope you have received "Three Soldiers" which I sent you a few weeks ago.[1] I like it very much and think it is much better than all the rest of the circus stunts the American Press has gone crazy about.

I have just signed my contract with Harcourt, Brace + Co. But I had to abuse them roundly first before I could get my way. By the way can you get me a statement from Grant Richards that the new "book is in no way a violation of any copyright belonging to any other party" for my publishers here. I have assured them that "Spring in New Hampshire" is practically out of print in England. Of course, I know it is hardly necessary to get a written statement, but the contract calls for it. It is odd, but true, that because I had first published in England, many publishers here would not consider the book. I am expecting to hear from you sometime when you have a little leisure. There is no news. Crystal [Eastman] has another baby. Max [Eastman] has written a book on Humor which I may send you next year.[2] The Liberator is in hot water and we are having a difficult time struggling along. I wish you would send us an article along the lines I suggested to you a few months back. You might think it over.

There is rather a slump and depression in radicalism here. The unemployment has hit all organizations so hard that they are all put to finding ways for mere economic existence while the bourgeoisie are planning how to save the world! Well, it[']s funny. I hope I shall get a chance to go abroad next year.

Sincerely yours
Claude McKay

CKOF ALS

1. John Dos Passos's *Three Soldiers* (1921).
2. Max Eastman's *The Sense of Humor* (1921).

To Hubert Harrison

7 January 1922

New York City

Dear Harrison:

I have just noticed your reference to me in the "Negro World" of today, which, in my opinion, is in extraordinarily bad taste. You are simply hurting me personally by such methods. It is not true that I am being "lionised at lunch" by "pseudo-intellectuals." I could not dream of referring to people who have had me as their private guest in such an indecent and uncalled for public way, nor have I given you any reason to make such a covert attack on them.

You have by your action, violated the simplest proprieties of social intercourse that even a kindergartner or an idiot would respect, and it is your duty as a newspaperman, if you have any moral obligation towards the professionals, to correct your statement in the next issue of the "Negro World."

You are very wrong to think that you can praise my work by a personal attack on intelligent minds, that whatever their faults, are working for the common cause in their own way.

Yours etc.
Claude McKay

NAACPR TLU (copy)

To Joseph Freeman

8 June 1922

New York City

[On Letterhead: *The Liberator*]

Dear Fellow Editor:

I have resigned from the executive editorship of the magazine and vice-presidency of the corporation and am going on four weeks' vacation from the 10th inst.

We are calling a meeting of all the editors at Bob Minor's house, 24 Charles Street, on Monday, June 12th, at 8:30 P.M. to consider and vote on the necessary changes.

Will you make it a point of duty to be present? The Liberator is again in extremely difficult financial straits and one or two of the editors have plans for meeting the crisis.

Yours sincerely,
Claude McKay

J. F.—Things are happening again for a change—and my resignation has not yet been accepted.[1]

I'd like to talk things over with you—for the sake of the Liberator—if possible before Mike [Gold] talks to you, but surely before the meeting. But I don't want anybody here—including everybody—to know.

[indecipherable signature][2]

JFP TLS

1. The postscript is handwritten.

2. McKay seems to have signed this postscript with an unknown pseudonym.

To Jean Toomer

27 June 1922

New York City

[On Letterhead: *The Liberator*]

Dear Miss Toomer

Thanks for your kind letter. I remember very well some of your things that used to come to the Liberator, and parts of them still stand out boldly in my mind for their bright local coloring and individual poetic power. However, none ever seemed quite to carry clear through from beginning to end on a high level and we had some lively discussion about them in the office.

Your opinion of the Liberator is mine also. It will always be a living force whilst it retains that free artistic spirit. I read your review of "Birthright" in the New Republic and thought it one of the very best.[1]

And now to your kind invitation: I should like to come. I need change and rest, but I am not sure what I shall do yet. I want to make a reading tour and I want to go abroad again—All depends on circumstances + conditions—but may I put your offer down for consideration?

Very sincerely yours
Claude McKay

[Left margin:] Hope you will continue sending in things to the magazine.

JTP ALS

1. McKay may be mistaken here. T. S. Stribling's *Birthright* was reviewed by Worth Tuttle for the *New Republic* in the issue of 3 May 1922, 288–89.

To Jean Toomer

11 July 1922

New York City

[On Letterhead: *The Liberator*]

Dear Jean Toomer

Now it's very interesting about yourself. I hope you will forgive my mistaking you for the other sex when you are altogether of mine, but it wasn't such a bad mistake if you are not anti-feminist. I put you in high company. If you have time I hope you will come to New York and before I go away—I should like to know you. Am sorry I could not go with you to Harper's Ferry. But I am tied to New York and will be for a few weeks—Besides trying to write more poetry and a little prose I am working out plans to receive money to make my trip to Europe possible. I am going to Russia—let me hear from you—

Kindest regards
Your Claude McKay

JTP ALS

To Leon Trotsky[1]

[20 February 1923][2]

Moscow, USSR

Dear Comrade Trotsky:

The stationing of black troops in Europe for the last three years has insistently demanded the international intervention of communists.

London and New York are the chief cultural centers of the West where Negroes hold mass meetings and discuss questions which interest them. At such meetings one can meet Negroes of all types—from the mulatto totally imbued with Western culture to the young son of an African tribe whom some philanthropist is educating with the aim of converting his tribe to Christianity in the future.

In the winter of 1919–20 the soldiers of various Negro groups from all parts of Africa and America met with one another in a London club especially set aside for them by the British government and separated from white soldiers. They spoke various European languages. They had all been disillusioned with the European war, because they kept on having frightful clashes with English and American soldiers, besides the fact that the authorities treated them completely differently from the white soldiers. They were deeply aroused by the propaganda of the policy of "Back to Africa" which came from New York. In place of their former pride because they were wearing khaki uniforms put on for "the defense of civilization," they had become disillusioned, had begun to look at things critically, and were imbued with race consciousness.

I was working at that time in London in a communist group. Our group provided the club of Negro soldiers with revolutionary newspapers and literature, which had nothing in common with the daily papers that are steeped in race prejudice. Moreover, we invited some of the more sophisticated soldiers to lectures at the socialist club.

In 1920 the great expert on Africa, E. D. Morell, and the London newspaper the *Daily Herald* opened a campaign of slander against black troops in Germany. In this campaign a class point of view was carefully avoided. "The black threat on the Rhine" was turned into some kind of purely bourgeois, biological problem having to do with sex. Such apologists, capitalists who had grown rich on cacao like E. D. Morell, turned to the British workers with an appeal to organize protest meetings against the construction in Germany by the French of brothels for black savages. Once, at a large meeting, a young Indian was driven out of the gathering by a crowd because he and some Negro students interrupted the speakers with remarks about the abuses of white, imperialist troops in the colonies.

I wrote to the editors of the *Daily Herald* and pointed out the falsity and harm of the propaganda which this newspaper was carrying out, but my letter was not printed and only appeared later in the *Workers' Dreadnought.* Klara Tsetkin also put an article in the *Dreadnought* in which she discussed the nature of the propaganda.

The campaign soon even reached America, where it was carried on with great energy by German-American nationalists and by native Americans who sympathized with them. Even the London *Communist,* in the edition of April 8, 1922, gave room for this obviously bourgeois propaganda, while Negro intellectuals and progressive Negro radicals found themselves in the same camp with American officers, the New York magazine the *Nation,* and the capitalist newspaper the World in defending the morality of the Negro race and the presence of black troops in Germany before German nationalists and the leaders of the Second International.

The harm lay in the fact that the capitalist press took upon itself the role of the defender of black soldiers before workers at the same time that the Negro masses had begun to see through their own experience all the hypocrisy of capitalist wars, and also the fact that their most progressive leaders in this war proved to be on the same side as the bourgeoisie.

This circumstance is only one of many specific problems of the Negro masses. As I have indicated, in a book which I am at present preparing for print, the Negro question is at bottom a question of the working class, which is being used by the bourgeoisie for philanthropic purposes at the same time that the leaders of the class struggle ignore it.

But at the present time the international situation is so serious, and French and American capitalists so nakedly use Negroes in their offensive tactics against the working class, that organized workers and communists cannot any longer treat the black masses with indifference.

If we look at a number of the radical newspapers and magazines that have been printed by Negroes in America during the last five years, then we will see that some elements among progressive Negroes have conducted large-scale communist propaganda among their race. Of course, little has been done; but even the steps undertaken were too timid, mistaken, and completely insufficient to take care of the huge demands. Black comrades feel this very keenly, but white comrades must recognize the justice of the assertion that I have made.

I have visited a tactical school for cavalry and infantry, and what chiefly struck me was the Spartan simplicity and order among the Red Army soldiers and also their understanding of that great ideal which has made the Red Army a military power which, more than any other power in the world, inspires fear and respect.

I thank you for your attention and your reply.

With fraternal greetings,
Claude McKay

NIA

1. Included in the volume, originally published in Russian, *The Negroes in America,* ed. Alan L. McLeod, trans. Robert J. Winter (Port Washington, N.Y.: Kennikat Press, 1979).

2. The original incorrectly dates this letter to 1922.

To Max Eastman

3 April 1923

Moscow, USSR

Dear Max,

The chapter which includes my experience with the Liberator group shall remain as it is, for in your letter I cannot find any convincing reason for omitting it; but, on the contrary, there is every reason for publishing it, if it will provoke stimulating argument and discussion, such as your letter reveals, on the Negro problem in America.

There are, however, a few knotty points in your exquisitely phrased letter which I have picked out—points insinuatingly questioning my motives and charging me with dishonesty, which I will take up with you in order as they appear.

You will understand that I do not intend to argue with you about my motives and honesty—to prove or disprove anything, I am only attempting to <u>enlighten</u> you.

(I) I have and had no intention of letting the public think I withdrew from the executive editorship of the Liberator solely because of a disagreement over the race question. As my letters to you and yours to me will show I was preparing to leave the work of active editorship of the Liberator months before I finally gave up the job. But I want to state emphatically, and to let those who are interested in the matter understand, that my colleague on the executive editorship made the race story in the June (1922) Liberator the basis of his attack on me, and his opinion, your letters, and the artist's, and the discussions of the affair by the Liberator group, revealed to me that the group did not have a class-conscious attitude on the problem of the American Negro.[1] I think it is very important that this fact should be published, especially if it will make for profitable discussion on the race question. The race matter was merely incidental to my quitting the executive work, but it was most important in that it disclosed the truth that the leading minds of the Liberator group did not, to me, have a comprehensive grasp of the Negro's place in the class struggle.

(2) Your write respectively in a single paragraph: "In your discussion of the disagreement which <u>did exist</u> about the race question, <u>you distort completely</u>

the nature of that disagreement.["] (second italics mine) and "There was never any disagreement between you and the editors of the Liberator, so far as I am aware about the proper communist policy towards the race question in the United States." I cannot reconcile these sentences. You know very well that you were virtually the boss of the magazine and that you made me your assistant and later announced it to the readers and the other editors. But, as is implied in your letter, you never discussed the Negro problem as a policy of the Liberator with me. Nor did any of the other editors. The Liberator group, therefore, could not be in "complete accord" with me as you write about my policy on the race question, when we never discussed it as a group. In fact as a group we never discussed the labour movement seriously. My position on the Liberator I discussed seriously only with the radical Negro group in New York. As I quite remember, I tried to discuss the Irish and Indian questions with you once or twice with a view of getting articles on them for the magazine, but with little sympathy you said that they were national issues. I never once thought you grasped fully the class significance of national and racial problems, and little instances indexed for me your attitude on the race problem. It was never hostile, always friendly, but never by a long stretch revolutionary.

However, I remember one day when you could not find a decent restaurant to accommodate us both on Sixth Avenue, and we finally had to lunch in a very dirty place, that you remarked, perhaps jestingly, "If I were a Negro I couldn't be anything but a revolutionist!" I don't know why, my dear Max, but the atmosphere of the Liberator did not make for serious discussions of any of the real problems of Capitalist Society much less the Negro.

(3) But you write: "You say that in joining the staff you were moved by a desire to further a solution of the Negro problem in the revolution. I refuse to believe that you were moved solely by that consideration, because I know that you were not a more simple person than others; rather you are more complex." You honour and flatter me by stating that I am more complex than others. You ought to know for you are a learned Freudian excelling in the judgement of human nature. However, I have not said anywhere that in accepting the job you gave me on the Liberator I was moved solely by a desire to further a solution of the Negro problem in the Revolution. I can afford to be frank. My first necessity on returning from Europe in 1921 without any money was to get a job so that I should be assured of shelter and food. My job on the Liberator secured me these. But my attitude was not very different from what it was in 1916 when I applied for a job as a houseman in a hotel in New Hampshire.

The manager told me that he could only engage me temporarily because all the other workers (about 25) were white men and women and perhaps they would object to my working with them because I am a Negro. I went into that hotel to work with the full knowledge that I was not merely an ordinary worker, but that I was also a Negro, that I would not be judged on my merits as a worker alone, but on my behaviour as a Negro. Up there in that little inn, nestling among the New Hampshire hills, the Negro (as in thousands of other places in America) was on trial not as a worker but as a strange species. And I went into that hotel to work for my bread and bed and also for my race. This situation is forced upon every intelligent Negro in America. In a few weeks I had won over the little hostile minority among the hotel workers; they all made demands on my company. For me to accomplish that, my dear Max, it was necessary to be complex! And I am complex enough to forgive your sneer at my saying that in joining the staff of the Liberator I was "moved by a desire to further a solution of the Negro problem in the revolution."

(4) I must repeat that you and I never had any tacit understanding on the race problem as you assert. So you could not have influenced me in any way on the subject. But you controlled the policy of the magazine as chief editor, and the files of the magazine are available to show what you, as chief editorial writer, said about the problem of the Negro in the Revolution. Nothing at all. In the December issue of 1921 you had a serious idea on the Negro of which you made a brilliant joke.[2] You say that I introduced too much race matter during the months of my editorship. You say this would not make the readers think about the Negro problem, they would rather "dismiss" it. Such is your opinion, which gives me a picture of you as a nice opportunist always in search of the safe path and never striking out for the new if there are any signs of danger ahead. I do not think you are a competent judge of my policy. The fact is that I received letters of encouragement and appreciation from working class leaders and Liberator readers as soon as I began printing those articles. The article "He Who Gets Slapped" which appeared in the May Liberator 1922 was reprinted in part in the New York World and syndicated all over the United States, even in some of the Southern States![3] It had the practical result of arraying certain members of the Theatre Guild against the Management on the issue of racial discrimination.

I still maintain that a revolutionary magazine in advocating the issues of the class struggle in America should handle the Negro problem in the class struggle in proportion to the Negro population and its position in the labour world. And more, I hold to this point of view because the strategic position of Negro labour in the class struggle in America is by far greater and of more importance than the proportion of the 12 millions of blacks to the 100 millions of whites. This obvious truth you would know, had you been in the least acquainted with the way in which the big capitalists have been using Negroes to break the great strikes in the basic industries during the last decade. Furthermore, I am quite willing to lay this debatable point before a jury of internationally class-conscious minds, but I certainly could not accept your opinion only as trustworthy.

Tom Paine was of his time and so is Lenin. To me there is no comparison. During the age of the French Revolution, Paine performed herculean tasks in England, France and America and if you had in your whole body an ounce of the vitality that Paine had in his little finger, you, with your wonderful opportunities, would not have missed the chances for great leadership in the class struggle that were yours in America.

(5) Again, you deliberately distort the truth when you say that [Boardman] Robinson said the Negro problem "will disappear with the disappearance of the economic classes." Robinson used no such scientific phrase as economic classes, but the poetic phrase "with the triumph of Labour"—meaning the rule of Labour. Hence your paragraph about the Workers' Government of Russia and the Jewish pogroms is ludicrous and untenable. First, because economic classes have not disappeared in Russia. What we have here is a dictatorship of proletarian rule under which the bourgeoisie are disenfranchised and shorn of political power precisely as the Negro workers of the South are barred from politics by the white bourgeoisie. I have shown your paragraph about the pogroms to a number of comrades and my translator and they have all characterized it as phrase-mongering. You write "The Commander-in-Chief (in the Red Army)[4] told me only two weeks ago that there never had been an impulse to a pogrom, even under the Czar, which was not instigated by the imperial Government. Everybody knows that pogroms disappeared automatically with the establishment of the working-class rule."

Firstly, I hardly think the War Commissar would have used that loose word "impulse." On reading your sentence, Comrade Ochremenko [P. F. Okhremenko]—who lived in the Ukraine (where there are great masses of Jews) before and through the Revolution, remarked: that the number of Jewish dead from the pogroms since the 1917 Revolution is greater than all that ever occurred under the reign of the Czars. Again the "Imperial" system in

Russia ended with the Revolution. Even the advanced bourgeoisie were against that system. All plots against the Soviet Government since then are the machinations of the counter-revolutionary bourgeoisie against the Soviets. These operations involve the instigation of pogroms against Jews, the inciting of the ignorant peasantry to sabotage, uprisings in remote districts against the communists, exploitation of the national differences[,] etc. The pogroms like the visible activities of the Mensheviks and Social Revolutionaries in Russia have "disappeared automatically with the establishment of the working class rule" because the Communists possess automatic machine guns and military control. If you would get out of your studio to see the strenuous feverish work of the Russian workers in competition against the NEP bourgeoisie, to study the work of the G.P.U., the Department of National Minorities and the numberless political commissars—the Communists alert against the "impulse" to counter-revolutionary tendencies—you would lose your romantic feeling about the Communist Dictatorship and get down to its reality.

You have read only one chapter of my book, but you assert that in it I say that the Negro problem is the chief problem of the Revolution in America.[5] When you come to read my book you will find that I have said no such thing. What I say is that the Negro question is an integral part and one of the chief problems of the class struggle in America, and I stand by that declaration.

If I am possessed of any "obscure emotion of resentment" it is merely that of publishing the truth as it appears to me. If what I write about the Liberator will "alienate from me every one of them" it would only show that, like you, they all have a personal rather than a social view of men and affairs. I am unwilling to believe with you that Robert Minor, Charles W. Wood and even Boardman Robinson himself would be of those alienated.

I cannot find in your letters that I have by me the paragraph which you quote and charge that I deliberately left out because it conflicted with my opinion. It may be in one of those left in America, but I don't see where it helps you in any way. It rather puts you in a weak and vacillating position. However, and finally, though I could not leave out the chapter, I am quite willing to publish your letter to me and my answer as an appendix if you want that; if not I cannot promise that if at any time after the publication of my book, a controversy should arise involving you and me, I shall not publish this exchange of letters.

Fraternally Yours,
Claude McKay

MEP TLS

1. "An Open Letter from Charles W. Wood to Hon. Richard Enright and Hon. John F. Hylan," *Liberator,* June 1922, 9–11.

2. This may refer to a short bit in an unsigned section called "Detestimonials" (*Liberator,* December 1921, 26). This appeared immediately after Claude McKay's critique of *Shuffle Along,* titled "A Negro Extravaganza," *Liberator,* December 1921, 24–26.

3. Claude McKay, "He Who Gets Slapped," *Liberator,* May 1922, 24–25.

4. Crossed out here: "(~~of~~ X the ~~Bolshevik~~? ~~Government~~?)."

5. Likely *Negri v Amerike* (Moscow, 1923), translated as *The Negroes in America* (New York: Kennikat Press, 1979).

To Max Eastman

18 May 1923

Petrograd, USSR

Dear Max,

I thought I would send a word to you before leaving here for the South. In your last letter you said something about persuading me from writing the truth (from the Communist point of view). The Communists, and especially the Bolsheviks of Russia, are too strong-minded, clear-headed and convinced of the sure triumph of their ideas, to be afraid of such facts as may not be very favourable to their programme at a certain period. Everything depends on the angle from which the facts are presented.

I see that you are confusing a revolutionary overturn with revolutionary constructive work. Do you think any fool could think that with the revolutionary overturn in Russia all class, national and racial differences would disappear as if by magic? Do you think the Communist leaders and the rank and file could by a single stroke change the minds of all the fossil-minded, stereotyped and mannikin wrecks of humanity that have been warped by hundreds of years of bourgeois traditions and education?

I have no more a [*sic*] "my solemnly consecrated political soul" today than at the time when I first went to the "Liberator." I still love to laugh, dance and wine and delight in pleasures. If you had seen me standing on street corners and selling red literature in London 1920–21, you would not make such a funny remark. If you had seen me doing propaganda work among the coloured soldiers you would modify your "opinion." And I never missed a single opportunity in enjoying living then as now. Do you think I was playing when twice in 1921 you saw coloured men and women at the

"Liberator" office discussing political and race problems with me—and you did not like it from fear of the Department of Justice? You have been entirely deceived about me, Max. I suppose it is due to this everlastingly infectious smile of mine.

Best wishes,
Claude

MEP TLS

To P. F. Okhremenko[1]

18 May 1923

Petrograd, USSR

Dear Okhremenko,

Perhaps you are thinking that I am in Berlin by now and making preparations to return to America. But I am still bound in Russia—quite a problem for me to get out but I have hopes of leaving in a few days. I should have written before but I just could not get that list ready and now that I have it, I find that I have more friends than books and I myself can only have 2 copies which I shall be obliged if you will send to me (under cover) to George Grosz 201 Hohenzollerndamm, Berlin, Wilmersdorf. Please remember to <u>enclose</u> my letter to him for if I stay in Berlin a month or 2 to do my Russian book I must be illegal on account of the American Secret Service.

I have hardly had any news of the outside world since I left Moscow—no English and American papers available here so far. But I have been busy writing[,] attending meetings and getting final observations and impressions for propaganda—of which Petrograd has a rich store.

When you write to me please give me some interesting facts + news of Russian events and of English and American guests in Moscow. I shall write to you at intervals—not very often but I will always write. Remember me to your wife and I hope the baby is O.K. And let me thank you for all the help that you gave me while I was in Russia—a real god- or party-send that I met you. And also be assured that you can always call on me at any time, wherever I may be located—in America or in England—to do any service for you that you may think me capable of doing.

With Communist greetings and fraternal wishes,

Yours sincerely
Claude McKay

RGALI ALS

1. Transcribed by Olga Panova, with revisions.

To P. F. Okhremenko[1]

30 June 1923

Berlin, Germany

Dear Ohremenko,

I hope that you got the letter and list of names I sent on to you from Petrograd. After a very long wait in Petrograd I arrived safely in Berlin a month ago, and after a very long wait and correspondence my documents arrived from Moscow only yesterday! I am hungry for some news of things since I left. I think I must have grown rather attached to the country without knowing it although it is Petrograd and not Moscow that holds my affection. Is there any news of my book, my articles and my play? I am also anxious to know if you can get the photographs of the plays from [Vsevolod] Meyerhold's theatre which I begged of you. I have not yet got in touch with my comrades in America. It is a great difficulty and the official channels seem cobwebbed with inefficiency! What has become of [Max] Eastman and [Albert Rhys] Williams? Many Americans here are asking for them—also Germans who met them in Russia. Berlin is a sadly depressing city for me. Here is plenty of civilization[,] gaiety and luxury. But such despair and obvious signs of decadence and demoralization I have never yet witnessed in my life in any great city. Moscow and Petrograd looking forward are infinitely better. In Berlin I see symbolized the complete crumbling of our false western civilization and all its false ideals. I wish you would write me a letter. The best greetings to your wife and the baby.

Warmest regards from Claude McKay.

RGALI

1. Transcribed by Olga Panova, with revisions.

To Walter White

8 July 1923

Berlin, Germany

Address under name
Eli Edward[1]

Dear Walter

I am back out of Russia after a great triumphal trip there. The more great because I went in unofficially and met with opposition from the American comrades. It was not race prejudice though. It was great and had tactics and because also although I am a Communist, I am a fearless champion of race rights even when that championship should reflect on the American Comrades. I want to hear from you. As you may have heard, I have done a book on the Negro in Russia treating the whole question from the economic end.[2] I have taken up every phase of it. It is translated in Russian and now I am trying to place it in America. I was always in demand for propaganda in Russia, such magnificent people, and so informed and interested about American Negroes from the right angle. I will do an article for the Crisis. Ask [W. E. B.] DuBois if he wants it. Do they pay anything? You see I must have money to live on while I am doing my impressions here. I wrote so many articles I could not do enough and all have been translated in Russian a few in German and French. I have just given [William] Pickens['s] article on the American Congo to the International News. It is good because it takes up the economic side in which the whole world is now interested. Send me three copies of it, also An American Lynching[,] Peonage in America + [Moorfield] Storey's Negro Question. Ask [Augustus Granville] Dill to do it.[3] And send me all your listed mutuals on the problem especially that which takes up the economic angle. I want to put over some propaganda here and send through things to Moscow. [Sen] Katayama has written to say that a Negro Congress will be called next year. How is the Garvey movement? Chandler + Owen?[4] What new progress in the N.A.A.C.P. Is the African Blood Brotherhood dead? Please give me all the news about the movement and of yourself. How is your book and your wife?

If any of your white friends want an article or two let me know. I have no idea of the state of the journalistic market and what is wanted now.

Will you be good enough to give this enclosed letter to Richard Moore? I have tried all ways to read him but don't know if I have. I should like you to give it to him personally. His telephone was Watkins 9180 working place—but I don't know if he is still there. Anyway, see. Is there anything new in the Literary Negro world in the drama—I read of the Negro players in Salome here. Name me to J[ames]. Weldon [Johnson], Miss [Jessie] Fauset, DuBois. Tell DuBois that a firm here wants to get a copy of his Darkwater also Souls of Black Folk sold for Translation (The Malik-Verlag) but the exchange is so sad he would hardly realise anything, but the propaganda value.

Sincerely—Claude

NAACPR ALS

1. McKay used the pseudonym Eli Edward for poems published in the *Seven Arts* in 1917.

2. *Negri v Amerike* (Moscow, 1923), translated as *The Negroes in America* (New York: Kennikat Press, 1979).

3. The National Association for the Advancement of Colored People's report *An American Lynching* (1921), Herbert D. Ward's "Peonage in America" (from *Cosmopolitan,* August 1905), and Moorfield Storey's *The Negro Question* (1918).

4. McKay likely means A. Philip Randolph and Chandler Owen, editors of the Harlem socialist magazine the *Messenger.*

To H. L. Mencken

17 July 1923

Berlin, Germany

Dear Mencken,

While I was visiting Petrograd last March a member of the intelligentsia remnant that is left there, showed me a copy of the November, 1922 number of the "Smart Set" with your writing on Blount's [*sic*] Diaries.[1] I also saw two of your Prejudices in Moscow and your big tome, the American Language, is known in Petrograd. One of the hobbies of Korney Chukowsky—the foremost Russian critic, who still makes Russia his home—is English idioms and American slang expressions. He knows more of them by heart than I have heard in my lifetime. Another well-known Petrograd poet, [Samuil Yakovlevich] Marshack[,] has translated some of the most dialecty of Kipling's imperial poems into Russian. And I was told that the translations preserve all the tang of the original, because the translator used the corresponding slang terms, which are even richer in Russian than in English. Translating from western literature is a hobby of the best of the Russian literati. You have been recommended for translation but it has not yet been acted upon. An officer of the Petrograd Department of World Literature, a well known author and translator, remarked to me that you belong to the school of Shaw, Chesterton and Ibsen, with the difference that you wear your social passion under the mantle of irresponsible and impersonal sarcasm. The Russian intelligentsia does not particularly like this school. It was never preoccupied with middle class social morality. Up until the time of the revolution it was always anarchistic and non-moral brazenly flouting all the social standards of the nobility and the bourgeoisie. Before the revolution, the social conscience of the intelligentsia which, besides the literati, comprised some of the keenest and most sympathetic-responsive minds of the princely aristocracy and the professional classes, was preoccupied with the unbearable economic and intellectual suppression of the little nationalities, the peasantry and the proletariat under the Tsarist bureaucracy. But, as the world knows, prominent members of the intelligentsia were persecuted and even martyred by the Government for their sympathy with the submerged masses. Inarticulate suffering is the background of the Russian intelligentsia. It likes high-class, artistic muck-raking and for this reason prefers, the Ruskins, Robert Owens, and Dickenses of English literature over the Shaws, Galwortheys [*sic*] and Bennetts of to-day. And it seeks to find the real expression of the United States of America in Mrs Stowe, Whitman, Jack London, and Upton Sinclair. The Russians are apparently primitive (simple) in their reactions and it is the quest of the intelligentsia for sincere artistic expression, I think, that has given the comfortable western worshippers of the East the catchy phrase: the Russian Soul, with its pseudo-mystic appel[l]ation.

This Blount article of yours was so much liked that it was marked down for translation. Before I went into Russia I thought there was a rigid literary censorship there, but no such thing exists. I have seen an Anarchist paper selling in the streets of Moscow, criticizing the communists in the most scathing language. I have heard [Grigory Yevseyevich] Zinowiew read long passages of lies from a white Russian paper printed in Berlin to a great proletarian crowd in Petrograd. And I have seen copies of Russian counter-revolutionary papers published in Germany lying carelessly about in two homes that I visited in Petrograd. The State Publishers translate all the recent work of H. G. Wells they can get hold of and Wells is definitely anti-bolshevist. Sherwood Anderson has been translated. Much of this translating work depends on what the translators themselves like and choose. But it was apparent to me that the chief business of the State Publishers (I visited both houses in Petrograd and Moscow) was to put out marketable books. The non-partisan intelligentsia is publishing through private channels. The various literary tendencies flourish vigorously in Moscow and Petrograd as they do in New York and Chicago. There are Parnassians, Romantic Classicists, Formalists, Proletarians, Futurists, and Imaginists [*sic*]. A member of the last-named school gave me a copy of his latest book containing a creepy poem, called: "Leprous Moscow" which [Maxwell] Bodenheim[2] might have written about New York, had he any vital power over the manipulation of words, but even if it were written, such a poem could not escape the persecution of [John S.] Sumner and the extra-legal Vigilance Committees of America.

I don't know whether your article was liked for its masterly analysis of the Western European and American political-economic situation, or for its transparently incorrect idea of Russian Bolshevism to which you gave a significant sentence. I copied it: "Nor does any intelligible scheme of reform appear in what is commonly called Bolshevism; it is even in theory, no more than the substitution of a new set of exploiters for those now in power." Now after living for over six months in Russia as a private citizen, with the utmost degree of freedom that my wages and my intellectual tastes could command, my enthusiasm for the Bolshevist theory as a a [*sic*] practical revolutionary means of social reform is far greater then [*sic*] when I over-idealised it a long distance from America. You are very pessimistic about reforming the highly-organised and complex world system of modern life. I share your pessimism and agree with you that: "The one way out is the way of disintegration and new growth." This is precisely what has happened in Russia—disentegration [*sic*] and new growth. And to the marvelously new and swift growth of Soviet Russia the Communist Dictatorship is ruthlessly applying the Bolshevist theory in reconstructive work.

Of course, the disintegration in Russia did not come of a sudden. The centuries-old seeds were implanted there as they are now in every state of Europe and America. But it was after the bureaucratic debacle of 1905 that the rapid disintegration set in like "galloping consumption." Fortunately for the little band of virile revolutionists, the middle classes became afflicted with despair and impotence over the Japanese victory and the fatuity of Tsarism and when the greater debacle came in 1917 the intellectuals of the proletarian movement were the only group that kept their heads and had a clear programme to deal with it. It is not even necessary for one to go into Russia to estimate the growing success and sturdy growth of the new system of International Cooperation against the International Competitive system of the western world. The opposition that comes from different interests in the bourgeois countries, interests antagonistic to each other, is indicative of the centralizing strength of the new Russia. The anti-government Anarchists and Communists declare that by allowing small private capital and trade to function under strict governmental regulation, the Bolsheviks have betrayed the proletarian Revolution. The Socialists are very angry that Bolshevism is not democratic. The New York Times says, in its dignified salesman way, that "Lenin points with pride" to the achievements of Russian Communism which has discarded all its ideals but the power of the Dictatorship.[3]

In reviewing the industrial world in this New's [*sic*] Year's issue [of] the London Times, glancing at Russia, remarks that the Bolshevists just saved themselves (The Russian Nation) by the New Economic policy, but their finance was still in a state of chaos, they were granting huge industrial concessions in Russia which the Western capitalists would not take on account of the political (labour) laws under which they would be bound to operate.

Thus the London Times speaks for European and American private capital and incidentally answers the Anarchists and petty bourgeois Socialists. Bolshevism is really the practical and theoretical centre of the International movement against International Imperialism. Communists believe in Government and they believe also that Democracy—after serving excellently the purpose of the middle class battalions of bourgeois society—has done its time and had its day. The politics of the Russian Communists is based on organised labour power.

Your indictement [*sic*] of the selfish policy of American labour is unanswerable. The powerful unions entering the banking business certainly indicates that the Labour Aristocracy will eventually swag it with the capitalists in exploiting the poorer labouring masses. But this selfish spirit is not peculiar to America, it has prevailed in Europe and it was especially strong in old Russia where the imperial policy of wielding power was to set all the countless nationalities at each other's throats. But Bolshevism sent that policy to hell in Russia after booting out the incompetent imperialists. To-day the most important department in the Soviet Government is the department of National Minorities. Every new law that is approved by the Communist party and passed by the All Russian Congress of Soviets is first sent to this department where its adaptation to the needs of each national minority must be tested; no nationality is neglected, however small, not even the little known Gherjes and Bashkirs.[4] This policy is the greatest asset to the political strength and entity of Soviet Russia. It is earnest of their increase in the immediate future. All the nations of the East are watching it. All the prostitute republics that were set up as buffer states against Russia by France and England, live in mortal terror of it.

The Communist Dictatorship in Soviet Russia is a ruthless aristocracy of brains. If you are a communist you have more chance of getting a place than if you are not. But if you have not the brains to make good you will be kicked out and that place will be given to any one not a communist who is capable and willing to serve the Soviet System. By its high-principled policies the Government is winning all the national, non-partisan elements to its support. The wages of officials is [*sic*] on the same scale of the skilled workingmen, but of course Communist officialdom has the compensation of social dignity and a deep pride in idealistic principles—and power! I don't think the Communist Dictatorship has any intellectual and practical comparison in history, except perhaps the period of the Holy Roman Empire. Russia to-day is the nightmare of the competetive [*sic*] capitalist system, because, with all her wonderful natural resources, she is beginning to challenge the bourgeois competitive system with a national labour cooperative. The American system is efficient as you note and its masters are competent, but as the greatest of industrial nations, the forces of social disintegration interwoven in the fabric of America is [*sic*] far greater than the present-day problems of crumbling Europe. America has its Plutocracy, its Southern Oligarchy, its Western Farming Interests, its Labour Aristocracy, a Proletarian Mass, a great body of unassimilated Foreign-born Labour in its Basic Industries, acute immigration problems, and a great body of Unassimilable Negroes. The outlook for America is certainly not at all Utopian. Its future is rosy as hell-fire.

You ought to take a summer trip to Russia, the beer is better than the German, the wine from the Caucasus most excellent and soothing and not at all dear. The hotels in Petrograd are very well appointed, the service leaves nothing to be desired. Moscow is just a little overcrowded. The native singing and dancing is as full of sheer fun and expression as jazz. The theatres are full of colour, joy, robustness and fine acting; so also is the general life of the people, who are good mannered. Railroad travelling is comfortable. You can go first-class from Moscow to Petrograd for five dollars. And about town the droshkys [*sic*] are very convenient.

Yours sincerely,
Claude McKay

HLMP TLS

1. Mencken discusses Wilfrid Scawen Blunt's *My Diaries* in his essay "Chiefly Pathological," *Smart Set,* November 1922, 138–44.

2. Maxwell Bodenheim (1892–1954), American poet and novelist associated with bohemian literary circles in both Chicago and New York's Greenwich Village.

3. "Lenin Points with Pride," *New York Times,* 23 November 1922, 20.

4. McKay likely means the Kirghiz and Bashkirs.

To H. L. Mencken

5 September 1923

Berlin, Germany

Dear Mencken

I am glad you are thinking of getting out such a review; the Northern states need such a publication, something that will take a good humorous fling at everything and everybody and you lead in critical opinion.[1] We've had nothing since the demise of the Liberator, especially the art feature of it. I think the Freeman wants to be a little gay and funny, but unfortunately it is too stuck on its own ultra-delicate sense of humor: afraid of speaking out lest the vulgar should hear its refined voice.

I am sending you a list of Russian acquaintances that would be overhappy to have your books—ticking off the most important. It was a pity you did not seize the chance of going to Russia. This reconstruction period, the flexibility of the people and government in adapting themselves to the lightning changes—is a stimulating thing to see. In a couple more years it will have passed altogether away.

Historically and imaginatively the collective force of the working class movement (its culture its writers, artists, politicians and financial backers) interests me far more than the well-being of the average worker. So long as people live collectively Labour shall always pay the cost of social administration. But it seems to me that society always reaches a stage where the class that monopolises the administrative trust wallows so much in corruption and effeteness that the rigorous brains on the outside begin to organise and attack it in its many vulnerable parts and that it must ultimately collapse. Shorn of propaganda and romance the workers individually are not better to me than other people, but it happens that their social status gives reformer[s] and agitators their weapon against opponents—and I suppose it always will.

The Nation's eulogy of Harding was very beautiful. I suppose it is impossible for the Anglo Saxon not to wax sickly sentimental in the presence of death. I wish Coolidge could die in harness, too, so that the Nation might find that, narrow and bigoted though he was[,] his mind possessed some of the noblest of New England virtues.

Now I am doing character impressions of obscure types I met in Russia and their reaction to the Revolution. At first an agent reported favourably about them but so far he hadn't been able to put them over. Would you like a couple?

Yours Sincerely
Claude McKay

I am sending you a copy of Trotsky's "Flight from Siberia" to me one of his best things full of acute observations + personal prejudices jotted down at the moment and sent to some person, formerly his wife. Are you translated in German? If not a friend of mine—John Heartfield, Der Malik Verlag Köthener Strasse 38, Berlin W9 (he published Upton Sinclair) might be glad to do something of yours. He writes a little English, too.

HLMP ALS

1. Mencken and George Jean Nathan's *American Mercury* began publication in January 1924.

To Arturo Alfonso Schomburg

25 September 1923

Berlin, Germany

Dear Schomburg: I am sending you an article which I sent to the World to make some ready cash and it was rejected. I guess it was too frank. When I was leaving America [Herbert Bayard] Swope told me that he might consider something, but would not give a definite pledge. Now I shall be very much indebted to you if you could sell it to any of the Liberal papers—The New Republic or Freeman, but you mustn't say the World rejected it. Eric Walrond of the Negro World might give you some hints and if he disposed of them, I could give him 15% [?]. I have no objection to which paper you sell[,] white or colored—whilst the article is not tinkered with. By the way, you might try the editor of the Forum, there is a man there named [Pierre] Coalfleet. Tell him you heard from his friend [Ma]rsden Hartley in Berlin that he would consider a[n article][1] on Russia.

"A Moscow Lady" is a late thing I have done.[2] You might be able to sell it at a good price for me—to [H. L.] Mencken of the Smart Set (but you should see him personally) or the New Republic.

This a great task I am putting on to you. But I am in a tight corner. I am trying to sell the book I wrote about The American Negro[3] in [Russia?][4] but the American market is bad for it, it seems. No report from agents. On the other hand I can't go home to America now, for I haven't the money. Besides I don't want to. I want to stay around and write some things. But I am quite broke—want to go to Italy where it is warm and cannot. Frightfully cold here—and must have some money next month. I am depending on you to help me all you can. Eric Walrond is a hustler, if you can get hold of him.

Sincerely yours
Claude McKay

[Ad]dress Festus McKay

AASP ALS

1. Letter is chipped and words are lost.

2. "A Moscow Lady: A Study in Prejudices" (by Claud [*sic*] McKay) was published in the September 1924 issue of the *Crisis.*

3. *Negri v Amerike* (Moscow, 1923), translated as *The Negroes in America* (New York: Kennikat Press, 1979).

4. The condition of the letter makes this word unreadable.

To Josephine Herbst

[29 November 1923]

Paris, France

Thanksgiving Day!

Is the American Mercury out yet?

Dear Jo

Your letter lay in the Agency over a week and I got it only yesterday with others. The office had changed clerks and the new girl was looking under "Mac" instead of "Mc" for my mail till yesterday when I insisted that there should be something for me. I can't tell you how happy your letter made me—not because you promised to help me a little (I did not ever imagine that you could spare anything) but because it gives me a chance to tell someone how I have been feeling these last months.

I am sick with a very dreadful disease and never knew until I came to Paris. Syphillis [*sic*]! A couple months after coming out of Russia I felt uncomfortable pains in my shoulders but merely thought I had contracted a cold there. Towards the ending of August I had the scabies badly but a doctor gave me some ointment and the itching sensation stopped, but in September it came back again this time breaking out in little pimples in my head and around my belly and thighs. A doctor said it wasn't serious that it was a common disease in Germany since the war and my landlord said the same, but the itching became unbearable and the pimples would not heal. So when I came to Paris a French comrade whom I had met in Moscow advised me to see a specialist but I had only 10 dollars, and went instead to the Public Hospital. Luckily the head doctor, [Edmond] Fournier, is a celebrated syphillitic [*sic*] expert and was much interested in my case.[1] It was so different from the general run. I never had the symptomatic cancre [*sic*], the doctor suggested that perhaps I had a sore throat but I haven't in years. Of course, I didn't want to tell them I had been in Russia, but perhaps I was infected when I had a very painful tooth pulled in Petrograd toward the end of May. The comrades gave two or three parties for me night after and there was much drinking and indiscriminate kissing between the men as is customary in Russia. I don't know if it came that way—it[']s a prevalent disease there—but I have had very little sex contact and the doctors also think it is such an unusual case. But what's the good surmising when the disease is a fact now. The next astonishing thing to everyone was my rapid recovery. Upon the first injection the itching stopped and within a week my skin was completely healed and the rheumatics gone. I stayed in four weeks and was very happy, peaceful and rested but for the miserable victims round me. Terrible! One young lad of 20 who had tubercular syphillis [*sic*] died an awful death. And there are others, who I am certain, have no chance of recovery—chiefly the men past their prime. I never knew that venereal disease could make peoples' [*sic*] bodies so hideous and I hope that I shall never be compelled to see such sights again. On the other hand I was touched by the general sweetness and kindness that the staff showed to all the sufferers—even those who were very unpleasant in manner and aspect.

My material troubles began when I came out on the 15th. I had to spend my last 10 dollars for a room so I just starved for some days. The French comrade is out of a job and living off friends and so he could hardly help me. I went to the Dome Cafe where the poorer bohemian artists (English and American) rendezvous and a few that knew and had heard of me treated [me] to wine and coffee. Fortunately I am not much of an eater. I felt very sensitive to beg, but I screwed up some courage to ask two persons and was turned down. You know Mrs [Josephine] Bennett of Brookwood College (Labour) I suppose. She came to see me in hospital, brought me literature to read, but never offered me a penny. I suppose she doesn't realize or don't [*sic*] want to. And since I came out she has invited me to dinner but I haven't gone. She would spend 50 francs on a dinner which would last me for five days—and I must pay for the dinner with my presence and tedious talk about politics when I am feeling in quite another mood. Another young American radical acquaintance says he can't lend me any money but he would pay for my meals for two weeks if I went to eat with him! Of course I couldn't—it's too humiliating. Funny enough there are a number of English and American here stranded it seems. I see them at the Dome waiting for some person with money to come in and buy them a drink and a sandwich. They say I should do the same but it seems to me demoralising and losing the last shred of self-respect. When I was in a bad way a Chinaman came to [the] rescue and bought my book of poems for 50 francs.

This week I am posing for some art students 3 hours for 10 francs and so I am saved. I am booked for three weeks but I don't know if I can continue, the hours are difficult and painful, for the treatment has left me with an irritating pain in the right ankle which sometimes suddenly prevents my standing or walking. On the 15th of next month I must return to the hospital for a blood test and another series of injections. The doctors say the cure for syphilis in this stage spreads over 2 or 3 years, but that as my blood is good and my health excellent, I may be quite cured in a year or perhaps much sooner. So there! I am glad to be able to tell some one about my troubles.

But one splendid thing! I wrote about 25 poems while I was ill—more than I have ever done before in so short a time. I am going to send them to [H. L.] Mencken and I wish you would write a note to him about them for I know he doesn't appreciate poetry. Perhaps he doesn't understand it. They are a record of my experience in hospital and I am sending you two to give an idea what they are like.[2] I don't know whether I shall go to Basel or not again. I should like to for I want a few days quiet to do some prose sketches that are clamoring for expression. I was to visit [Franz] Welti one of the men that prosecuted [Maurice] Conradi.[3] I met him in Moscow and he has been urging me to go to visit him. From Berlin I wrote him that I would come from Paris and he wrote back that I should come right after the case was tried. But after my case was diagnosed I wrote him from hospital telling him frankly what was the matter that I should like to come up after I got out. But he hasn't replied. He may be a little shocked and afraid. But if he should write me and I go I will go to see [Andrew] Bernhard. I am so sorry for him. He didn't look very healthy to me in Berlin and I thought he was unwell. If you give me his address, I will write to him. He is lucky to find out what is wrong in time. I feel glad too that my sickness came here and not in America. Although I have no money, I feel much safer. I should feel much relieved if you could send me next month[']s rent. Two comrades in America have promised to keep me, but I am <u>still</u> holding out the promise. Am not a bit down[h]eart[ed], but the whether [*sic*] is rotten enough to make one so. Rain + sleet and terribly cold and for the first time since I left the tropics I find myself longing to return.

Claude

JHP ALS

1. Edmond Fournier (1864–1938), doctor and researcher who specialized in syphilis treatment.

2. Under separate cover (postmarked December 17) McKay sent Herbst "Convalesing" [*sic*], "The Needle," "Legacy," "Affirmation," "Retreat," "An American Patient," "Pageant," and "Escape."

3. Maurice Conradi, veteran of the Imperial Russian Army during the Bolshevik Revolution. Conradi and a collaborator attempted to assassinate the Bolshevik delegation to the Conference of Lausanne on 10 May 1923. He was ultimately acquitted.

To Grace Campbell

7 January 1924

Paris, France

Dear Com. Campbell:

I hope you received my letters. You are just as bad as all American correspondents. They never answer letters. I had the bummest holiday of my life. I was down with the grippe for 10 days and only forced myself to get up on New Year's day. I suffer because I am not properly clothed to stand the winter. I am wondering if anything can be done over there to raise a little money to tide me over these bad times. I nearly got turned out of my little room but for Mrs. [Josephine] Bennett of Brookwood College coming in while I was ill to pay the rent and buy me some fruit.

I suggest that one of you go in the name of the group to Eugen Boissevain, 137 Front. St. or Dudley Field Malone and see if either of them will help a little. You might show them that I have been working here—not idling[—] and that so far it was impossible for me to sell anything to the bourgeois papers. I would write to them directly but I think an interview may be more effective. My life here is very unsatisfactory for a propagandist—cadging a meal off people who are not at all sympathetic to my social ideas. There is so much work to be done if I am helped a little, but no one can work against such odds single handed, especially when he is not even guaranteed a little food and a bed!

Sincerely,
Claude McKay

NAACPR TLU (copy)

To Arturo Alfonso Schomburg

4 February 1924

La Ciotat, France

Dear Schomberg:

I am obliged to you for the cuttings, but the truth is I am very disappointed and disgusted with you folk. Not because none of you could afford to give me anything when I was broke, but because all of you Miss [Grace] Campbell, [Richard B.] Moore and yourself, stopped writing when a word of encouragement from a member of my own would have meant so much to me. I wrote you two letters that you haven't answered and I am sure you got—the same with Miss Campbell. Moore, I won't mention at all. And I was so worried about my trunk. How could Moore have fooled you when he does not write to me. So far, he has nothing to do with my trunk, and all I wanted you to do was to break into it and send me a dozen of Spring in New Hampshire. The first books you sent were a great help to me for I sold some of them at $2 each which helped me out considerably at The French exchange[.] Miss Campbell had promised to take care of the trunk, I wrote to you about it, and you might have telephoned her—Grace Campbell—a matter of 10 minutes rate. I merely wanted you to send me some more—to help me to help myself when I was very down and out. As it is if a few American people had not helped me to get away to this little town in the South of France to cure my cough I should have passed out in Paris. I am blaming you all because you refused to put yourself to a little trouble to help a friend in a strange land—merely the matter of my trunk, a few books and sending me some Negro literature. The white friends in America whom I thunder against send me all of their interesting literature. Some Negro magazines + papers would give me an insight into what is going on in the Negro world and I could write some articles from them to make money. I couldn't write to white strangers to look after little matters like my trunk and yet if I did I think I would get better treatment from them.

I am sending you a card on which I would like you to put the season of those West Indian fruits. You might get it from [W. A.] Domingo[1] or any Jamaican country man. I should be obliged if you will do this and return the card as it is important to what I am doing now. I am writing a novel to be published this year. I do hope you won[']t neglect this card as everything else has been.

Yours sincerely,
Claude McKay

AASP ALS

1. W. A. Domingo (1889–1968), Jamaican writer and activist living in Harlem at this time who was editor of Marcus Garvey's *Negro World*.

To Josephine Herbst

12 February 1924

La Ciotat, France

Dear Jo:

This letter of yours is away the best thing I've got out of you yet, if I except material help. I love it.

I am very much interested in that Bennett family,[1] and as a writer, you must be too, even though they touched you so very closely. But your temperament may be very different. I always manage to stand people off a little even those with whom I have the most intimate relationship, so that I may examine them with an artist's aloofness.

Unfortunately, I don't know Toscin[2] but the Bennetts seem to me such a typical composite American family. Self-centered you say, but it's more than that. There are many self-centered people who have the sensitive faculty of feeling. But the Bennetts are such an unconsciously unfeeling family. Yet they <u>think</u> they are sensitive and cultured and that they feel deeply. They are just like Ruth [Allen] except that their superficial culture is real—not such an obvious painfully acquired thing as Ruth's. (The way she takes a cigarette out of her decorative case and lights it—like a converted bourgeois performing a religious rite of bohemianism[.]) But the Bennetts don't rub me that way. I can stand their company when I couldn't Ruth's. The first are artistic vaudeville, the second bad burlesque. Of course, I have no sympathy to waste on them. My interest is artistic curiosity (I wish I had another word beside the stock "artistic" to use) and materialistic necessity. But the whole clan of Bennetts know just what they want, go after it ruthlessly, win it if they can, pass it up if they can't, or chuck what they win when they grow tired without any feeling of compunction. A devouring tribe. You never should have tried to be "nice to them" afterwards. They are the typical bourgeois that dominate all progressive movements in America. In their little country town, hedged in by social convention, they find it impossible to live with any liscense [*sic*] whatever, and so they take to "movements" chiefly the radical + proletarian where they endeavor to find that liscense [*sic*] their only society denies them—without contributing anything of intrinsic worth to such "movements"; for they have given up nothing of their old selves. There is something of the Bennetts in Max

[Eastman]'s nature except that his strong, lucid thinking saves him from their ignorant mistakes.

Our Bennetts will never learn, even through the most tremendous defeats, for they possess such an unhealthy athletic assurance about life—they are the Christian Scientists of Radicalism. But there is no doubt that their influence and contact ruin many promising minds of the lower classes that have not breadth of outlook enough to make them aware. Young Katz to me is ruined forever. Here was a boy that might have amounted to something taken up by a wealthy self-opinionated and self-contained family that had its own "right" views about everything under the sun. They pretended that they were superficially free of bourgeois traditions and encouraged him to be free. And of course this Jewish boy from the slum had no background to rest against as they. Why, they just used him up, took everything he had and gave him nothing. The freedom he has acquired is very bad manners in talking, eating and general demeanor that no cultured person (who is not in love with him in the way Jo Bennett is) will tolerate. He's so neurotic now, I don't think Freud could help him—cannot see the fine distinction between the commonplace prostitution of Paris and the more disguised prostitution of Jo's world. Of course, he now naturally despises them, for he has seen through them, but he cannot readjust himself. They have robbed him of all standards of balance and given him a false attitude of self assurance that he has not the education or money to support. And he drifts around with the lower class pimps and prostitutes of Paris—utterly lost.

Jo says these pimps are after her money through Oscar. I told her frankly from hospital that I thought it was her job to help right him—perhaps send him back home. But she won't see [seem?] just as unbalanced as he, except that she has a background to lean against and he hasn't. The boy always liked me in New York, but frankly I am a very sensitive sort about vulgar manners, and like Mike Gold, he had a way of scratching the private parts and spitting, that always made me want to vomit. But he was useful to me in Paris for he had acquired the language and when Jo learnt that he had found Claude she just sailed down on me with attentions—and the farther he sailed away from her. She wanted me to save him (for her) and I shouldn't let him know as he would be offended. I had lots of amusement. She came to the hospital one day and had only 10 minutes to spare, but he came in as she was going and she just simpered all over and stayed an hour out.

He has the upper hand (without knowing, poor devil he's just <u>running away</u>) but she is the cleverer. For months he slept on the floor of a cheap prostitute (girl) in Paris and Jo knew; they starved some days. She was willing for him to sleep in her hotel and she would feed him in good restaurants—but she was no dafty old widow about giving him a little money to throw away on prostitutes. At last I got him to take a room and induced Jo to pay for it for 2 months. He won't even take money from her now. But he is safe now, I think, driving a car and ought to find his level among such people as drivers etc.—However, he was out of a job—and Jo has just written to say she's been "presented with a little car—belated New Year's gift!"! [*sic*]

If your letter was catty, mine is tigerish, dear Jo. Here is something good from Andrew [Bernhard?]—but he ought to get away from that Anglo-American colony of Montparnasse. No good for anyone but the artists who must bum an existence from the curious bourgeoisie that generally come around. And they will take Andrew for an American bourgeoisie. I wonder if I could tell him this!

Have you forgotten the magazines? Doesn't matter how old. Have seen nothing since Berlin. Began my second treatment in Marseille last Thursday. It is nicer than the first—injection in the arm + not painful. Doctor says my reaction is superior-positive. I must go every Thursday + will. Going to live till 100. It is rumored you know that it was what Wilson + Lenin had. Neglect during first stage—so it worked its way after a seeming cure to the brain as it always does.

You know Ruth sort of took me in altogether—because of your recommendation and then she told me you had shown her my first letter in a sort of tremendous voice so I thought you must be very intimate. But she said you had both lived together in New York. I asked her if you ever quarrelled and she said: No, both knew how to avoid that. And I remarked I thought it was strange for most good friends do have a quarrel.

CM

JHP ALS

1. Likely M. Tuscan Bennett and Josephine "Jo" Bennett, American activists associated with Brookwood Labor College.

2. Likely M. Tuscan Bennett.

To Josephine Herbst

29 February 1924

Toulon, France

Dear Jo

Here's a letter from Ruth [Allen] that you must share with me. It is so self-revealing.[1] That "mending my clothes" phrase is perfect from her. And she's after my "ego" for which I'm searching myself. I don't quite get her line. It seems she's piqued about something and want[s] to show Cincinatti [*sic*] what she can achieve. I did tell her in my answer that her desire to go back there seems rather a petty sort of ambition.

I've heard from Andrew [Bernhard?], too. I suggested to him in my last letter that he should open an art bookshop. I don't know I think he has the combination of qualities to do it and he seems to love books so much. But I said it in a half joking half serious way. But I really think it is a good idea.

Funny how Ruth has the same qualities as Jo Bennett if she wasn't third-rate. The latter has too small rooms in a little tenement house in the Rue St Jacques—just off the Boulevard Montparnasse. She has painted and curtained it up Greenwich Villagy and she thinks it's so wonderful to have such a place for only 200f a month! Of course the entrance to the rooms is narrow and dark—but once you get in—why a princess of royal blood would be glad to have such a place. But Jo Bennett thinks it[']s so romantic to be living in a slum. She invited me up twice with a French acquaintance and did <u>all</u> the cooking and waiting herself—wouldn't even let us help her remove dishes. And she always have [*sic*] a crowd there—people she really despises, too. I asked her frankly how she could do it. And she says she is going to write a novel and is getting material! Don't be offended Jo, but I think your radical women need more emancipation than the proletariat.

Jo is a strange mixture. I owed her 200f. Bob Minor sent me $25 drawn on Paris and she was the only reliable person I could think of asking to change it for me. So I told her if she really wanted the money now she could take it + send me the change. I knew from her nature she would take it then—but the funny part she also sent me an indifferent lot of new American magazines costing about 125f! And I'm going to write and tell her she is certainly the Grande Dame. Yes you ought to put them in your book, but I think you should laugh at them. I hear the family is unbalanced on both sides. Two frightful suicides and a bad case of lunacy. Living in a small town with all the neighbors of standing whispering about them + they very conscious of it. It is easy for such a family to develop a devil-may-care attitude toward society and try to shock it by taking part in radical movements and all that. And Jo is rather peculiar in spite of her front of perfect poise.

For example she told me that Fritzie (know her?) and all the women at Brookwood "did her dirt" because they were jealous of Kate. She was so beautiful and athletic going out in the fields with the men, with all of them crazy about her, and yet she did nothing with them! I think the only girl she really likes is Genevieve Taggard.

Thanks for that Guardian with the Lenin report. I had missed it. Isn't the Bookman rotten! Not one good thing and I hear the circulation increases every month.

See my address! Am moving next Monday. For a week I couldn't work—the cold wave numbed my fingers. I slept with my old overcoat next [to] my skin + yet couldn't keep warm. The little houses here have no chimneys. At last I found one + moved ten days ago, only to find the fire place was walled up. Awful for me with this chronic cough. I have found a room in Toulon where I can burn wood. I tried Marseille but it is a nasty repulsive city. And the French trading class is terrible. They cheat me going and coming. I hear too you're having snow in Florence. We had two falls here.

Sincerely
Claude

I like your orange paper: it is fine.

JHP ALS

1. Includes a letter from Ruth Allen.

To Arturo Alfonso Schomburg

1 March 1924

Toulon, France

My dear Schomburg: If you won't write you are doing the next best thing by practical help so I won't quarrel with you. Thanks for Moore's book but I am not appeased.[1] I would still write to him if he would send me even a card or if I knew he had any interest in my letters at all. But to other things.

I warned you before that I shall make many demands of you to finish my book[2] and do it well. (1) I want a little map of the United States with the boundary of each state clearly marked (2) Then I want the fauna and flora of Alabama[,] Texas and Florida—especially the chief garden flowers. (3) Please ask Moore the facts about Bebel the German Socialist.[3] Is there a life in English (4) What is the salary of the governor of New York (5) Can you tell me if Smith, Vassar or Wellesley take coloured girls and the exact location of each college (6) and hardest I should like to have a copy of the novel called White and Black.[4] I think Moore had it and I don't know how you will manage it, but I think it is essential that I should have Jessie Fauset's book but you mustn't beg her for it in my name! Please don't. And I want Walter White's too when it comes out. Do break your silence and tell me what you think of Jessie's "There is Confusion[.]"

I have had a very nice letter from her recently. She is charming but rather schoolmarmish in expressing her opinions.

And now Schomburg, please do not fail me. It is absolutely necessary for me to have that map with the states all marked off clearly. I have finished the first half of my book and want to revise it. But I cannot do it without that map and some clearer knowledge of the flora and fauna of the South. I have forgotten so much. The heroine of my tale is a Spanish-West Indian girl who goes to school in Alabama—a coloured Catholic school for girls, I make it. Is there any such in America? We have many in the West Indies of course, + I know the mixed schools in the U.S. but I don't know of any exclusively for our coloured girls. If there are let me know.

I had to move here on account of the cold. Am working hard and have no need to worry now for I am expecting some money to carry on for three months.

Yours gratefully loyal + Sincerely—
Claude

Tell me, too, when did the suffragettes picket the White House during Wilson's presidency and when was the 19th amendment giving them the vote signed.

CMcK

AASP ALS

1. Presumably Richard B. Moore, though the book in question is unknown.

2. *Color Scheme,* McKay's first attempt at a novel, later destroyed.

3. August Bebel (1840–1913), founder of the Social Democratic Workers' Party of Germany.

4. Hubert Anthony Shands, *White and Black* (1922).

To Alain Locke

2 April 1924

Toulon, France

Dear Locke

It was a pleasant surprise to read your review of Jessie Fauset's book in the February Crisis.[1] Of course you haven't given me any idea of the scope of the work, however I gather it is about better glass [*sic*] coloured folk and that Joanna Marshall has an artistic purpose, but you did not give the drift of the story which to me seems essential for coloured readers—something of the mind outlook and contacts of the characters.

If you can afford it, I wish you would send me a copy of the book. I should be very grateful.

I answered your post card from Berlin but you never wrote again. I also sent you a letter from [Arturo Alfonso] Schomburg and you never even mentioned the receipt of it! I didn't even know whether you had gone to Egypt or not.

I left Berlin in October—just in time to enter hospital in Paris. I grew ill again with pneumonia just after getting out round Christmas time—and I really thought I was going to die then—my whole system was so debilitated. But a couple of friends rescued me and sent me here to the South of France where I am also working on my novel. I have just finished the first 10 chapters and am entering the New York phase of the lives of the three foremost characters.

I am having a good laugh at everybody and everything in America myself included—but there is the inevitable tragic side. I am assured of three months more support here and am working like mad.

The gang all went to pieces in Berlin[,] some went to America, others to Italy—Charlie Ashleigh arrested + deported to London[.] I find Toulon interesting. Dirty and quiet but good to work in. I have much to say to you when I am sure of your getting this letter.

Sincerely yours Claude McKay

ALP ALS

1. "The Younger Literary Movement," *Crisis,* February 1924, 161–63.

To Langston Hughes

16 April 1924

Toulon, France

Dear Langston:

I sent you a card just a moment of the receipt of yours. It was addressed to Thomas Cook. I am very sorry and disappointed about your trouble. I was anticipating a pleasurable time with you. My book is finished, thanks. If you are going to be there for any length of time I thought I could afford to come down before going on to Paris. I haven't been any place since I came here. Let me know[.]

—Claude

[Alain] Locke showed me a couple of your poem[s][—]would like to talk about them.

LHP APS

To Alain Locke

1 May 1924

Toulon, France

My dear Locke

We may have been thinking of each other and fired off those first letters nearly at the same time. I don't think I accused you of neglect. I only wondered why I never heard from you—we having so much in common. It is very possible your letter miscarried. Other correspondence of mine also went wrong in Germany. And you should be careful by the way to spell my name exactly right—McKay—I have trouble with the French postal employe[e]s when it is not just like that.

You know some parts of your first letter mystify me rather. I thought I was persuading you all the time not to take that Washington disappointment so badly but I never reckoned on your entering upon experiences of "diffused emotion."[1] The first phase seems to me infinitely better than the last. I need not argue you supply the answer yourself when you write: The only thing that worries me is that there seems to be little creative energy derivable from it! A highly preserved and guarded emotion is absolutely necessary to creative effort. As a philosopher you must be quite aware of that. The person of diffused emotions belongs to either of two extreme types—that of the common prostitute or the gentlemanly rake. Each of those types by deliberately abusing the natural emotions has lost the taste for any rich morsel of life's sensations—just as the common drunkard loses a discriminating taste for rare wines.

If ever I sink to the level of "diffused emotion" I know I shall lose the creative gift. But on the other hand I am not a sentimentalist hopelessly longing for lost fruits and spilt water. We all suffer setbacks and disappointments in the various ways of life. Should we allow the sap of emotion to dry up within us like the ascetic or dribble out into the barren places of dissoluteness because of a broken love or a lost ideal? Every artist answers that by preservation of the emotion. But I must not forget that emotionally the artist is a self-protective animal.

You quite missed my wave in Berlin. I love criticism and advice from friends. I wasn't so reckless after all—my own body is a sort of instinctive protective agency against unclean types and although I went around to all sorts of places I was quite discriminating and had fewer affairs than you imagine! But the best of persons get caught sometimes.

My skin broke out in pimples all over before I left Berlin and the doctors never found out what was wrong. The treatment in Paris went like magic, the doctors said the disease was only incipient and in six weeks my flesh was sound again. I am strong and look healthier than ever, but I must take treatment at intervals for about a year or two for the germs in the blood.

The French are experts in the disease and I am glad I happened to fall sick in Paris. They are certainly a courageous people. My few French friends in Paris thought nothing of my illness. Two or three of them came here to spend the winter season. Toulon you must know is a naval port. Last week the most interesting one left and gave a stag at which I was present. Everybody was drinking indiscriminately and I said something about individual glasses. But Jean said it didn't matter: <u>Nous sommes tous malade</u>.[2] I was frankly startled at such an anarchistic view of hygiene. But compared to other civilized people the French seem to have no sense of hygiene. In the hospital I watched the visiting relatives kiss the patients as if they were not ill of a dangerous malady.

I like Toulon. It is small, quiet, bracing—a good tonic for work after Berlin and Paris. And I am getting much done. More than half the book is finished which I am now trying to get typed in Paris. I also finished another book of poems, half of it from my hospital experience, and sent it on to Harcourt, Brace + Co. I told them to send it to [Arturo Alfonso] Schomburg if the m.s. was not available for them.[3] You can hardly do anything for me in that line if you are leaving as early as June. But I am obliged for your offer.—Jessie [Fauset]'s is a readable narrative but I resent how she makes light of discrimination against Negroes in America.[4] Better she hadn't touched those points than glossing them over like that. Why, just a little prejudice, has killed and enervated artists among the white races. The nerves of Negroes are not made of wire. What a story she might have made writing about the reality of a Negro artist's struggle for experience in an American environment! Instead, she is so intent on making a business success of the artist Joanna that we get a perspective of a nice land but no heights—no depths. The book was sent to me by the publisher. Hope to <u>see</u> you this summer.

Ever
Claude

ALP ALS

1. According to Jeffrey C. Stewart, this is a reference to the end of a relationship between Locke and his young lover, William. See Jeffrey C. Stewart, *The New Negro: The Life of Alain Locke* (New York: Oxford University Press, 2018), 431.

2. "We are all sick" (French).

3. Unpublished as a collection during McKay's life, these poems appear in the section "The Clinic" of Claude McKay, *Complete Poems,* ed. William J. Maxwell (Urbana: University of Illinois Press, 2004), 197–207.

4. Jessie Fauset, *There Is Confusion* (1924).

To H. L. Mencken

1 May 1924

Toulon, France

Dear Mencken

I was glad to have your note last January. I did not write again as I had nothing of importance to say or to offer.

I have been writing furiously ever since and now the better half of the book is finished. I am having it typed and shall let you have a look at it before this month is out.

I didn't stay in Paris to work. I left there the middle of January. But I think it is a much nicer city to loaf in than London or Berlin and infinitely preferable to any American city. It is more congenial to an anarchist temperament.

Of course I hate the French waiters North or South; they are too impudent and familiar—fresh and the little traders will cheat a man every time he winks. But when he points out he is being treated the French will hand back the change. They don't tell him he's an auslander[1] and should be overcharged as the Germans do.

Again the night life of Paris may be enjoyed by everybody. I love roaming around cities by night. And French city life seems to be organised with loopholes for everybody. A man may not like French manners and customs but he can group himself or be eccentric in clothes or manner without being pestered by policemen or a crowd of cads.

But the night life of London is awful for anyone not having lots of money to spend. No means of conveyance after 11 except high-priced taxis no cafés open—only the swell clubs for swell people. If one wants a cup of coffee anywhere in London after 11, he must go to a coffee stall and drink that poisonous substitute. Of course the people speak one's own language but one is glad to get away from that scourge sometimes. I am, at any rate. No, except for wealthy people London is a horrible city.

I am feeling much better and stronger and hope to return to America in the Fall.

Yours Sincerely
Claude McKay

HLMP ALS

1. "Foreigner" (German).

To Arturo Alfonso Schomburg

16 June 1924

Toulon, France

Dear Schomberg,

I'm sending you another list of questions that will undoubtedly put you to a test but I hope you will honestly forgive my plaguing you so much. But as I go forward with the book I find that there are many small things I need references for and here I am cut off from every available source. So I hope you will try to supply my need.

The first half of the novel is entirely finished and being typed. I had a very good reader go through it for me and she praised it very much. I shall finish the whole early next month I hope. Then I shall devote the rest of the time to revision.

I was down in bed again and now the doctor says my lungs are affected. However I am putting on a brave front and working as if nothing is very wrong with my health. It is the best way and there's no use worrying. I did not receive that book "White and Black" and I would be glad to have it. Let me hear from you once in a while and if there's any newspaper or magazine clipping—anything of interest in the Negro world please send it to me. How is the Garvey Organization? And do you ever see the Messenger?

Ever yours sincerely,
Claude

1. What Year Iowa went Dry?
2. Did Lord [George Brydges] Rodney die in Jamaica?
3. When did the first sale of Liberty Bonds begin?
4. When did the first Negro regiment reach France?
5. Was it the 15th?
6. What is the name of the principal coloured Lawyers' street down-town?
7. How much was the soldier's life insurance?
8. About how many pages of the N.Y. "World" go in advertising?
9. Do Smith, Vassar, Wellesley, and Bryn Mawr colleges admit coloured girls?
10. Can you give me the nick names of some of the chief southern states. For reference Virginia is "soreback[,]" South Carolina "Tar Head" among colored people. Could say what it is for Texas, Georgia, Mississippi and Louisiana?
11. Will you send me a Map of New York?
12. What is the number of coloured women in America?
13. In suicide cases in New York is the body always taken to the Morgue, or, in the case of people of means, direct to an undertaker? How soon after suicide is a coroner's inquest held? Is the suicide given Christian burial?

[Left margin:] Have you heard anything about my trunk and all my books at No 25 East 14th Street? I'm anxious about them!

AASP ALS

To Josephine Herbst

7 August 1924

Toulon, France

You note that I always give the title for I think it is essential in Europe. It saves odd difficulties. On Monday I received money from Paris by letter—cabled from America + the envelope read: Monsieur Madam or Mademoiselle Claude McKay!

Dear Jo:

You shouldn't use a phrase like "presumptious [*sic*] enough" in helping me critically. That should go between formal acquaintances but I'm sure we are more than that. I regard you as a literary comrade.

I'm not kidding or pretending when I tell you I'm quite ignorant of modern prose technique. It is a fact. I have the natural feeling for fine rhythm in poetry and I've been interested in all the various forms ever since I was a boy. But prose I've read always haphazardly and only for esthetic pleasure. Then I haven't even done much of the haphazard reading since I came to America in 1911. For after I left college I never had any time for that. I used to follow up poetry at the library but prose was a hard thing to tackle, living as I was. When I was on the Liberator I was doing the spade work of weeding out mss—so I hadn't any time either. You know what that is. I am having the wonderfullest period of living now that I've had for thirteen years. I only wish I had some stuff to read.

Of course I know the people who count in modern prose—through the reviews—but I've read very little of them. One book each of Norman Douglass and D. H. Lawrence in 1920, two of George Moore's, Jurgen,[1] which I didn't like, some heavy forgotten thing of [Theodore] Dreiser's, one Knut Hamsun, [John] Dos Passos, Floyd Dell's second which was bad—and that's all! Besides not having the time to go through the hard procedure of getting new books from the libraries I've never had the money to buy them. [James] Joyce I've never read at all. I do want to get at him and [Aldous] Huxley and all of Lawrence's some day.

Don't you know that on the Liberator Max [Eastman] used to discourage me from writing prose? He said I would never do it well for poetry was my forte. But Mike Gold thought I should do prose. And Heywood Broun, Sherwood Anderson (whom I've not read) and people in London whose opinion

I value, said that I ought to write prose. Ruth Hale thought that I might do better in it than in poetry.

All this to let you understand that I'm not "digging" you in any way. I can't do that with friends. I am most sensitive to criticism by <u>responding</u> to it and trying to find out just what is wrong, where a faux pas or cliche spoils otherwise good writing. I used to pounce on such things very quickly myself on the Liberator. But they often get by in one's own work and only an eye coming freshly to it can pick them out. I think it[']s almost impossible for this not to happen when one is doing anything as long as a novel.

<u>I am finished</u>!! Got through last night. This second part is a bulky lot and while piecing it together I see more and more where your criticism of the previous dialogues hits the exact mark. I shall have to cut out more of it than you indicate I think[.] Because most of what is <u>argued</u> is <u>developed</u> in the series of events that follow. Thus the argument is unnecessary. In fact that real book is the second part, the first I see clearly now is only the introduction and it must be shortened considerably so that it shall fit on to the second.

I'm glad that you're swinging away now into your own work without any further troubles. When will you be finished? Mrs [Anna] Davis <u>hints</u> that I should go home but I really don't want to yet. For two weeks, I haven't gone swimming. I had a ferocious onslaught of colic and dizziness and am just getting over them. Do you ever get a heavy cloud on the brain? I wonder if it comes from too much mental exertion.

I am going through this + shall pack it off to you soon + you'll have to <u>laugh</u> at my horrible picture of New York. It's the only thing to do. Mike wrote to me from London. He was staying with Charles Ashleigh + I gave him your address. Best regards + thanks—Claude

JHP ALS

1. George Moore (1852–1933), Irish naturalist novelist and influence on James Joyce. He is also referring to James Branch Cabell's *Jurgen* (1919).

To Arturo Alfonso Schomburg

14 August 1924

Toulon, France

My dear Schomburg,

Thanks for your last letter and the rib-tickling pictures you sent along. I have been waiting thinking that you would send me that map of New York City and other small things I asked you for! I have finished the novel and the map etc are necessary for me to fill in blanks during the correction—so I shall be much obliged if you can send them to me.

About the poems—I have no terms.[1] You must find only what the publisher[']s terms are and inform me—then I could tell you how I would like the book to appear and so on. I couldn't not [*sic*] make out the name of the person you said would publish. What is it? In the meantime as the novel is finished, the poems might wait until I can make the number up to 100! Let me have your opinion about this. It is a big book I've done and it might be difficult to get it published for I have not been over circumspect and reputable in presenting my scenes and conversations. I wanted to be as true as truth itself and I had to write as I did. What I have been careful to do however is to use fine language and that covers up many an unpleasant scene and word.

[Alain] Locke is here—rather in Paris. He sent me a note from Southampton but I have heard nothing further. Thanks for information about the fruits[.]

With many thanks and sincere feelings,
Ever Yours Claude McKay

AASP ALS

1. A reference to the collection "Miasma," which was forwarded to Schomburg by Harcourt on 28 April 1924. This likely included the poems McKay eventually called "The Clinic," collected in McKay's *Complete Poems,* ed. William J. Maxwell (Urbana: University of Illinois Press, 2004), 197–207.

To Josephine Herbst

18 August 1924

Toulon, France

Dear Jo: Today is a week since you wrote that you had sent off the package but it isn't here yet!

I may leave for Paris anytime in a week or two for I am not so well again. I won't say what it is for it sounds alarming on paper when I don't think it[']s serious[.] But it will be better in Paris where Pierre [Loving?] can interpret for me and I am certain of a friend if I should get worse. It maddens me for I was hoping to do all corrections here.

About that Confusion book: I thought it awfully written—no attention to plot and bringing out of details, quite a Confusion in itself.[1] But I never could see what Jessie [Fauset] was driving at though I tried to read it twice. Seems to me her chief purpose is to show the whites that there is an exclusive Upper Ten of Negroes and how they live. The writer is typical of that clan of colored people and you'll find that I show something of their <u>real</u> thoughts and ways in <u>relation to the whites</u> throughout my book. They are awful people and you'll find the type in every subject race. But worst of it is that among American Negroes they are the [*sic*] practically the <u>only</u> articulate ones and they have behind them that awful gang of New England and Quaker philanthropists—the people that read the "Nation."

On the other hand, I don't think Jessie wanted to show the white characters as <u>bad</u>. She is writing a Sunday school self help tract for good behaving Negroes and it works out that way. She's something of my Richard Blair sans his fine character.[2] She has no perspective, no social, psychological, not even a humanitarian outlook on the Negro question. I don't think she <u>feels</u> even—for instance she makes Joanna an <u>artist</u> while her reactions to the life around her are precisely those of a clod-hopper!

I think I am much more <u>bitter</u> than she in the presentation of my facts, but I don't use my facts (at least I try not to) for propaganda value. For me the facts are not final entities by themselves, but atmosphere against whose lights and shades move my characters in whom I am much more interested as people.

The root of the race trouble in America is entirely economic—no sane observer can deny that. In ordinary propaganda language we say white vs. black but we know that it is more than that. The Irish and Indian peoples hate the English nation because they visualize it as the Power oppressing them. It is only from that point of view that their nationalist movement is at all tenable because when we look at facts we find many members of the English nation working for Irish and Indian Independence. And it is thus also with Negroes—the whites en masse represent a system that oppresses Negroes, but it is a system that a great body of thinking whites were accidentally born into and would like to change—perhaps more than many Negroes who view it only from their own acute angle. But it isn't an easy matter and in the common fight we use the ordinary phrases—black vs. white and working class vs. bourgeoisie—that are not at all correct. For life isn't narrow and definite like that.

After all, Jo, the best of the whites—the people who think—as well as other races have no need to apologise for being what they are. I often had to say that to correspondents when I was with the "Lib"[3]—sometimes people wrote to me saying they "were ashamed of being white!" And I wrote back that they should not be any more than I was of being black. Of course the really fine people in this world are so few and so powerless that sometimes one is seized with a fit of despair in contemplating life. But there is this much consolation, that it is the old, old world struggle we are in and that black, white, yellow and red are merely concrete examples of it—and we may fight and hope or we may not—but the trouble will remain long after we are gone.

Ever Claude

Did Max [Eastman] arrive? Have you heard from Mike Gold?

JHP ALS

1. Jessie Fauset's *There Is Confusion* (1924).

2. Richard Blair is presumably a character—representative of the "Talented Tenth"—in McKay's destroyed first novel, *Color Scheme.*

3. The *Liberator.*

To Josephine Herbst

22 August 1924

Toulon, France

Dear Jo,

I sent off the rest of the book to you yesterday. You'll notice where I made some hurried notes using your suggestions as the cue. Of course I have been more careful since your first criticism and I think I've done better with this half. The Railroad part I consider the best in the whole book. The part called The Congo I'm satisfied with least of all. I'm doubtful whether it[']s in good taste and good form! I did want to spit out something about Vachell [*sic*] Lindsay and that nasty Jewish critic (He thinks he is a critic) but I'm not sure if I've been able to fit The Congo in—make it belong to the whole.[1] Let me know what you think. The whole point to me could be lifted out without the book losing anything thereby.

The example "A" was just what I wanted all along to set me right in the presentation of my conversation. I knew that something was wrong which made me choose the stage way in those long dialogues but I couldn't find out what it was you see. I've changed the conversation to suit it some—where I have educated people talking. Do you know Jo it is altogether an educated American way of talking! As I read that little bit, it all came back to me how Agatha did talk like that. But the English are more formal and less vivid and direct and the ordinary Negroes have a way of dragging one sentence over into the other. They never use the reflective way of conversation. I think I've done best with Richmond Joe and Dixie Pride—except that I haven't made them too dialecty. I've gone slow on the dialect and the "slangs" because I think there's a tendency now to overdo them. I find for instance that so much of the novelty in dialect and slangs is quite in the spelling[,] when one pronounces them they are good everyday English.

But the biggest hint of all you've given me is [John] Herrmann advising that I should read the talks aloud. I never did before, you know. And as I read on I found out how many impossible words and phrases I had been using. Things that the most pedantic bores would not utter in real talk. I've cut out many as you'll see. But I'll have to get after them again after the typing for errors and bad breaks to me always stand out more clearly in typewritten form. You'll see that I have only one of that stage conversation in this last part. I've thrown out all the rest. Except that which introduces Blair to New York + makes him tell Alfred about himself. I think it is quite in place. Another thing—I don't know if I've handled Bonita's return adequately. It is painfully real and fresh and I did not want to paint it too much for fear of falling into sloppy sentimentalism. So I gave it a "lick and a promise" and finished.

And now I might tell you that I think I passed through the biggest crisis of my illness during the last 10 days. I though[t] I'd have kicked the bucket so I wrote 2 little notes to you + Pierre [Loving?] where my patrone would find them. It came on the very day after I finished. I don't know if I overworked myself. But I hardly think so because I have an instinctive way (or used to) of roping myself in. However on the Saturday after I'd finished I went to the beach to run + bathe—a solitary part of the littoral where I always go alone + sometimes take all my clothes off—no bathing suit. When I went in to bathe I was seized with a frightful pain in my head + had to get out. When I went home + for three days it was as if some devil had got into my head stretching it to breaking point. And sometimes my skull felt so much like a mash [mask?] of celluloid I thought it would break when suddenly it contracted and I felt as if a great hand had squeezed my head up so small that I had nothing but neck on my body. Tuesday my left side was completely paralyzed. Wednesday it moved up to my face twisting it up like a coil of rope. I could not eat [and] could hardly talk. Thursday I went to the hospital in Marseille. What happened I think was the doctor letting me stay too long—two months—without treatment. Judging by experience I seem to get well rapidly + to go to the devil on the other hand easier than the average white person. In Africa they say the disease will sweep a multitude of blacks off in three months while the whites seem to stagger on for a long time. Of course the doctors say it wasn't serious—but it was <u>serious in my bones</u>. The French are a little like Negroes—apt to make light of serious things until calamity is down on them. I was going to run away to Paris as soon as I had the strength where at the hospital one of the internes speaks English—but I'm a little better for the last two days. My face has twisted out normally again. And today I ate for the first time in 13 days. Oh what a meal I had!

And Pierre has written advising that I should finish the six weeks['] treatment here since I began it. So I think I will stay—going to Paris next month where I shall have a thorough examination.

Max [Eastman] has written me a nice letter. He's in the next province here by Var. He says he is unwell also—but not serious. Writes that Mike Gold is going to Russia leaving his book unfinished. Strange boy. The bolshevists would respect him more if he had a name as a writer in sympathy with their cause! But let him go and see for himself.

I rather think Mrs [Anna] Davis will be shocked out of her wits when she reads my book. Her letters sound so terribly respectable. But I wish she would give me a little more money to finish the correcting of it. Did she answer your letter? I'm afraid it was after she got it that she hinted I should come home. Because she has not mentioned your writing. But I don't want to go home right yet. I don't know whom I should send the book to. You remember my poetry publishers Harcourt, Brace. They said they would be glad to see it, but I don't like them at all. And would much rather try somebody else. Their claim to be radical publishers is all bunk. I remember their leaving out a perfectly harmless love lyric of mine. But I'm out of touch with everything. Who is going to do your book? I might try the same firm. Or do you have an agent in New York?

I must take a rest now—the doctor says I must "repose" for a few days so I haven't looked at the first part since you sent it back. But when I do I shall have lots to knife in it. When will you be finished? And what do you think of Andrew [Bernhard] now. You haven't mentioned him for some time + he's written me just twice in a long, long while. Thanks again to you and Her[r]mann for helping me and tell him that reading-the-talk idea just got me right.

Ever, Claude

JHP ALS

1. The critic mentioned here is likely a character in McKay's destroyed novel manuscript *Color Scheme* and may be based on an actual critic who wrote about Vachel Lindsay's controversial 1914 poem "The Congo," the title of which McKay references in the section of the *Color Scheme* manuscript described here.

To Walter White

2 September 1924

Toulon, France

Great Congratulations!

Dear Walter

Correspondence with friends is one of the special interests of living for me. So I am glad to hear from you after such a long interval of silence and to write again. You must be extremely busy with your duties and doing creative work also. I don't know how you manage it. Miss [Jessie] Fauset also. You have something of modern machinery in your physical make-up. Twelve days! You've beaten all records, and here I am envious—not yet finished! But I must plead illness. I have finished the narrative itself. I am doing the revision now. Cutting out, making additions, welding to get a complete, compact story. It is a job.

I finished the first week in August and came down a few days after with a paralytic stroke. Thought I was doomed that time. But I've partially recovered. I still have however the most alarming and excruciating pain in my head and I am going to Paris in three weeks where a friend is arranging to have me thoroughly overhauled by a specialist. It's no use dragging on a half invalid like this. I want to know what chances I have of permanent recovery. Don't tell this to anyone but I suffer from cloudiness of the brain and get the vivid and definite feeling sometimes that I shall become insane. Some friends say I should have an intellectual rest. But I don't think that is the cause of my illness. Writing is nothing[,] also reading. To have an intellectual rest is not to think and I cannot help thinking.

Well—I am glad I have finished the book[1]—whatever happens! My book presents the expressions of two intelligent colored youths trying to find ordinary decent work in a Northern city. There are photographs and sketches of the life of the average city Negroes—also of the sporting set. The white world that the chief characters touch is also shown. It is really a series of situations through which these young colored men pass. One finally commits suicide and the other remains a problem. Nothing is solved. In between I pour my loves and aversions—ideas. But everything belongs in the story. It is a second of reality—without any regard for sacred cows: white, brown, black. I don't know who I shall send it to—perhaps your publisher Knopf. I am not keen on going to Harcourt Brace again although they write that they would like to <u>see</u> it!

I am eager to read your work. I always felt that you had a real story to tell—from your investigating work, from your Evening Post articles. I don't know if you will do it for only you yourself know how much you can do. But apart from what I think you have in "The Fire in the Flint," I think you have the inside material for writing one of the greatest psychological American novels. And psychology is <u>the</u> important factor in novel-writing now. There are few people in America who employ your unique position. Perhaps there are a few, but who have not like you the gift of articulateness. You can write a romance—the real thing—of the true soul of the lyncher—the individual who lives respectably, has wife and children. You can show his life—turn his guts inside out—before and after a lynching. The workings of his mind, his personal conduct, respectable appearance. Is he human or infrahuman? Does he think he is doing the will of God or the Devil? You could do a wonderful work Walter. Something that no white man could ever write—however noble he is—because he could not feel the reaction of Negro blood. And also something that no black man could write (I mean any man that is obviously Negroid) because the white man will not allow him to see into his normal consciousness. But you have the incomparable opportunity of getting the very normal reaction of white to white and coloured to coloured. Your situation alone is a romance. My head aches I must not write more.

Ever
Claude

I wonder why Miss Fauset hasn't written to me! I hope I did not offend her in my letter about her novel. I tried to be frank—showing her where she wasn't seeing effects. And I expected her to respond and write more. So much to say. Tell [Augustus Granville] Dill I wish he'd taken a subscription of the remittances he sent me for the Crisis. I miss it. Get no news of the Negro World without it. I heard from [Alain] Locke + [Langston] Hughes. They are coming to see me next week. I agree with you entirely about propaganda. Truth itself and artistry in presenting it are the greatest of propagandists. We are every man a propagandist according to individual interests. But some people put the stuff over too raw. Bad propagandists. That's all[.]

C

CMCA ALS

1. McKay eventually destroyed the manuscript of this novel, titled *Color Scheme.*

To Josephine Herbst

7 September 1924

Toulon, France

Dear Jo:

I am very happy over this your letter and what you and John [Herrmann] think. I was afraid you both would not like the last part as well as the first as it did not have the idyllic touch and most of the New York and Railroad things were so sordid. Now I feel confident for I value your judgment greatly.

No: I think that as you're so busy the revising might wait till I get back to Paris under there unless there are whole paragraphs you think would be time + paper wasted for Pierre [Loving?] to do. I am slashing so much of this first part—at least a third of it.

I am glad you're nearly done too. I wish Mike [Gold] had stuck at his and perhaps we could all blossom out together and show Floyd [Dell] there is such a thing as radical writing different from the stuff he's doing. I did not imagine you were going back so soon. Well I couldn't think of anything more ideal than your taking my stuff along and if it's accepted soon I could work at the proofs over here. There's another novel on the Negro and, you know, I shouldn't like mine to be puffed as a "race problem" novel. For it isn't merely that.

I may come to Paris sooner if my head don[']t [*sic*] stop this constant drumming—it drives me crazy. Max [Eastman] thinks I've busted a blood vessel. He did too last winter and is rather unwell he says, but not serious. I hope to see him before I leave here. I just had this letter from Mrs [Anna] Davis. It might interest you.

Regards and thanks to you and John—

Claude

JHP ALS

To Langston Hughes[1]

22 September 1924

Toulon, France

Dear Langston:

I may not manage to get over to Genoa after all. For since living here in Toulon I have accumulated a number of books and other things that are of some value. In all I have two suitcases of things that I cannot lug around with me. I wanted to send them on direct to Paris—but I find that the cost is extraordinarily high. So I may have to go direct to Paris from here taking the bags [?] as personal luggage when I would not have to pay. However, I'm expecting some money from America and if it comes, I'll send the damn things on to Paris anyhow and come down to see you. Anyway, I'll send you in telegram whether I can come or not. If I don't come my temporary address in Paris is

Thomas Cook et Fils-2 Place de la Madeleine. You must write me there how you are. Especially if you should go broke before you find a ship. It's dreadful business that. I have more experience of it than I care to remember.

I want to talk to you about your writings.[2] Your stuff seems the most sincere and earnest to me of any that young Afro-America is doing. Of course, [Countee] Cullen is facile and more fluent than you but he lacks depth. [Alain] Locke showed me a few things of yours. You ought to pay more attention to technique I think. That blues thing for instance I thought remarkably good but you should have made the whole of it more colloquial. You having in some literary words which appear strange in such an atmosphere.

I thought your prose in the Crisis was very good—some of it better than some of your poetry. I am sending you that September issue of that magazine, two copies of which have just arrived. I see [William Stanley] Braithwaite has a reference on me among others. I resent it not because of what he thinks but because of the spirit of the man's thought. I hope that [W. E. B.] Du Bois will let me reply to it some day. Braithwaite is the Booker T[.] Washington of American literature—a bred[-]in-the-bone sycophant—perhaps an unconscious one by necessity and environment. I think his influence on American literature both bad and worthless. And he is a warning to every young Negro of artistic aspirations of what he should never emulate. But I want to work all of these strictures into an article and take a crack at Miss [Mary White] Ovington who perhaps thinks that her <u>leadership</u> of the NAACP entitles her to give authoritative advice to Negro artists. I am afraid Du Bois may not be able to print it! But what Negro artists need more than anything is to succeed, in these days of psychological effects in literature, is a daring independence of mind and spirit. Especially when the competing avalanche of expressions is so overwhelming. Braithwaite, frightened by the aggressiveness of the whites, would caution the young Negroes to go easy to take the Booker Washington's [*sic*] path in literature—the very line that has made Braithwaite himself such an unfortunate mediocrity.

When you get back home, please write to me. I may return in the winter. I am not sure yet. I'll have to find the passage. I'm sick to death of knocking about. I hope you don't fall into that state of life voluntarily. It can't do you much good, I think. You should try and take the most of such material comfort that you can get to enable you to write. That is also necessary to good writing. I must stop preaching and I am hoping still I shall be able to see you again.

Sincerely yours
Claude

Say my last name is McKay not Mac[.]

LHP ALS

1. On the reverse side of this letter, Langston Hughes has drafted a poem with the title "Me and America," which appears to be an early version of his famous poem "I, Too."

2. Paragraph not indented in original.

To Alain Locke

22 September 1924

Toulon, France

Dear Locke,

Got your telegram and card[.] Too bad it was not possible to know before hand, we might have had three leisured days together with some amusement thrown in.

But don't mention thanks and future returns over a simple matter of camaraderie. That was merely a gesture of friendliness and sincerity and it was such a treat for me to talk intelligible and intelligent English again! I wanted to go to Genoa just to talk with [Langston] Hughes of things that I know I won't find anyone in Paris to talk to very soon. But I've had to cancel the plan. I don't want to lug two suitcases to Italy and the cost to send them direct to Paris is enormous. So I must forgo the pleasure of meeting Hughes until I return. I leave at the end of this week for Paris by Bordeaux. Hope you had a good voyage over. Charles [Ashleigh?] was pleased that I gave you the photograph. I have been hiding from him. He wants me to give him my address in Paris, but he might come to my room when he is finished here and embarrass me with my not-so friends. Another thing, he may think I have money and expect me to go halves on his expenses. His people are well off but they won't give him money to fool away his time in Paris I am sure. He knows I haven't money but you never can tell what these people think when one is a stranger among them and not working in the ordinary way. They hear what you have to say all right, but wink behind your back at each thing.

On Saturday, however, I'm going to make a punch for about half a dozen of them. They have been mighty good chaps in their way. I tell you Locke there were times when I would go crazy working here alone with no one to associate with—if it were not for them. The best sort are the casual aristocrats of the world. To them the little differences of colour and language etc.—that seem so insurmountable to "nice" people—don't matter at all. The punch will cost me about 20 francs but it's worth doing it.

With best wishes Sincerely Claude

You'd better destroy this letter—

You know if you're neurasthenic you ought to see a psycho-analyst—if you cannot help yourself. At any rate you know yourself. Dr. S. A. Tannenbaum of New York is a fine understanding chap. He's a friend of mine—slightly neurasthenic himself which makes a better + more sympathetic analyst. He cured Floyd Dell according to the latter's word. C

ALP ALS

To Alain Locke

7 October 1924

Paris, France

My dear Locke: you know of course that I am suicidally frank. Your letter has angered me. Your attitude towards the "Mulatto" poem is that of Booker T. Washington's in Social Reform[,] Roscoe C. Bruce in politics and William Stanley Braithwaite in literature. It's a playing safe attitude—the ultimate reward of which are dry husks and ashes! Why mention the Liberator? It's a white paper and "Mulatto" is not stronger than "If We Must Die" which the Liberator first published. I guess if the Liberator had not set that example not a Negro publication would have enough of the "guts" you mention to publish it! It isn't the "Survey" that hasn't guts enough. It is you. The Survey editors would not mind. There are many white people that are longing + hoping for Negroes to show they have 'guts.' I will show you by getting a white journal to take Mulatto.[1] Send it back to me at once. No wonder the Negro movement is in such a bad way. No wonder [Marcus] Garvey remains strong despite his glaring defects. When Negro intellectuals like you take such a weak line!

Send me back that Mulatto poem. And the others also[.] I would not have the Cradle Song[2] published without being accompanied by Mulatto to strengthen it. The Crisis my dear Locke will be glad to take "Mulatto." Send me back all the things—and I do not care to be mentioned at all—don't want to—in the Special Negro number of the Survey. I am not seeking mere notoriety and publicity. Principles mean something to my life. And if you do publish any of the other poems now and leave out "Mulatto" after this protest you may count upon me as an intellectual enemy for life!

I am angry as I say. Certainly Jessie Fauset would show more courage than you have in this case. Damn it Locke—I am surprised—yet not too much. You are a dyed-in the wool pussyfooting professor.

Claude

ALP ALS

1. "The Mulatto" was published in *Bookman,* September 1925, 67.

2. This poem may be "Africa," which features the phrase "Cradle of Power!" This poem had been previously published in the *Liberator* (August 1921), the collection *Harlem Shadows* (1922), and *Opportunity* (May 1924) and was later featured in Alain Locke's anthology *Four Negro Poets* (1927).

To Langston Hughes

28 October 1924

Paris, France

Dear Langston

I wrote to you from Bordeaux. I don't know if you got the cards. I did not get here until the 5th.

You know I am very very sorry I could not get to you, but I hope that we shall get together soon. I'm anxiously looking forward to that time. I am quite lonely here. It is cold and raining all the time and I cannot get a good cheap room. My two American friends went home last week and I am altogether by myself. I am working on my book though. The typing is nearly done. My friends could not wait any longer to take it along. But I hope to send it off by the end of this month.

Some Crises have just come to me with more of your poems. I wish we could get together for a talk fest about your stuff. That "Night come tenderly dark like me" is exquisite with beauty but to me you spoil it with that quite prose line in the first stanza—"That is my dream." I have not the poem here therefore I am not sure if I quote you write [*sic*]. But my point is that the poem is enough a dream by itself without your breaking the artistic unity and telling us that it is.

Let me know what you expect to do now that you are back in America. [Alain] Locke + I ran into a snag since he left. Nothing serious only a little matter of tact—method and principle on the great problem of America—a little matter but of big significance to me.

Ever Claude

LHP ALS

To Alain Locke

4 December [1924]

Paris, France

Dear Locke: Now to it. I hope you don't think I have foolishly stayed angry, sulking and not wanting to write. But I've been most busy finishing my book. That is all done at last and I'm happy to tell you that Sinclair Lewis is reading it before I finally send it off. That's a stroke of good luck. Walter [White] arranged it for me. I've been getting the most charmingly fresh and frank letters from him. I don't know of any one in America I really love so much. He is so kind of naive. And he has too I think a beautiful mind. In spite of the dynamite in his book[1] I am sure he has none of the bitter contempt for American civilization that settles in my soul.

Walter says he asked you about my book and what you told him "did not amount to much when boiled down[.]" I suppose you did not want to tell too much but there is a tendency to vagueness in your talk and in your letters. Hope you won[']t get mad at this. I felt this in that letter about the Mulatto that I answered in such a raw style. And I don't like indefiniteness. It annoys me, kind of makes me feel that the person is putting a blind between his auditor and what he is telling him. A deliberate blind. Get me?

I don't get yet what you're diving at about Charles [Ashleigh?]. You don't mean he has gone to America, do you? But even so there is no reason why he should be on your hands. He could make his way among German-speaking people. Of course you must know how to deal with such a situation in a country like America and a place like Washington—if it should develop!

"Prancing Nigger"[2] was forwarded to me from London by a reporter friend of Philadelphia. And it makes damn diverting and strange reading. Of course it is nothing like the islands—but the dialogue is half-good and the natural scenery excellent.

Your last word about Mulatto is quite precise. And I agree with you. But as you know Locke, I as an artist am not concerned with placating Public Opinion, white or black, vicious or sympathetic. I hate the blessed Public. What I want to show is the feelings of a certain type of New World mulatto—to lay bare his soul. How he feels toward the white man. There is no doubt that there is a great big difference between the soul of a [W. E. B.] Du Bois and that of a Paul Lawrence [*sic*] Dunbar. I can't help if white fools make bad propaganda of a psychological truth. The truth will gain in time. The part that there are great black leaders can never be disputed again after Toussaint L'Ouverture.

Well I hope you send a copy of the Survey. I have seen Jess[i]e Fauset but she has not had much to say. She's busy attending lectures, meeting people etc. I am busy sleeping and thinking. I can't do much going around for I have no money. Jess[i]e is as prim as ever. Her book I hear has been published in England.[3] Walter has certainly stirred up a hornets' nest and he has sure written a vigorous document.[4]

Sincerely yours
Claude

ALP ALS

1. White's novel *The Fire in the Flint* (1924).
2. Ronald Firbank, *Prancing Nigger* (1924), also published under the title *Sorrow in Sunlight.*
3. Jessie Fauset, *There Is Confusion* (1924).
4. White, *Fire in the Flint.*

To Walter White

4 December 1924

Paris, France

[On Letterhead: Brasserie Des Papillons, Paris]

Dear Walter: I am very glad to have your long letter. I took a sly dig at [Alain] Locke over that reference of yours. That fault you mention is in his talk, his letters, his writings. It's so hard to nail down what he's driving at. It's a fault of many coloured writers. I don't know if it can be traced to the long years the black race has lived in America without being allowed to express its own thought and feeling. I met [Jean] Toomer here for 10 minutes and felt something of that evasion and confusion in his talk to which I see so clearly in his book. He could really do wonderful things if he would be simple and clean and not confuse the reality of Negro life in the purple patches of mysticism. If we're going to do anything in literature and art we've got to stand good straight-out criticism and not allow ourselves to patronized as Negro artists of America. Another thing that might hurt Negro writers is too much indiscriminating praise from Negro journalists. [William Stanley] Braithwaite's "scholarly" article some time back could not have been worse. He is a nice man, appreciates literature, but as a critic of high discriminating tasks he's pitiful and hopeless.

I've met Jessie Fauset. Her book has been published in England, but we don't see much of each other. I'm living over in Montmartre—away from the Anglo-American raw rendezvous in Montparnasse, which I detest. But I go over there once in a while as it is the only place where one can pick up interesting people.

Day before yesterday I met Sinclair Lewis + wife. He's a good chap. I had dinner with him again yesterday + we were out drinking all night at the N.Y. bar. I have given him my book to read as I am sure he can give me some good tips for publishers. I also showed him your letter to me and he was clearly pleased by your reference to him. He loves you immensely—also your wife. You're lucky in making friends. You're so altogether charming and fine: I'm a son of a bitch—I like really well so few people, that those I can like, I prize dearly and I always feel happy when I can possibly like some new freak of God.

I hope you'll be having some substantial royalties on your book and that it will be published in England and France and Germany. If I get mine out, I want to supervise myself the French translation. I'm interested in that more than in any other. As a people, I've not been much able to <u>see</u> the French yet. The little trading clan treat you in a way that Germans, Americans, English + Americans of the same clan do not. The French are really sharper, wit like the small Jewish trading clans of America. But I do like the immense elbow room that French civilization gives the individual. You're left alone. You can do so much as you like within the wide limits. You can take the country + ignore the people if you want—and I don't think that is possible in any other country. France has them all beat.

You ask about my pecuniary matters. Well, I am just now in low waters again but I've sent off three frantic begging letters. I had promise of help for a definite time but I have gone beyond that—so I am not sure what's going to happen. I can only hope. Thanks for the map. It gave me the location of some down-town streets I needed badly. Would you mind telling me one thing: What is the name of the streets in which the colored lawyers chiefly have their offices downtown? I think it is Fulton, but am not quite sure. I hope you take a holiday + come over here before I get back. Best luck to you + wife[.]

Greetings [to] James Weldon—Again thanks, Claude—

[Upper margin:] I send you a letter about your book from a good Dutch writer. I am lending it again to a writer on the Paris Times, a good publicity paper. Then other people want to have it. It[']s being talked about in the quarter + they all ask—who are you? I am asking a friend in Philadelphia, he sailed from here a week ago[,] to look you up.

I don't know if you know that I had a paralytic stroke in Toulon last August. It is worrying me rather + I want to go to London to see a nerve specialist. Tell me—who do you think is the better fellow to send my book to—[Joel E.] Spingarn or [Donald] Brace?[1]

[Left margin:] Can[']t find that Hollander's letter—Sorry[.]

NAACPR ALS

1. Donald Clifford Brace (1881–1955), American publisher and founder of Harcourt, Brace & Howe in 1919.

To Walter White

15 December 1924

Paris, France

Wishing you a bully [?] Xmas

Dear Walter:

I forgot to say this in my last letter: That if you are convinced about that raping business[1] you should also have convinced us—all of your most sensitive and critical readers. For it is one of the most prominent and striking things in the whole book. Miss [Mary White] Ovington has the very same sort of thing in her powerful short story "The White Brute"—the best thing by her I've ever read—if you've never read it you should. And she convinces. You make your rape take place right in the heart of a pretty populous city. After all raping is not an instinctive thing to average men. It arrives from special conditions—you may find it for instance among soldiers and sailors who are sex starved and somewhat brutalized in nature. And so I suppose you could find it sometimes among southern whites who want to enact their savage masculine and race superiority over a reserved and respectable colored girl or among blacks who are tabooed from consorting with white women. But in Maimie's [*sic*] case—it comes down on us so painfully sullen and gives us an unbearable feeling that not a colored girl who wants to can hold herself away from brutal white men in the South. If you had sent her out walking over the Central City country road, brooding over her unhappy state in Georgia, have her wandering home through a field path then the attack—I think your case would have been by far more effective. For if those things happen as you assert and as I am found to believe the world should see them in the true light—not in a melodramatic atmosphere.

I'm worried about my book. I am afraid it is not good enough to publish as it is. I want to do tons of things to it. And I don't know how I'll ever get the finances to go through with it. If you could convince some publisher—but not bloody likely—not yet. I'll write you about that later.

In the meantime I must make a strange request of you. Could you send me a hymn book that is used in the colored baptist churches and one of the African Methodists. I have some hymns in my book but I think you might ask one of your boys in the office to get them for you—old ones will do fine as well. Here's a little secret between us—I've met Jessie [Fauset] twice. At the Montparnasse cafe frequented by English + Americans and at a tea party. But I've made no effort to meet her again. I guess I'm hopelessly off but Jessie is too prim, school-marmish and stilted for me. You know I got something of that professor-manner in Joel Springarn too—Gee I'm always running away from that sort of thing. It[']s all right I guess if you[']re brought up to it—but I wasn't + if there's any good to it—I'll never find out my dear Walter—I'm too old to learn now. Sinclair Lewis is all praise of you + your lovely wife. Ah you were lucky to draw such a handsome one. He likes the whole N.A.A.C.P. crowd. [W. E. B.] DuBois' article in the Mercury was clever—not like his old way—a little Menckenistic I thought.[2] Ever Claude

NAACPR ALS

1. McKay refers to the plot of *A Fire in the Flint*, in which the main character's sister Mamie is raped by white men.

2. Likely W. E. B. Du Bois, "The Dilemma of the Negro," *American Mercury*, October 1924, 179–85.

To Walter White

27 February 1925

Toulon, France

Dear Walter

I must not accuse you of not answering my last letter for perhaps your responsibilities are so great—what with your old work and your new—that time is playing tricks with you.

I wonder if you got that letter of mine in which I asked you for a hymnal of the A.M.E. Church and a collection of Negro Spirituals (the latter without music or music not essential as words)[.] I asked <u>you</u> because I thought that you could do it better than [Arturo Alfonso] Schomburg or [Alain] Locke as (being in an office) you might just ask one of your employees without worrying yourself too much. Let me know, please Walter, if I can expect these things of you for I've just reached the stage in the revamping of my book where they are necessary.

You know it's impossible to get your book in Paris. It was reviewed way back in November in The Paris Times the newest English paper in Paris but it could not be had neither at Brentano[']s, the Shakespeare Bookshop in the rue de l'Odeon nor at the American Library in Paris. Mrs Fred Howe[1] (her address is 20 rue Jacob-Paris) was very anxious to get it. But my copy was going the rounds + could not get to her before she left for Cannes. And it is still in Paris now in the hands of French friends.

I don't know how long I shall be here for it seems I cannot get the money to go on. I am doing a short story about Jamaica that I'd like you to try and sell to one of the better paying magazines. Let me know if you can, for by such means I may be able to keep on here until I finish.

Sincerely Claude

NAACPR ALS

1. Marie Jenney Howe (1870–1934), American feminist activist and author of the biography *George Sand: The Search for Love* (1927).

To Alain Locke

1 March 1925

Toulon, France

[On Letterhead: Gd. Café De La Paix Et Des Sports, Toulon]

Dear Locke:

See I'm back here again and working like hell remaking my book. Had a hard time getting the dough to come back and so it's necessary for me to put the whole show across this time.

I got the poems back from [Arturo Alfonso] Schomburg + I hope I did not offend him. He couldn't get our point of view for not publishing them now and it is so hard to explain everything in a letter. I've worried you all so much you might be getting tired. And yet there's more to come.

In one chapter of my book I have a scene in a colored church and for this I need a hymn or two from an A.M.E. hymnal + for something else some of the very old Negro spirituals (without music or music not essential). I wrote asking Walter [White] if he could help me get them but I got no reply up till now. Perhaps he must be frightfully busy! Could you get in touch with him Locke + see if he is sending them? If not, can you do it? I suppose Walter could get at them much easier than you? But please don't fail me this time between you both for those hymns are absolutely necessary to my book. I hope you'll answer before I go further on near Nice. I only came here for 2 months + one is already gone. I'm expecting a friend from Paris later on + he does not like Toulon. And I myself want to be [indecipherable] the life of the Riviera though not to be in it.

I visited that Pierre Levee[1] place before leaving Paris. Entertaining, but how dirty, disgusting, slimy! I never saw anything so sordid in Germany. When the French go in for filth they can swim deep in all right. But I found two other places that would be interesting to you. Are you coming over this summer? What I mean is that I love small rough commonplace hangouts like these here around Toulon—but I can't stand nastiness—shit!

Tell Langston [Hughes] for me that I shall write to him very soon. I was worried and unwell one half of the time in Paris + did not know whether I should have to hurry back home to America—which I didn't want to do. What is he doing + how is he getting on. Give him my fraternal + professional love.

And how is the Survey number. I see you scored by dropping Mulatto after all.[2] But how can I fight you from way over here? How can I? So better let it be as it is. Tell me about yourself.

And please Locke don't fail me please.

The A.M.E. hymnal + the spirituals—just very cheap copies will do—

Yours always
Claude

ALP ALS

1. Rue de la Pierre Levée, Paris.

2. Locke did not include McKay's poem "Mulatto" in either the special "Harlem" edition of the *Survey Graphic* or in his *New Negro* (1925).

To Langston Hughes

8 April 1925

Toulon, France

My dear Langston

I suppose you are thinking that I am a very poor correspondent. Well the fact is that for a chatty casual letter I have wanted to write to you more than any one I know except it is [*sic*] Max Eastman, but I've been having a hell of a time since last Christmas which destroyed all my initiative for friendly and intimate writing. You know how it is with a so-called intellectual who is bumming and begging his way through life. Sometimes I wish I'd stick to manual work and insured [*sic*] that material security and comfort for myself which is the premise essential of any decent existence. But I don't stay in that sort of dependency for long, life still remains an adventure with me and I won't balk at erasing any aspect of it even though I do it with fear and trembling. You see my funds were cut off just about Christmas time and I was adrift in that damned damp and cold city of Paris. I was put under discipline, my dear boy, because my patrons had heard I was not living right. I don't know how anyone could live wrong in Paris on forty dollars a month!

I borrowed 500 francs and came back here at the end of January and for two months I have existed on bread and water only. Not such bad results physically for I'm afraid of an inclination to rotundity. But mentally it was a horror—I could not work. Now I have the chance to go on for some weeks—so I must stop complaining.

I've had to rewrite my book, every word of it. It was bad as a novel—no form to it and I didn't want to publish a novel by "a Negro Poet." I wanted to publish a novel. I have three-quarters of the new one done and whatever it may lack in content, there is nothing lacking to its having the form and shape of the novel.

Well, I hope you were able to make the University. I think you know exactly how you feel about it. It's the man-adult and poet in you fighting against being a regular student. I had the time of my life trying to become a regular student when I was twenty two after publishing a book of poems and I never succeeded. I think I am quite unfit for any regular academic work in any sphere of life. But I do hope you'll be able to get through and get a degree. It might mean so much to you in this highly specialized age, (or Germanised) where there's no place for free lancers.

Say I do wish you['d] pull yourself out of the dumps and laugh at yourself and life a little. It isn't such an awfully bad affair. I regret more than ever now that I missed meeting you out here. It was a great loss to me. I met [Jean] Toomer for five minutes in Paris and I must confess I could not like him in that awful atmosphere at the Dome. It may be that I impressed just as badly. People are never natural under such conditions. I went one night with Max Eastman + Jo Bennett to Zelli's[1] + we took in Florence's[2] for 10 minutes. But the others did not like her. I'm afraid she's changed since I saw her last year and not for the better. The white Dome cats say she's never been the same since she danced with the Prince of Wales.

I've received copies of the Harlem Survey Graphic which is an excellent number except for (to me) the pictures. They're poor, lacking individuality. I liked the lay of your poems, I did not like the <u>sentiment</u> of, "I too" nor the form. "Our land" I love, for it is lovely. You've got a great gift of poetry color, clear vision and simplicity but you have a tendency to jam in an absolute prose line among your most beautiful lyric lines. That spoils a poem, of course. It is strange that you do it. Countee Cullen whose work I consider quite inferior to yours never does it. He's a born rhym[e]ster. What I loathe in Cullen is his sickly religious twist. It's ugly. Your Jazzonia is a lovely wild thing but "In a Harlem cabaret six long-headed jazzers play" is a <u>bald</u> prosaic statement of fact. Perhaps, though you could not feel as lyrical about the players as of the girl. Dream Variations is also very beautiful. But in the very midst of that lilting loneliness, you bring in the prose fast, "That is my dream." Why Langston? We know it[']s a dream without you telling us[—]you ought to leave something to our imagination + intelligence. Take that line out + you have a very perfect lyric[.] The last two lines classic in their beautiful simplicity.

Don't get mad at my opinion—it[']s friendly—

Claude

LHP ALS

1. Zelli's Club, located at 16 bis, rue Fontaine was a fashionable Paris cabaret owned by Joe Zelli and featured in Ernest Hemingway's Lost Generation novel, *The Sun Also Rises* (1926).

2. Chez Florence, located on the rue Pigalle until 1926, was a fashionable Paris nightclub owned by Louis Mitchell and named for African American performer Florence Emery Jones.

To Arturo Alfonso Schomburg

8 April 1925

Toulon, France

[Upper margin:] You'll find the poem on 4th page of the letter. If you don't like it I can send another—

My dear Schomburg,

I was very glad indeed to have your letter for I had kept on wondering why you had not written to me. I did not mean to be offensive in any way about the poems but when I heard that you were still thinking of publishing them I was terribly afraid because I had been convinced by competent observers that I would be making a very great mistake by publishing the poems at present not from a literary but from an individual point of view. I hope you understand everything now and if I've been offensive in any way I withdraw and beg your pardon and hope that you forgive me.

I am pleased that you like Miss [Pauline] Rose. I was slightly acquainted with her in Russia and in Paris I got to know more of her as she typed my work.

The Pushkin in the Crisis[1] was not precisely for you but [Augustus Granville] Dill has got all the originals of my Russian photographs that were published in the Crisis and I had asked him to guard them for me—Therefore if you would oblige and humor me by calling for them—I think you would get them all—the Pushkin included. You have only to tell Dill that I asked you.

About the paintings in the Louvre I don't know what to do—if I were still in Paris I could ask any of my artist friends to go there with me and make a search for them—then I could pay to have them photographed. I am sure it would not cost very much. But I left Paris at the end of January and I am sure that nobody I know there will trouble himself—They will all be lazy just as you were writing to me. The most I can do is to ask a little friend I have there who is very reliable. He's a young French Communist and knows nothing about art but he may be of use.

Concerning that poem—I shall send you something along with this letter. But—as you must know I have been very busy with prose and have written no poetry of late. I can only send you one of the old ones which I hope you will not mind.[2]

AASP ALU

1. This image ("Pushkin, The Russian Poet: An unusual picture presented to Claude McKay by Yasinsky Yeronimavitch") appeared in the *Crisis*, March 1924, 227. Other photos from McKay's time in Russia accompanied McKay's two-part essay "Soviet Russia and the Negro," *Crisis*, December 1923, 61–65, and January 1924, 114–18.

2. Letter survives in incomplete form; it breaks off here.

To Arturo Alfonso Schomburg

28 April 1925

Toulon, France

My dear Schomburg:

At last I have finished my book in the way I want it to be and I am having it typed. The next thing for me to have now is a publisher who will pay me something in advance "a few hundred dollars" for I'll soon be at the end of my rope. Being so long away from America, I am out of touch with the publishing market. I therefore want to trust the placing of my book and the driving of a good pecuniary bargain with you. I will tell you the most likely publishers.

If you are willing to undertake this hard job please let me know and I will send you the m.s. as soon as it is typed off. I think the best firm to try at first is Alfred A. Knopf's[,] failing that Harcourt + Brace my poetry publishers, and failing them Boni and Liveright. I am certain to suit one of the three. But Knopf first of all as you might get an advance more easily out of him. I want that advance to live on while I am waiting for the proofs and planning my novel of a West Indian near-white in America.

Now when I send you the m.s. Schomburg, great though the temptation is, I hope you won't keep it by you to read it. Unless you can do it in one night! I want you to rush the placing of it—because my future as a writer or anything—all depends on my getting that novel published as quick as possible.

I have reached the point where I can no longer expect to get charity from anyone. I must make good by my own worth. Another thing—I want you to guard the secret of the title of the book—also that I have sent it to you.

It is necessary that no one should know that I have finished—especially certain groups of liberals so-called in New York, until the book is announced by the publishers themselves. If it is known that I have finished my precious supply of bread-and-butter may be cut off entirely.

Not the least of persons that should know anything of it is that Miss Pauline Rose. If you should say anything about it to her, I am sure that it will find its way back in a very garbled form to the N.A.A.C.P. and others. That girl is after all only a gossiping little kike. One must not be afraid of calling a spade a spade even though we might belong to the suppressed Negro race! That kike girl took back the stupidest and quite untrue stories about me to New York which caused me endless suffering for three months—my allowance was stopped because the sender said that she had unfavorable reports about my activities in Paris! Whatever one can do in Paris on a few paltry dollars.

I am waiting now to hear from you. I may be leaving Toulon before your reply but your letter will be forwarded without delay. I shall not be going near Paris, however, as I cannot afford it.

I think you will like my novel. It's a comedy[,] a satire in white and black and I don't make virgins of my colored girls. No sir! It will shock some of our ultra-reputable hypocritical Negroes, but I think I'm nearer the truth and tragedy and gaiety of Negro life than Miss Jessie Fauset.

Ever your friend
Claude

By the way if you will place the m.s. for me, you should take it to the manager and get an interview. That is better than mailing.

AASP ALS

To Arturo Alfonso Schomburg

On or after 29 April 1925

Toulon, France

Dear Schomburg: I've just got another letter from [Alain] Locke in which he mentions that you are still thinking of publishing those poems of mine privately.

I write back to you post haste because I do not want the poems published now in any form. I thought I told you that expressly in a letter some time back. I am acting on good "white American" advice so it is a matter of material urgency to me that those poems should not be published for some years when I have a measure of security and can do as I please intellectually. Nor do I want the poems shown around to anybody else Schomburg. I hope you understand it would be better if you sent them back to me. Best regards + thanks, why don't you write?

Ever yours Claude

AASP ALS

To Langston Hughes

9 May 1925

Toulon, France

My dear Langston

I was very happy to get this letter of yours. I have had no real news of our country for a long while. I wrote to Walter White and [Alain] Locke twice each asking them small favors—a couple of things I wanted to refer to in doing my book. I had counted on their expressed friendliness towards me but neither of them has deigned to reply. I don't know if I unwittingly offended Walter or what. I did give Locke a hell of a calling down over a poem of mine called the "Mulatto" which he thought was "too strong" for his special Harlem number, but we settled that difference between us. I must then suppose (to be fine and noble) that their silence is due to overwork! However, I don't need the references[.] I made use of other things hot out of my head which I consider better.

I think, my dear Langston, I can guess something of your social trouble. Locke had hinted to me in a letter to Paris that you had been warned against him by busybodies and were keeping shy of his place since you got to Washington. I wanted to say something to you about it but I couldn't find a nice way of saying it, so I didn[']t. I felt about you then and still feel that you are capable of nosing your way by instinct, intelligence and balanced judgment. I've had all sorts of bothers myself on account of my conspicuous boyishness and my airy-free attitude toward people and things, but I always manage to hold myself the way I want to. You see I know many, many persons who are friendly-disposed towards me (some of them perhaps call me friendly), but I have very few real friends—certainly not over half a dozen intimates scattered all over earth!

Friendship is certainly the most exacting and selfish sentiment in the world—I at least have found it so. We make friends because certain individuals have something of value to contribute to our life, mental, social, physical, intellectual, bestial, enervating, as our bent may be. I myself have found friendship possible only by instinctively and heavily appraising my friends and weighing just how much of my mind and my time I can give to them and letting them comprehend instinctively just how much of their vagaries and other things I could possibly stand. And that has worked well. Max Eastman and I, for instance, have remained the closest of intellectual friends although we differ radically in our ways and our general outlook upon life.

So, old boy, don't lose faith in friendship, but be sure always to know that you're making the right friends. Don't let yourself be imposed on because you have become somewhat of a public character. Don't be forced into friendships sprung out of race or professional sympathy. To me they are worthless. I rejected many such while I was on the Liberator especially pushing Jew opportunists, made enemies—better though than mushroom friends.

I never expect or want to be personally popular, for certain types are so terribly objectionable to me physically and psychically that I could never pretend to like them. You will find lots of people trying to use you to their own little ends. You must learn how to use them for your ends.

Now, what you have stated about your poetic style forms an iron wall around any criticism that I may let fly at it. You of course have your own conception of what is good and what is great poetry. I am sure that you have read much and formed comparative judgments. I am sure too that, even though unconsciously, the rhythm, style and accent of the great masters have influenced yours. All of us artists, however revolutionary and progressively modern we may be, are traditionalists to a certain degree. I myself, although quite in sympathy with any novel trend that is worthwhile, am rather a classicist. But that is my natural bent. Nevertheless, the great remembered phrases in poetic literature (even the anonymous folk things that fall from the tongues of the people) are those phrases that combined the most perfect marriage of words, rhythm, movement and atmosphere. A dead, flat stock phrase may manage to hold in the regular rhythm of strong vigorous verse without falling to pieces from dry rot and over work, but the fine, keen eye or the soul that is moved by color will not find any color in that dead stock phrase and to such a poetry lover, the rhythm is more than broken[,] it is murdered.

I didn't like any of your things in the Workers' Monthly.[1] They all seemed to fall short of your good work. I love when you say you write to amuse yourself. I hate when you deliberately write "propaganda stuff for the Crisis or cheap stuff to buy a meal." I don't mean that you shouldn't write journalistic verse for a living if you want to, but your poetry is not that. It is not Walt Mason, Edgar Guest or Berton Braley. You are not doing light comedy. Underneath everything of yours I've read is the personal, tragic, profound note that is the essence of great poetry and if you deliberately turn that into cheap material, then (I hope I do not go too far when I say) you would be cruelly prostituting your highest natural gift.

It's a relief to hear that you are in with the right people so far as a job is concerned. And it may be better for you, of course, to stick Howard jusqu'au bout.[2] And it may not be. You and Fate hold the key to the situation. Of course, I see by your letter you are determined not to get spoilt in that silly monkey-society atmosphere[.] But on the other hand my dear on top the folks may consider your refusal to attend their functions intellectual snobbishness[3] on your part! I know that you want to be simple and ordinary as all true poets are, but talented people cannot help themselves in that, much less geniuses! The world is so empty of real achievement, real intellect that the hungry masses and classes are ever ready and waiting to set up gods to worship. The half gods in their extreme vanity have this ignorant worship. I don[']t see how the genuine ones can stomach it.

However, if you're interested at all in satirical prose those society affairs are not entirely to be ignored, I think.

I give you the Paris address because I don't know where I shall be for some months. I'm leaving here in a few days for Marseille whence I want to get to some other points. I've finished the book and want a shift of scene to clamp it up a little. I'll let you know where I am from time to time. If you have any Crises from December I should like to have them. And tell me—how did Walter's book + Prancing Nigger go? And what are the new things of worth on the Negro Horizon? I am cut off entirely from everything. I didn't know [Countee] Cullen had a book out. He has in my opinion, a higher sense of form than you. I think that most of his stuff could hardly hold together if he didn't lace them in form. If you would do that with all you have to say I would predict anything about you. Tame the anarchist a little. Say what is Phi Beta Kappa? Jessie [Fauset] is that too, isn't she?

To finish I would like to knock around with you but I won't give you any bad encouragement. If I had a pocketful of money. . . .

Why don't you marry one of the race's heiresses? I am coming back to look the prospects over—for the benefits of art my dear Langston[.]

Claude McKay

LHP ALS

1. Hughes published several poems in the March and April 1925 issues of the *Workers Monthly:* "Drama for a Winter Night (Fifth Avenue)" and "God to Hungry Child" (March) and "Rising Waters," "Poem to a Dead Soldier," and "Park Benching" (April).

2. "Until the end" (French). McKay references Howard University.

3. McKay inserts a stray *X* here, something he often uses for a marginal insertion, but no insertion appears to exist.

To Arturo Alfonso Schomburg

3 June 1925

Marseille, France

My dear Schomburg,

Your letter came just in the nick of time preventing me sending the ms direct to Knopf. Now here it is and I want you to drive the hardest bargain for me. Try and get me a thousand dollars or failing that 500 on acceptance. And the book must be published on a royalty basis. I hope it will be on the bookstalls by September.

Don't worry about the N.A.A.C.P. You fellows ought to organise and fight their baneful influence. Their social work is splendid but in the artistic and literary sense they are a harmful lot. [W. E. B.] DuBois knows good prose but he knows nothing about poetry and art, his is the same type of mind as [H. L.]

Mencken's. And that woman—that virgin New England tabby Miss [Mary White] Ovington, who boasts of leading the movement—I'd better not write what I think of her.

If Knopf does not take the book—I think you'd better take it up to Mencken before you see anybody else. He might give you good advice. But I don't see how you can appeal to my compatriots. Nothing can be done that way, I think. I must make good with my own stuff. Am anxiously awaiting results. Write to me at Thomas Cook et Fils 2 Place de la Madeleine—Paris[.]

Ever Claude

AASP ALS

To Langston Hughes

6 June [1925]

Marseille, France

Dear Langston

I've just had your splendid letter a couple of days after Walter [White]'s telling about you and your book[,] [Countee] Cullen and others. I'd given up Walter and was rather sorry that I'd sent off my novel before getting his letter. However it's off already and the next news I want to hear is a cheque.

I'm damned pleased about your book. I'm sure that seeing your own work in printed form and being reviewed will be of immense value to you. I should like to see the Contest number of Opportunity with your poems.[1] The magazines are not here yet. Many thanks for them. Thanks too for the hymn book. I haven't received it + two that Walter is sending but I guess I shall. I can't use them as I had thought of but they may do for my next book. . . . .

Now, if you don[']t want to marry an heiress for the benefit of art, you might for your own benefit. No artist can exist unless he has some sort of subsidy in any sort of way either from his work or any other source. Anyway if money in any form should be showered upon you don't dodge away from it, nor take my homilies more seriously than they are intended to be! Alas I cannot marry an Ethiop heiress for fear of the bigamy penalty, but if any is ready to break through the barriers of Afro-American respectability and try a little free living with me for awhile well. . . . that depends. But I'm always ready for any adventure that I can work up the slightest interest in! And I'm not afraid of ties as God Almighty himself cannot hold me when I want to cut loose.

I'm now three weeks in Marseilles doing the Vieux Port and whore houses with a Mexican artist, a young Californian and a beachcomber. It's great fun. I should be in Bordeaux really according to my plans but the Californian has cancelled his Paris trip to remain some time with me and we want to do Corsica and a few interesting places together. Next month I shall go to Brittany where I must begin work on my new novel. I have written some poetry this spring—the first in 2 years but Provence is so beautiful, poetry just flows out of one. I have enough for a book but I don't want to publish any poetry for a long time yet. I don't know if I'll see [Alain] Locke or any one. I certainly shall not get to Paris before September if I do go there. I may even go home in the Fall—I don't know.

By the way there was one thing of yours in the Worker's Monthly I <u>did</u> like, "Death is a Whore," it was bold and fascinating.[2]—I'll let you have some news of me wherever I am. Cook's remains my forwarding address. A firm "Viking" has written to me about my book. It was Walter's suggestion—Here's a letter from a strange guy. Do you know him?

Congratulations, Claude

LHP ALS

1. The *Opportunity* contest was established by the journal in 1924 "To stimulate creative expression among Negroes and to direct attention to rich and unexploited sources of materials for literature in Negro life." This $500 award was discontinued after winners were announced in 1927. Although McKay submitted the poem "Desolate" (later titled "The Desolate City") in 1926 and the stories "Bad Boy" and "Redemption" in 1927, he never won the award. "*Opportunity* Literary Contest," *Opportunity*, August 1924, 228.

2. Hughes's "Poem to a Dead Soldier" opens with the epigraph "Death is a whore who consorts with all men." *Workers Monthly*, April 1925, 261.

To Arturo Alfonso Schomburg

[early June 1925][1]

Marseille, France

My dear Schomburg

This enclosed excerpt from [Alain] Locke's letter worries me extremely.* I have <u>never</u> said I don't want <u>Walter</u>[2] [White] to know about my book for Walter is really one of my best friends. Certainly you could not have said that to Locke. Did you?

Do, my dear Schomburg, try to keep yourself out of all backbiting gossip. When we must fight our enemies or friends—let us come out openly and do it—but you know how the Negro belts are just rotten-crazy with spiteful nonsensical malice and if we get mixed up in that sea of shit we shall never be able to do any real revolutionary work along artistic or social lines[.]

Best regards
Ever Claude

* I am worried because once gossip begins it never ends + so many Negro intellectuals are like old maids[.]

[Left margin:] In February I wrote to Walter + Locke asking them for a colored hymn book + Negro spirituals. They have never replied until now when my book is finished—they have sent them—just now!

AASP ALS

1. White posted the hymnbook on May 20.
2. Triple underlined.

To Walter White

15 June 1925

Marseille, France

My Dear Walter

Your letter was a surprise but a good one. I am always happy to have news of home especially when one like you can make them so interesting. I am so happy about the aroused interest in the creative life of the Negro. It is for Negro aspirants to the creative life themselves to make the best of it—to discipline themselves and do work that will hold ground besides [*sic*] the very highest white standard. Nothing less will help Negro art forward a boom in a splendid thing but if the wares are not up to standard people turn aside from them after the novelty has worn off.

About my book—I sent it off to my faithful old friend [Arturo Alfonso] Schomburg just a few days before your letter came. There was nothing else to do because you nor [Alain] Locke never replied to me! Locke has just written to say that a letter of his must have missed me. Something always goes wrong with my Charming Locke's mail but in spite of such accidents I like him immensely—we have quite a little in common. So back to Schomburg and my book. I should be glad if you will consult with him and give him some advice. I wrote him to that effect. I told him first to get the m.s. to Knopf (and that he might ask [H. L.] Mencken's advice)[.] The latter wrote to me a year ago asking to see the ms. I had a letter from the Viking Press who mentioned you. Thanks. But I should prefer a more established firm. However, failing Knopf—Liveright + my own publishers—H. B. + Co I should try the Viking.

I was interested to hear of [Countee] Cullen's book—I don't care much for what I have seen of his poetry but Langston Hughes is a real poet[,] strikingly original if he will only work hard and take his work seriously. I'm so glad his book is coming out. We correspond with each other.

Locke tells me now that he is sending a hymn book—Langston says he too is sending one and you! Overwhelming thanks. I can't use them now again—but perhaps some day I will. I have a short story some place that I might send to you. Poems—I don't care to publish any of what I've got for a while yet. I sent one story to America and never heard tell of it[.] That was about the same time I wrote to you.

I hope to come home at the end of the year and get things together myself. One can do so much more on the spot oneself. I regret I did not keep the Paris Times review but when I get back to Paris in the Fall I shall remember to look up the files for September or October for that review.

In Bretagne I shall think up the characters for a second novel. And when I've done that I shall start in on poetry again. The Harlem number of the Survey was an excellent thing but I did not care much for the illustrations[.]

I wish you had told me how your book went financially + in general also Jessie's. It's all right to have the boom but are the people buying? Artists must exist say I and not forever be begging for handouts—Regards to James Weldon [Johnson] + others.

Warmly [?]
Ever Claude

NAACPR ALS

To Arturo Alfonso Schomburg

[late June 1925][1]

Marseille, France

Dear Schomburg:

Here's a letter from Walter White and another from a new publishing firm. Will you make the most of them for me? I got Walter's letter right after mailing the book to you. And I am writing to tell him so. You might consult with him about the ms. He's an awfully nice chap—if <u>my novel will not shock him!</u> For it is <u>not</u> a "moral" book. I make my Negro characters yarn and backbite and fuck like people the world over. So it's up to you to use your <u>discretion</u> as I am not on the spot. I am sure Walter can give you lots of good advice. About the new firm Viking—I think I should see Knopf or Harcourt Brace first. An <u>older</u> firm can always <u>sell</u> a book better than a very new one. Especially if the book is of merit.

The thing for you to do for your friend is drive a hard bargain. As I am writing to you now I have only 500 francs—of course I have promise of money but I can't get it. I am still in Marseille but I shall leave anyday as soon as I get the dough. Let me know whether you received the m.s. o.k. and how it is going. I'm anxious about that.

I would also say don't be afraid of asking advice about the book. [H. L.] Mencken, to me, seems the best man of anybody, because his standard of judgement would be entirely literary.

Yours sincerely
Claude

AASP ALS

1. References a letter from Walter White dated 15 June 1925.

To Arturo Alfonso Schomburg

[late June/early July 1925]

Marseille, France

Schomburg:

Here are two very important mistakes I picked up going through the m.s. since I mailed the publisher's copy to you. They are mistakes in French[:]

1—page 66. Alfred asks Mark s'amusez seul? That is wrong. Please make it amusez vous seul?[1] Cross out the s' before amusez + insert vous. This mistake occurs in the fourth line—

2—page 138—line 14. Lucilynda says Je s'amuse—I don't quite remember. Make it Je m'amuse[2] crossing out the s + putting in m[.]

Sincerely Claude

[Left margin:] About the novel again I should advise you to take the publisher that will give me the highest figure as advance—Claude

AASP ALS

1. "Are you having fun alone?" (French).
2. "I'm having fun" (French).

To Max Eastman

"Friday" [20 June 1925]

Avignon, France

Dear Max

I came in here from Arles today. This is the nicest of the smaller French towns I've struck. It looks out on a wonderful valley and doesn't seem overshadowed and oppressed by its past like so many "historic" places. It has a throbbing life of its own and the river air is a marvellous thing.

I finished your Lenin and Trotsky coming up.[1] I like the spirit and time of it much more than the Trotsky youth.[2] If you'll let me I'll tell you frankly why I don't like the latter so well in spite of the fine flowing writing. It is because you seem to take it for granted that your reader should be of Communist Revolutionary persuasion. That sort of thing irritates me immensely—although I am a revolutionist of the Communist persuasion because it happens at this period to be the most progressive and reasonable from the proletarian viewpoint which I accept. And mark you it's not because the thing is Communist that I object. I need hardly say that. But if you were [a] prancing idealist like Upton Sinclair, [or] orthodox Catholic like [G. K.] Chesterton I would object to your writing as if the whole public believed with you. It's a trait I never find in [George] Bernard Shaw although he is so outstandingly socialist, trotting out his theories in all his works. Yet one is so carried away by his argumentative skill and passion that one wants to keep on reading + reading, forgetful of the fact, if one is anti-socialist, of the author's faith.

Perhaps I'm quite beside the mark in my strictness + if I am I hope you won't get mad. It seems to me however that when I read the great historians [Edward] Gibbon, Macauly [*sic*][3] our own Van Loon,[4] I am never suddenly jerked up in my reading to the fact of their being Christians or Liberals, etc. I couldn't say the same of [Thomas] Carlyle or H. G. Wells, they make me throw a fit every time.

In the Lenin + Trotsky where one should expect more of what I object to because of the nature of the writing there is so much less. There was only one little thing I did not like and that was when on page 97 in the footnote you seem to take an uncalled for crack at "bourgeois reviewers" to put yourself right with official Communist critics. At least that is how it appears to me, but it won't help you with the latter as the dirty tactics of the Editor of the Worker shows. The bourgeois critics have their own economic point of view—many of them are chockful of liberal theories—and can afford to be fairer to you in a review than rabid Communists on the one hand or tigerish fascists on the other. Both these groups are partisan to the extremes of dishonesty and would give you a fair hearing but will distort everything you say to their own ends.

That makes your position all the stronger. I don't know how you think of your position in the movement, but you certainly know that you are intellectually mountain-high above any American leader. You occupy on your own ground as sure and important a place as did Lenin + Trotsky themselves. You have done what no other writer has ever done. It seems to me that you've given us one of the finest and most balanced political treatises of these times, a crystal-clear analytic study of the cooperative work of Lenin + Trotsky—their faults—their weaknesses[—]their greatness. And whatever happens to Trotsky this little book of yours will live and interest the world so long as it remembers Lenin + Trotsky. You must have learned to love Trotsky a lot. Nothing less could inspire such a warm passionate piece of writing. It is amazing. An electric thrill runs through it from beginning to end and it reads like a romance. It is a great little book. Trotsky will love it, every warm-blooded person will. Even the official communists will secretly gloat over it and wish they could write one page of it. Lenin himself would have been startled by it.

You must expect the official Communist International to attack you precisely as the Russian officialdom attacked Trotsky. If you had any high place in the American section you would have been excommunicated. I'm glad you haven't. Perhaps you would have had to remain dumb like [Boris] Souvarine + others who tried to stop you. Incidentally you're doing more than anyone can imagine just now for the Proletarian movement—you are helping to lift the clumsy hand of Moscow off of it. Something will have to be done. At the present moment there are thousands of revolutionists who cannot go to the Menshevik camp because they are not Mensheviks intellectually yet they cannot go to [the] Communist International so long as it remains dominated and corrupted by Moscow. We find ourselves standing between as Trotsky did between Lenin + the Mensheviks—except that there is nothing now that looks even like the shadow of Lenin.

Personally I think the headquarters of the International should be removed from Russia if it could set up legally in another country. I feel about it that Russia has already had her Revolution—and that because so many of the Russian leaders of the International are connected with the Russian government, the International will always consciously or unconsciously be over-influenced by Russian governmental politics internal + external—to the detriment of the proletarian movement. Wherever I look in the Communist International I see nothing but dry rot—the little leaders of Western Europe and America mere ventriloquists vying each with the other to repeat the words of Moscow. To me it seems bad for every body all round and even worse for Russia. Fancy a great wonderful country like that using a ventriloquist show to scare the great lords of International Capitalism. I must stop—Again please don't get mad if I displease you with my criticism—it isn't worth anything after all—can't hurt you—one little thing. There is a sentence of Trotsky's which seems to me to contain practical political wisdom of the highest order where he says "One must not be right against the Party." It has a flavor of cynicism + seems to have been learning [?] when it was too late. I admire Stalin—he is finer than brutal—has all the cunning of the fox. If he were only flexible what mightn't he do? You certainly make [Grigory Yevseyevich] Zinoviev the most detestable braying ass in the world. I can see him working in the Petrograd Soviet. I go to Bordeaux soon. Will write. Had a letter from Betty Hare. Says you don't write often wants you to come home—Claude—

[Upper margin:] Miss Hare also says that your picture with something (I can[']t make out her writing) was in the World.

MEP ALS

1. Max Eastman, *Since Lenin Died* (1925).

2. Max Eastman, *Leon Trotsky: The Portrait of a Youth* (1925).

3. Thomas Babington Macaulay, British historian and author of the five-volume *The History of England from the Accession of James II* (1848–61).

4. Hendrik Willem van Loon, Dutch-American historian and author of works like *A Short History of Discovery: From the Earliest Times to the Founding of Colonies on the American Continent* (1917), *Ancient Man: The Beginning of Civilizations* (1920), and *The Story of Mankind* (1921).

To Langston Hughes

20 June [1925]

Avignon, France

Dear Langston

I was awfully glad to see these poems. They're really the finest thing of yours I can remember seeing grouped together. If you did these carelessly as you hinted to me in a previous letter, if you did not work them over with great care then you're a wonderfully clever poet. The second, The Cat and the Saxophone[,] is a perfect piece of cleverness. You ought to do the score for that jazz opera you told me about. Nude Young Dancer did not hit me much but it is a good poem for that sort of sweet-romantic thing.

I heard from [Alain] Locke + Walter [White] all at once. They're sending me those hymnals when I no longer have use of them. I'll be all cluttered up with baggage. Yours I did not get either. But don't worry yourself, thanks. I shouldn't need that sort of stuff for a long time yet. Next week I leave for Bordeaux en route for Bretagne. Locke writes that I did not get his letters[.] Tell him he must have mislaid it in Washington, he's always getting messed up—I laughed at him so much last summer when he came to me from Genoa + he said you were always getting at him too!

I sent my book over a few weeks ago and I do hope that it will be ready for fall publication.

Poetry doesn't sell much it's true but you have a good publisher + with poems like these you['ve] shown me and good publicity you might establish a record [?].[1] A woman has written me about a new group in Harlem with [Jean] Toomer + [Paul] Robeson.[2] Do you know what it is like? The letter was very interesting.

Good luck and dreams + all for the present.
á bientot
Claude

LHP ALS

1. May be "second."

2. Jean Toomer led a Gurdjieffian group in Harlem beginning in the spring of 1925. See Cynthia Earl Kerman and Richard Eldridge, *The Lives of Jean Toomer: A Hunger for Wholeness* (Baton Rouge: Louisiana State University Press, 1987), 143–45. There is no evidence that Robeson participated in this, but he did meet Toomer in early 1925.

To Langston Hughes

6 July 1925

Bordeaux, France

Perhaps you would like this great river port. It's the most interesting I've struck yet—exceptionally clean + attractive. And the townspeople are nicer than what I've met in Provence and other parts of France. They have a certain dignity and good manners. Less excitement, gestures, posturing,—and less spitting! Oh how the French can spit! Anywhere, everyplace. Today the 4th I went for a long walk along the docks and many French boats flew the Stars + Stripes with the Tricolor. But the English didn't. One dock was specially decorated for Henry Ford's ship which is not yet in port.[1] I've been unwell again but not seriously as I've taken myself [indecipherable] in hand. Bordeaux is a marvel after dirty Marseille. I shall probably stay here a week then to Bretagne where my mail goes + I hope I shall find something from you[.] /C/

LHP APS

1. The freighter *Oneida,* carrying five thousand Ford motors and other automobile parts, departed 20 June 1925 from Hoboken for the Ford plant in Bordeaux.

To Arturo Alfonso Schomburg

19 July 1925

Brest, France

[On Letterhead (crossed out): Hôtel des Voyageurs, Brest]

By the way explain: How could [Alain] Locke know what was in the m.s. when he never saw it? Did you show him? If you did I wish you hadn't, because he's the most gossipy person in the world! Macmillan would be much better than Knopf, or any of the young publishers.

Dear Schomburg: Just got your letter. As I said when I sent the m.s. I leave the business of the book entirely in your hands (I could do nothing else when I am far away this side [of] the waters) and whatever suggestions I offer concerning the marketing are merely suggestions. You are on the spot and must be allowed your own discretion in the matter.

I never expected you to mess with that N.A.A.C.P. crowd, I have nothing against officers white and black, although [Joel E.] Spingarn and Mary Ovington are mes bêtes noires—can't stick them as individuals—but as I said in a previous letter the influence of the organisation may be bad for aspiring Negro artists and other individual Negroes who believe in exercising freedom of thought and action that may seem contrary to the aims of the N.A.A.C.P. That's why I welcome criticism of them whether it comes from the Garvey group, the Owen and Randolph paper[1] or The Amsterdam News—fair, keen criticism and protest is good for the souls of organisations and people.

In the matter of the medal, however, I think you're flogging a dead horse. The very thought of a Spingarn medal to reward the Intelligence of American Negroes annoys me.

(you may quote this whenever you want to) I should have liked to be an American Negro first for the chance of refusing it in ringing words. Put any other race or national group of America in the position and see how ridiculous it looks. For a Negro to win real achievement of any sort in America is reward sufficient, the recognition of a Negro's merit by any intellectual group in America is medal enough. The Spingarn medal therefore seems to me the cheapest of decorations (and I hold all such baubles as trash)[,] an insult to the intelligence of the American Negro—like a tick attached to a thorough bred horse. But if it pleases the vanity of the Springarns and the N.A.A.C.P. to recognize Negro talent by such a showy smug gesture let them have their peacockish pleasure. Let the whole colored officialdom of the N.A.A.C.P. have the medal. Doubtless they are working for it (and many others outside of the organisation) working to show the pompous professor Spingarn how much they merit him notice.

The fact, my dear Schomburg, merely demonstrates how far below the general average is the American Negro's feeling for genuine self respect for real achievement in contemporary thought as expressed in science literature and art. Just picture the Spingarn medal being offered to any other race or national group in America—even the Jews of the ghetto world resent the words accompanying the reward. You and the Amsterdam News have missed the real point. It is not a joke, it is an insult to the intelligence of 15 million colored Americans—a people bigger than Belgium.

White (Walter) however is a good personal friend thinking of friendship from the personal point of view—when I was sick broke and alone over here he organized a little charity for me to which Joel Spingarn kindly contributed 50 dollars. Walter likes me personally and so could be of help with the book if it didn't offend him personally, but it might—for he's a propaganda angel when I am not. However much I resent organized cruelty against weak peoples or individuals, I always want to write the truth about things as I feel and see it. American Negroes have been living their lives behind closed shutters (I mean the better off ones) not allowing the light in for fear of Cracker insults and mind. For the sake of artistic self expression the light should be let in. I am never afraid of light. I love sun and truth as I see it.

I am terribly anxious to hear what you have made for me. I'm almost broke and don't want to stay in Bretagne very long. But I must stay till I hear <u>definitely</u> from you. In the meantime if I get some cash I will pull out again so continue to write to Thomas Cook et Fils 2 Place de la Madeleine, Paris[.]

—Ever Claude.

AASP ALS

1. Chandler Owen and A. Philip Randolph were editors of the *Messenger*.

To Arturo Alfonso Schomburg

22 July 1925

Brest, France (?)

My dear Schomburg

I was rather disappointed not to get something from you in my American mail which came today. Of course, I know you're frightfully occupied with different things: your lodge, your library, your work but then you will forgive my anxiety when you realize the agitated, half-nervous-and-half-hopeful state that I am in at present.

Here's another letter from Walter White. I think he is wrong about the Viking Press, the older firms of good standing have all the advantages of selling books, a good selling agency developed for years. I was a magazine editor and I know. The new firms on the other hand have to develop everything in the selling line and that is why they have to push struggle and advertise so much to put over a success. I was a magazine editor and I know. Walter seems to have forgotten that little bit!

I hope, however, that you don't let any publisher keep the book over 10 days or two weeks for a decision. It is absolutely necessary that I should get in on the Fall market and the proofs will all have to be sent to me here. You see how short the time is. Therefore, it is absolutely necessary for you to give the reader a time limit and not wait at his leisure. You can easily do that when you have four interested firms! Also the excuse of my harrying you from over here! I think I forgot to mention how necessary it was to get the Fall market in my previous letters. So I hope you do not wait "too patiently upon Mr [Harry C.] Block."

I don't understand about [Alain] Locke. How too friendly? Do you mean that he took the side of students against a reactionary faculty or something else. From another source I learn that he is out of Howard because he was with the students in their strike against militarism.[1] Which is which? By the way he wrote that he was coming to France two months ago but I've heard nothing further.

A request! Will you send me the full name (all and each of them) of Dr. [W. E. B.] DuBois. I hope I shall have had some good news before you get this so that I can make plans for my next work—in my present state of

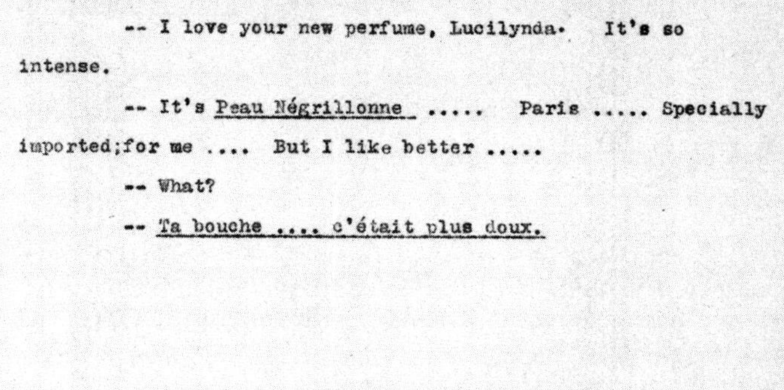

205a.

3.

-- I love your new perfume, Lucilynda. It's so intense.

-- It's Peau Négrillonne ..... Paris ..... Specially imported;for me .... But I like better .....

-- What?

-- Ta bouche .... c'était plus doux.

Fig. 1. Fragment insertion for McKay's *Color Scheme* manuscript, enclosed with the 22 July 1925 letter to Arturo Alfonso Schomburg. (Arturo Alfonso Schomburg Papers, Schomburg Center for Research in Black Culture, Manuscripts, Archives and Rare Books Division, The New York Public Library)

mind I can't do a thing. Yet there's so much to be done! Thanks for your good works and write soon.

Sincerely Claude

[Left margin, page 1:] This enclosed bit was left out by the typist. I found it going through the duplicate. It should begin part 3, page 206, coming after page 205. CMCK.[2]

[Left margin, page 2:] I thought you and Walter are good friends. I heard that you had been at several affairs with him.

AASP ALS

1. Locke had battled with Howard University administrators over faculty salaries, but after he supported students striking over the university's ROTC requirements, he was fired by Howard in the summer of 1925. For details, see Jeffrey C. Stewart, *The New Negro: The Life of Alain Locke* (New York: Oxford University Press, 2018), 477–503.

2. This one-page, twenty-seven-word insert is all that remains of this novel.

To H. L. Mencken

2 August 1925

Brest, France

Dear Mr Mencken,

I have written a small novel that my friend Mr [Arturo Alfonso] Schomburg with the assistance of Walter White is now trying to place in New York. And I'm drawing your attention to it (emphasized by the enclosed letter from the firm of Knopf) because, perhaps (I may be mistaken) a word from you, if it should take you favorably, may make the route of the m.s. a little easier.

I could not, of course, think of sending the whole thing to you at first for you are a busy man and I wanted to try it out on its naked merit.

I need not tell you that in the writing of the book I had no intention of bringing [John S.] Sumner on to me or its publisher. I tried as hard as I could to evade that! But I also hewed hard to the line of sincerity. However, being away from America for quite a while and responding to a different environment I may have put over certain phrases that might be too raw for the American public. Although I tried to avoid that by putting certain French phrases in the mouth of my characters. That's an old trick and I thought it might go pretty well in this special case.

The book itself is a realistic comedy of life as I saw it among Negroes on the Railroad and in Harlem. The motif by itself is bizarre, but I thought it would have a happy effect to drape the harsh reality on such a romantic skeleton. And I am quite ready to tone down any passages that may be considered obscene.

If you could do anything to help I should be very grateful. Mr [Harry C.] Block kept me waiting nearly 2 months for his decision and now I may lose the Fall season. I know the stuff is uneven as he says but it is a first novel on which I've worked hard indeed under unpleasant (to say the least) conditions and I should like to have it published so that I may have the chance to continue writing.

Yours very sincerely
Claude McKay

HLMP ALS

To Arturo Alfonso Schomburg

3 August 1925

Brest, France (?)

My dear Schomburg

I am terribly disappointed! Not because Knopf did not take the ms. (I gave you a list of firms as I was not banking on <u>one</u>) <u>but because you allowed that blockhead</u> [Harry C.] <u>Block to keep my novel so long.</u> He has had it over six weeks when more than 7 days were unnecessary! Of course you understand my situation is desperate and I'm entirely in the hands of you people. I really have no money at all and I can't even work because of anxiety. I thought you would try next that Macmillan fellow who wrote to you from the New Republic.

<u>Between us</u> my only fear of the m.s. getting in Walter [White]'s hands is that as Block hints the book is not moral and the N.A.A.C.P. folk may frame up and prevent me getting a publisher. Walter <u>to me</u> is a loyal friend but I don't think he would put me before the propaganda interests of the N.A.A.C.P. So you see the situation. As for his letter, I note its slightly complaining tone but I am writing to tell him that he has nothing to complain about!

I wonder if it is a mere coincidence that Block sent back the m.s. to you on the 22nd of July and Walter wrote on the 23rd? Did you think of that? Perhaps Walter <u>knew</u> that it was being rejected. Of course, for 5 months

Walter never wrote to me—I even asked him for certain materials to help with the novel and he never responded. You were the only person that stood by me. [Alain] Locke also never responded until after they heard that the novel was finished. You know the tribe.

I wish you would get in touch with [H. L.] Mencken. I begged you to. He is not actually connected with Knopf but they publish his magazine, The American Mercury. I have sent him Block's letter and if you see him, he can do anything he will. He is absolutely free from wire pulling[.] I am marooned here in Bretagne until I get some money. Keep me informed how things are going. Will you?

I wish now I had come back home with the m.s. but it is too late. Of course I'm quite willing to tone the stuff down whenever they think it is too strong or without the law—

Ever Claude

I am very worried about the m.s. being published because I hear that Carl Van Vechten is publishing shortly a novel of Negro life in Harlem![1]

AASP ALS

1. White author Carl Van Vechten's controversial novel *Nigger Heaven* (published in August 1926) was a bestseller. Because of its title and sensational content (including scenes emphasizing the Harlem underworld), it was the subject of vicious debate and criticism in African American literary circles and among Black writers who were friendly with Van Vechten. McKay was concerned that the themes of Van Vechten's novel overlapped significantly with the novel he was working on during this time.

To Walter White

4 August 1925

Brest, France (?)

Dear Walter

I wrote to you in a hurry when I was feeling quite unwell and there are a few things requiring clarification.

First, I was not blaming you for not writing to me in any way. The fact is that I had the novel finished and not knowing what to do I had to write and ask Mr. [Arturo Alfonso] Schomburg if he would handle it and wait for his reply, which only came after I had left Toulon!

I suppose [Alain] Locke was as busy as you. I wrote telling him that perhaps you were busy and he would be doing me a big favor if he sent me the hymn-book—but, like you, he never answered until long after, months after, when the novel was finished! the truth is that I was rather peeved because I felt that either of you might have sent me a card saying that pressing duties made doing anything for me at the time impossible!

About the novel itself, my chief regret is that Knopf's reader was allowed to keep it so very long. I don't mind the rejection at all but I am hoping that the book gets published for the fall season. I also hear by a roundabout way that your friend Carl Van Vechten is doing a novel on Harlem Negro life and I don't want him to get in ahead of me because he would hurt my chances, being a white man and a popular novelist known to all the gaudy crop of bleating reviewers, who are all log-rollers hoping some day to be kindly reviewed for the novels they intend writing.

Another (to me unpleasant) fact is that I am up against it right now for money, my allowance is at an end, and there's no chance of my getting anymore. That's why I told Schomburg to try his best to get me an advance on the book. And I hope you'll try your very best so that I may be able to get back to New York without appealing to charity or having to work my way over as a stoker again. It is dreadful work and I am no longer strong and fit as I used to be.

Lastly, I'm all all [*sic*] willing to take out anything illegal that might involve me with the Laws of the Land. In reality, I tried hard to avoid anything of that sort but something may have slipped up and of course I am not quite posted about libel cases etc. However, I should not like harmless innuendoes and jokes that flavor the narrative to be touched at all. If people who can stomach Miss Warren's Profession, Nana, Jurgen, can't stand Color Scheme it would only demonstrate that the White literati cannot stand for a black author laughing at White folks['] foibles.[1] That would be at the the [*sic*] bottom of any objection to the theme of the book. I hope that such a supposition has no validity that, benighted as America is with all its Great White Ways, there is yet a silver stream of intelligence that remains unpolluted.

I hope that in trying to place my book you are not cheating your own. I'm glad you've started in again upon another. I myself have another novel all planned out—but I really can't begin work until the first is off my hands and my mind.

Hoping that everything is clear and straightened out now.

With the very best of wishes
Sincerely Yours Claude

NAACPR ALS

1. McKay references several controversial texts about prostitution and sexuality: George Bernard Shaw's *Mrs. Warren's Profession* (published 1898), Émile Zola's *Nana* (1880), and James Branch Cabell's *Jurgen* (1919).

To Langston Hughes

18 August 1925

Concarneau, France

You mustn't write such extravagant praise to me. Of course a sweet juicy word is honey to the heart but . . . no one can afford to live on past achievements—if he is a real artist. It must be work, work always and I do by far <u>too little!</u> Of course there are reasons! Only a <u>very very</u> few things I've done I consider satisfactory. I am not modest (I know I am a poet) I am merely discontented with my achievement. Will write a long letter when I get to Brest. I am travelling with a young French man who likes those poems you sent me and I told him to write and tell you so.

—Ever Claude

Your letter went all over Bretagne and finally reached me here. [Harold] Jackman, a nice chap I once met in N.Y. sent me a card from Paris.

LHP APS

To Langston Hughes

25 August 1925

Concarneau, France

Remember to stamp your letter properly the tax is a bother + holds up the mail when the proprietor will not pay.

Hello Hughes: First news of my novel unfavorable. I heard that I was "without the law" too often—and it[']s so long since I've been able to get near any mail I don't know what's happening. Hope you are doing well with your sheaf of poems + all. Will write more at leisure [?][.]

LHP APU

To Walter White

7 September [1925]

Concarneau, France

My dear Walter

I am, to say the least, disappointed—not that I expected you to work miracles but because it is a month since [Arturo Alfonso] Schomburg said he was sending you my M.S. and, according to your letter, it seems that nothing has been done in the meantime. From Schomburg himself I have had no word since. As I told him in my <u>first</u> letter, when he agreed to try and place the m.s. for me, I didn't give a whoop what publisher took the m.s. But the chief fact was my getting an advance on it by the end of August as I would be surely short of money then with no one to turn to.

What you say about to [Harry C.] Block is of interest. It may be that he is so prejudiced in favor of the Negro that when he is confronted with a work of art that touches on the life of colored people, he immediately approaches it in terms of propaganda and <u>not</u> of art and life. That's the great trouble with Jewish art and literature in America (I don't know if Block is Jewish) indeed with the whole field of American art and literature. We are made impotent by the press and misgivings of minorities and by the harsh judgement of majority opinion, and thus we became emasculate[d] in ideas and the expression of them.

I know what I'm talking about. Every work of art is in reality personal propaganda. It is the way in which the artist sees life and wants to present it but there is a vast chasm between the artist's personal expression of himself and his making himself the instrument of a group or a body of opinion. The first is art the last is prostitution and that is the sole difference between art and propaganda whether the field be that of conservative or radical politics, national or racial questions!

I don't know about Block's conversation but in his letter to Schomburg he writes: "There are a great many passages which, as they stand, are certainly not within the law and, while I have no objection to them myself, on moral grounds, we certainly could not publish the book without considerable expurgation."

So there you are! I am in a hell of pecuniary fix! No, thanks, I don't expect you to help me personally and I [am] fed up with begging! I have tried my best working as hard as ever but everything goes against me and I am awfully discouraged. If I were in New York I could do much better. As I was an editor for a short while, I know how much success in the competitive literary field depends on personal contacts. I had a nice note from [H. L.] Mencken in which he said he would ask you to see Harcourt or Holt. It is cold here in the village I have been staying near Brest. And being at the end of my rope I am going to Marseille or Bordeaux to see if I can find a boat. I leave tomorrow. But until I do find one my address is still through Cook's[.]

Yours Truly
Claude McKay

I have been working on some short stories as poetry pays nothing and I must have a living and I have two completed but I'm losing heart + can hardly care about perfecting them. I feel all paralysed. Perhaps Louise Bryant (Jack Reed's wife, now Miss Bullitt) could help. She's interested that my book should be published. Don't think I am careless, unsympathetic of the fact of your working hard! I know what it means for you too to write under such circumstances with your hard driving work of secretary of a great organization + I honor and commend you! But my position is tragic. I am always working under the shadow of insecurity and it paralyses one's best efforts[.]

—Claude

NAACPR ALS

To Arturo Alfonso Schomburg

9 September [1925]

Concarneau, France (?)

Dear Schomburg,

I've just had a reply from Walter [White] dated August 28. And that is the first news I have had about the book since your note of July 24! If you knew what an anxious time of it I am having you would send me a card at intervals to say you were doing something, even though you are unsuccessful. I hope you are not allowing any friction between you and Walter to militate in any way against my book. Placing a book is a most difficult job and you will need all the help you can get.

I feel sure that Eric Walrond could be of great help to you. He knows lots of literary flies and is a very pushing person. Unfortunately I haven't got his address or I would send him a note. In my first letter from Marseille I gave you a list of the firms you should try in turn—Boni + Liveright, Harcourt, Albert + Charles Boni, I know Albert personally, and there was the Viking Press whose letter I sent to you. I know you are busy with your daily work and your official duties as a mason but you know how things are with me—I couldn't be any worse off now—and with no friends no one to help me.

Louise Bryant (formerly Mrs Jack Reed now Mrs Bullitt) is in New York and she is interested in the m.s. She knows Boni + Liveright and would help all she can if you can find her address. I don't have it. It is cold now in the village where I am staying and I am leaving for Marseille where I shall wait around the port until I can get a boat back. That is all I can do unless you manage to make a turn with the book. I hope it has not been lying idle at Knopf's all these weeks. Walter's letter has made me afraid it has. But I feel sure you could not do that knowing the state that I am in. Please let me hear from you through Cook's. I shall still have all my letters forwarded until I get the boat and if not a boat I shall have to find some sort of a job here in France, I don't know doing what. How can a man do literary work under such circumstances[.] It is tragic.

Ever Claude

AASP ALS

To Walter White

25 September 1925

Cagnes, France

My dear Walter

Here is my first of those series of short stories that I'm working furiously at just now to save myself if I can, from a strange foreign gutter. I am on the edge right now. Please do your best with it for me. Perhaps the Mercury or Century or some decent-paying magazine will take it. I've read it to Max Eastman, an American novelist, and two English critics that I met at a cafe in Cannes, and everybody has praised it enough to give me a big head. I have made it as decorous as possible without sacrificing its originality in any way. The m.s. is not as good as it should be but I have no typewriter. A friend in Paris typed this and sent it back and afterwards I saw that it was necessary to make corrections. However I've made the whole thing quite clean[.]

Hope you will be quick in your response to this Walter and if you can't handle it yourself, please send it to Eric Walrond although I do hope your duties and your own literary world will yet give you time enough to handle this yourself however[,] as you can do more for me than anyone else.

I am pinning my hopes on it and upon some poems that I've sent over. Since I got down here I've been living from hand to mouth. Max lives in an imposing sem[i]-charitable institution at the Cap 'Antibes about 5 miles from here and I go there every day nearly to eat with him without paying anything. But he is leaving in a short time at the end of this month and if I can't get some money by my literary efforts I shall have to try for a job as garcon de cafe or something. On the other hand if I can sell a series of short stories, I may save enough up to get back home by way of Canada or Detroit.

Hope your novel is coming on strong. Remember me to your wife[,] James Weldon [Johnson] and any friendly enquirer. And I hope I am not entirely forgotten over there!

Ever yours
Claude McKay

NAACPR ALS

To Walter White

15 October 1925

Cagnes, France

Dear Walter

I went down to Marseille to see if I could get a boat home and to get in somehow. Then Max Eastman invited me up here and read my novel. Of course, he put his finger (from his long experience as editor) on every point that he thought objectionable and impossible for the American market—and there were many!

I showed him also my short stories and he has shown me with great patience and care what I should do to make them acceptable for the market. I have done that and within a few days I shall send you the first one called

Within the Belt which I hope you can place for me either with the Century, the Dial, the Mercury or anything. [H. L.] Mencken said in his letter about my book that he could not use a long story in the Mercury. Well, everybody thinks this short one extremely good. I hope you like it. Curiously it is about an octoroon girl in Harlem and the first part of [Rudolph] Fisher's story which I've just read in the Crisis treats the same subject but from a different angle to mine.[1]

I hope too, if you sell it, you will see that payment comes quickly as at present I am living on good will and credit which can't last over long! I am willing to pay an agent to handle it if you can't.

In the meantime I have sent poems to the Century, Mercury and Nation and asked them to forward to you if unavailable. Hope you won't be offended with this liberty. I think the current Crisis a great number and the competitions are from my point of view the finest work of the Crisis. I'm going to send Dr. [W. E. B.] DuBois some poems also.

By the way do you know what has become of the m.s. of my novel. I can't get any word from [Arturo Alfonso] Schomburg but I should like to have it back. It's a terrible disappointment but one must put up with the inevitable, is it not? I was discouraged and demoralised at first. But Max Eastman has put heart into me again to continue. Wish you great luck with your novel.

Sincerely as Ever
Claude

[Left margin:] You haven't written since your August letter whether you did try Harcourt and what was their decision. Did you!

NAACPR ALS

1. Rudolph Fisher's "High Yaller" appeared in the October 1925 issue of the *Crisis.*

To Langston Hughes

23 October 1925

Cagnes, France

My dear Langston

I have been so unwell and unsettled during the last months that I couldn't write. I left Bretagne about two months ago and was staying until 2 weeks ago with Max Eastman at Antibes. Then I got a little room here from a painter because Max had to give up his house but I don't think I shall be here long. I was on the point of going to Bordeaux or Marseille to try and get a boat that would land me over the pond sometime but Max's invitation made me change my plans. I had to do that because evidently my novel could not be placed[.] From all accounts that I was able to get it is either too obscene in parts or too poor a novel, I didn't know which. Max thinks that I might have sold it if it were not for certain passages and he thinks that the fact of my race makes it necessary for me to be careful and not to give full play to my imagination + draw too freely upon all experiences because although there is an interest in Negro writers—the puritan prejudices are there in America to overcome and they may be much harder in the case of a Negro writer—I don't know. You ought to be able to tell. At any rate I am retouching my short stories to make them acceptable to standard magazines and I hope I shall succeed in selling some as I am awfully broke and sick.

I don't know where the novel is so far. I sent it to [Arturo Alfonso] Schomburg and the last I heard from him was a letter in July saying that [Harry C.] Block of Knopf had decided against the book. Since then, I have written about 4 times to him without getting a single reply. The very last thing I heard of the book itself was a letter from Walter White at the end of August saying that he would tell Schomburg to send it to Harcourt. But I don't know if anything was ever done. Walter has not answered any of my two letters since. He is busy he had said to me with his own novel. But perhaps you might find out something and ask that the m.s. was sent back to me at least. I am enclosing a note for Eric Walrond which I should be glad if you'll forward. I can't get his address from anyone.

I was in Paris for two days this time and I saw Vanity Fair with your poems but I could not afford the price.[1] I congratulate you. I also read of your essay in the Crisis. I like [Rudolph] Fisher's story—the first time I have read him. Curiously I have also finished one about an octoroon girl but it[']s a different thing altogether. I am sending it to Walter to ask him to sell it. Everybody here likes it. I have never seen your Weary Blues and should very much like to. [Countee] Cullen's prize writing poems did not make the slightest impression on me. They are things I should expect to find as a filler in any Munsey magazine.[2] But he's young yet and may do good work although one ought to find some sort of original expression in him I know.

When you write please tell me something about [Alain] Locke. You know I like him very much but I haven't heard since I got news of his being fired from Howard. I expected him over here according to your letter but he didn't come! Let me hear and also how you are making it in the University[.] I saw no American visitors colored or others this season because I was hiding—away from the regular tourist places[.] If I stay here in the Midi however I shall go to Nice which is cheaper to live in—Claude

Wish—if you have any spare one—you could send me some magazines containing something of interest—I have to send this through the Crisis because I see that I have left all your letters with my books in Paris chez mon ami[.]

LHP ALS

1. Hughes's poems "Suicide's Note" and "Fantasy in Purple" appeared in the September 1925 issue of *Vanity Fair.*

2. The Frank A. Munsey Company published a number of magazine titles (including *Munsey's Magazine* and the *Argosy*), which, like other pulp magazine titles, were associated with low-brow literary tastes.

To W. E. B. Du Bois

27 October 1925

Cagnes, France

Dear Dr Du Bois: I was happy that someone sent me the October "Crisis" with its fine literary features. That is to my mind the greatest work the "Crisis" has ever done yet! Although it may be that I am prejudiced in rating creative work too highly—and above social work even as highly as I do rate the second. I say this despite the fact that in competitions, like examinations, I've never had any interest or faith even though they do produce fine results sometimes.

I am sending you a sheaf of poems (five) that you might be able to use and pay me something for them. I had a setback and have been ill again. I am staying in a little town here in the Midi and am without any money. To help myself I have sent out a number of things to a couple of liberal New York magazines including yours and I am anxiously awaiting the result.

With kind regards
I am
Yours Sincerely
Claude McKay

The poems are taken from a collection that I am making for another book but so far I have not enough good ones yet and publication in magazines may help me now as well as the hoped-for greater event—

CMcK

WEBDP ALS

To Walter White

25 November 1925

Cagnes, France (?)

My dear Walter

I haven't heard of you since last August, nor of [Arturo Alfonso] Schomburg since July. I feel as if I was entirely deserted by everyone just at a time when I have failed and am down and out. It gives me a terrible, bitter feeling. If you are displeased with me or with my work I wish you would be frank and tell me so. And then I should no longer be hoping you might do something for me.

You must forgive me. I know you're busy with your official and private work, but I feel so utterly let down by everybody.

Last week I received a cheque for $10 from the Nation for a little poem.[1] I was down to my last sou and it has saved me for 2 weeks. I have finished another story better than the first one I sent you, But I don't know whether I should send it to you or not. Because you haven't even acknowledged "Within the Belt" I have also sent more poems to the "Crisis," "Mercury" and "Century."

On Saturday I saw the [Paul] Robesons with Frank Harris and Max Eastman. They were extremely nice and I love them. Mrs. Robeson said she had just had a letter from you and that your new novel was accepted by Knopf. I congratulate you. I thought I should have a note from you too but I received nothing when I went to the Agency.

With Sincere wishes
Yours Claude
NAACPR ALS

1. Likely "Home Song," which appeared in the 24 March 1926 issue of the *Nation.*

To Alain Locke

2 January 1926

Nice, France

My dear Locke

I was so happy to have your letter. It gave me, of course, all the needed information about my book[,] Walter [White][,] [Arturo Alfonso] Schomburg et al. I have made up my mind to the fact that the book must be bad, so I must do another. This time by way of short stories. I have already done five and they have been praised by two or three discriminating persons that I met here. I am not depending alone on the American market, I have also found an agent in London. I should always remember that London published my book of poems before New York was ready to accept them. I have read the advertisement of your New Negro in the Nation[.] Real congratulation[s]. By the way I hear that that poem Mulatto that I put on the gloves with you over has been published by the Bookman after all! In my Russian Cathedral you have the 13th line reading "Bow slowly down." It is not slowly but "lowly" which makes the poem entirely different and I do wish you would correct for me in any further editions.

Of course I don't know anything about your case because you throw no light on it. 2 or 3 correspondents also mentioned it but nobody gave particulars. They seemed to take the whole matter in a very bigoted way. But, of course, when you fight in any cause, you must not expect gratitude from the masses or from a timid intelligentsia like our Afro-American. I think it is only in Europe where you have an old strong aristocratic class that you find a few individuals participating in unpopular causes. In the American Democracy you may identify yourself with something unpopular so long as you keep on the safe side of public morals. I saw the Crisis mentioning Kelly Miller[1] + others but no mention of your case.[2] I don't know why. [W. E. B.] DuBois is funny. When I came out of Russia with plenty of publicity he was glad to pay for my articles. Now I am broke + send him a few poems + ask him to pay for them, he does not reply nor return the poems.

If you can send me any current literature I shall be very happy. Europe is, of course, all right if one has a little money, but if one is broke as I am now it is no good. I want to come home to sell a book of short stories and make enough to return to France and write for a year. That's my only reason for coming home. And I want to refresh myself with the American atmosphere. Wish I had seen you this summer. It was beautiful in Brittany—well you mustn't expect too much of the younger generation. They have their future to safeguard + they must need get on the band-wagon of respectability to succeed! Thank Langston [Hughes] for his card—Success for his book + Happy New Year to all—Ever Claude

ALP ALS

1. Kelly Miller (1863–1939), African American mathematician, sociologist, and dean at Howard University. He was a regular contributor to the *Crisis*. During the conflict between the faculty and administration at Howard in the summer of 1925, Miller was removed as dean.

2. W. E. B. DuBois, "Opinion," *Crisis*, August 1925, 164.

To Alain Locke

15 January 1926

Menton, France

My dear Locke

By the way I've just gotten a cheque from Boni + Liveright for my poems in the Masses Anthology.[1] I don't know if you pay twice but perhaps A.+ C. Boni may be willing to give something for book rights also. Of course I'm only suggesting this to you[.] You mustn't think me a pig but you know how hard it is over here to live. I'm doing a book of short stories that are going to "go over the top." Wish I could get a copy of your book + [Countee] Cullen[']s.[2] Wish you success on yours + I hear that things have taken a better turn for you. Glad. I have an agent in London + [Eric] Walrond is doing his best for me in America. I must try to regain my old stride + go farther. I saw the Crisis + was interested in [W. E. B.] DuBois' review of your book.[3] What he says about your Beauty cult is right in principle but DuBois is wrong in practice. There are no hard + fast rules about Beauty + propaganda—Intuition + Time are the final judges of Beauty in creative work—

Ever Claude

ALP ALS

1. Genevieve Taggard, ed., *May Days: An Anthology of Verse from* Masses-Liberator (1925).

2. Countee Cullen's first collection, *Color,* was published in November 1925.

3. W. E. B. Du Bois, "Review of *The New Negro,*" *Crisis,* January 1926, 140–41.

To Louise Bryant

10 February 1926

Menton, France

Dear Louise Bryant: Sometime ago I wrote to you in America enclosing a story of mine called High Ball. I didn't have your address, so I sent it through The Nation. I don't know whether or not you got the story and my letter. But a couple days ago I saw Max [Eastman] and he told me that you were back in Paris. He said too that you were in a sense broke and couldn't help me materially, but if you can't yourself you might be able to suggest something.

As I told you in my American letter I had to scrap the first big prose thing I attempted to write in 1924. Last year I did another and sent it over. But it wasn't good[,] for all the publishers turned it down. Although I had the subsidy for six months whilst I was doing it, I was more worried working then than now when I can't raise any money from any source. I certainly had a very self-conscious time of it with Mrs [Anna] Davis sending me a sermon everytime she felt like advising me to be careful and dutiful "because of my race" and to see that "not a drop of me was wasted."

However, I wasn't discouraged because I didn't put the book over. I was more worried because I felt that all the friends who believed that I had something to say would feel that I had my chance and lost it and cease to interest themselves in me. That is precisely what has happened. Nevertheless, I pegged away as hard as my anxiety and pecuniary worries would let me. I chose the short story medium and wrote about a dozen of them. It has been difficult for me to master a form + get my stride in prose, because I've been training myself to verse form all along. But now I've found the manner I want. Max has been reading my stories and he has the highest praise for 8 of them. He read the last one last week and said something like: "That is your novel. It's a shame for you to throw away material like that on a short story for that is what you should make your novel out of." He said I ought to publish the short stories in book form and then start in to make the novel. Of course, Max knows all about me. I've been bumming him, too hard a time as he has! So I told him that I had written to you in America and I asked him if he wouldn't write and tell you about these stories and perhaps you might do something more for me. But he said he had already bothered you about [Boris] Souvarine's Bulletin.

Max's praise makes me feel especially confident. Because he has never liked my prose—never encouraged me to write prose[.] He always said: write narrative verse, which I had no inclination for. Personally I always felt Max did not "get" my prose because it didn't have that special, lively quality that is characteristic of Masses-Liberator prose. I feel confident too about Max's criticism because he didn't like the recent novel I did. And he predicted that it wouldn't be accepted for publication. There are many things that I don't see in the same light as Max. But he has had experience and can always put his finger on weak spots and unpublishable phrases. If he was an authority in the sphere of fiction I could get him to write his opinion of my work for some publisher and perhaps I could get an advance on these stories to tide me over six months. But he hasn't. He sent one of the stories to [H. L.] Mencken but Mencken says he has enough stories to last three years! He Mencken wants an article which would bring me in something. But I have no vivid experience of France to put into an article! Perhaps you might be able to interest Boni and Liveright. I should so like to get these stories out this Fall. As they have a Negro wave on in America now, something good may be carried over in it.

I have only 3 of the stories typed! And I've sent them all out. I haven't a typewriter and I can't afford to pay for typing. Max has been reading them handwritten. My only financial hope is three competitions—one story + two poetry—in which I have entered. I was staying at Cagnes near Max. I had to move to Nice to get cheap food. There I had a room for 200 fr with fireplace. But I couldn't afford it—so I moved to Menton where I got a room for 3 fr a day. But it is so cold I cannot work in it. Last week I got a job as an "actor" to appear in the dance of Rex Ingram's "Magician." So I'm learning new steps.

If you cannot <u>do</u> anything for me this time you might be able to suggest some way out. It was your beginning at any rate that started me off year before the last.

Yours very Sincerely
Claude

I'm sending you one of the stories to give you an idea of what I'm doing. I wish you <u>would send</u> it back as it is the only typed copy I have. I sent the original in to the short-story competition that a Negro magazine has organized. CM

LBP ALS

To Louise Bryant

13 March 1926

Menton, France (?)

Dear Louise

I do hope you'll let me dump this burden of my stories on you and entrust you to get them to a publisher for me. Together they seem to me a favorable ensemble. I thought of doing ten in all. Here are nine (except one—The Human Race that Max [Eastman] has somewhere and which I shall ask him to send you.) I haven't seen him since you wrote. He's having a hard time eking out a living and is in Corsica now I think where things are cheaper.

However, I took your advice + went slashing through my things myself and what I miss perhaps you will pick up for me! There's nothing like a frank + friendly critic to help me.

It's awful presumptiuous [*sic*] of me to send these stories to you but I've struck an impasse and must find some way out and because of your genuine interest in what I'm doing I felt you were the only one I could do this too [*sic*]. I must find some kind of work—anything at all. I am going to try Nice. Marseille—the ships again—anything anywhere. And I couldn't carry these about with me like this because I think they stand a good chance of a publisher. Not having any money for a typist, you might take an investment in them and if I make anything I shall surely try to pay you back! The same girl who did my other things will do these. She is Miss Jessie Hyde 8 bis rue Campagne Premiere—Paris. She understands my writing very well and makes very few mistakes. I already owe her 100 francs more or less which I've never been able to pay. But she is a very nice woman + considerate.

I have two more stories planned to complete the series but I've slipped up on them. I'm sorry I couldn't finish one. However, if I don't get to sea + get a job that will give me a little time for writing I shall finish it.

I give you carte blanche on the stories. I hope I don't go to sea. I hate it + would prefer anything on land. But if I do go, please send them off to New York as soon as they're typed.

Hope it's all right my depending on you about these + please forgive me any inconvenience I may be causing you. Hope your trip to Austria did you good. Best regards ever + many thanks,

Sincerely
Claude

Oh: I have originals only of High Ball + Home to Harlem.[1]

LBP ALS

1. The first mention of "Home to Harlem," the story McKay would adapt into his first published novel.

To Louise Bryant

3 April [1926]

Nice, France

My dear Louise: Your pneumatique won't reach Max [Eastman] to be of any use in my case because he left for Austria via Venice this morning.[1] I enclose his letter as proof.

I am glad you have the stories. My mind is at ease now. I want to get them over to New York as soon as I can. Because I would like to get some money, which would ensure me the leisure to enter the competition for a Negro novel. If you could make the time and would read the stories for me I could rely on your judgment. I know precisely the sort of criticisms I want. And I know you're absolutely capable of making them.

I enclose a letter from my typist, Miss [Jessie] Hyde. Very nice letter and I wish you could see her for me. I haven't had time to write. I work from seven till nine. When I'm through I am just fit to sleep.

Yesterday I went to see [Rex] Ingram + [Harry] Lachman. Both of them were cordial. I may get a job there when my month as houseman is finished a week hence. The trouble is I have no clothes to begin in. Max left me a shirt but it[']s twice as large as I am + it would cost as much to buy a new one as to alter it to my fit. I work now in a houseman's uniform.

I told Lachman I was a good writer and willing to take any sort of job. He was sceptical. Said he had too many poets around the plant already. That is a sort of handicap. People who know you as a friend never want to employ you. Think you'll presume on their friendship. And I've never been like that. Try to make good at anything. I put my hand to [it]. <u>Oh please Louise, don[']t send [indecipherable] to Austria</u>. Forgive all the letters thanks for prompt reply. Claude

LBP ALS

1. Max Eastman attempted to see Sigmund Freud in Vienna but was unable to meet him until the following year.

To Langston Hughes

24 April 1926

Nice, France

My dear Langston

I had the book allright and beg your forgiveness for not thanking and congratulating you too before. But for three months I've been going around with your letter in my pocket (that nice racy one about your party at [Carl] Van Vechten[']s) with the intention of writing you a real letter. But I have been so worried and unsettled I could not settle down to the job. I picked up a hundred francs here, a dollar there, trying to live in a way you can't imagine. With me, trying to live became a job, a problem. I moved from Juan-les-Pins to Cagnes from Cagnes to Nice from Nice to Menton and back again to Nice, wherever I heard of a cheap room I hunted it up. But you can live cheap when you have the teensiest bit of sure money coming to you. When you haven't, it's stupid to bother. When I came out of hospital I found a job as valet-butler to a civilised cracker doctor and his Russian wife. I stayed with them a month. The experience was so interesting I kept a diary of it. When I say civilized[1] I mean it in the typical cracker sense. I couldn't stay over the month and I stayed it out simply because I'd lose my 200 francs if I hadn't. It gave me an insight into what the French "bonne a tout faire" has got to do. You work from 7–10 at night without any letting up. You get indifferent food[,] a bed etc. That is, it[']s little different from what a slave domestic was doing in Virginia a hundred years ago. I quit it to work on a building—(but I had almost forgotten to tell you that the old cracker told me that if I were a good boy and stayed with him I could have all his clothes when he was finished wearing them! That would be a part of my wages. I used to hear of that in America but I had to come to France to prove it for myself!)[.]

I stayed on the building a week and through Max Eastman's influence I have a temporary job with Rex Ingram. He is a very nice man, entirely taken up with his work of course, but devoted to fine and artistic things. I gave him your book because he was so interested when I spoke to him about you, [Countee] Cullen, the New Negro and the intellectual Negro movement in America. So you may imagine how happy I am to have this other copy with the nice words you have written in it. I am reading stories for Ingram with the idea of perhaps finding a good scenario for him. The job is really a sinecure, just to help me out over these hard times, but I find it interesting enough—I do read a little. And up at the Studio I peep around to see what's going on. Highly fascinating a cinema studio. I get 40 francs a day—enough for my meals and a good room. I am more than content. This you can see from this long letter. As an assembled whole, I love your book immensely.[2] Oh, I wish I had a chance to review it somewhere! First, I love the cover—jacket I mean. It is daring and vivid. I like the title poem, the proem, Jazzonia, Negro Dancers, The Cat, Nan, Banjo Dance, Blues Fantasy, Cross, When Sue Wears Red, Water-Front Streets, Port Town, Young Sailor, Disillusion and more and more. And if you want to know the ones I disliked intensely I name The South, Caribbean Sunset, The White Ones. That God having a hemorrhage is a most vivid but intensely nauseating image to me.[3] I don't know why. I am not religious in any of the orthodox ways. Guess I would be affected in the same way if you had written a bull or woman having a hemorrhage. Cross is a beautiful poem for me, perfect[,] exquisitely done. It shows that while others are vainly prating about artistic freedom among Negro Writers, you have won out over all obstacles. You have opened up new vistas by touching a subject that thousands of Afro-Americans feel and yet would be afraid to touch. Oh but it is as dull and painful to <u>recite</u> about what creative act should be as it is to <u>read</u> about it.

You were lucky in Van Vechten's introduction.[4] He is a sophisticated man and wrote just the right thing. Nothing overdone. In my case (it is the first time I am saying it) there was very, very much overdone. In some parts it was like screaming my merits from a mountain top. I don't like too much of that sort of thing myself. The quiet, subtle unobstructive is more to my state of mind.

All that may surprise you considering my politics! But that is nothing. In spite of my politics I don't like politicians, red, black, pink or white. And while I was on the Liberator I was never in with the very political set. I always preferred the Bohemian dilletanti and the more decadent they were the better I liked them.

Now the news you give me about yourself change[s] like a chameleon. First I thought you were working with that Negro History man and going to Howard. Next I heard of you in a Washington hotel. That was astonishing. Now Lincoln. Of course Harvard sounds better to me but you must have your reason for preferring Lincoln. Guess you'll find it difficult to stick to any sort of university work—being a poet! But one of the Negro colleges might make of you what Michigan made of [Robert] Frost. That was a very fine gesture indeed. You should be bothered about the whims and prejudices of the Negro intelligentsia. They are death to any would[-]be Negro artist. A plague on them and however hard hit and down I am they won[']t get their claws on me.

I must stop now—the cafe is closing. I have written a book of short stories—sending them to New York next month. More about that anon. Congratulations. Wish you could come to Europe this summer! We would continue to have some fun. Give my warmest regards to [Alain] Locke. Tell him I would feel it an honor to have a copy of the New Negro. I can't afford the price from way over here.

Ever Claude

LHP ALS

1. McKay shifts between English and British spelling in this letter.

2. Hughes's first book of poetry, *The Weary Blues* (1926).

3. The opening image of "Caribbean Sunset."

4. Carl Van Vechten provided the introduction to Langston Hughes's first volume of poetry, *The Weary Blues.* Hughes, in turn, would provide original blues lyrics for Van Vechten's novel *Nigger Heaven,* published a few months later.

To Louise Bryant

"Monday" [26 April or 2 May 1926]

Nice, France

Dear Louise

Your letter makes me happy. You're indeed my patron saint. That's the only way to say it.

I quit my model job and went to work in a building. It was harder but better. Then I got a call from the Rex Ingram company and I worked there for a week as an errand boy. At the end of that week Mr Ingram set me to read stories for him. I shall continue to do that until the end of May. I read mostly Arab stories. The studio closes down in May for two months. I don't know what I shall do, but I feel hopeful that I shall surely keep on finding something to go on with.

My address will be Cook's in Paris as previously[.]

That you're taking the stories to America without sending them back to me makes me feel better than ever. Of course there must be many changes to make. I always find them after I have a story typed. I think I ought to cut down the foreword to "Gigolo"—way down to two sentences. Maybe you have something to suggest about it. I have a little more leisure since I started in on the stories for Ingram and I am using it to do the two stories that were not in with the lot. The Human Race (the semi-socialist thing that Max [Eastman] disliked so violently and which we almost quarreled over) I am rewriting. The novel I have all planned, in part half written. And I do hope you manage something so that I could start working on it for that prize. If not possible, it must wait until I can do it.

Wish you good luck and bon voyage and no words by pen or mouth can ever express my gratitude to you. I'm never very good at expressing myself that way, but I do hope you'll understand.

If I tried to express what I really feel it would be banal. I know.

Sincerely yours
Claude—

LBP ALS

To Louise Bryant

24 June 1926

Marseille, France

My dear Louise:

I feel pretty certain that if you really understand my present desperate position—my hopes, my aspirations, my fears, you might have acted differently about those stories.

Useless I should recite how I have been struggling to exist this last year when I sent the stories to you in March I had just reached the end of my rope. I had been getting 5 dollars for a poem now and then, but a friend had urged me to do some stories and get in on the Negro vogue—so I dropped the writing of poetry altogether. I wanted to send those stories either to you or to Francine [?]. I decided on you because you were nearer and interested in what I was trying to do.

Soon after I sent the stories from Menton I found a job at Nice as general servant for 200 francs and keep such as that was. I worked from 7 in the morning until 9:30 at night. I quit that place after a month to work in a building. I found out that work in France was much more exacting than in America—

I had no time to think much less to write. What was I to do? Give up or what. I decided to try to write even if I starved.

My hopes [*sic*] then was to get my stories to America as soon as possible. John Farrar of the Bookman was interested. [Eric] Walrond urged that I should try + get even one story in. That might help to straighten out my problem.

When you said you were taking the stories to America in May I was happy—even though I was anxious to see them in type; for I always do my best rewriting <u>after</u> seeing my stuff in type. I had no choice, on account of my desperate straits, except to let you take them along as I felt that you wanted to help me in the quickest possible time.

You are an artist and you can imagine how I felt about my stuff being read by editors without knowing in what form they were in!

I know I must not, I have no right to complain, when you have taken upon yourself the burden of looking after the stories—generally giving of your time and money when I have not the slightest claim on you. I know it is your love for literature and art[,] for seeing obscure talent recognised, that makes you do it. Besides you have been ill—you have duties—other things to do.

But it is four months since I sent you the stories. And here I am—hoping and waiting on them to help me—existing, trying to write, in swarms of flies and bugs and filth, when, maybe, my stories corrected and sent to America might change my wretched situation a little. Just might—I don't know—but isn't it better to hope? Now I am terribly disappointed, utterly despondent, absolutely fed up. Before I left Nice you promised the stories in 2 weeks. I figured on running through them—sending them off. Then I came here and rented this place for a month. Thought I could get something done in a month. It is now more than three weeks—nothing done. I am discouraged, of course, miserable.

You say I am too impatient—the stories are not finished. It is not so much impatience as it is sheer misery. If you have no time to finish the stories, I will finish the correcting on the lines you have suggested in your previous letter. Marseille is my last and cheapest stand. I don't want to be driven out of here by hunger and want as I was out of Cagnes, Nice and Menton. After all the few things I manage to turn out are the only joy I have. Before I must leave Marseille for God knows where I want to work at those stories—to feed the joy of having completed something—Otherwise I'll always carry along with me the haunting feeling of work uncompleted. You know what I mean and how I feel.

My month will be up next week. I don't know if something might happen to keep me on another month. You will understand then why I want the stories right away—no matter what shape they are in—

Yours Sincerely
Claude McKay

Miss [Jessie] Hyde said you gave Gigolo to some editor. I never heard anything from it but I wanted to make more changes in Gigolo than any other story[.]

CMP ALS

To Alain Locke

27 July 1926

Marseille, France

My dear Locke

I am sorry that "because of your much abused candor in the past" you dropped corresponding with me also!

Well, of such stuff is the artistic temperament composed. I must be satisfied.

Am staying here in Marseille which is the cheapest place in France for a man like myself without resources. Hope I shall have a chance of seeing you.

There are things to be done. I have the m.s. of my ten short stories in Paris. Want to get them over at the first opportunity. You or [Arturo Alfonso] Schomburg—the first to return—might take it for me. I mentioned that to Schomburg.

Congratulations and more over your New Negro. I never received a copy. I am working very hard on my novel. But I don't want to enter in for that prize. Prizes are bad things for anyone that takes his work artistically. And if the stories are accepted it means that I shall have enough money to continue without sending in the novel to the competition. Another thing—I am afraid I must tell you frankly of the Afro-American judges. I am afraid of their influence. Although I have strong social opinions I cannot mix my art and racial propaganda. I must write what I feel what I know what I think what I have seen what is true + your Afro-American intelligentsia won't like it. I know that.

How was Walter [White]'s new book?[1] Better than the first? Nobody in America writes to me now. I suppose I am in disgrace—a back number. Only Langston [Hughes] keeps up any correspondence with me.

Please let me hear from you soon whether you can get here or not—

Sincerely
Claude

[Lower margin:] What is Jessie [Fauset] doing?

ALP ALS

1. Walter White, *Flight* (1926).

To Arturo Alfonso Schomburg

27 July 1926

Marseille, France

Dear Schomburg,

I sent a letter to you Poste Restante, Madrid. You may not have received it therefore I am writing again to Paris. I should like to know when you are returning to America. My m.s. of short stories is in Paris and I want to get them to my publishers as soon as I can for this year's publication. Perhaps you or [Alain] Locke might take it back for me. I think it will turn out better than my Color Scheme which you acted so inexcusably about.

It was not a matter of an acceptance or not. But simply that as a trusted friend you should have written to me saying frankly what had happened and what had become of the m.s.

I am living here in Marseille which [is] about the cheapest place in France to live in when one has no resources[.]

I hope you enjoy Paris. Please let me hear from you.

Yours faithfully
Claude McKay

AASP ALS

To Louise Bryant

30 July 1926

Marseille, France

Dear Louise

Please note the address carefully as I had quite a little trouble over the registered mail you sent me recently.

Miss [Jessie] Hyde has all the stories. I told her to tell you and I did myself in a previous letter. The Revelation Blues I sent her just yesterday. I've changed it very much according to your suggestions and I think you [will] feel a little more sympathetic about it now, nevertheless it is a thin story. The novel is almost finished. About three more chapters to do. Then rewrite and revise—that will take all of August I think. I could have most of it ready for you but it won't do for you handwritten and I can't think about typing it—not unless I get a little advance on the short stories.

Miss Hyde has a bad arm and great difficulty typing but the stories should be ready for you. I had even thought of sending them before. Did you hear anything from Harcourt, Brace?

All of this month I have worked wonderfully. Only bothered by the heat and mistral these last days. The novel you know I have made out of two short stories. Max [Eastman] thought the theme was too good to be wasted on a short story. It's about an octoroon girl who could not make up her mind whether she should marry her black lover and resign herself to the Black Belt or whether she should throw in her lot with an octoroon adventurer with whom she could have an easy time free from petty prejudices and discriminations. Circumstances are too much for her and she loses everything and is broken in the end.

Thank you for remembering me so soon again[.]

Yours Sincerely
Claude

I asked Miss Hyde to get Home to Harlem from you to get it in the series. As a title I have thought of <u>Speakeasy Nights</u>.

LBP ALS

To Alain Locke

1 August 1926

Marseille, France

My dear Locke

I received a copy of the New Negro a few days ago. Many thanks to you and the Bonis.

However, I am displeased about my representation in it. I remember writing to you that "White Houses" was not the title of the poem published under that title in the Survey Graphic. In the Liberator it had appeared under the title "The White House."[1] That is a symbolical title. When you change it to "White Houses" the poem immediately becomes cheap, flat Afro-American propaganda. What does a man of sensitivity, a poet, care about entering a lot of uninteresting white houses? The whole symbolical import of my poem is lost under the title you have chosen to give it + allowed to remain after I had called your attention to it. If you understand how an artist feels about the word that he chooses above other words to use—if you know that artistic creation is the most delicate of all creative things—if you want to pit it against how a craftsman—a goldsmith—an engraver—might feel about someone changing his design—then you will understand how I feel about "The White House." I do hope you will set this matter right in future editions of your book.

I also wished you had asked me about the "Negro Dancers" in the Liberator. As the magazine was defunct there was no one but me to ask and, of course, I would have vetoed their publication.

Dear Locke—in your letter you mention petty differences and misunderstandings. I wish you would see how these are the things that make for discord between people who should stand together on a common platform. I eliminated "Negro Dancers" from my "Harlem Shadows" because I did not consider the poems up to the level of my other work. The process of elimination reflects the growth of an artist + that process is his inalienable privilege. By printing in 1925 poems that I eliminated from Spring in New Hampshire in 1920 and Harlem Shadows in 1922 (and without any commentary note) you've broken up the artistic pattern that I have been trying to work out. I cannot understand why you have done it. You knew my address. You might easily have consulted me. That is the very ordinary and usual procedure among literary people. Besides we—you + I are something of friends + friendship calls for higher courtesy—I hold—than between strangers! I hope you enjoy Paris. I am working hard on my novel—Hope to have my book of short stories out this year and my novel will be finished this month—If you're having a new edition of New Negro I should like Negro Dancers eliminated + other poems that I have substituted[.]

Claude

ALP ALS

1. *Liberator,* May 1922.

To Arturo Alfonso Schomburg

1 August 1926

Marseille, France

My dear Schomburg: I am sorry you could not come to Marseilles[.] Together we should have seen something of this great, vile, rotten and sordid port town. But you will enjoy Paris I am sure. I love Paris. I haven't been really there for a year and a half. When I got back from Brittany last August I stopped there for two days only—to see a friend. I had no money to stay longer.

I am indeed glad of your invitation. There are many things I should like to see in Paris—especially at the American library. And I should love so much the opportunity of talking over my affairs with you . . . Yet I hardly have decent clothes to make the trip. Let me know when you want me to come. I am very happy—like a kid—about it. Who couldn't over the idea of Paris?

I am also happy about the job of writing out "Harlem Shadows" for you. I need the money badly. But I wish you could wait until I finish my novel. I am on the last lap of it (hand-written) and it will soon be finished. Then I must revise and rewrite. I shall probably take it to Paris with me. It's different from anything I have done and there are no obviously naughty things in it. So I am hoping for a real success. I want to get it on the market immediately after my short stories are published (Before the Boni Competition)—The story tells of an octoroon girl of the Black Belt who cannot decide whether she should marry a young black business man and live in the Belt or whether she should pass over into the white world whose amusements and fashionable things + people she adores. The scenes are set in Harlem and I evoke a whole galaxy of types—West Indian Afro-American and white. Into the pattern is woven a young white man that the heroine falls in love with and whom she gives herself to, two interesting brown girls and a young near-white adventurer. Between the young white man, the black, and the near-white the heroine is finally broken by inexorable circumstances.

Please, Schomburg do not mention or show the plot of it to any person. Not even [Alain] Locke. Plagiarism is so frequent nowadays and you know what I [*sic*] struggle I have, unaided, to get along. I have been working as valet and houseman in Nice . . . the m.s. of "Color Scheme" was finally returned. Perhaps that is better so. It was a sort of tour de force. It would have been different had I myself been in America. Hope you enjoyed Spain. Want to go there when I get money although my real objective is America for more material. Thanks for 100 francs[.]

—Ever Claude.

AASP ALS

To Louise Bryant

[mid- or late August 1926]

L'Estaque, France

Dear Louise

Are you really sailing on the 1st? If you are I don't want the stories left behind. Miss [Jessie] Hyde has been slow with them because she had a bad arm and she wrote she was overwhelmed with work and couldn't get at yours.

The time is so short I don't think I can see the m.s. again before you leave so I would suggest that you take it directly from Miss Hyde. The novel is practically finished. I wish I had a typewriter now to rough it out. I have started in at it by hand. I think I have about sixty thousand words. Wish I could show or read it to some critical person.

Didn't you hear from Harcourt Brace? I had an offer for a colored collector to copy out by hand my book of poems for fifty dollars. I jumped at it. But it is over a month and I haven't heard from him again.

After you sent me that money I went to live in a little fishing village called l'Estaque about 10 kilomettres [*sic*] from Marseille. I worked better. It is quiet. Nothing to bother but mosquitoes. Cezanne used to paint there they say.

I envy your going home. Wish you success with your play.

Yours Sincerely
Claude

LBP ALS

To Louise Bryant

23 August 1926

L'Estaque, France

Dear Louise

Miss [Jessie] Hyde had promised me not to charge you for the duplicate copy, as it is in a way a luxury. She said it would hardly amount to more than the cost of paper so I told her to go ahead and make if for me and give me credit until I sold something. I guess she thought the chances rather risky and so made sure of you. I hope you don't mind. It is a big bill.

You'll see I made many changes in the stories. I took the cue you gave me and made bigger slashes than you suggested. It is remarkable how just one incisive comment can wake you up to pages of bad stuff you were hitherto blind about. For instance, the best part of Coral's Buffet Flat was bad simply because I had projected it wrongly. I took my cue from a note you made in another story about "too much author" and made that right.

That's why I am so anxious about the novel. It's on a different plane from the stories—all about the upper circles (the restrictions, taboos, comic-tragic existence of the New York Negro)[.] But <u>no</u> propaganda. It is a story first of all.

It is finished. I banged through it easily enough, but rereading important parts I find an appalling lot of things that must be re-written—cheap words and phrases that come inevitably in the first telling. Roughly I have upwards of seventy thousand words.

Are you sending me the duplicate or do you think it better to take both copies along. You might do what you think best about that.

Thanks again Yours Sincerely
Claude

LBP ALS

To Arturo Alfonso Schomburg

26 August 1926

L'Estaque, France

Dear Schomburg: I have waited most anxiously for a word from you about the handwritten copy of "Harlem Shadows." My novel is so far finished and I have the time to give to that work. Another reason is I am now absolutely broke—in debt and in trouble—and 50 dollars would lift me out of the rut like magic and make me fit for creative work!

My situation is this: At the time when you wrote to me about copying out "Harlem Shadows" I had just put the finishing strokes to my manuscript of short stories and intended to ship as a cabin boy to Singapore. The job was promised to me. And as I had no hope of further resources, I was going to make the trip. I calculated that by the time I got back to Marseille I would find an advance from the publisher of my stories awaiting me.

But your letter changed my plans. I went to a little village a little way out of Marseille and took a pension for a month to finish my novel[,] thinking that you would respond in time and that I could also finish your work there. I am in a dilemma now. My month is up on the 3rd of September and I have not a sou.

I was promised 1000 francs by a woman interested in the stories but on the strength of your letter I told her to take the money and pay for the typing of the manuscript and its dispatch to America. She is a publisher's reader and has got a letter from a publisher saying that he will send me an advance as soon as he gets the stories. But that will take a month at least and meanwhile I must live. I also have a story with the Bookman but it will be a month before I hear from Farrar also. If you have changed your mind I wish you would let me know, please. And if you could give me instead a loan on the stories to be published I should be very happy. I am sure about the stories for I have got the best criticism on them. I am in the tightest corner, believe me, that I've ever been in since I came to Europe and I've been in very tight ones!

I wish you would send me a telegram when you get this—

Claude McKay
Golfe Hotel
L'Estaque (Marseille)

Letters as usual go to Cook's—

Sincerely yours
Claude McKay

AASP ALS

To Louise Bryant

[late October/early November 1926]

Marseille, France

Dear Louise: I wonder if John Farrar would consider any of the stories you have? He has always been friendly and might be able to help you out with suggestions! I wonder why he couldn't use "Gigolo"? Sets me thinking there might be something "obscene" in the stories. I never thought of that before. I was always conscious of sordid, ugly and sinister aspects in the tales I tell—had never [thought] of obscenity. But now I imagine there may be that too from the conventional point of view. I don't know. But I feel sure if there were anything really offensive you and Mr [William C.] Bullitt would have pointed it out to me and, if unsure, I would have taken it out.

I have roughly done two other things but they are not typed. I would look upon it as a special favor if you gave me Jack [Reed]'s typewriter.[1] Couldn't you send it for me? It would be such a help for then when I did a little poem or story I could send it out and perhaps have a small cheque coming in at needy moments. I think I should like to do a novel about Marseille. The life of the devilish sailors here is like some horror out of the Middle Ages. It seems almost unreal. At first I thought it was too ugly to dwell on. But close contact has changed my mind. I met a woman beach-comber—a half-breed—the first I've ever seen anywhere. I haven't done a thing about it yet I am so unsettled.—but the story is big in my mind and growing bigger every day.

Max [Eastman] has taken a home at Antibes for a little while—he has made a little money I think. And he's made me an offer to come down and help Eliena[2] (his Russian wife) with the work. She wants to paint. I would get my food and about 400 francs a month and the use of Eliena's typewriter. That would solve my problem and I could go on working without being worried about immediate acceptance and payment. But I hate that region (I suffered so much there last year) and all the hivernants that Max knows. However I wrote him asking for a week's wait—and if I didn't hear anything satisfactory from you I would go. Thanking you for everything.

Sincerely Claude

[Enclosure: Included—a letter (dated 19 October 1926) from John Farrar of the Bookman rejecting the story "Gigolo."]

LBP ALS

1. McKay presumably means John (Jack) Reed's typewriter. Reed, journalist and author of *Ten Days That Shook the World* (1919), was Bryant's second husband and died in Moscow in 1920.

2. McKay routinely misspelled Eliena Eastman's name. The spelling here is difficult to make out.

To Louise Bryant

22 October 1926

Marseille, France

My dear Louise

I hope my two last letters that you must have received together did not make you thoroughly mad and disgusted with me. But Max [Eastman]'s letter threw me in a hopeless state. To think of Paris on three hundred francs without an overcoat and half crippled with rheumatic pains. It sounds whining, but I am in a terrible state with a pain in the right side of my neck running down the shoulder blade. Day + night it's there and all the aspirines I swallow will not scatter it. And my teeth are always on edge. And it[']s so depressing with the beachcombers day and night. They're just rotting in hell here on the docks. White, black, brown, yellow[,] every race is here. The police beat them up and kick them like dogs. I used to think New York's Irish police were brutal but these Marseille ones are the cruellest I ever saw. They pick up the beachcombers on the breakwater and in the box cars beat them up thoroughly and let them out again. They won't keep them in prison for they'd have to feed them. Nearly all of them have lost their papers and the consuls will not help them. Some of them speak English—Finian [?][,] Scandanavian [*sic*] deported from America. But all the <u>real</u> Americans [*sic*] ones are helped by the consul here and sent back. Every cent they get they spend on red wine. I am afraid when I talk to them for most of them are healthy appearing normal fellows and it[']s puzzling that they just deliver themselves up to rot like this.

Some of them are of course ill and the stuff they scoop up off the shops is horrible. I went down a few times and I couldn't eat although I was very hungry. If [I] get any money I'll have to give the chaps I stay with a raise. I wanted to get a room by myself after I got your first letter but I couldn't risk it as I wasn't sure about the decision on the stories. A good thing I didn't then! If we only had a real window and some natural light it would not be so horrible.

Your second letter has sent my spirits up again. Thanks for the 5 dollars. I agree with you about the Bonis. I met Charles [Boni] in Berlin when I got back from Russia and his views were reactionary—Menshivists [*sic*]. He was just about to start his publicity business then and was negotiating to buy a plant to print his books in Germany because the mark was worthless. I prayed God something would happen to smash up all these cheap little speculators. The next year the Dawes plan was established so I don't know what happened to Charles' scheme. That fellow Max wants me to go to in Paris is also considered a spy. He is Russian and a fellow of the lowest character—what the French call "voyon." He was also doing the charge [?] among other things in Berlin. He claims your acquaintanceship—but I don't think you remember him. He used to be with another Russian—one of the Dome crowd—named [Peter] Petroff. I hope the Viking people decide favorably. I should be so happy to get out of this. I wanted to tell you of them. But I heard that one of their readers of Negro stories was a colored official of the National Association for the Advancement of Colored People. They don't like me neither from the point of view of politics or [*sic*] of art[.] And they would never endorse my stories—because they deal with the black underworld. Perhaps Surprise + Revelation Blues would please them, but nothing else. My novel too will make them mad because it deals with the sex conflict between black and yellow Negroes. I sympathise with their sad respectable aspirations of course—but I want to keep out of their claws.—I hope you sell your play. I myself have ideas for two—But know nothing of play writing technique. If I were in America I would surely find a collaborator. Could you not send me some magazines: Nations—Time—Mercury—Century—+ if you could send too the copy of the New York Times with Max's article on Russia. Been cut off from all news for months. Again thanking you[.]

Sincerely
Claude

LBP ALS

To Louise Bryant

21 December 1926

Antibes, France

Dear Louise

In that list of names I sent you I forgot to put Eric Walrond. He is a young Negro who recently published a book of short stories called "Tropic Death" with Boni and Liveright. He is a friend of mine. Sold a couple of poems for me last year when I was broke. He is on the staff of "Opportunity["] Magazine published at 127 East 23rd street.

I know that your trying to place the stories must be dreadfully irritating work for you and taking up so much of your time. Sometimes I am pretty despondent, so despondent that I feel light-headed. And I am unhappy here with Max [Eastman]. He expects me to be smiling and charming when I must stay in all afternoon washing dishes and making beds while they go off to play tennis. I am not ungrateful. It is better to work for my food here than to starve in Marseille, but I cannot pretend that I am happy. I think Max regrets he asked me. It is awkward. We've known each other too long and too well for this arrangement to work happily.

He is coming home in March. I wish I could finish type [*sic*] my novel that he may take it along. But I don't think I will. I get so tired after I have finished my work at the villa, I have no joy of sitting down to the machine. It is more the novelty of having one to use that keeps me at it. It isn't that the work is hard. But as I told you some time aback [*sic*], I am all broken up inside with rheumatism. It grips me like a vise everywhere and at all times—feet, back, fingers, shoulders, neck.

If I could sell a story for fifty dollars, I would stop working and devote my time entirely to typeing [*sic*] my novel. I do wish it was possible for you to sell one separately for me: I eat so little. A mess of food turns my stomach, perhaps because all my life I have been obliged to slop about in all kinds of food for gluttonous people.

I have finished two more stories and I shall send them to you as soon as I have fair-typed them. They ought to be with the others. One of them I think is the best short story I have done yet. I have the use of the machine until March whether I work for Max or not.[1]

Greetings for the New Year
Sincerely yours,
Claude

P.S. I wish you could ask the firm of Harcourt Brace to send me a dozen copies of "Harlem Shadows"—please. I cannot ask myself because they sent me a dozen last year and so I owe them money. But the suit-case in which I had them was stolen with all my poems and other manuscripts, dictionaries, theaaurus [*sic*], all my valuable books—from the Seamen's mission at Marseille. You can imagine how difficult it is for me to write without a thesaurus. If I have a few copies of my book I can sell one sometimes. I could have sold three since I came here.

C

LBP TLS

1. This sentence is handwritten.

To Charles S. Johnson

11 January 1927

Antibes, France

Dear Mr. Johnson:

As the announcements of the contest that you sent me did not give the necessary details of forwarding material, I am sending this story, Bad Boy, personally to you. I want it to be entered instead of Yellow Fever which (if Mr. [Eric] Walrond has entered it) I should like to be withdrawn. I began also to work on a poem after getting your letter, which I hope to finish in time for the contest.

The story, Bad Boy, is not typed as well as I should like to have it. But I am not a good typist and I could not afford one. I hope the corrections and crossing-outs will not irritate the reader and count against the story itself. I think it is my best yet in that line. I put my address in pencil, so that it might be easily erased.

I was wondering if you could remunerate me for a series of articles on the life of Negroes in Marseille. I got to know it while I was stranded there last summer. It was terribly exciting, sad, picturesque, and cruel in many aspects. Negroes from every part of the world are flung together there in the old port. Sailors who have lost their ships, many of whom, apparently, never intend to go to sea again. Living on the great breakwater, always bumming, sometimes working and spending their time between the Quartier Reserve and the piers.

French, American, English, Portug[u]ese and former German Negroes—all are there. I am planning to go back there and do a book about their life (if I get the opportunity) and bring it back to America.

Again, let me thank you for your letter. I was very touched by it indeed.

With kindest regards:

Sincerely yours,
Claude McKay

P.S.
The story is sent under separate cover. I have not yet heard from Mr. [Countee] Cullen. I hope he did not also write to that address in Nice!

CM

CCP TLS

To Louise Bryant

13 January 1927

Antibes, France

Dear Louise:

Your letter quite stunned me. I had given up thinking that the stories would pass any of the young publishers in their present form and now you tell me that a firm like Harper[']s is interested. Oh I feel so relieved and revived again. I have been down with the blues since I came down here to Max [Eastman]'s. A French bonne took my place there three days ago, and I am staying in my room in the old town, working from eight to twelve hours a day, typeing [*sic*] my novel. I wish I could have enough of it done to show Professor [William A.] Bradley when he comes.

I am sending the other two stories, BAD BOY and REDEMPTION. I had sent in the best fair copy of BAD BOY to the OPPORTUNITY (Negro) Magazine Contest before your letter got here. I would not hold[1] the duplicate back to do another as I type slowly and you might want to see both stories immediately. I wrote BAD BOY when I was alone in Marseille doubled up with rheumatism and did not know what in the world was going to happen to me.

I had also sent the story ALSO LOVE to Egmont Arens of the New Masses just the day before your letter came. And I also asked Eric Walrond to give him the copy of BACK TO HARLEM which he has had since last year. I received a letter from Arens asking for them. Max had written to Mike Gold about them when I was at Marseille. If you succeeded in getting [H. L.] Mencken to take either of these two, you might just let Arens know that he can't use it! I don't care what the rebellious young men think, but I should'nt [*sic*] like to lose a chance in the MERCURY to the NEW MASSES.

I want to change the title of GIGOLO to SWEETMAN. That is the regular word among Negroes. I heard them use it at Marseille last summer and remembered that it was commonly used in Harlem. All through the story, whenever gigolo is used I will substitute sweetman. That Psyche and the Swan in CORAL should be Leda. And I want to change a whole page in that story.

Did'nt [*sic*] you tell Professor Bradley and [Albert] Boni that I had a novel all about the real life of Harlem? I thought of BLACK BELT as a title for it. I don't think that with a doughboy as my subject I could render the life more thoroughly than I have with the three principal characters in BLACK BELT,—a young black man studying to be a lawyer, his high-yellow fiancee and a high-yellow sweetman. What I could do however, and I think it would improve the novel, is to make the black man a returned doughboy. It would be very easy to make the change. What do you think of that?

I want to go to Paris as you suggest and type the novel. It will take me a little time, of course, as I am still quite slow. But it is better that I should do the first typeing [*sic*] myself as I make so much better emendations. Then I'll send it to you to get your advice, and go back to Marseille in the meantime to draw up a plan and make notes of places for the book I want to do about the life of the Negroes there. It is all so vivid, so fresh in my memory, I don't want to miss doing it.

I think I can get an English passport. I had one of the old ones and can furnish proof. But to get home to America I have to get in on the West Indian quota, and I have no idea how that works. I don[']t think it is as rigid as the old world quotas. Maybe the State Department has forgotten about my being in Russia! My appearance always deceives official people, so if I could get in under the quota, it would be better than making a problem of my getting in. At any rate, I think we should try the simplest and smoothest way first. Perhaps, you could find out for me about the West Indian quota. As soon as I get to Paris, I shall make my application.

Thanks very much for my present. Max is pleased that something definite has happened at last. He has written a novel too (this is a secret) which he intends to bring home in March.[2] He is making little additions to it and may show it to Professor Bradley, if he comes down.

Thanking you for your warm, encouraging letter,

Yours Sincerely
Claude

LBP TLS

1. The words "not hold" are handwritten.
2. This is likely Max Eastman's *Venture* (1927).

To Harold Jackman

14 January 1927

Antibes, France

My dear Jackman

It was very charming of you to write. It does me good to be remembered like that—unexpectedly. Also your little cheque was warmly welcomed as I am always in a state of chronic indigence, but I value more your fine sentiment that prompted it.

Oh yes, I hear from time to time of the big color wave breaking over New York and I am excited and curious in a thousand varying ways. I want to come back—for a time at least—but it's no good taking a ship and working a hard way over to be stopped from entering. I have so many things to count against me—alien and Bolshevik and a name that gets quite embarrassing at times. However I hope to get in in the regular way some day.

I am glad you like Desolate.[1] Everybody that read it in ms loved it. I was disappointed that it did not take the "Opportunity" prize. However, I have deserted poetry altogether for prose. Poetry is too limited a range for all I've got to do. I have been working on a novel. Indeed I finished it last summer. But I had no machine to type it and no money to pay. So I've just been right up an impasse. When I ran completely out of pocket and clothes and all pawnable things at Marseille, I came down here to Antibes and got a job as a valet. So here I am—for a while.

May I ask you a very important favor? And depend on your help? I want to know if there is any book or pamphlet about the enlistment and service of American Negro Soldiers in France during the war. If there is, could you possibly get me one. If there is not, could you get me this information.

When did the Fifteenth Regiment arrive in France?

When did it return to New York?

How long were ex-soldiers allowed in foreign universities at government expense?

Did the ex-soldiers receive any pay after demobilization? If so, for how long?

How is the bonus being distributed?

Does it apply in totality similarly to colored as to white ex-soldiers?

What good does the American Legion or War Veterans (I mean economic good) accomplish for the ex-soldiers?

Is there a colored branch of these organizations?

I want the facts to clear up certain points in my novel. There is an ex-serviceman in Harlem named William Service Bell who might supply you with the information if you mention me.

In addition I should like to know how many Negro regiments were organized and sent over.

Were all the colored officers of the Fifteenth Regiment removed from their positions?

And any other facts you can find up. I hope it won't be an awful bother to you.

Again, many thanks. I hope we shall meet if you come over next summer or if not—if I manage to get back to New York!

Sincerely yours
Claude McKay

[Left margin:] "Fire"[2] has not yet arrived—but I am expectant. I want to know what the different groups are doing and be with them—CM.

And let your friends know that I am doing better work than ever in spite of all hardships.

CMP ALS

1. "The Desolate City," originally published in *Opportunity,* November 1926.

2. *Fire!!*, a controversial literary magazine edited by Wallace Thurman, lasted only one issue, dated November 1926.

To William A. Bradley

7 February 1927

Antibes, France

[On Letterhead (crossed out): Majestic Café Bar, Cannes]

I don't think the short stories will be any use when I have done the novel, because I find that the background and most important settings from them are coming quite naturally into the novel. I thank you very much indeed for giving me the right idea.

Dear Mr Bradley

Here are two chapters of "Home To Harlem" that I have done.[1] I think I am going on in the spirit of the original story. Please let me know what you think. Perhaps you remember "Home To Harlem" enough, so I don't enclose my only copy.

I am having a real picnic doing it. Everything is clear and I can see through the whole story to the end. I ought to have the thing done by the end of March. I am uncomfortable in my new place however—the chimney won't work and I cannot heat it.

I should have sent you "Spring in New Hampshire[,]" the only copy of my poems I have—but we are holding it now to show the police. Max [Eastman] promises to go with me everyday but some how it is postponed. I am trying to get a reduction card and the little book comes in handy as it has my photograph. But you will have it when you come down.

I hope you wrote to Harper[']s for me for I am in a pretty tight hole.

Yours Sincerely
Claude McKay

WABLAR ALS

1. After his first meeting with Bradley, McKay began to develop the short story "Home to Harlem" into his first published novel.

To Louise Bryant

17 February 1927

Antibes, France

Dear Louise:

I waited to find out something definite about the new plans before writing to you. Mr [William A.] Bradley came down and saw me and he was very nice and helpful. I had done some fifty typed pages of the novel, but neither he nor Max [Eastman] liked the scheme of it. Although it was upon Max's suggestion that I began the novel. I admit it was done on an elaborate scale and the characters did not come through as clear-cut in the first chapters as they should. But they became very real as you went along. . . . . . .

However, upon Mr Bradley's and Max's suggestion, I am doing a novel out of the Home to Harlem story. I already have fifty pages done. I showed the two new chapters to M. and B. and they are both enthusiastic. I enclose Bradley's letter as I feel you might like to see it. It is such a very simple story and the scenes and people stand out so clearly and easily that it is like a picnic writing it. I never thought as much of the story myself as of others—like Also Love and Coral's Buffet Flat—but I daresay it had qualities I overlooked! In its elaboration I naturally strike deeper down, but I am holding it throughout in the same simple and easy form. Maybe I am unconsciously more myself like that. I think Bradley is a good critic as he isn't tied up with any school or problems and has, it seems[,] a keen eye on the market.

Except for a little loose change and an uncomfortable room (it is raw weather) I am very happy working now. And of course, I could never express to you how deeply I feel about your help and encouragement. No one else encouraged me as warmly and finely as you. And I suppose only my mother, if she were living and able and understood, would do as much. If the book comes out I want to show how much I feel about it, by doing the only thing I can do, if you will let me—inscribing it to you.

I want to finish by the end of March—at least not later than April. Then I hope Harper[']s will advance me enough to do the Marseille book. I spoke to Mr. Bradley of the life there and what I wanted to do. And he thought it was a splendid idea. He is also arranging to get me back home. He thinks it will be easy. There are some initial things to do—seeing the British Consul and writing a letter to be shown to the American Consul. But I am too busy now to see the consul, and Max thinks I shall have a better chance in Paris.

I saw Albert Boni at Cannes. Bradley told him about Max's novel and he came down from Paris and made a deal with Max about it. He said if Harper[']s didn't take mine, he would be glad to have it. That sounded odd to me when he had the chance to do something about it and didn't.

I don't think I shall want to publish the short stories again, because I am working all of the striking scenes into the Home to Harlem story. They fit in naturally without any straining. I am working like mad.

Thanking you for everything,
Yours Sincerely,
Claude

LBP TLS

To William A. Bradley

1 March 1927

Antibes, France

Dear Mr. Bradley

I thank you very much for the cheque and for your letter. It came just in time as I had no money and Max [Eastman] is short at the moment.

I had the chimney mended a fortnight ago and have been working more comfortably. I have now exactly 72 pages completed. In about ten more pages[1] I shall have the first part of the book done and I will send them to you. That will be sometime next week. I am working in the same fine spirit I started in and the story is working out quite smoothly.

I wonder if you will get back for me the chapters you sent to Harper's? They have some corrections that I haven't on the duplicate. I should also be much obliged if you could send me the ms. of "Bad Boy." It was the only fair copy I had left and a Frenchman thinks he could sell it to a publication called "Europe." He really wanted Home To Harlem and I was sorry I couldn't give it as I am doing the novel from it. Do you think it would be allright to give it?

Thanking you very much again for arranging this matter for me and so quickly[.]

Yours Sincerely
Claude McKay

WABLAR TLS

1. The word "pages" is inserted in pencil.

To William A. Bradley

11 March 1927

Antibes, France

Dear Mr. Bradley

I did just manage to get these chapters off "next week" as I promised, but not in time that you should get them before the week was out as I had intended. It's all because I went to Marseille last week-end. I just had to have some little jaunt away from here after getting a little money and I wanted to know how the boys there had fared through the winter. The number was diminished by about one-half. Two had died in hospital and three others, after being very ill in hospital were sent home by the American Consul. The guitar and banjo players were hired by some kind of travelling show, but a few remain rather sad, dirty and scantily-clothed, but hanging on the beach all the same and having no desire to leave it.

I want to go there as soon as I finish Home To Harlem, to start that book. Max [Eastman] thinks I should even go there before as he is leaving here next week and it will be lonely for me when he goes. I don't know just what I shall do. It will be cheaper to live in Marseille after Max and Eliena are gone. I hope Harper[']s will like Home To Harlem well enough to keep me doing the Marseille thing. It's going to be better, I feel it more vividly.

If you think Harper[']s will print the book from the copy they have and the others to be sent, without demanding a fair-typed manuscript, then I shan't need to have back that copy that I asked you for. It will be enough to do the corrections in proof. And I should be glad to be let off the expense of paying a typist.

I am in quite a quandary about a typewriter. I am using Max's, which he is taking with him when he goes next week. Mrs. [Louise Bryant] Bullitt had promised to send me an old one from America, but I suppose she forgot. If we can't find a cheap second-hand one I shall carry on by hand all the same until something turns up.

I should be very relieved if you could help me about my carte d'identité. My present one is a student's from 1924. Since the new laws I have made several applications for a special writer's card, but never received any reply from Paris. At Marseille last summer the application was turned down by a prefe[c]t. They tell me here that I must get a special attestation from some responsible person proving that my claims are en regle. I thought you might help me. Unfortunately I haven't a copy of my book, Harlem Shadows, to show. But I have a couple of magazines with poems and the booklet with my photograph that was published in London—the one I spoke to you about. I was sent from the bureau here to the bureau at Nice. There they said I should show them a journalist's card to prove that I write, but I told them I had no such card and I wasn't a journalist but an ecrivain. My chief concern is to get away from paying 375 francs.

I do hope that you will like these new chapters as well as the others. I also wish that you would tell me whether you think any of the phrases are too strong. I don't at all want to get out of bounds, so please tell me just what you think. I thought you would be coming down here, but Mrs. Michael. . . . . told me you had changed your mind.

I wonder if two hundred pages would make a presentable book? I don't want to drag the story out, nor pad it too obviously.

Thanking you[1] for your letter
Yours Very Sincerely
Claude McKay

WABLAR TLS

1. Handwritten from "Thanking you . . ."

To William A. Bradley

9 April 1927

Antibes, France

Dear Mr. Bradley

Thank you for the cheque for 200 francs.

I am returning the contract, because I think clauses 1. and 14 should be changed and explained before I sign.

First, I had no idea that Harper's was intending to contract for the short stories after I had come to an agreement with you to lengthen "Home To Harlem" into a novel. In the novel I am using material from the best of the stories, "Yellow Fever," "Coral's Buffet Flat," "Gigolo," "Prince of Puerto Rico," and "He Also Loved" I am including in its entirety. I had sold "He Also Loved" to the NEW MASSES and stopped its publication after seeing you, although I badly needed the money. If the stories are published first, they will kill the novel, and if they are published after, they will only make me ridiculous. Later on I could write some more stories to make a book with "Bad Boy," "High Ball" and "Redemption." I have not drawn upon any of these for the novel. But it is important that I should know now whether Harper's really want[s] the short stories (the title I had in mind was Speakeasy Nights) or the novel. If it had been clear to me at first that the stories were to be published, I should have written a very different sort of novel.

Second, I was under the impression that you were acting for one book only, viz: Home To Harlem. At least Max Eastman said so. But as the contract stands, you are acting for any other two books that I may do. I suppose that is just a general way of putting it when one is represented and that you had not made the matter definite to the firm. I should be very much obliged to you if you would and have the clause altered for me. I think you will agree with me that as I am going home immediately after doing the Marseille book, and taking it with me, I'll be able to make direct contact in New York and won't then need a representative over here. That would eliminate the difficulty of my being in New York and having to refer everything concerning getting out the book to you in Paris.

May I also ask you, personally, to make a clear financial statement of Clause 14 for me? As clear as Clause 12? I ask because I have never had a representative for my other books and I do not know what the arrangement is.

If I were sure that the clauses would be altered as I hope, I would sign now as you suggest, for I am very much in need of the money to go on with my work. But I don't know if I could ask for changes after signing, so I think it is better to wait until they are made. I must confess I am unduly worried perhaps about the two points, and I won't be able to carry on as smoothly as before until they are settled.

Yours very sincerely
Claude McKay

WABLAR TLS

Plate 1. Claude McKay, frontispiece to *Spring in New Hampshire* (1920). (James Weldon Johnson Memorial Collection in the Yale Collection of American Literature, Beinecke Rare Book and Manuscript Library)

Plate 2. Nicolai Bukharin, Claude McKay, and Grigory Yevseyevich, ca. 1923. (Claude McKay Collection, Yale Collection of American Literature, Beinecke Rare Book and Manuscript Library)

Plate 3. Claude McKay, "Speaking from the Throne Room in the Kremlin," ca. 1923. (Claude McKay Collection, Yale Collection of American Literature, Beinecke Rare Book and Manuscript Library)

Plate 4. Claude McKay in Russia, ca. 1923. (Claude McKay Collection, Yale Collection of American Literature, Beinecke Rare Book and Manuscript Library)

Plate 5. Claude McKay in L'Estaque, France, 1926. (Claude McKay Collection, Yale Collection of American Literature, Beinecke Rare Book and Manuscript Library)

Plate 6. Claude McKay, 1928. (Louise Bryant Papers, Manuscripts and Archives, Yale University Library)

Plate 7. Claude McKay, 1928. (Louise Bryant Papers, Manuscripts and Archives, Yale University Library)

Plate 8. Claude McKay in Paris, 1929. (William A. Bradley Literary Agency Records, Box 43, Folder 8, Harry Ransom Center, The University of Texas at Austin)

Plate 9. Claude McKay in Morocco. (Claude McKay Collection, Yale Collection of American Literature, Beinecke Rare Book and Manuscript Library)

Plate 10. Claude McKay in Morocco ("Tangier-Bahlia"). (Claude McKay Collection, Yale Collection of American Literature, Beinecke Rare Book and Manuscript Library)

Plate 11. Claude McKay in Tangier ("The river running by my house at Tangier-Bahlia"). (Claude McKay Collection, Yale Collection of American Literature, Beinecke Rare Book and Manuscript Library)

Plate 12. Carl Van Vechten, "Claude McKay," 13 April 1934. (Carl Van Vechten Papers Relating to African American Arts and Letters in the Yale Collection of American Literature, Beinecke Rare Book and Manuscript Library)

To Louise Bryant

[mid-April 1927]

Antibes, France

I finally took it to a place here in Antibes where they discovered that some spring was missing.[1] I had to pay another 100 francs and that ten dollars you sent me just in time to help me out. Thank you. I went back to the man I bought it from at Nice. He had given me a guarantee for six months and ought to pay the cost of repairing. But he said the guarantee was for reparation by himself!

I am sending you a letter from [William A.] Bradley, copy of my reply to him, and the paragraphs from the contract that I object to.[2] Max [Eastman] says I am too blunt in writing but I tried to make my letter to Bradley as diplomatic as I could. You told me to put myself in his hands and I did. But he never told me he was going to make himself my permanent agent. I don't think that is necessary, especially as I am soon returning home. And I don't want to tie myself up to him for three books.

I wish you would call to see Mr. [Eugene] Saxton of Harper's about the matter for me. I am sending him a note to that effect. Just hear what is his decision between the short stories and the novel[.] And you might broach my objection to Clause 14. In the meantime I am in a pickle. I must give up this old sunless room in two weeks. I had planned to go back to Marseille, to live in the atmosphere of what I am going to write about. But I shan't have the money to move as I have not signed and I cannot ask Bradley while the matter is pending. And now that Max is gone there is nobody to suggest an [*sic*] anything. I leave it to you, then, after reading through the stuff to advise me. If you think it is O.K. and I should sign as it is, won't you cable me 15 rue du Saint ESprit [*sic*], Antibes[,] France "Sign" or if you think otherwise "Wait." You have experience about these matters.[3] I hope I haven't made a false step.

I am very glad to hear about your play getting over. I hope it will be a success. Thank you very much for your letter. I think Mr [William C.] Bullitt will know right away if I am right about that Clause 14.

Sincerely Claude.

Egmont Arens of the New Masses wanted a story. Do you think you could sell him cash one of those I sent you? That would help solve my immediate problem until this thing is settled.

LBP TLS

1. Letter survives in incomplete form; opening page or pages are missing.
2. The letter from Bradley is dated 8 April 1927.
3. Handwritten beginning with "these matters."

To William A. Bradley

15 April 1927

Antibes, France

Dear Mr. Bradley

I was very glad to hear from you right away. I felt this about the first part of the contract: That if after your representations and recommendations, Harper's did contract for those short stories, then it was safer not to sign before it was definitely agreed that the short stories should be set aside.

Louise Bullitt had written that I should put myself entirely in your hands. Therefore I knew that your interest in me was not that of a mere representative. If I thought so, I could not have written to you always as I did, nor expected so much of you in other matters.

That's just why I was pulled up by the last clause of the contract. It read very sharp and business-like and final. (I suppose a contract must be very matter-of-fact.) But I would have felt different about it if you had given me beforehand some idea of what it would be like. It is a pity you did not talk the point out with Max Eastman, so that I should not have had to bring it up. When Albert Boni came to see Max about his novel, the matter was touched upon (I wish you were here then) and Max assumed you were acting for one book only. He has had representatives in London and New York. As I said in my last letter I have never had any, and I don't know the rules. Now that you explain, I am entirely willing to hold by them.

I am sorry you had to write the last paragraph of your letter. Because I could not dream of being dishonest with you and slip anything over, after all the real interest you have shown and the work you have already done for me. I could not, if you were even an agent only. But I have been thinking of you all along as [a] friendly critic who knows his stuff, and not as a mere representative. I know too well from experience that one doesn't meet such a person everyday, and I should hate that anything should happen to break off a contact just begun.

It is over a year and a half since I tried to place my first novel, Color Scheme, in New York and did not succeed. I got disgusted and burned it. I am quite sure that if you had seen it, it would have turned out differently. For in feeling, it was very much after the pattern of the story that I am doing now. It was after that failure that I started in on short stories, hoping thus to reach the magazine market.

I wish Max Eastman had been here to act for me. He is so suave and diplomatic. I hate business matters, and the fact that they have arisen irritably between you and me. I regret it.

Yours very Sincerely,
Claude McKay

I think I shall leave for Marseille at the end of next week.[1] I may as well live in the atmosphere of what I am going to write of next.

WABLAR TLS

1. The postscript is handwritten.

To Alain Locke

18 April 1927

Antibes, France

Dear Locke,

I see by Miss Gwendolyn Bennett's column, that you are again writing something about me.[1] I don't know if it will mean anything at all to you if I say that when Louis Untermeyer was putting me in his anthology, he specially looked me up in Paris and told me just what he was going to do. I am always forced into the unpleasant position of making comparisons between white gentleman [*sic*] and black gentleman [*sic*] to the disadvantage of the black ones.

I am hoping that this time I shall not be as badly presented as I was in your "New Negro." I picked up quite a number of mistakes before the volume was stolen from me at Marseille. And what you mentioned in your last letter concerning immigration and the title of my poem that you unwarrantably changed (making me appear as a ridiculous, angry person hankering after the unattainable flesh-pots of the whites) seemed so utterly irrelevant that I was dumb-struck. I could not think of any third-rate white editor and critic, who puts any value on a work of art as something worth more than a mess of

American corn bread, who would deliberately violate an artist's work in the way you did. It seems to me that if you thought my poem dangerous from political motives, you should have left it out of your collection altogether and not violated it the way you did.

I write strong words because I felt strongly at the time about your action and still do. I must say frankly that from my experience, I do not think any of the American Negro intelligentzia [*sic*] have any real interest in art, Negro art, except as a decoration for their special social affairs. I would much prefer if you could drop me out of your contemplated book. I do not think that, as a poet, I have penetrated deeply into that racial experience that I have seen mentioned by you somewhere. There are many others to that heritage born and more deserving and humble and grateful, that you can find to put in my place.

I don't want my name nor my work to be deliberately massacred because of the exigences of false, momentary racial aspirations. We are so far apart in ideas, I don't know if I can explain this to you. But I am a man and artist first of all. The imprisoning quality of my complexion has never yet, and never will, move me to bend to[2] flunkeyism and intellectual imprisonment with the sorry millions that are likewise tinted.

Yours Sincerely
Claude McKay

ALP TLS

1. Alain Locke, ed., *Four Negro Poets* (1927). This was mentioned in Gwendolyn Bennett's column "The Ebony Flute," *Opportunity*, April 1927, 122–23.

2. The words "bend to" are added in handwriting.

To William A. Bradley

24 [April] 1927

Nice, France

[On Letterhead (crossed out): Café Notre-Dame, Nice]

Dear Mr Bradley

Thank you for your letter and card, I am glad Harper[']s answered promptly and that everything will be right now in the new contract. I could not go to Marseille broke, so I came here to a little hotel where I stayed last year in the expectation that something would turn up to straighten me out. It will be easy for me to leave anytime as it is by the day.

In the meantime I should be much obliged if you would send me another 200 francs (in bank notes) please.

I shall finish "Home To Harlem" in another week, at most two. I wish you would get back the short story "Home To Harlem" and also the last chapters you sent over, I want to see under my own eyes all of the original together and add some notes that I have. I am also dividing it in 3 parts. I really should have culled that ten days ago but the contract business threw me into confusion. I don't want to pencil in new things on the duplicate because I should have to move them again to the original. I am sorry now I had forgotten about it for I shall be finished long before you get them here.

Thank you for the address of Ford Madox Ford and of Blaise Cendrars. I saw the "Anthologie Negre" in Paris but did not get the time to read through it.[1]

Yours Sincerely
Claude McKay

WABLAR ALS

1. Swiss-born French writer Blaise Cendrars's collection of African folk tales, *Anthologie nègre* (1921), appeared in a second edition in 1927.

To W. E. B. Du Bois

28 April 1927

Antibes, France

Dear Dr DuBois

Thank you very much for your letter and cheque for ten dollars. I knew I was right in thinking that my letter and the poems had not come under your personal attention.

About my return to the States. The real truth is that I have never made any definite application to get back since I returned from Russia in 1923. Intellectually I have been working very hard; economically I have been drifting. None of the more ambitious things I did were favorably received by publishers. Maybe that was because of my limitations, maybe it was because I was not in New York to push my own stuff. At any rate I have been going on as hard as ever, without being mentally discouraged. . . . . . Perhaps, if I had gone straight home from Germany, existence might have been just as economically difficult for me in America as ever. I hate platform propaganda, I have not enough interest in an assembled crowd to try and put myself over in its favor and I saw no prospects of anything more congenial; and so I felt that I may as well knock around in Europe, for the new experience at any rate, than to return to America and repeat the old business.

I am hoping to return again very soon, however. But I do not want to make a political or racial issue of it. A friend of mine in Paris thinks he could get me over through a well-placed friend of his in an important department at Washington. I shall let you know in case his representations are turned down.

Again thanking you very much for your kind letter,

I am sincerely yours,

Claude McKay

WEBDP TLS

To Harold Jackman

28 April 1927

Nice, France

My dear Jackman

I thank you very much for your letter and the information. It was just those skeleton facts that I wanted. Scott's book would be of very little use to me, thanks.[1] The American administration is welcome to it. Have you heard anything of a book or pamphlet called: two colored women with the A. E. F. I think it was written by one Hunton.[2]

I have seen no copies of Ulysses in the book stores here at Nice.[3] I came down specially to see. But I did see some at Marseille. And as I am going back there in a few days I shall no doubt manage to get one for you. The price in France is 50 francs, about two dollars just. I would buy it myself but I am living a very precarious existence in the pecuniary sense. I have found a publisher and am on the point of signing a contract. But the agent who managed it has not yet touched any money for me. You will have to tell me how to get the book past the customs. It is big and bulky and I am sure it will be opened.

I was very ill when I wrote that poem "Desolate." And as the essence of good writing is to put over your thoughts and feelings in a vivid way, I suppose

"Desolate" must be well-written indeed. I am glad you like it. Countee Cullen writes that he likes it too. But it was written in 1924. When you wrote to me on your trip over here I was very much better. And I am still looking as well as when you saw me in New York, except that I don't feel physically so fit and I have periodical fits of depression. But some money and a little change of air and that will disappear in a short while. When are you coming back over again? Please thank [William] Service Bell and tell him that I hope to drink [to] his health some day with bootleg. And you too. You have been so splendid about this matter. You shall have one of the first copies of the novel, but I am afraid it won't be signed as I am away over here. Are you thinking of travelling again soon?

I did not get Fire. Yes, I sent Opportunity a story and a poem. But I have no faith in competitions. It all depends on one doing something more spectacular than inherently fine. Also the humor of the judges decides much. No harm trying, however. I hope your mother is better. By the way, forgive my asking, are you Southern or Northern or West Indian or a mixture of all? How is [Alain] Locke and [Langston] Hughes and [Carl] Van Vechten and his Nigger Heaven and the group of Young Negro Intellectuals? Won't you give me some news? I should have written to Langston and I must soon. He sent me both his books and he is a charming correspondent, but I have been too inquiet of late to write. . . . Why did Jessie Fauset leave the Crisis and what has become of Jean Toomer? And is Gwendolyn Bennett pretty? Amazing questions, but all of the hours thoughts.

Thanks again for your kindness
Very Sincerely Yours
Claude McKay

CMP TLS

1. Likely *Scott's Official History of the American Negro in the World War* (1919) by Emmett Jay Scott.

2. Addie W. Hunton and Kathryn M. Johnson, *Two Colored Women with the American Expeditionary Forces* (1920).

3. James Joyce's *Ulysses* (1922), published in Paris by Sylvia Beach's Shakespeare & Company, was banned in the United States until December 1933, when a court case determined the novel was not obscene. Before this, American writers and intellectuals sought out creative ways of smuggling the novel to the United States. Jackman had previously tried to have Gwendolyn Bennett acquire a copy for him. See Belinda Wheeler and Louis J. Parascandola, *Heroine of the Harlem Renaissance and Beyond: Gwendolyn Bennett's Selected Writings* (University Park: Pennsylvania State University Press, 2018), 198.

To Langston Hughes

30 April 1927

Nice, France

My dear Langston

I should have written to you long ago, I was unhappy not being able to, because your letters have such a fresh, charming interest; but I was passing through such a sad, doleful period, it was impossible and would have only been farcical, to try and write warm responsive letters to my friends. I know you will understand this. My correspondence was limited to purely necessitous matters that could help me out of my difficulties. And all my time, aside from working here and there for a bite, was concentrated on such literary work as I could do it to lift myself up out of the rut by the boot strings.

I have received a copy of your second book of poems and I thank you for having it sent to me. Personally I seem to like the form and manner of this book even more than the first. To me there are fine individual lyrics in the first book that stand out boldly all by themselves. But here in the second I seem to find a definite plan of weaving verses out of the common everyday words of the American Negro of to-day and the ensemble is a complete and worthy achievement. This is no dogmatic assertion. I am merely stating how the book strikes me personally as I might tell a friend how I feel after looking at a painting. I hope you sell many copies.

Did you make your contemplated trip to the West Indies last summer? I should like to know what you think of the islands that you touched. When will you be finished at the university?

I am thinking of coming home next fall or winter. I write of America as home. I am really a poet without a country. Maybe that is why I have an international mind. I am on the point of finishing my novel and I think I have a publisher now, although I won't shout until the contract is signed. I shall have the contract, I hope, in a few days. Then I shall go on to Marseille, where I intend to write another and then if there are no obstacles—a visit to America.

I am now at Nice, But I don't care much for the Riviera landscape. I came down here from Marseille last fall, because I was flat broke and a friendly American offered me a job as a "bonne[.]" I did not make a good one this time and so I gave it up after two months['] trial. A dollar or a few francs coming in at times from various sources kept me going. And I could go and eat free whenever I liked with the radical gentleman for whom I had worked. So that was why I stayed on in this strange, shallow-rooted region of rich hivernants, their arse-licking lackeys, and swinish commercants.

Marseille I really love more than any place in France. It is the most vivid port I ever touched. Wonderful, dirty, unbeautiful, rolling in slime and color and hourly interest. There all the scum of the sea seems to drift on to the natural soil. I love it more than any of the English American or German ports. Do you know Antwerp? It is even more interesting. Well I am hungry and I gues[s] you will be tired so—

Good luck and my best wishes Ever Sincerely
Claude

LHP TLS

To William A. Bradley

14 May 1927

Nice, France

Dear Mr. Bradley

Thanks for your letters, the 200 francs and also the cheque. The cheque is smaller than I anticipated on account of the extra 5%. The error you noted was not overlooked by me. But I thought that for the sake of my passport I had better let it remain as it was. I did not know there was an income tax on such small amounts! And as all honest people are dodging this abominable thing, I was not at all unwilling to join them. You see I have received money for literary work at various times from America—in one case amounting to 200 dollars and I never paid any tax. However I am leaving all business arrangements entirely in your hands. Max Eastman wrote advising me to and I always take Max's advice. I only want enough so I can go on picking up material and writing. I shouldn't mind getting some idea of the format of the book and what the cover will be like. I chose the cover myself for my book of poems. I should also like to know if I am not entitled to a duplicate of the contract.

I haven't any good photographs with me. But, if you have no objection, you being in Paris, you might get some very good ones of me from Miss Ber[e]nice Abbott. I don't remember her address. I think her studio is in the rue du

Bac, but I am sure you might get it from Sylvia Beach. Miss Abbott took some very good photographs and everybody liked them. I did not take any of them from her for I could not afford to pay for them. She might let you have them very cheap, for she had offered them to me at a low price.

Max Eastman's preface to my book of poems, "Harlem Shadows," gives exact information about myself. Perhaps that might suit Mr. [Eugene] Saxton and he could use that material in any form he likes. He might change "born in Jamaica" to "born in the West Indies" until I get back home. There are United States West Indies also, and sooner or later she will take Jamaica from the English, for that little island is in the direct route of the Panama Canal. Of course, what I have been doing since I came to Europe is not in the preface, but I think that information should be held over for the Marseille novel. Don't you?[1]

I have finished the novel. And as soon as I have reread and emendated them, I shall send you the remaining chapters. I am leaving today for Marseille. Lloyd's had to telegraph to Paris to verify the cheque and that was expensive. But I did not want to stay a day longer than today (Sunday). My temporary address there will be Thomas Cook and son, until I get settled.

Thanking you for everything
I am, Yours Sincerely
Claude McKay

WABLAR TLS

1. This question was inserted in handwriting.

To William A. Bradley

23 May 1927

Marseille, France

Dear Mr Bradley

Under separate cover or covers I am sending you the last chapter of the novel.

I am worried about pp. 140, 141, 152, 156, 217—not being sure if they can go through—and would be much obliged to hear your opinion. The contract said something about not putting in "illegal matter" and as I have a peasant fear of contracts and litigation I want to be on the safe side. I am always puzzled about obscenity in literature—something that seems obviously pure filth to me may get by while a brutal innocent phrase may spoil a book's success. I wish you would tell me what you think personally before we go to Harper[']s. I couldn't wait for the other parts as time is slipping by so quickly. I wonder if I couldn't make the corrections and the division [?] on the proofs! The chapters of course will have to be changed + the numbering. And I've got to get in a little dedication.

I am also sending you a letter from Opportunity magazine which you might be able to deal with better than I can. The editor, Mr [Charles S.] Johnson, has I think five of my short stories including "Home To Harlem" which I am almost certain he will publish unless you send him a strong protest. A former assistant of his, Eric Walrond, was acting for me in New York, trying to place my stories. I think he submitted some of them to the Opportunity competitions but they did not win prizes. That was two years ago but when Walrond left recently he also left my stories there at the office. I have written asking the editor to return them to me and this letter is the first answer I have got. Of course they know now, I am sure it has leaked out, that Harper[']s has accepted the stories and they will publish all of them that they hold, including Home To Harlem, thinking that I am helpless over here. They add insult to injury by paying nothing. I can do nothing with them. Negro editors are in a class by themselves and do not follow any of the rules of journalistic decency. I think if you write to them as my legal representative they will send the stories back and promise not to publish anymore. John Farrar of The Bookman also has "Gigolo." I have written twice for it but he has not replied. You might be able to get it out of him. I am very worried. Publication of the stories does not only seem like a breach of faith with Harper[']s, but, in their present form, it works against the novel.

I also want to hint here that after Harper[']s have had the rest of the book I should like your suggesting (if the completed thing satisfies them) another #200 advance. That would total #500 and that is what is generally given for a novel I understand. I mean advancing this on the Harlem and not on the Marseille novel. That would give me enough to get some essential things and settle comfortably down to work. And I won't be worrying every day about how long this 200 francs will last. Today I am going down by the port to find a room. Then shortly I shall begin working at "Marseille." I have been staying in a hotel of "du centre[,]" a quiet place where I could re-read + correct without distraction.

I am afraid there are too many ugly corrections. I am willing to type them over if you think so. In a day or two I shall send [an] auto-biographical note. I know the time is slipping—but I can't today. I am too tired headachy and "bouleversé."

If I should have left Leon standing anywhere in the story it should be changed to Ray. I grew to dislike Leon when Ray is the actual name of a railroad pal of mind. It is also allright to use it. He is dead. I think Ray helps to balance Jake. I had to bring him in to get the railroad stuff "pat" and I hope his "high brow" ideas have not retarded the flow of the story. I think the contrast is good and it is really based on fact. The character of Ray also gives me a chance to let myself go a little.

Finally I stand ready to take out anything that might be considered offensive[,] obscene or in any way illegal. I have not the slightest wish to publish a novel that may be suppressed.

Yours Sincerely
Claude McKay

WABLAR ALS

To William A. Bradley

[postmarked 25 May 1927]

Marseille, France

I forgot to mention the most important reason for suggesting a further advance. I have a number of clues to follow up, places I knew of last year that I couldn't afford to visit. And if I am to do something about Marseille better than "Home To Harlem" I must have a few spare notes to "blow" me into these places. As I am fixed now I have nothing to spare over strictly living "en pauvre [?][.]"

Yours Sincerely
Claude McKay

WABLAR APS

To Harold Jackman

4 June 1927

Marseille, France

My dear Jackman

I hope you got my letter. I am now in Marseille and have finished my novel and sent it to New York. You will get a copy, of course, as soon as it is out. There are a few other things I want to ask you, which I can straighten out in proofs. Namely: What universities and colleges graduate doctors in New York and New England. And, please find out from [William Service] Bell if he could give exact information on what company, or regiment, the colored boys who stevedored at Brest during the war belonged to. Also, if the big building at the foot of the rue Siam overlooking the bridge and the port was a Y.M.C.A. canteen or some other organization's. How were the colored boys treated at the Y.M.C.A. recreation rooms etc. Ask Bell why the Col. Young Post was abandoned and if colored legionnaires are invited to the annual conventions of the American Legion. And anything else of importance you might think of will be welcome. These facts are not fundamental issues, but I want to be sure before I even hint at them.

I never got "Fire." Yes, I tried Opportunity again with a story and a poem but I don't think I won this time, either. Of course, I do not take the results of literary competitions seriously—intellectually they never mean much—but I think a great deal of the money awards. That is my only object for entering. If I do get a chance this time of putting my novel over, then I would be free to continue writing for my publisher only and leave competitions to those who have not yet had their chance.

Hoping you will write to me soon and not keep me waiting so long this time as I have only a month before the book must be placed in the hands of the publisher.

Ever Sincerely Yours
Claude McKay

CMP TLS

To Alain Locke

4 June 1927

Marseille, France

Dear Doctor Locke

Preliminary note: I would state quite blandly that my correspondence is safe at any Cook's agency in France and sure to reach me. You are the only person whose letters to me seem to go astray periodically. As for the letter you mention it has never reached me. Amazing fact: I have been living at Antibes since November of 1926 until May 1927 and getting my mail at Nice at Cook's, which is just ten minutes ride from Antibes so—

After getting your letter and reading it, and re-reading it, reasonably and dispassionately I must say that it's [*sic*] effect upon me is to destroy every vestige of intellectual and fraternal understanding that may have existed between us. It is not for you to talk about my intellectual position. By your actions you have done everything to injure it. You have used poems of mine that I had dropped out of my collection, you have changed the title to one of my most important poems (thinking, I am sure that as a doctor of philosophy, you have a finer comprehension of a poet's ideas than the poet himself)[,] you refused a poem that a conservative white man was not afraid of publishing, you ignored the date of my birth that was given in "Harlem Shadows," (my latest and most authentic biographical note is printed there) and you went and dug up an anterior date. It was after the publication of "Spring in New Hampshire" that my sister verified the date (it had been set back at Grade School so that I could be allowed to act as assistant to the school-master) and wrote me about it in London. But I suppose that you have such a passion for discovering things and acting upon your own initiative that you never considered it polite or expedient to ask me for the facts.

You say "poets are anthologized on publisher's permission." Very well, but a poet or writer can refuse his publisher to go in an anthology, I, personally, know of cases of refusal. Boni and Liveright wrote to me personally before they attempted to put me in the Masses Anthology. Besides "Like a Strong Tree" and "White House" are not included in Harlem Shadows and I have the right, legal right over them. I gave you those and certain poems of your choice out of "Miasma" for the "Survey." That permission does not carry over to a pamphlet published by Simon and Schuster. I entirely fail to see how on the 27 day of

April, when your pamphlet is already published, you can be giving me "the courtesy of notice and request for cooperation." There is no question but, that, in spite of your doctor's degree, you have not acted as a man of honor.

I will now give you my notice. It is that I am very much alive and that at the first expedient opportunity I shall assemble all the hodge-podge that has been written about me and repudiate it. In fact I have been twice approached to do it, but I refused, simply because I did not want to splash about in the hog-water of Negro Journalism.

The "movement suffers," you write. I won't comment on that except to say that perhaps the movement would suffer less, if the individuals who pretend they are leading it displayed a little more intellectual solidarity and disinterestedness. I never told you that I was seeking any "Abstract universal recognition" as a poet, but I think I may have my ambitions without being catechised about them by Doctor Locke. I would not suggest at all to you if you might not have preferred to be known as the doctor of philosophy at Berlin or Cambridge than at Howard. That would be your business, depending on which you think, perhaps, would better help forward—the movement. . . . . And as to your opinion concerning the ultimate appraisal of my life and work—keep it, my dear Doctor Locke. Keep your opinion and, forgive me but, I don't care a damn for it.

Yours Sincerely
Claude McKay

ALP TLS

To William A. Bradley

4 Junc 1927

Marseille, France

Dear Mr Bradley

I was very pleased to get your letter and to know that you like the second half of the novel. I had planned to bring Ray in the Marseille novel. That was why I sent him off out of the scene like that. It wouldn[']t have served any real purpose keeping him to the end. I am not going to have too much of him in the next novel, because I cannot handle him as objectively as I can a character as Jake and thus I am likely to get away from the main telling of the story. I was not even so sure he did not obtrude a little too heavily in "Home To Harlem[.]" I am glad you like it as it is. I did have Ray as the principal character in my two other attempts to do a novel and I don't think he stood up as well as he does in a secondary role. Maybe I was more interested in his ideas than in his life. I think I've found out how to get at him now.

I hope you got the photographs from Miss [Berenice] Abbott. Supplementary material about myself: During the war I worked for a time on the railroad. Previous to that The Seven Arts and Frank Harris' Pearson's Magazine published some of my poems. In 1919 I went to Europe visiting Holland, Belgium, and London, where I stayed over a year and brought out a little book of poems, "Spring in New Hampshire" with Grant Richards. I returned to America in 1921 and Max Eastman engaged me to help on the Liberator. Harcourt, Brace published "Harlem Shadows" in 1922" [*sic*] and in the fall I again left for Europe working my way over as a fireman. I landed at Liverpool and went up to London. Crossed over to Berlin where I met Eden and Cedar Paul who were going to Russia.[1] An English writer, friend of mine, managed to get me a passport to go to Russia also. I stayed there about six months in Moscow + Petrograd + had a good time going around with the drunken poets. I came back to Germany in 1923 and stayed there six months. I wrote a number of poems during this period but I lost all of them at Marseille last summer, when my suitcase was stolen. In 1924 I went to Paris. I was flat broke and posed for a time as a model. Then I fell ill[,] caught cold posing naked in a cold studio. A group of liberals got me away to the Midi. I went back to Paris in 1925. I had written a novel but it did not "get over." In the fall I returned to the Cote d'Azur. Spent the better part of 1926 here at Marseille existing any way I could, doing a day's work on the dock and sometimes touching a small cheque for a poem. I lived most of the time in the Quartier Reservé with Negroes from America, British, French, Portuguese Africa + the West Indies. It was then I put the idea of doing a novel around them with the Vieux Port as background. I wrote the short stories in 1925–26[,] some during the Marseille period. Mrs [Louise Bryant] Bullitt took them to America for me in the fall of 1926 and, of course, "Home To Harlem" the novel grew out of your suggestion that I should expand the short story of that name. I am sorry I have to write with a pen, but my typewriter is gone wrong again.

I am sending you a copy of "Opportunity" with an article of Pierre Mille's.[2] If they didn't pay him they ought to. They are a rich philanthropic organization.

John Rockefellar [*sic*] Jr is in the board, but they won't pay for contributions if they can get away from paying.

It was merely a suggestion that matter of a further advance, and it depended, of course, on whether you thought it wise or not. I won't worry but will go on working and waiting and see how things work out[.]

Yours Sincerely
Claude McKay

WABLAR ALS

1. Eden (1865–1944) and Cedar (1880–1972) Paul were British socialists who together translated many works in the early twentieth century.

2. Pierre Mille's "The African Work of Alexander Jacovieff," *Opportunity,* May 1927, 132–34.

To William A. Bradley

24 June 1927

Marseille, France

Dear Mr Bradley

I shall have to get the photographs elsewhere, Miss [Berenice] Abbott is too high-priced. When she did me over two years ago (she was then assistant to Man Ray and did not have an establishment of her own) she offered the photographs to me at 30 francs a piece and said that the regular price was 50 francs—but I could not afford to take them even at 30.

I would take some cheap ones here, but even that I cannot afford now, for I am down at 500 francs, just enough to carry me 20 days more.

I wonder if you did suggest Mr [Eugene] Saxton's subsidizing me through the Marseille book. I haven't commenced the actual writing yet, but I have taken a composition book full of notes and done some scenes and made true plans of the Vieux Port and Juliette[,] the two principal places where the story is centered in [*sic*]. Please let me know so that I may be certain where I stand. You were not very precise in your answer to that letter in which I asked you about a further advance on "Home To Harlem." I had to mention the facts then because I had already felt my pocket flat after repaying the various small accounts that I had "tapped" of friends over the winter.

Yours Sincerely
Claude McKay

There are many of the poems in "Harlem Shadows" I would cut out if I were doing the book again, I have grown so much beyond them.

WABLAR ALS

To Harold Jackman

27 June 1927

Marseille, France

My dear Jackman

I have called my friend in Paris to get your "Ulysses." There at Marseille they had only a sample copy in the book-store I mentioned and it has been sold. I asked you for some facts on certain items in a letter that must have crossed yours. They are for my novel—to go in the proofs if I had made mistakes. I shouldn't like to be tripped up in trivial points.

Oh yes, you did tell me about Countée Cullen when you came to see me in 14th street. Don't you remember? We have been corresponding for some time and he has just sent me a copy of "Color" as a reward for my efforts in "Opportunity's" contest. It is a very beautiful book. I have also just heard from Langston Hughes. We are old friends and I love his personality and his work.

The "Crisis" is an entirely different magazine from "Opportunity." There is so much fallow ground in the Negro field to be ploughed in America that I have never been able to see why the interests of two such discriminating publications should clash, when there is nothing in common with their policy. Dr. [W. E. B.] Du Bois, whether one likes him personally or not, is one of the most powerful propagandists in the U.S. and so his editing the "Crisis" will always make it worth reading. There are many things he might do better of course. But so could "Opportunity." But everything depends on the viewpoint and personality of each editor. Have you ever thought what a great Negro editor with the outlook, "pushfulness," resourcefulness, and thick-headedness of a Jew might do to wake up America? Suppose you had a man with the energy of [Marcus] Garvey who was not ignorant and narrow and hard headed withal as Garvey was!

Thank you for your picture. I saw it in the Survey Graphic, I think, or in "The New Negro" before the volume was stolen here last year. No I don't think it looks very much like you. As I remember you, you were by far handsomer, your lines were softer and classical something like old Grecian—and your eyes in the picture have not been rendered at all.

I don't like Weiss[1] [*sic*] in any form.[2] I think he is a very weak artist. The curious thing is that American artists never seem to get the real spirit of people of color in their work. None of them ever could get me. Maurice Sterne, I think, has done the best with non-white types. He has real insight and understanding. On the other hand I have seen splendid things of Negroes (some quite ordinary things mere posters) here in France and in Germany. I think European artists do better with Negroes because they feel freer and less self-conscious about them.

I like Weiss [*sic*] less when he takes pains to prettify his Negroes as he evidently did in the "New Negro" volume. The Mexican who did the jacket for Langston's "Weary Blues" is a much more definite and powerful artist.[3]

Thank you for sending Gwennie Bennett's photo. She is "cute" as we say over there. Tell her that Mrs Robeson spoke to me about her in Nice and gave me a card for her, (I was flirting around with a French cocotte then and Mrs Robeson was rather disgusted.) and I was sorry that I couldn't rake up any cash to get to Paris so that we could do a little of Montparnasse together. I like her Ebony Flute. It is spicy and peppy. Ask her why didn't she put some of her Paris glimpses and contacts in the Ebony Flute. That ought to be very interesting[.] Is she ever coming back.

Glancing through your letter I find I have misspell[ed] Winold Reiss, but <u>he</u> is the one I mean quand même.

Yes "Nigger Heaven" was very interesting to me. As you say I don't think it is well written[.] It certainly does not read as well as [Carl] Van Vechten's "Blind Bow Boy." It is almost apologetic and plodding in parts. I think it is because Van Vechten was not <u>sure</u> just <u>how</u> he should write about his characters. It seems to me he missed a wonderful chance of writing an amazingly humorous and vivid book. What couldn't he have done with Adora and why make Lasca so romantically barbaric and unreal? Mary does not live, but he is at his best with Byron. There he seemed to find the character that really interested him. But I don't think he knew what to do with him at the end. And then you know, I am sure that Van Vechten has been too "nice" with some of his characters. He should have done something to make DuBois highorse-crazy instead of just angry. I am sure from what he has hinted he left out many things that might have made the novel much more <u>real</u>. Yet they say he has abused the kindness of black folk. Of course I don't know if Vechten has sympathy and insight enough to handle Negro material. He shows not [a] trace of these things in Nigger Heaven. But one can see that he really <u>means well</u>. I hope your mother is better and that you will come to Europe this year. I should be happy to meet you again—

Sincy [?],
Claude McKay

CMP ALS

1. McKay is referring to Winold Reiss, whose illustrations (including a portrait of Harold Jackman) appeared in Alain Locke's "Harlem: Mecca of the New Negro" special issue of the *Survey Graphic* (March 1925) and his *New Negro* (1925).

2. Paragraph not indented in original.

3. Miguel Covarrubias did the illustration for Hughes's *The Weary Blues* (1926).

To Langston Hughes

29 June 1927

Marseille, France

My dear Langston,

I was very pleased to hear from you again. Funny, I thought from some of your poems that you had been South. I have spent a few days in the three of the big cities Atlanta, Charleston and Birmingham, but that was long ago, and I should like to go again. I hope you are enjoying your trip. I don't feel as enthusiastic as you do about the river boats of course—but that is because I have had so much of the rough-and-tumble of life—physically I have never cared much about myself, but temperamentally it has been hell enough.

My novel is completed and with Harper[']s and I am now awaiting the proofs. Then in the meanwhile, I am taking notes and sketching plans of the next one which will have Marseille for background. My representative who is also a critic is full of praise for the Harlem book, but I think I'll do better with Marseille. It will be more clearly [?] built [?] on action and scenes.

I ought to have started already but I am worried about the money to go on with. That is always the trouble. I used up all I got on the first advance and my representative is not sure if he can get any on the Marseille book before Harper[']s see[s] some of it. And I am in no mood to start in before I have the assurance of the cash—so you see how it stands—I have sent an S.O.S. to New York to an old friend who might help if her bonds are bringing in anything.

Oh there was nothing to be ashamed about. Others who really should be + whom I had some claim on, were not. It has been a hellish time but I don't regret the difficult steps and moves that brought me along. There is nothing I cannot make use of in the future. My health has started worrying me again. That is the only thing I regret. I could not afford to look after myself as I should.

I've had some interesting letters from Countée Cullen. I hope we shall all meet together if I manage to get back. I want to sometime this year or early next. [Harold] Jackman has also written to me. I met him once + did rather like him. I don't know if I shall ever be resigned to live in the States again. I feel as if I want to wander over the world forever.

Sincerely
Claude

LHP ALS

To William A. Bradley

3 July 1927

Marseille, France

Dear Mr Bradley,

I wrote to Miss [Berenice] Abbott reminding her that she had promised to let me have the photographs at a reduced rate and that I was paying for them[,] not you nor Harper[']s. I also asked her, if she would reconsider her price, to get in touch with you again. She might as I used to know her around the studios in Montparnasse.

Although you told me not to worry about money in a former letter, I cannot help worrying, especially when I find myself with just enough to carry me over another week. And, naturally, I cannot do any creative work in this state. I must either have the definite assurance of pecuniary help or face the fact that I must be looking round at once to find some sort of job before I get down to my last franc. If I had about 50 dollars a month until I am finished, I should be perfectly contented.

The novel will take me about four months or so to do. As soon as I am assured that I can go on with it without financial harassment I shall knuckle down to real writing and in about a month I shall send you an adequate representative portion of it. The second part of "Home To Harlem" was better, I believe, because after you sent me the first advance I knew that I could give my time to writing and worry about nothing at all. I have the new book very clearly planned out from beginning to end. The principal characters (a West Indian and an American Negro) belong to the same world as Jake and I am writing the story in the same simple vein of "Home To Harlem."

Thanking you for writing and hoping I'll soon hear from you again,

Sincerely Yours
Claude McKay

P.S.

May I remind you too of your promise to show me how to proceed about getting the passport for America? Mrs. [Louise Bryant] Bullitt said I should keep her in touch with developments, because, if it proved difficult, her husband had friends in the State Department who might help. I don't know how long it will take to get it and I should like to be able to get back towards the end of this year or the beginning of next to look the old ground over for my third book, i.e. the one I scrapped to write "Home To Harlem." I think I could make a simple interesting thing of it, if I spent a few months observing the new life of Negroes in New York and Washington.

I am sending you a little photograph of myself—the only one I have. It isn[']t much like me. It was done in New York before I left there. But if you don't get one from Miss Abbott you might send it to Harper[']s. If you do get one I shall be very happy if you return me this.

CMcK

WABLAR ALS

To William A. Bradley

30 July 1927

Marseille, France

[On Letterhead: Bar Auzas, Marseille]

Dear Mr Bradley

I was very happy to get your letter today and I am very grateful to you. I wasn't over depressed about my plight this time, simply because I felt confident you would do something for me.

I feel ready to begin work right away and I wish you yourself would advance me 300 francs to get my typewriter until the money arrives. By the end of August I shall send you the first chapters.

The idle weeks were not altogether fruitless. A Senegalese came back from America with a little pile after 10 years and bought a bar down in the ditch and the Negroes around dance there every night. It is very amusing to remark the difference between the Senegalese + the Martiniquan + American Negroes.

I posed for a set of photographs and as soon as I get the money to pay for them I shall send some to you. Thanking you very much[.]

Sincerely Yours
Claude McKay

WABLAR ALS

To Harold Jackman

1 August 1927

Marseille, France

My Dear Jackman

I wanted to reply to your first letter giving me all the precious impressions I begged for but I was waiting a little to hear from Sylvia Beach about "Ulysses." I enclose her card. You see the cost is much more than I estimated exactly the amount you mailed me.⁺ And I could not order the book at the moment, either. Because I got broke and had to use your money. I had kept it all along, but I could not do otherwise when the small advance I got from Harper[']s in the winter had dwindled down to nothing. I had hoped to pull through until September when Harper[']s, as promised, could advance me something in the new book. [Charles S.] Johnson of "Opportunity" promised me a cheque for my story and I was banking on that (one can live decently over here on #50 a month) but the cheque has never arrived. He wrote promising it on the 2nd June. He did the same thing about my poems last year. Wrote me a nice, kind letter saying "it was vital that I be kept alive and my voice be heard" and he was appropriating a certain sum to pay me for the poems, although the magazine did not usually pay. I wrote thanking him gratefully. Two months passed and I received nothing. Then I wrote to [Eric] Walrond and to Johnson again. And he (Johnson) sent me a ten-dollar note saying that was all he could afford! I was working then in a kitchen in the Cote d'Azur and any relief from that would have been most welcome.

To be frank with you, it is between us and I hope you will forgive me the liberty, I think the colored editors are rotten bastards. I feel about them just as Lasca felt about the Negro leaders.[1] Carl Van Vechten certainly said a mouthful then. The colored editors are simply hiding behind the Negro movement to exploit the Negro artists as much as they can, using fine phrases without giving them any material aid unless they are compelled to. Of course it is an economic problem with the little Negro editors too. If, like in the white world, we had wealthy Negroes running Negro publications competing for profit, the cream of Negro talent and genius would come to the top. But we have little men with literary ambitions themselves and all more are[2] [*sic*] less afraid of "art" and forthright artistic expression, dependent as they all are on some white philanthropy.

I've had the same trouble with [W. E. B.] Du Bois. In the fall of 1925 when I was ill and penniless at Cagnes-sur-Mer, I sent poems to four American magazines telling them I was ill and asking them to help me. Two of them (white) replied promptly and paid me a dollar a line. But Du Bois never replied. I thought he did not get the poems until in the summer of 1926 I saw one in the "Crisis" and another in February 1927.[3] I immediately wrote to Du Bois—Feb 9. He answered March 16, sending me 10 dollars and saying Miss [Jessie] Fauset probably overlooked the poems. I wish you were here to see my correspondence with the guardian-angel editors of my race. You would laugh because it is as funny as tragic. Then the doctor [Alain] Locke. He put poems in "The New Negro" that I had discarded, changed the title of another, for political reason he informed me when I protested and put me in his pamphlet series without even the courtesy of notifying me. I first learned of the pamphlet series from Gwen Bennett's column. There ought to be some payment too and I am writing to Harcourt Brace Co to take the matter up with Simon Schuster. Finally Walter White whom I really loved and admired as the head of the N.A.A.C.P. gang. He called me Claude and I called him Walter. I knew he had contacted with several white editors, so I sent him one of my stories (Scott Fitzgerald had praised and thought it very saleable) and asked him to try and do something for me. Walter never replied. I could not understand. Never even acknowledged the story—I had asked him for personal comment. I was very hurt, because he had always been friendly, and just when I returned from Russia and was ill, collected about 100 dollars for me. If he had even written to say he was busy—a word—a friendly word would have helped me so much, for I was broke and sick and lonely and very sad. Not a word until during the winter 1926[.] I met Paul Robeson at Nice and he showed me a nice cordial note from Walter. So I wrote Walter telling him I had seen Robeson[,] we spoke of him and I was still alive. No reply.

But last Saturday I got a letter telling me he (Walter) had been down at Harper[']s and seen the dummy of my book. It was beautiful etc etc. He had sent a notice about it to 250 Negro newspapers and he and his wife were coming to France and would be happy to meet me again. Of course I didn't want to meet him. You can imagine my feelings. I have had enough to keep me wise to the end of my days. I am now settled down on the individualistic wagon and I am not going to be used as brushwood for any of the selfish propaganda fire of <u>any</u> of the gangs.

I hope you are not over weary of this tale of woe.

I am sorry for the delay of "Ulysses" but I shall send it as soon as I get a little extra money. I didn't want to strain our friendship over such a little thing and it is the little things that break friendships.

I checked up on your notes and found that I was all right and did not have to change the trend of my novel. Thanks again. I hope you scan my fist all right. It's not so good since I started to typewrite. But I had to do it this way because I was compelled to put my typewriter in the municipal pawn shop for 300 francs[.]

Ever sincerely yours
Claude

+ I was so long away from Paris and out of touch with things that I got way behind prices!

CMP ALS

1. Lasca is a character in Carl Van Vechten's *Nigger Heaven* (1926).

2. McKay likely means "more or less afraid of 'art,'" but he has mistakenly written "are."

3. The *Crisis* published "A Daughter of the American Revolution to Her Son" in March 1926 and "In the Hospital" in February 1927.

To William A. Bradley

3 August 1927

Marseille, France

Dear Mr Bradley

I thank you very much for the cheque for 300 francs. I have just put it through Lloyd's Bank (Nat'l Prov. [?]) here much more easily than I did the other at Nice. They were very courteously obliging and if you will make all other cheques payable through them I shall not have any difficulty—nor delay in putting them through.

I didn't refer to [Eugene] Saxton's editing me because I thought it was understood between us (you and me—as you mentioned we both thought some blue-penciling would be necessary) that he should. I only hope he will not be over cautious and cut out stand-up phrases that would leave the passages flat and inconsequential.

Thank you for "Gigolo." [John] Farrar wrote that he liked it very much and was sorry he could not use it in a publication like "The Bookman[.]" He has always been very friendly. I also received at the same time three others, including "Home To Harlem," from Mr [Charles S.] Johnson's secretary. According to the marks on the letter it has been set up in 10 pt type, so I suppose we just acted in time to prevent its publication. The other stories are all retyped. Johnson wrote that he was friendly with Harper[']s and could straighten out the matter with the firm, but I have replied, courteously, that my representative would take care of that.

I shall get back my typewriter today and I am looking for a room on the quieter side of the port—a private one which will be cheaper and more to my taste than a hotel. I am very happy and thanks again for arranging everything.

Yours very Sincerely
Claude McKay

WABLAR ALS

To William A. Bradley

30 August 1927

Marseille, France

Dear Mr Bradley

I am worried about seeing the proofs of "Home To Harlem" before it is published. The time seems very short and, if you haven't received them yet, I should be glad if you call Mr. [Eugene] Saxton's attention to the matter. The galley proofs would do. I should hate to have the book published, without seeing proofs, <u>especially</u> as cuts are being made. With best wishes.

Yours Sincerely
Claude McKay

WABLAR TLS

To William A. Bradley

1 October 1927

Marseille, France

Dear Mr Bradley

I am sending you herewith, the first chapters of the new novel, "Banjo" as I promised. All the characters are presented, except Ray, who, as in "Home To Harlem," will enter in the middle of the book, but continue to the end.

Please let me know frankly what you think of it. Any criticism or hints will be welcome . . . I have enough material to make it a full-length novel, longer a good way than the first. I did all this in a month, beginning just after I got back my machine. Some of it is rough and will have to be done over. I had everything quite ready and planned and had no difficulty in going on smoothly as soon as my little financial troubles were settled.

One thing that worries me is that I am not well. I have been suffering from vertige, I suppose that is what is known as High Blood Pressure, for over a year. When I was at Antibes I had some treatment from Max [Eastman]'s doctor at Nice. But it is worse since I came to Marseille and the other night I became unconscious for a while in a café. I suppose I ought to see a specialist, but I want to hold out until I can afford a good one. I am rather worried about it. . . . . I hope you received the new photographs on thin paper that I sent you.

Yours Sincerely
Claude McKay

WABLAR TLS

To William A. Bradley

24 October [1927]

Marseille, France

Dear Mr Bradley

I shall be much obliged if you could send me 100 francs against the 30th inst. I am still going on with "Banjo," having reached the point where Ray comes in, but I don't feel so sure about all the material that I want to include and the general plan of the book (e.g. whether the indiscriminate throwing together of white and black characters might be too much for the American public to relish. I have had misgivings about that.) And so that is why I am so anxious to have your critical reaction to the opening chapters. I don't want to spoil the chance of being heard by insisting on situations that might be left out or inferred without any material harm to the book.

I have been wondering also if there might not be a possible chance of my selling one or two of the short stories that I have by me. You know the collection. Perhaps you are posted about the more select magazines and could put me on to some favorably-inclined editor. I am thinking of different ways to help myself over the winter. . . . . . The revue "Europe" did accept "Bad Boy" but I suppose they will not pay before publication. Louise Bryant had also promised to get the ear of some of the more advanced New York editors, but it's a long time since and I have never heard of anything. I have a couple more short stories in mind that I could get done in a couple of weeks if I knew any of the magazine editors that might be favorably disposed to them.

The rainy weather has commenced here and I am a little out of joint in consequence. Hoping you are well. With best wishes[.]

Yours Sincerely
Claude McKay

WABLAR TLS

To Harold Jackman

[late 1927][1]

Marseille, France

contemporary people and things in general.[2]

Don't be despairing about "Ulysses." You will get it some day. I regard it as my first obligation to settle when I make a raise. I don't know when my book will be out, some time next year I think. I have not had the proofs yet! Of course, I should like to see it out, simply because it would perhaps help in some way, direct or indirect, to solve my desperate pecuniary problems and give me a chance to concentrate on creative work. Indigence or the fear of it sterilizes all creative activity.

Thanks for sending me [Lothrop] Stoddard's ravings. They are at least amusing, yet without spice because Stoddard's Freshman rhetoric is so superannuated. The Nordic cause is in a bad way indeed if it can not produce a more competent and discriminating apologist. If I find my white critics amusing, I cannot say the same of my colored ones. They are often inept to the point of downright pettiness. I do hope that the Voice of the Negro in artistic and literary expression will carry farther and be saved from the brayings of Negro apologists. I have had the distinguished attachee [*sic*] of the Boston Transcript up at me in the "Crisis" and the Honorourable Oxonion [*sic*], Doctor [Alain] Locke, and now comes your friend, Mr [Countee] Cullen, who in the Anthology of Negro Poets cannot find anything more appropriate than the journalistic word "vituperative," synonym of the police court term "abusive," to express his opinion of my hortatory poems.[3] Even the worst of my white critics, the Stoddards and [Thomas] Dixons, have never used such a contemptible word as "vituperative" to show their disapproval of such of my poetry in which a race cries out against murder and suppression. I have always felt a certain hostility on the part of Afro-American intellectuals toward me. I don't know why. Maybe it is because when I write, I express the things that they feel so deeply and yet are forced from social and economic reasons to damn up in themselves. Yet I think they might extend to me a certain racial indulgence as I am so far outside of their field. Somehow I am glad I am not in on any of the groups, so that I can see them all from a detached standpoint. I want to see Negro artists express themselves to the limit. They should exclude nothing, limit themselves to nothing. They should make their voices as strong, sweet, broad, strange, sad, happy and varied as all Negro life itself is. I don't think they should tie themselves up in movements and tendacious [*sic*] groups with their petty artistic quarrels. Negro life has always been an "open-shop" life and Negro art to be worth-while will have to reflect that, from sweet cabin-door psalmody through irregular rhythms of modern cities to rebel shouts.

I am not expecting any servile praise from any of my critics. I welcome straight, clean criticism at any old time. But I am disappointed in Mr Cullen's adjective. It speaks volumes and it is interesting and illuminating that it should come from the author of "Heritage."

Of course, I write to you as a friend, giving my personal reaction. If you have any of the writings of Wallace Thurman and can spare them, I wish you would send them to me. I liked his story in "Fire" and his criticism of "Nigger Heaven." I should also like to have any magazines outside of the "Crisis," "New Masses" and "Opportunity" which I get regularly. If you see Langston [Hughes], ask him if he got the letter I sent to him through

CMP TLS

1. Possibly a response to Jackman's letter of 14 September 1927.

2. Letter survives in incomplete form; opening and closing pages are missing.

3. Countee Cullen, ed., *Caroling Dusk: An Anthology of Verse by Negro Poets* (New York: Harper & Brothers, 1927), xiii. Cullen writes, "Claude McKay is most exercised, rebellious, and vituperative to a degree that clouds his lyricism in many instances, but silhouettes most forcibly his high dudgeon."

To William A. Bradley

3 November 1927

Marseille, France

Dear Mr Bradley

I was very very glad to get your letter at last and extremely relieved after reading it through. When after the first few days you did not write I felt certain you had a little adverse criticism to make and I am glad you did it frankly.

I have finished one hundred and twenty-five pages and would have gone much farther if I had not been very put about since last week. I can recast the story and preserve the best of what I have written and I think it is better I had not gone any further since your letter came.

You see, I had my doubts also.[1] I thought that by planning the story as I did, giving a short history of all the characters, and then projecting them on the Marseille scene, I was symplifying [*sic*] matters for my readers, but I was uncertain of the effect.

I had two plans for the novel. One to have Banjo lose everything and fall in with Latnah (who was a real person on the beach last year) and then put him through a series of adventures in Marseille. But with that plan, which would undoubtedly make a more rapid and close-knit story, I would have to rush him to his death and I did not want to kill him. With the present plan, beginning grimly, I meant to end it up happily by sending him back to America. My own objection to the first plan, his losing his milkmaid and then finding Latnah, was that it was a little like Jake's adventure and I did not want to repeat myself. However, I shall be glad to talk the whole matter over with you. . . .

The atmosphere and feel of Marseille itself, you will see later, I was giving by degrees. I wanted that to come naturally into the story without my going out of it to give any detailed description. I thought I was getting all of that in and if I haven't I shall have to concentrate more on that.

I thought "Home To Harlem" was held up because the time was too short to get all the work done. So did you I suppose when you suggested Louise Bryant doing the proofs. Of course it is all right if Mr [Eugene] Saxton think[s] the book will go better later on. They must know better about such things + I should not have written to Louise if I had known that that had been definitely decided upon. I have not heard from her yet.

Oh I nearly forgot to thank you for that 100 francs!

Yours Sincerely
Claude McKay

WABLAR ALS

1. Paragraph not indented in original ("You see" appears to have been added).

To William A. Bradley

25 November 1927

Marseille, France

Dear Mr Bradley

I am sending you herewith my new version of "Banjo." I feel quite satisfied with it. It[']s a complete story as it stands in which I have compressed his wish to come to Marseille, his motive, his intention and his luck. So technically it is like the opening chapter of "Home To Harlem." Now I feel free to go on building up on this a series of incidents and situations just as I did in "Home To Harlem," which was really a long story version of the short stories. I shall reverse the theme a little, making Malty the one who hankers after Latnah, but I shall use all the important points in what I have already written.

I was glad you came down and I thank you for the treat. If you come back in January we will spend a day down the docks, doing both sides of them. Then if you could spend a little longer time, we could see some of the quarter in the daytime and afterwards see the same places again at night. I find it interesting to compare it that way.[1] I have an interesting Martinique friend who runs between here and Madagascar and Reunion. He ought to be ashore in January and would go round with us.

There were a few things I forgot to talk to you about. The short stories above all. I had hoped to give them to you to save postage and also to talk about the ones that would more likely find a market. Then I wonder if you could send me some money by the first. I am broke and had to borrow a hundred francs from [T. F.] Tracy. I wanted to tap you here, but I felt you had spent rather heavily on the trip.

If you don't mind, I think you might get Mrs. [Louise Bryant] Bullitt to do something for me. She did promise to help me when she came over if I still needed help, but she hasn't written. She could help me to get out of this room. I want to, but I can't because the rent falls due on the third week of the month and I never pay until the first week of the next, so I am always owing. It is cold without heat or sun or air. I have to keep the window closed all the time to keep out the carbon gas from the two kitchens that wall in the rear of the hotel and the smell of the garbage that is pitched below. The proprietor says he can give me a sunny room looking out on the sea for 300 francs. If I could get the sun I wouldn't mind the lack of heat. It's only a hundred francs more than what I am paying and I would like to take it and feel that I was really living in the Midi. I think that if you explained it to Louise, she just might do something about it, as she's rather interested in me. I am inscribing "Home To Harlem" to her. But if I ask again myself she might think I am just "working" her because she's married rich. She wrote me once that all the people she used to know expect her to help them.

I wonder if we could not sell this opening chapter of BANJO? It might be better to call it "Banjo in Marseille." I think about this because if I am not comfortable during the winter, I want to spend all the mornings in search of the sun and I do all my work in the morning.

With best wishes, Yours Sincerely
Claude McKay.

Please remember the books + the Nations if you can find them + any other American magazines you can spare.[2]

WABLAR TLS

1. This sentence was inserted in pencil.
2. The postscript is handwritten.

To Josephine Herbst

29 November 1927

Marseille, France

Dear Jo Herbst

I have been wishing to get in touch with you for some time, but hadn't your address. But I think I will reach you now through your review in the New Masses.[1] I wrote to Andrew [Bernhard] nearly a year ago at the Tribune in Paris, but he never replied, although the letter, which had my address on it[,] was not returned. I had neglected to answer a letter of his, but he had happened to write at a time when I was way down in hard luck, just grubbing along in the gutter with no spirit in me for friendly correspondence.

Are you back in New York? Tell me, what became of your book? And what are you doing for yourself? I saw a story of Herman[n]'s in the New Masses.[2] Was his book published? I get no magazines at all except the New Masses and a couple of Negro monthlies, so I don't know what is going on in the American literary world. You know, after you went away, I put aside my first autobiographical novel and wrote another from a more objective and lighter point of view. It was a sort of satire, no, really a comedy of smart Negro life in Harlem, and a satire on the fashionable white people who took them up. I sent it to Knopf, but after some hesitations, they turned it down. Nobody would take it and so I began doing short stories. These at last got to Harper[']s and they gave me a small advance to do a novel of Harlem's Negro life. I did it and they liked it very much and now I am doing another about the Negroes here in Marseille. They gave me $250 dollars to do it and the money is finished and I have just one decent chapter to show for it! So, as usual, I don't quite know where nor how I am going I make the best of the present, that's all. It was an unpleasant summer for me, and I suffered from severe head troubles.

Please write to me and if you have any Mercurys with [H. L.] Men[c]ken's blab, please send me some. I have an old machine now which has served me well, beside my work, at the Mont de Pietè[.]

Good luck, happy Xmas
Sincerely
Claude

JHP TLS

1. Josephine Herbst, review of *Profane Earth* by Holger Cahill, *New Masses,* November 1927, 29–30.

2. John Hermann, "The Story of the Lead Pencil," *New Masses,* July 1926, 28–29.

To Harold Jackman

29 November 1927

Marseille, France

My dear Harold

Thank you so much for sending me your photograph. It is a well-made photograph, but I think it makes you look rather fierce. On the other hand the reproduction of [Winhold] Reiss' portrait which I have before me also, makes you excessively melancholy, but I prefer it as it brings out character or personality, which the photograph does not. None of them has the faintest touch of charm, which as I remember from our slight acquaintance, was the outstanding trait of your features, but that is something very difficult for [a] photographer or painter to get. You ought to get Maurice Sterne to paint you, but he has grown rich and famous since the time I knew him and I don't think he runs now with the old crowd of Greenwich Village rebels. He used to do charming things of Eastern people, chiefly Indians and Malays I think, and as you run something to these types, I think he would make a real picture of you. I don't think American artists are good at doing colored people, and I believe that this is due to the popular American idea of non-white peoples. Artists are often influenced by the vulgar popular mind without realizing it. These reproductions of the German artist on the covers of "Opportunity" could not be better.[1] And I have seen little amusing caricatures of colored types in French journals that make attempts in "Life" and "Judge" and like publications, look banal and cheap.

I wish you had also dropped me a line about yourself and Knopf's.

I hear Paul Robeson is in Paris. I did not hear anything of [Jean] Toomer. We met once, but we have never been friends nor corresponded. When I was on the "Liberator" I think I wrote to him once or twice. Funny Robeson didn't play in "Porgy." No, I have never read the book. Would like to. Was shocked to hear of Florence Mills' death. What has become of [Charles] Gilpin? I am sending you a couple photographs that I too[k] for Harper[']s. Not very good, for they are cheap. You remember you sent me one of Gwen Bennett's, so you can give her one and thank her for hers.

I didn't have much for a summer. I bathed a little, a couple of weeks with an Ecole Normalien[2] who came down from Paris, but otherwise it was nothing but hard work. I am doing a book on Marseille. It[']s a tough, picturesque old city and I should love to show it to you some day. There are many Negro seamen from all over the world here and I spend my leisure time among them in their haunts.

Ever Yours Sincerely
Claude

CMP TLS

1. Walter von Ruckteschell provided illustrations for the covers of multiple issues of *Opportunity* in 1927, after the artist was profiled in Louise Herrick Wall, "Walter von Ruckteschell," *Opportunity*, May 1924, 147–48.

2. A student at the École normale supérieure in Paris. Possibly Georges Friedmann (see p. 421).

To William A. Bradley

3 December 1927

Marseille, France

Dear Mr Bradley

Thanks for the fs. 100, which I immediately invested in meal tickets, and Louise [Bryant]'s address. I have already sent off an s.o.s. to her. I am sorry I wasted four francs on that telegram.

I am worried about my room, the landlord watches me with such a mean eye, but I have shown him your letter and said that I expected money soon, which, of course, is very uncertain. If I had known that I was going to get so badly in, I would have given up the room, because I can always find a temporary bunk with one of the fellows in the Ditch.

However I hope Louise will do something.

Banjo is unfolding all right now along the lines of a straight story, with the tedious conversation cut out. I am getting in the best of it, but always short, pithy and to the point, and it is finished before you begin to think about it.

The proofs are late and I don't see how it will be possible for Mr. [Eugene] Saxton to get the book into January. I am sorry to see it thrown back late in the season, because I rather think we are missing the best selling months. I shall drop [T. F.] Tracy a note telling him what you say. I don't see them so often. He told me a story that was excellent, he told it so well. It seems to me he talks a little better than he writes. We shall certainly be glad to see you again in January. It was a pleasure to know you a little more. I met the patrone of the Martinique in the Place and told her you would give her joint a literary boost one day. She was gratified to know that she had had a literary man from Paris at her place and she said that if I had told her she would have had things much nicer. Maybe it is better I didn't, she might not have had the soldiers playing. I took two people there last summer and she stopped the dancing and I had to tell her we came there more for that than to eat before she would let them go on. She won[']t believe that I write. They really think I am a sort of an adventurer.

Thanking you again.
Sincerely Yours
Claude McKay

WABLAR TLS

To William A. Bradley

12 December 1927

Marseille, France

Dear Mr. Bradley

I received the proofs on Saturday direct from the manufacturing department with an envelope and note to return them to one Mr Rusholme. I am sorry it is not possible for us to go through them together. They haven't chopped it up too badly. Only it is surprising to me that they leave in all the local Negro phrases that I thought would come out and take out bits that seem quite all right to me!

I am sure you must want to see it, so as soon as I am finished I will send it to you with the forwarding envelope. I am rather baffled about a few minor points. The word "pimp" for example. In one place they take all the significance and punch out of a paragraph by cutting it out. But they leave it in where it is repeated twice in the conversation that follows and which depends altogether on the conversational use of the word where it is cut out in the first place. I think I will restore it and you might make a note for Mr. [Eugene] Saxton, leaving it to him to take it out again if he sees fit.

It is late already and so we cannot be losing very much time by sending it through you.

About Banjo I think I will put the first part aside for a little while. Yes it is better without the first paragraph. I don't think it will be difficult to incorporate the breakwater scene in it, but Latnah will have to be left out of it. Her coming in after the risque on the Bum Square is so much more interesting.

I have the whole thing fairly planned out and will send you a synopsis. I can't make a sentimental affair of Banjo and the first girl for Banjo is really heterosexual and the thing that he is most sentimental about is the Ditch. All my chief characters are pretty free and pagan, emotional, sensual, but not sentimental. And if I tried to make them sentimental I don't think I could do them justice. Unless I did a satire. Even Latnah. She is not jealous of Banjo in the possessive sense. She is Oriental and sympathises with a man being polygamous. What stirs her and finally makes her hate Banjo is when she discovers that he prefers chair blanche to chair noire. I think that is a much more important point to bring out in the book, don't you? I mean the kind of instinctive, animal feeling that's so different from the sentimental home and social and pseudo racial conflict that motivates color-problem stories. I will send you the ensuing chapters a little after I finish with the proofs.

Yours Sincerely
Claude McKay

WABLAR TLS

To William A. Bradley

[received 19 December 1927]

Marseille, France

W. A. B.

I have taken out that paragraph about [George Bernard] Shaw. I don't like it as it stands in print. I want to say something like that but not just like that so I think it's better to cut it out altogether and wait until I have the right thing to say + the right place some day.

I think "tout" which the English use in some sense for "pimp" might be substituted. In one place where it was cut out I had to put "filthy parasites" just to give some sense and meaning to what follows—but I hate the word parasite—it[']s so overworked.

Will send short stories soon.[1] Now that I have interrupted my work on Banjo to do the proofs—I might just as well read + correct the short stories again[.]

C.McK.

WABLAR ALS

1. Very mild indentation here. It could be part of the previous paragraph.

To William A. Bradley

19 December 1927

Marseille, France

Dear Mr Bradley

I am sending you the batch of stories under another cover. Reading them again I find two outstanding faults. Too much obvious sentimentality on one hand and obvious "propaganda" on the other. When I wrote the stories I was really pot-boiling for two markets, the New York magazine market with the cabaret-speakeasy stories and the Negro magazine field with the others. I know that I couldn't break into the first without the sop of sentimentality to offset the bawdiness. I could make them "right" now but that would throw me off "Banjo" + I suppose they are better as they are for the magazines you are going to try! So I send them as they are with slight changes. One of them[,] "Within the Belt[,]" you have never yet seen. It was the first I wrote and I still like it. I haven't a duplicate so please look out for it for me.

It is very cold here, frozen water pipes and ice in the streets and foggy. My room is so cold I can do no work in it. I am hunting for another and hope to change before Christmas. I think the Provençals are more afraid of cold than any people I have seen. The terraces of the cafes are all deserted. I went to see that bon [?][1] of the Marseille underworld that Pasien [?] sent me a letter to see. He's a rather dull wine-shop keeper + had nothing to show me but the houses—all of which I already knew. Indeed I knew more of Marseille than he. I asked him about the Camorra[2] but he says it does not exist, or if it does it is in a small scale port as in any other big port. However, a few days ago, I saw in The Petit Provençal an item which said that a custom patrol boat had been fired on by a small mysterious boat which got away in the fog + darkness. It could not have been significant as it appeared in the "faits divers" column.

Only two American boys + one South African are left in the beach now. And they are trying hard to beat it away. It is so cold. The African chap stowed away last week + was sent back from Barcelona.

Wishing you a merry Christmas
Yours Sincerely
Claude McKay

WABLAR ALS

1. This could be "boy."

2. Organized criminal organization based in Italy. McKay may mean organized crime in general.

To Louise Bryant

31 December 1927

Marseille, France

Dear Louise

Thank you very much for my Christmas present. It was just in time and made it possible for me to pay down the rent in advance as they demanded before moving into this French-warmed room.

I have asked [William A.] Bradley to tell [Eugene] Saxton to replace the inscription by the one you sent me. And I have written Saxton about it myself as I want to make sure that it is done. Your letter didn't arrive until some days after I had sent on the proofs to Mr. Bradley. I worked very rapidly on them. Yours is so much superior to mine, which I was not contented with at all, but I wanted to say something more than "To Louise Bryant" and just couldn't think of anything as fine and simple as yours.

Well, I am so surprised by what you hint about the Harper's prize that I am trying hard not to think of it.[1] Besides, I thought that only novels that were entered specially could be considered. It certainly would be a treat and I would treat myself to a really interesting voyage.

In another letter you said you knew Saxton well and would write to him for me. I do wish you would. You might tell him you have been talking to me, which you really have been doing by correspondence, and that you think if I were left alone to choose my stuff instinctively and write without remembering there were censors, my work may turn out better for all concerned, publisher, public and myself. . . . I enclose his letter.

I shall let you see some more of "Banjo" next month.

I think it is allright to feel grateful in the finer sense. It is really nothing less than to feel happy when someone makes you happy. But the word itself is degraded by charity-minded people and so I am glad we are not using it.

Happy New Year
Sincerely
Claude

LBP TLS

1. The Harper Prize was a biennial prize awarded to novels from 1923 to 1965. The prize novel was chosen for "conspicuous merit and the underlying purpose of the award is to give prominence and success to a writer who has not hitherto found a wide audience." McKay did not win this award.

To Louise Bryant

31 December 1927

Marseille, France

Dear Louise: Just a moment after mailing my letter to you I received this from Mr [William A.] Bradley. I thought you had urged on him as you intimated to me, to give me a little unhurried time to do the book + I will send it to him in parts as I did "Home to Harlem[.]" He let me entirely alone when I was doing it. I cannot work if I haven't some little feeling of pecuniary security, but am kept in a state between expectancy and disappointment from month to month. Here I was expecting January's payment in a few days only to hear that it is not sure and, perhaps, depends on my forwarding immediately for Harper's man to see, the two chapters of "Banjo" that I have done—since you saw the first and which I have not yet worked over. You know I was busy on the proofs, going over my short-stories to try + sell something + hunting for a room.

I have written a long letter trying to explain to Bradley. But I do wish you could get at him in some diplomatic way + try to help me. I know that you can and I am glad you are in Paris. I don't think I shall have anything ready to show until the end of January. And now I can't work—as soon as I find myself in a pecuniary fix, I lose my balance + cannot work until I am certain of the outcome. And so I lose some of my best working moments + my head which is chronic [*sic*] bad, starts drumming away again—

Sincerely Claude

LBP ALS

To William A. Bradley

31 December 1927

Marseille, France

[On Letterhead: Brasserie Carnot, Café Parisien, Marseille]

Dear Mr Bradley

One of the packets contains the typed m.s. of "Home To Harlem," which you said should be returned to Harper's with the proofs, and a letter. I thought I'd marked that envelope specially!

I haven't enough of "Banjo" done to send to you to show Mr [Thomas Bucklin] Wells. I shall, I hope, by the end of January. You know I had to stop to do the proofs and go through those stories, besides hunting for a comfortable room to work in.

I thought you had taken up the matter of the payments with Mr [Eugene] Saxton, and working, I was feeling confident that January's was near at hand as you know how I can barely carry on from month to month. And now my monthly rent is 100 francs more.

I must confess to you that so soon as I am up against immediate pecuniary problems, I am thrown off my balance and nervous and cannot work until I know exactly what I am going to do. I cannot help that. It is a state of mind. Last summer I did not get anything done at all between July and the time the first payment arrived at the beginning of September. For two months I worked furiously day and night so that I could have something to show you. You know the result: bad work with little patches of good things. I also worked in a hurry to give you that revised first chapter of "Banjo." It was different while I was doing my short stories. When I sold a poem or an article I would settle down to write—or when I received a gift from some friend or a little royalty from my publishers. When I had no money I stopped writing to find some kind of job or bummed awhile. I was different too with "Home To Harlem." I quit working and started in with a little money + borrowed from Max [Eastman] until your first cheque came. Then I finished the first hundred pages or so and sent them to you. From then on I worked steadily but quickly until I finished, cutting out many things, splicing bits and rewriting many pages. I am afraid that if I am kept at a jumpy nervous tension from month to month, I shall never be able to make a good story of "Banjo." I was very glad you came down here and talked to me. I have profitted [*sic*] by the criticisms I got from you and from Louise [Bryant], but I need a little time to work things out without being confused + worried by other problems. I am not a facile writer. I know my limitations + the things I have to surmount to put myself over. But I am quick at getting under the meaning of criticism and picking up suggestions. For instance, in that brief moment when we were alone together last February at Antibes I was able to seize the essentials of your comment on "Home To Harlem" and see the difference between your criticism and Max's. I saw too where you missed a little of what I was trying to do, but I brought it out as I went along and you liked the new note that I introduced. I think I will do the same with "Banjo." The material is richer but I do need time to work it out in definite periods of tranquility. I think that as we are so close to each other in this work, you will like my explaining myself at length—if you should have to explain more to Mr Saxton. I really thought the matter was about settled by now.

Best New Year's wishes
Sincerely yours
Claude McKay

WABLAR ALS

To William A. Bradley

[received 3 January 1928]

Marseille, France

Dear Mr. Bradley

I am sending the m.s. of "Home To Harlem" ~~separately~~.[1] Had quite forgotten that it should be sent back. Could not remember whether I did with my poetry mss. Thanks very much for reminding me. I thought it better to send it to you as it may arrive in time for you to forward with proofs and you might want to see yourself just what was cut out.

Will you please ask Mr. [Eugene] Saxton, if you have already sent the proofs, to change the dedication as following:

To My Friend

Louise Bryant.

She prefers it like that and as it's hers, I would like it to be what she likes. Besides, it[']s so much simpler and better than the first.

One other correction; Chap. 11, Galley 38, line 69. "It's a great life if youse is on it." should be "It's a great life if youse in on it."

Stories sent under another cover.

Have moved. Found a warm room which will catch the morning sun when at last we begin to get it again at Hotel Brager 83 rue de la Palud. It's a hundred francs more, but I must find some ways of paying it, for it was senseless staying on at the Natioue[2] [*sic*] when it was too cold for me to work.

Will now knuckle down to Banjo again and hope to send you some of it shortly. Thank you for writing,

Sincerely
Claude McKay

WABLAR TLS

1. The word "separately" has been crossed out in pencil.
2. Likely the Hotel Nautique in Marseille.

To William A. Bradley

5 January 1928

Marseille, France

Dear Mr Bradley

I have your letter today—but I had to put my typewriter in this morning for 100 francs after trying to hold out on café au lait and croissants since last Saturday. I was so nervous + upset + the clerks got me worse by not wanting to take the old thing, because I have not a Marseille address on my "carte."—I heard from Louise [Bryant] a few days before Xmas. She sent me 200 francs which I used to pay for my new room. I am writing to her again but I am afraid she will get tired now. I was doing too one of the best of my chapters—doing it around that Shake That Thing version of the Jelly Roll which you liked. I cut out all that heavy conversation and made a fine voluptuous blues poem of it. It is the best thing that I have ever done—better than anything in "Home To Harlem[,]" and "Banjo" will have to stand or fall by it. But you will judge when you see it.

I felt so rotten this morning after putting in the typewriter as if I did not want to see it again but just go away and try to find some other work + never think of writing again until I had some real means of continuing. It was the same feeling I had when I had that breakdown in 1924.

But your letter cheered me up a lot and made me feel that everybody was very interested and wanted to help me. And I am right up out of the dumps now + thinking of the next chapter.

I hope Mr [Thomas Bucklin] Wells will come across so that I can carry on. Since I have got into the habit of the machine I hate the feel of the pen. I have 60 pages done, but that first chapter is still to be done over again you know.

Sincerely
Claude McKay

WABLAR ALS

To Le Directeur en Chef of La Compagnie Fabre, Marseille[1]

13 January 1928

Marseille, France

Dear Sir,

By a happy chance I discovered today that you were Consul for Liberia, whose President, Mr. King, I happened to meet some years ago at a banquet that was given in his honor by the Negro intellectuals of New York.[2]

May I therefore, bring to your attention the case of a poor West African boy from Nigeria who stowed away last winter on one of your boats going to New York and had the dreadful misfortune of having his feet frozen in the place where he was locked up, so that they had to be amputated in the immigration hospital at New York.

The affair was published in the newspapers of New York and a [lawyer] took it up in [*sic*] the boy's behalf. The lawyer negotiated a settlement with the Fabre Line in New York, and the boy received a certain sum in compensation that was paid to him through the British Consul in New York. He was also returned by the New York Immigration authorities to Marseille, to be sent home to Africa.

But on the day of sailing he was arrested on the ship for a clandestine[3] embarkation and is now held at the Prison Chave. I went to the offices of your company to see what could be done for him, and I was cordially invited by Mr. Croisy, who told me that the company's charge against the boy, Nelson Simeon Dede, would not be pressed if he paid the cost of his passage, aller et retour, Marseille-New York.

I went to see Dede yesterday and he told me that he was willing to pay, so that he could get out of prison (where he is very miserable, after having gone through a whole year of sickness and suffering) and get home to Nigeria, Africa, as soon as possible.

I happen to know about this case by mere hazard and am not interested in it from any personal motives. I am a Negro myself, a poet and writer, have published books in London and New York and I write for the best of the Negro Monthlies in New York. A story of mine has also recently been accepted by the French revue "Europe," the Editors of which I know.

I met Dede accidentally, when I stopped off at Marseille on my way from Paris to the Cote d'Azur towards the end of 1926. He was one of a group of Negroes from all over the world and I became very interested in their vagabond and romantic means of existence in the great port of Marseille. I conceived the idea then of doing a book about these Negroes. I wrote about it to Harper Brothers, my New York publishers, and they were enthusiastic. I went down to Antibes to finish a novel about the Negroes of New York, which has just been published there and I returned here this summer to do the Marseille book.

I was very shocked when I ran into Nelson again with both feet amputated. You may imagine how interesting his case is to me[.] He was one of the liveliest of the stranded black seamen and the best dancer in Charleston and Black Bottom, for which he was much admired indeed by the girls of the Vieux Port quarter. Now he will never dance again!

Naturally, I should like to write something about Dede. His case is so strange and striking. The great literate body of American Negroes and the increasing influention [*sic*] party of liberal white opinion, are very much interested in the welfare of Negroes in the civilized world. But as a writer I am not an opportunist propagandist, interested in publishing a sensational journalistic story. I should like to write a <u>happy</u> story, showing that the Compagnie Fabre stood honorably by Dede after his accident. But I could only do that if the boy is speedily and unconditionally released and sent on home.

I feel certain, Sir, that a word from you will effect his immediate release. Trusting, therefore, in your generosity,

I have the honor to be
Sir,
Yours Sincerely

CMP TLU (copy)

1. Possibly Paul Cyprien-Fabre (1870–1955), president of the Compagnie Cyprien-Fabre. This letter details the case that inspired McKay's posthumously published novel *Romance in Marseille* (2020).

2. Charles D. B. King, president of Liberia from 1920 to 1930.

3. Two words in original (hyphen may be present but not visible in the carbon).

To Louise Bryant

18 January 1928

Marseille, France

Dear Louise

I was sorry to hear about your cold and hope it is better. Still to be frank I had been hoping to hear from you again as you promised. I took a hundred francs, with five extra for interest, of the 150 you sent me to get my machine out. But how can I work if I am anxious + hungry and disgusted. [William A.] Bradley has not written again and that 200 francs—well I couldn't do closer with it if even I were put on rations. Perhaps rations would be better for I feel just like a tethered animal that is allowed one step and one bite at a time. My room is as cold as an ice-box, the woman stopped giving us a fire the same week I moved in. And I dare not say anything for I am powerless to threaten to move to another place. She might tell me to go.

I had a chance to go to Singapore as a steward's boy. I sent an Egyptian fellow in my place because the desire to write got the best of me. Now I am sorry finding myself in the same old damnable fix and having to write you another frantic letter. Anything was better than this room again. And such an opportunity doesn't come every day—

Bradley came here in October + he said he would write [Eugene] Saxton + things would doubtless be allright. And this is January. I don't know how he manages—I think his hands are so full of little business that he forgets a fellow.

Yours truly
Claude

LBP ALS

To William A. Bradley

18 January 1928

Marseille, France

Dear Mr Bradley

When your letter came with the two hundred Francs I was just making up my mind to go on a fly [?] voyage to Singapore as assistant steward to a Demeraran. It was a unique opportunity and the second like it to offer itself (the other was in the summer of 26 when I had the chance to go to Central America on a yacht) since I have been knocking round Marseille, the steward was a likeable person, my work was light and we were sailing for warm seas.

I didn't think going mattered much although I had taken money from Harper[']s to do the Marseille book. I had just reach[ed] the cracking point under the periodic pecuniary harassments and the frantic letters of appeal every month. I felt it was better to go, that if "Home To Harlem" had any success, Harper[']s could repay themselves the advances + I would know whether I would have a decent chance to do any further writing. For the trip would have taken me away for three months or longer.

However your letter came. And because I want to write now more than anything else I decided to stay. And then it said definitely three months and anything may happen in three months. In '26 when, curiously, I had almost the chance, I had an offer from Max Eastman to go down to Antibes and help Eleina and use his typewriter for the four months they were going to stay there. It was my Russian friend that decided I should go down to Max[,] and the real result of going was "Home To Harlem."

This time I decided myself. As between jobs + writing, there were many times in New York when I threw up good jobs, good for a proletarian, to gratify the whim for a stretch of writing.—I have lost the best part of January and at a time when I was in my best form. It would be impossible for me to recapture the spirit, and make it breathe through my writing, of the easy-going vagabonde existence of the boys I knew here in 1926 if I am not enjoying a modicum of physical contentment myself. Because we are all living in a certain state of animal happiness, although I was staying in a chambre noir with two of them. But it was different from having to keep up a respectable front + worrying about 300 francs rent. What made me discontented a little about your letter was that Mr [Thomas Bucklin] Wells could not find it expedient, after his decision to help, to send himself the first payment from Paris. I let an Egyptian boy take my job and right afterwards I regretted it and could have kicked myself for not having gone. However, I am still waiting[.]

Yours Sincerely
Claude McKay

WABLAR ALS

To William A. Bradley

10 February 1928

Marseille, France

Dear Bradley

I should have thanked you for your registered letter and your promptness and thoughtfulness in getting the double allowance for me, right after receiving it. But I am feeling all out of joint in this weather, turned bad again since a week. My throat has been bothering me for quite awhile, giving me the sensation of the grippe coming on, which I have been fighting off with aspirine and eucalyptis [*sic*], but the worse thing is a dull irritating pain under the skin of my hands which troubles me much working at the machine.

I have put off going to Nice until the weather clears up but the real deterrent is my working on another lap of "Banjo" which I want to complete altogether, so I can feel myself free for a little lay-off.

I am mighty glad that you like the chapters I sent you. That makes me feel more confident to keep right on chopping along. The whole thing will be much longer than "Home to Harlem[,]" about thrice as much as what you already have and will keep me working, I daresay, all through the Spring. I have it all planned out in four sections and will forward each to you when completed.

In the meantime, I shall be glad if you will write me more[1] about the first part, stating frankly where you think I am strongest and where a little weak and pointing out the things that were most interesting to you. Any such criticism will be very helpful as I can use it to balance myself as I carry on. You see that I turned all your first hints to good account! It was better to rewrite in most instances than to patch.

I think the work went better this time too, because I have been so very comfortable. It was so cold at the Nautique and the hotel I moved to from it.

I found a cheap little room in the Place d'Aix with a fireplace. I do the cleaning myself—no bonne to tell me I must stop in the midst of important work so she can clean up—and I can make the room as hot as I want with that splendid "boulet." It's a Negro quarter too.[2]

Funny case. The fellow out of whom I was creating Taloufa got back here in January with both his legs cut off below the knees. He had stowed away on a Fabre boat to New York towards the end of '26, and was locked up in a W.C. where his feet were frozen. The doctors cut them off at Ellis Island and one of those Jewish accident lawyers sued the Fabre company for the boy and obtained a settlement of 17000 dollars of which the boy got twelve thousand. The British Consul in New York sent 10,000 dollars for him to Nigeria and he was repatriated by way of Marseille. But on the day of sailing for West Africa, the Company Fabre had him arrested for clandestine embarkation and thrown into prison. We got him out two weeks ago and he is gone home. It[']s a very amazing humorous case and I cannot give you the details now, but you will see it in the story.

I received 6 copies of Home of Harlem and shall send you a signed copy on M[onday.]

Very Sincerely[3]

[Left margin:] I like the format—there are some corrections to be made.

WABLAR TLU

1. The words "me more" were inserted in pen.

2. This sentence is handwritten.

3. The final sentence and closing are handwritten. Damage to the letter obscures "Monday" and the signature.

To William A. Bradley

"Tuesday" [received 20 February 1928]

Marseille, France

Dear Mr Bradley

Thank you for both your letters received today (one enclosing cheque for 1,071.10) and the dummy, which was sent on to Cook's. I left the hotel Brager during my little financial panic, as I did not want to be caught there when my month was up + the money did not arrive. I like the cover of the book + the color of the jacket but I don't like the drawing. It looks so much like the stiff skeleton of a black ape. Has no life and one looking at it will naturally link it with Jake. [Miguel] Covarrubias could have done something striking + sympathetic, but I suppose I should not grumble + criticise but be loyal and patriotic as the artist is a colored man.

Do you know why in the notice to the Trade the book is listed as a collection of short stories + not as a novel? I thought you had settled about that with Mr [Eugene] Saxton + he had plenty of time to correct the first draft. Or are they really calling "Home To Harlem" a collection of short stories?

Am very happy about the arrangements for the payments. All that was going on too when I was having about the hardest pinch of it ever over here! I suppose some good will come of the whole of January last. I am rather [a] fatalist optimist, insist everything in my life is for the best. Thank you very much for putting it through finally.

I am in a very excited way—working hard on "Banjo[.]" You will have the first part of it this month. I had a long letter from Mr Saxton about it, when I sent him that list of names of people who might help boost "Home To Harlem[.]" He thinks I should get back home just when it is published—"Banjo." A good idea. Apropos of which I enclose a letter from [James Weldon] Johnson. You might help me about an answer! That is the second letter from the N.A.A.C.P. about my return. I don't want any racial or political issue raised about it, if I can avoid that. Those liberals always want a little cause to take care of and that man [Lothrop] Stoddard who wrote "Rising Tide of Color" has been calling me a dangerous black bolshevik in a recently published book, because I went to Russia.[1] Maybe I could try the quota or go to Canada when the time comes. At any rate we ought to [text missing] now that the book is [indecipherable][.]

Yours Sincerely
Claude McKay

Do you want back the dummy—I should like to show it to [T. F.] Tracy—

What about cuttings?: I suppose I could get mine through Harper[']s?

WABLAR ALS

1. Lothrop Stoddard called McKay "the most notorious member of that group of firebrands who are to-day busy spreading the sparks of a racial conflagration" in *Re-Forging America: The Story of Our Nationhood* (New York: Scribner's, 1927), 280.

To William A. Bradley

25 February 1928

Marseille, France

Dear Bradley

Many thanks for your letter of the 20th with enclosure. I think the quietest way of returning to New York will be the best. If the N.A.A.C.P. or any other association does not have to make an issue of it, it will be all the better for me and my work. In fact I don't know if it would not be better not to try at all, if there is going to be any trouble with the authorities, and enter by way of Canada or under the six months permission.

I haven't the slightest inclination to get back into any movement. Not that I am no longer interested, but, happily, I have been close to so many movements and gone so far in life on my own, I have learned a lot and know that my writing, where I have more liberty of expression than in anything else, is the real thing for me. And I know that the farther I stay away from actual contact with movements the better work I will be able to do. I'd prefer any little job with a chance to write than working in a "movement."

I've had a letter from Mr [Eugene] Saxton, which might interest you, and as it is one of those nice letters I like to keep I'll be pleased if you send it back. I'm very happy about the arrangement and feel relieved and entirely free now to keep on pegging away at "Banjo" without any worry.

I have finished the first section and you will have it during the coming week. A hundred pages. I could have sent it with this letter, but I haven't recasted [*sic*] the first chapter yet. I have been looking it over and find it much easier to do after finishing the other chapters. And it will be quite easy to start in with the breakwater scene as you suggested. You know it[']s very much harder to do than "Home To Harlem" because I have to keep all my characters concentrated in one place and make them act more and talk less than in the first draft. I have no chance to run Banjo all over the shop as I did Jake.

Yes, I think my first opinion on the cover was wrong. It is effective and grows on me. The Senegalese fellows at the cafe were enchanted with it at first sight. Maybe my plastic sense is a little corrupt and sentimental. [T. F.] Tracy also liked it. He was here a few days ago and, by the way, he says he is preparing a collection of short stories for you.

Thanks for sending off the stories. I hope one or two of them finds a market. I could do with a little extra cash. I want to go down to Nice to get my identity card. I have the receipt only here. I have been warned to renew as I am liable to a "contravention," but I cannot without the real card and if I write for it, I think it will involve a lot of red tape. Maybe you might arrange for me a special payment of two months at one time? That would be a solution of the matter, for I cannot find a way of making the trip out of my monthly budget.

Do you know whether "Home To Harlem" is actually out? I have no news yet, but a paragraph in this month's "Opportunity" said the publication was postponed until spring. Perhaps they count this month as Spring. Will write again next week sending ms. With best wishes[.]

Yours Sincerely,
Claude McKay

WABLAR TLS

To Harold Jackman

10 March 1928

Marseille, France

My dear Harold,

It was so charming of you to put that little gift in your letter of Feb. 2. It was one of those little gestures that are very big to me because they always remain to convince one in moments of bitter reflection that there is a kind of friendship that is more than an empty name. What you did, after my letter, is so beautiful, that I am constrained, (in spite of my pecuniary state and the fact of my poetic inability, although I am by no means spendthrift, to keep any money in my hands) to practise a little self-denial and feel a little finer for it, by using the order to procure "Ulysses" for you.

Herewith the covers and I do hope that [James] Joyce's splendid heavyweight as I have sent it will reach you camo[u]flaged under the light-weight protection of Monsieur Paul Morand whose facile cleverness may be innocuous enough to make his name acceptable to American puritan imbecility.

I regret to hear you are not well, but if I may be allowed to say it, you should not take <u>little</u> ailments over seriously. Just go on living healthily as much as you are physically and psychically able and don't worry. I have had so many real illnesses that I would be a perfect ruin I think if it were not for the vigorous optimistic state of mind that just holds my body strong together. So much for advice that is the easiest of all things to give!

When I published "Harlem Shadows" I did have a letter from a Negro Clipping business, somewhere out Chicago way asking me to subscribe, but it may have gone out of existence since. You might find out from some official of the N.A.A.C.P. By that way too, I have recently had a cordial letter from [James] Weldon Johnson inviting me to come back home and enjoy some of the benefits that Negro artists are obtaining through the general public interest awakened now to the Negro Literary Renaissance. You also hint at something of that in mentioning the Harmon Awards.[1] I have no objection in the world to receiving money, which I can always use. But I cannot <u>write to please</u> a body of charitably disposed people. My work must be judged as it is written and if I am awarded something other than public favour for it, all the better, but personally, I could not lift a finger to further my own cause along those lines. About going back, I should love to look in on the States again. All these laws and rulings since the war are very irritating to the vagabond soul, especially an outlaw soul, that cannot reconcile itself to the fact of limitation to any one country, or allegiance to any one nation. But maybe those are the factual forces, irksome though they may be, that help to make an artist of a vagabond.

I am obliged for the two songs. "Shake That Thing" is fine. Is it popular in the cabarets? I had the two last verses and have already written a riotous thing about it. It won't be necessary to remove anything but only to add something. Why don't you shift your machine to give the black type? Do you like the red? I hate it.

And you know, I don't like the idea of your showing my private letters to your acquaintances. [Wallace] Thurman, in a nice clever, smart-alecky letter to me, said you showed him two! Now what have you, my dear friend, to say about that? Of course, I'm not dictating what you should do with my correspondence, but if I mention any small thing personally to you (like my note on [Countee] Cullen, for example) and you show it to the Harlem gents, eventually and inevitably it will be all over Nigger Heaven as Mr Carl Van Vechten might say or Nigger Hell as Gin Head Susy[2] would say; And by this to remember Young Thurman, please tell him that I shall most surely write to him, but just now I am flooded with more correspondence than ever since the last five years and, as I shall have to invent a special key in replying to the style of his ultra-sophisticated professional handshake across the pond, he must give me a little time. But tell him however that he must be careful when he gets his "aching critical claws"[3] into "Home to Harlem," as he hopes, that they are not painfully broken off in it!

I had a few copies of "Home To Harlem" the same time I had your last letter. It is a neatly made book. [Eugene] Saxton wrote me he sent out the copies to all the names I gave him and as you have yours I shall not send another. You must wait until we get together and I can sign it. I wish you could come over this summer. I shall have finished my new novel by then and we could swim and poke around the low quarters of this town together, if you care about those things. I know Langston [Hughes] does. He has sent me a fine cable about "Home To Harlem."

There are a few mistakes to correct in the book, but there is one very important that must be made right away. And I want you to help me again. I cannot find the correct thing in the library here, but I feel sure you will in New York. It's in Chapter 10 p. 135, 1st par, referring to the Kings of Africa. <u>Behanzin of Benin</u> is wrong. Behanzin was the big fighting king of Dahomey that the French defeated and deported. What I want is the names of the King of Benin, (there were two outstanding ones in the fifteenth and sixteenth centuries when the Portug[u]ese traded with West Africa). And there is another very important one when the British conquered the country in [the] eighteen forties. You will find the information in two or three books on Benin in the Forty-second Street library—one a massive thing with the reproductions of sculpture and ivory carvings written by an Englishman.[4] If you send me the names in order of their importance with a little note on each, I shall choose the one I want and forward the correction to Mr. Saxton. I hope this job won't be too troublesome to you as you tell me you are working so hard at your new lecture course.

I am happy to hear about the creative activity of Negroes in New York. I have never once doubted that recognition and monetary reward would come for the Negro as soon as he produced work of merit and the public was aware of it. I did not take a pessimistic race-conscious view of "Home To Harlem" because it did not sell. Poetry in general is never a selling thing. There are exceptions—like leap years!

About Cullen's note on me I must say that "vituperative" has nothing to do with "raillery." In the peasant atmosphere in which I was born and reared our stock of words were strong words, direct and meaningful. As a boy I loved literature because it spoke the words of life and all my best friends with whom

I have loved literature love it with me above all for the realness of words. And I have always been identified with those people who hate looseness in literature, holding that words should mean what they say! Any cub reporter knows that "vituperative" is "abuse." Go down to the night court where it is called abusive language! If Mr Cullen doesn't know the common meaning of the word it shows an amazing ignorance. And as a worker in words, I must tell you frankly that I have no love nor sympathy for loose milk-and-water meaningless use of words either in prose or in poetry. Personally I have the friendliest feelings towards the young man, but I am one mean bastard who does not think of personal or racial considerations when I am dealing with artistic wares. Please write soon and give me some news and—gossip! Thanking you for everything,

Yours "vituperatively"
Claude McKay

CMP TLS

1. The Harmon Awards (also known as the William E. Harmon Foundation Award for Distinguished Achievement Among Negroes) were given in several categories from 1926 to 1930. In 1928 McKay received the $400 first prize (or gold medal) for literature "for his power, skill and originality in both poetry and prose, especially his 'Harlem Shadows,' which were considered to voice in tragic force many of the deeper feelings of the Race: also his 'Home to Harlem,' with its pictures of certain phases of Harlem life." "Twelve Get Awards for 'Good Work,'" *Chicago Defender,* 5 January 1929, 1.

2. A character in McKay's *Home to Harlem,* Gin Head Susy lives in Brooklyn and hates Harlem.

3. Quotation marks around this phrase are inserted in pencil.

4. Above the word "Englishman" McKay has handwritten "(over)" and on the verso "George Pitt-Rivers—Benin." McKay likely means *Antique Works of Art from Benin* (1900) by Lieutenant-General Pitt Rivers (Augustus Pitt Rivers).

To James Weldon Johnson

10 March 1928

Marseille, France

Dear Mr Johnson,

Thank you for your kind letter of January 26. Naturally, I always think and long for America as the place where the most interesting formative years of my life were spent and, as much as I can I follow eagerly the trend[s] and tendencies of the literary and artistic life of the country, especially among Negroes.

However, this life is such a crazy, complex, onward-pitching business, that I have never definitely thought about "going back." But I would like to feel that I can go to the States again when I want to. I know that the immigration laws have changed since I left in '22. However, I have never tested them by applying to return, but I should like to return towards the end of this year when I have finished the book that I am at present working on. The ordinary course, I think, would be the best for me to try, by putting in my application at once. But I am not familiar with the quota rulings, therefore, as you say you are willing to help, I should be glad if you will give me the ruling for the British West Indies and some information about the form of application. My passport is made out in a way that might enable me to get in on the quota, without my being made a special case. Don't you think that that would be the best way for all concerned?

That was a very charming sketch of me you did. Mr [Eugene] Saxton sent it to me, saying he was going to release it to the Press. I was so chagrined, because of an important point that was inexact and that I preferred to have left out, that I had to cable Saxton to hold it up. And I do hope it hasn't gotten out. It is about that restaurant. It would have been better, I think, if you had asked me for the correct information before writing about it. I never owned a restaurant in 53rd Street. I did own a business, including a restaurant, in partnership with another person; but it was not in the 53rd Street district. Nor was it the scholarship money I used to come to New York and buy the business. The scholarship fund was exhausted when I left the Kansas college. The money came to me from an English admirer of my "Songs of Jamaica," which had a big vogue and sale too when it was published.

But the point is that it is better that my business venture should not become public property, especially if I am to get back to America, because there are certain details concerning it that might be aired and make a very embarrassing situation for myself and others. I hope, then, you will do all you can to suppress what you have written about the restaurant.

With my deepest regard, and again thanking you for your interest, Sincerely yours

Claude McKay

JWJP TLS

To Langston Hughes

30 March 1928

Nice, France

[On Letterhead (crossed out): Café "Moderne" Bar 14, Avenue Félix-Faure, Nice]

Dear Langston,

Your cablegram was the first notice I had that the book was actually published, and I was very happy to have it. I quoted it in a letter to [Eugene] Saxton of Harper's telling him he could use it if he wanted to! Then it was a great treat to have your long letter. I brought it down here with me to reply to it. I came down for a week or so to fix up my carte d'identité and take a little time off from my second book. But I haven't been able to get away from working at the book! The change of scene does me good however. I must keep right on at the book until I have finished—some time between spring and summer. That is what I am working at now (I think you asked)—a novel of Negro beach-combers, chiefly English-speaking on the docks and in the whore quarter of Marseille. I have about a third of it done and [William A.] Bradley, my reader-friend-agent in Paris, is in raptures over it. I don't think the National French Respectability will love me anymore than the Negro Racial Respectability when I have finished + published this book. Like "Home to Harlem" the bite comes in the second part. Of course I am merely painting scenes as they exist + using my brains to link them up with a story. But the French literati will not like it. They have never touched Marseille, I understand, except in the romantic sense.

I am now chuckling over the reviews I am receiving.[1] That one in the New York Times was certainly a scream. I liked it as much as the reviewer liked Jake. The most entertaining thing for me about getting out a book is the reading of the reviews. Hardly any of the white reviewers like Ray yet I think he is the one character the Negro intellectuals will like!

I don't know [Pío] Baroja's[2] or [Francis] Carco's works. I met an American girl last winter when I was working on Home to Harlem and in talking about my work she mentioned Carco + promised to send me "Jesus la Caille."[3] She did but before I could read it, somebody "borrowed" it and I haven't seen it since. But now you have mentioned them I want to read the best of both

Baroja + Carco after getting this book done. I am very glad you like it so much. Honestly I value your opinion above any of the Negro intellectuals—next Wallace Thurman in whom I find some real independent thinking and strength. As critics, the others merely second the leading whites' fiddle—but what more can we expect when our magazines even our entire social existence follow the standards set by the solid well-followed America Babbitry.[4] They don't like you for your stuff won't do for the Negro rotarian + Elks—neither the white I suppose[.] All this means that I don't give a damn what they say. Their opinion will be conditioned by that of the whites + the success, if any, of the book. Whether you give them revolutionary thought or revolutionary depiction of life there is no difference in their attitude. If they accepted, "If We Must Die" it was because a radical white organ printed it <u>first</u>. [Alain] Locke wouldn't use my "Mulatto" for his Anthology[;] he said it was too strong. [John] Farrar printed it and Locke changed the title of my "White House" which was symbolic to "White Houses" which makes the poem cringing + whining. I protested (<u>he did it without consulting me</u>) and he went over my protest + did the same thing in his pamphlet for Schuster. Then I just got mad and wrote and cussed the shit out of him telling him that he could take his damned anthology + Negro renaissance + my part in it and dump the whole show in the can! He has not written since, that damned Oxford doctor, and I guess he won't ever. I don't blame them for compromising—everybody has got to—artists + all revolutionists + the whole damned gang—got to to live. But I hate their damned imbecilities + dishonesty. If we've got to compromise let[']s do it, but not with a damned sanctimonious darky prayer.

It would be wonderful if you could come over this summer. I shall have finished my book + we could play around together + root around Marseille + I would love to go down to Genoa to get its background for a short story—+ I couldn't go with a better body than you! Locke told me when he came to Toulon that you had some of my taste for low-down places—so I think we could knock around without getting on each other's nerves. I'm a born bastard of moods, but I am sure you are too + so we could adjust moods for a holiday together. I am a good fellow in the mood, but when I am out I don't torture + vex my friends—I run away from them like a cat + hide. I want to go down to Barcelona too. I am getting tired of Marseille + only the book holds me there. I have no plans. I want to get back some day but not right now. Johnson (Weldon) writes that he is asking his friend the under secretary of State to facilitate my coming back. But I don't think it will be any easy matter—except I go in on the six month permission. I had a letter from the under-secretary rather a copy that he sent to Johnson + the whole business is so difficult + full of red tape I feel discouraged about tackling it. And I don't want to worry about anything while I am doing this book—I wrote Harold Jackman asking him to try + come over this summer. Wouldn't it be great if we could all get together! Thank you for sending that clipping.

I am pretty well, strong and feeling fine. I have only head trouble a kind of dizziness and my doctor says it is because I have been such a hard drinker. I have to give up drinking—practically! And that is awful for I love the smell and taste of good red wine. I take a little with my meals however + I enjoy the boys swilling around here even though I can't. Once in a while I break the rule + go on a drunk + then I must stay in bed for 48 hours! I will send you a photograph when I get back to Marseille. We took some swimming last summer + they were very good.

Again I am glad you like "Home to Harlem." My characters are the people you sing about, the people I really love + significantly they were the people I sang about when I was your age! When I told you I liked "Fine Clothes To the Jew" as a whole even more than the first book I really meant it. The first book had better individual lyrics than the second, but the second had more of a folk portrayal of life in it. That was how it seemed to me. I would like to do a play but I cannot alone because I don't know the theatre enough. Let me hear from you again soon. I will send cards if I am too busy to write + you can do the same.

Sincerely Claude

LHP ALS

1. Paragraph not indented in original.

2. Pío Baroja (1872–1956), Spanish novelist and member of the "Generation of '98."

3. *Jésus-la-Caille* (1914), Carco's first novel, about a gigolo in the Montmartre district of Paris.

4. Derogatory phrase for empty middle-class values, a reference to Sinclair Lewis's novel *Babbitt* (1922). This expression is associated with H. L. Mencken's cultural criticism.

To Harold Jackman

1 April 1928

Nice, France

Dear Harold: I know many Negroes, ordinary Negroes, Africans, Americans, West Indians who prefer their "brown" to any white girl. I myself do! That does not mean that they would not "have" white girls. All men are curious about women of other races. I know fellows who wanted to get "next" to white women not because they cared for "white" but because they wanted to break through the taboo. In a way it was because they hated the ofays why they wanted to have their women. I cannot go with the matter here—some day I hope we will talk it over. I know there is a strong feeling for white women among Jamaican Negroes—but it is because of the taboo. In the West Indies it does not exist. You have a big black society, a "high yaller" and a white—Individuals who are not conformists mate according to their inclinations but the big average is conformist. However, as open miscegenation is a rare thing in America, I think literature should treat life more as it is than as it works in the imagination of those who want it to be otherwise! Get me!

However you are quite wrong about Jake. The young buck has had it all—seen it all—in France-in England where he was nearly killed for white flesh! All that is given in the very first chapter of the book. After such an experience is it not natural that he should turn for love and peace to a little "brown" of his own race? It serves me he would!

I am convinced by experience that educated Negroes worry themselves much more about miscegenation than the average working Negroes. The workaday Negro never thinks about the thing. In his daily life and conversation, he refers to white women in the carnal joking way. If he is a servant in a white house + has a chance at the stuff he would take it of course without bellyaching—but the woman he is always saying amorous sweet things about is, "mah brown," the woman of his daily life! That is a simple enough matter to understand—

For example, the half a dozen colored girls here in Marseille do a wonderful business among colored seamen. They have white too, besides. And they are much higher-priced than the white girls of the quarter.—Again I did not think myself that I had made my characters oversexed. Perhaps that fault lies in me! However I do not find them more sexy than the characters of white modern authors! [Aldous] Huxley, [James] Joyce, [Paul] Morand, Michael Arlen, [Jean] Cocteau, and all "les Jaunes." This, my dear boy, is the Freudian era of freedom in sex. If the Negro is virile, it is all to his credit. He is no more so than the Italian! My characters are characters + not the whole Negro race. I rather think the thing appears over-sexy to you because I have so many brothel scenes, which is unusual in literature. But I was dealing with a certain milieu + had to use that environment. You will see there is not much difference between the black + white side of it when I have finished the Marseille book except that the black is cleaner + more human.

I am glad you like the book as a whole. I am getting some nice notices. I did not like Heywood Broun's saying I write down my contempt of "all things white."[1] That is not true. There are many white things I appreciate as I do yellow + black—yes you will see Ray in the next book. Glad you like him—the white reviewers don't. He will be more interesting in the new book—I must stop now. I came down here to see about my identity card + take a little time off. I am going back in a couple of days.

Sincerely
Claude

CMP ALS

1. The phrase "contempt for all things white" appears in an unsigned review of *Home to Harlem*, "Banana-Ripe," *Time*, 19 May 1928, 47.

To Langston Hughes

3 April [1928]

Nice, France

Here is a page about [Francis] Carco that might interest you. I understand he is regarded as quite second-rate in France. But I won't be prejudiced. I am going to sample him for myself. I have been reading [André] Gide + [Marcel] Proust. Gide I don't overlike [*sic*] but Proust is wonderful—the greatest writer I have felt since [Leo] Tolstoy.

The news of the Guggenheim awards has just reached me. I am very sorry you were not included. It might have made you getting over here easier + more comfortable!

I am more concerned about what the Masses group will think about "Home to Harlem" than the opinion on the Negro Press. I don't think the New Masses crowd will like the book <u>if it becomes a success!</u> For them anything successful in Capitalist society must of necessity be bourgeois! Max Eastman will like it I think.

You remember the first novel I sent to Knopf's! It was written around the type of people in [Carl] Van Vechten's "Nigger Heaven." You had told me that Van Vechten was doing Harlem for material for a book + I knew then that it would be no "nice" little book to please the exquisite taste of the Negro intelligentsia. So I was trying to beat Van Vechten to it. I knew those people well. I met most of them when I came to New York from the West with plenty of money and I lived with one family of the "muckty-mucks" over in Brooklyn. But while I was doing my book the people who were giving me a little money began harassing me about returning to America and I could not resist the temptation of satirizing them in the novel. That spoilt it and my introduction in it of French argot which I was at that time learning.

When I got over my anger I thought I would write a straight thing about the Negro smart set + leave the uplifters + French argot out. But "Nigger Heaven" was published while I was doing it + took so much of my ground + atmosphere I just had to do something else. I had written some short stories—the first two chapters of Home To Harlem was [*sic*] written for the first Opportunity contest. All the critics here loved it + one of them suggested my doing my book from the short story "Home to Harlem" + so I just continued Jake through the Harlem scene! But he did not even receive honorable mention from the Opportunity contest! I am going back to Marseille tomorrow, after a well-needed rest. Let me hear from you[.]

Best wishes! Claude—

LHP ALS

To William A. Bradley

"Thursday" [likely early April 1928]

Marseille, France

Dear Bradley: Received your letter yesterday afternoon. I expected you to send the first part of Banjo to Harper[']s—did not know you hadn't nor think it was necessary to tell you.

I suppose you held it by misunderstanding a little my motive in sending you [Eugene] Saxton's letter. I sent it because it was a nice friendly letter but had no idea of acting on it and not letting him see "Banjo" before he was finished. I thought it would be better for him to see Banjo at any rate so that if I should want any more financial help before it was done he would feel confident sanctioning it!

Thanks for cuttings. What they say about Ray is amusing. They don[']t see of course that he is just Jake's other self—so much so that I am just realizing, I haven't made him do anything <u>real</u> like loving or gaming [?] in the story. I shall look out for that in Banjo, but nevertheless Ray must second-fiddle all through the narrative. The only way to make Banjo <u>the</u> character.

Some colored college boys have written praising, naturally, Ray. He'll be the only character that the Negro intelligentsia will like a little.

If you have anything important ever you might telegraph me at the Hotel Miramar, Place d'Aix, Marseille—but no letters please as there is no real bureau with someone always in attendance.

Yours Sincerely
Claude McKay

Will finish by the end of May I hope[.] I don[']t want to spend the summer here by no means.

WABLAR ALS

To William A. Bradley

12 April 1928

Marseille, France

Dear Bradley

"Banjo" is moving along like a crazy patchwork to its happy-tragic end. I'll have the middle lap all done by the end of this month. I see "Home To Harlem" like an impudent dog has nosed right in among the best sellers in New York! That's more than we reckoned on I think, but just the stuff to spur me on with "Banjo." I am working carefully, however, + so much slower than I did on "Home To Harlem[.]"

I am sending you a statement from the clipping bureau. You might, if I am not bothering you too much, ask [Eugene] Saxton to stop them. A friend has just written that she has asked the "Argus" bureau to send me cuttings and I suppose it is as good as the other.

Oh yes! I hope you don't come down until I have this lap of "Banjo" done.

Sincerely
McKay

WABLAR ALS

To Louise Bryant

22 April 1928

Marseille, France

Dear Louise

I am so glad you're feeling better. I have a hunch you will get well in spite of the specialists' dictum if you take care of yourself. And happily you have the will and the means to do it thoroughly.

I am enclosing the note for [Carl] Van Vechten. I have read a couple books of his and some articles but, frankly, I didn't know what little right thing to say about them as he and I are so far apart intellectually. I put in a set of photographs too and you might choose one for him and use the others any way you want to. They are all bad. I took them for Harper's and apparently they did not use any. Although the sketch of me that I have seen in the reviews (I don't know where they got it) is quite worse.

About the passport, it is not a British one I want. I have an old one which is quite good to get me a new [one] when I have the money to spare for it. What I want made easy for me is the way of returning to America. You see I left there before the new immigration laws were passed and although I thought of staying away only six months when I went to Russia, I have stayed six years! I even did sublet my room in Fourteenth Street with my two trunks and sticks of furniture in it and I don't know what has become of them. But unfortunately I have no proof to show what my intention was! And as I have been listed as a Bolshevik (Senator [Henry Cabot] Lodge read me into the senate records as an agitator and our Nordic hyena Lathrop [*sic*] Stoddard, has raked up the worse [*sic*] he could about me for his recently published book, "Reforging America") I am sure I shall have trouble getting back unless the way is paved for me.

I think you told me long ago that Mr. [William C.] Bullitt knew somebody in the State Department at Washington that might help.

[James] Weldon Johnson of the N.A.A.C.P. spoke to asst. Secretary of State [Wilbur John] Carr, who is a friend of his, about me. And Carr sent him a note on the matter, a copy of which was forwarded to the Consul General here. It said that if I could show proof of my first entry into America and that when I left in '22 I intended to return, I could take the matter up with the Consul General, but if I hadn't the proof I would have to try the quota, which is filled up for years ahead.

I sent both letters to [William A.] Bradley, but I haven't been to the Consulate, because I have no proofs and I should like to feel certain first that my re-entry is not objected to in official quarters. I have however written to the immigration commissioner at Charleston, for the record of my first entry. So that's how the matter stands.

I am working hard on my new book and it is half-finished. I hope that after you have finished your "cure" you'll be able to pitch right into yours and clean up with it. . . . . I have had about as much of this town as I can stand and would like to get away from it before it becomes an unpleasant thing in my memory. But I must finish the book first. I am getting my last monthly allowance on the 1st of May so I hope "Home To Harlem" will bring me something by June! Bradley is trying to market some of my stories in America, but we haven't heard anything yet. The revue "Europe" published "Bad

Boy" last month and all they sent me for it was fs. 133.[1] And I was banking on a thousand!

I hope you have a good time when you get back and please remember me to Max [Eastman] and Crystal [Eastman] and tell them I should like to hear from them.

Yours Sincerely
Claude

LBP TLS

1. This story was published as "Mauvaise Tête," *Europe,* 15 March 1928, 343–61. It appeared in *Gingertown* (1932) as "Truant."

To James Weldon Johnson

30 April 1928

Marseille, France

Dear Weldon Johnson

If you have no objection we might drop the mister since I have known you so long and [Eugene] Saxton in his letters mentioning you also dispense [*sic*] with the formality.

I haven't been to see Mr. [Wesley] Frost, the Consul General, yet. I sent your letter and Mr. [Wilbur John] Carr's on to [William A.] Bradley, whom I burden with all my affairs that he will handle, so as to leave myself free and unworried for writing. He is also looking into the matter of my getting back some time and he will be glad to use your influence with Mr. Carr either in Paris or here in Marseille, if he comes down, to ensure the easiest and most certain way to put the thing through.

First I want to get my hands on all the necessary proofs and information that may be asked for. To this end I have written to the immigration commissioner at Charleston for the record of my arrival. I could also prove, if I could get hold of the people, that when I left America in 1922 it was with the intention of returning in about six months. For instance, I subletted my studio at 25 East Fourteenth (which I rented from a Frenchman named Perrier) to Nancy Markhoff, a girl that was doing secretarial work on the "Daily Worker." And I left all my worldly goods there! My two trunks, two or three sticks of furniture and my books. I haven't been able to get into communication with Mrs. Markhoff, but perhaps you might for me through Louis Engdahl, one of the editors of the Daily Worker. A note from her indirectly verifying what I have stated might be helpful.

From a purely personal cause I am a little loth [*sic*] about going to the Consul here on behalf of myself. Simply because I have written to him a few times and gone to the Consulate too on account of colored American seamen who were stranded, especially one fellow who was expelled and thrown into prison and brutalised by the police. They were very courteous to me at the Consulate, I think one of the men I saw the second time was Mr. Frost himself, and now I am a little diffident about going to him with my own trouble!

Did you ascertain, in talking to Mr Carr, that my going to Russia would not be held against my entering the States again?

I am glad you like the book. I value your criticism because I have known it to be well-balanced and clear ever since the time I used to read you on [*sic*] the New York Age. It is surprising those hidebound Negro papers do not chastise you for puffing me on the jacket! I have seen cuttings from the the [*sic*] "Amsterdam News," the "Tattler" and "Pittsburg [*sic*] Courrier [*sic*]" only of the Negro papers. I wish I could see the others. Lady Nicotine is very amusing and I like her style![1] But the Rev. ole [William H.] Ferris surely surpasses himself when he accuses me of obscenity and selling-out after his hand-and-knees crawling before [Marcus] Garvey, while that personage was obscenely selling out and wasting the wealth of the Negro masses.[2]

In writing "Home To Harlem" I have not deviated in any way from my intellectual and artistic ideas of life. I consider the book a real proletarian novel, but I don't expect the nice radicals to see that it is, because they know very little about proletarian life and what they want of proletarian art is not proletarian life, truthfully, realistically, and artistically portrayed, but their own false, soft-headed and wine-watered notions of the proletariat. With the Negro intelligentsia it is a different matter, but between the devil of Cracker prejudice and the deep sea of respectable white condescension I can certainly sympathise, though I cannot agree, with their dislike of the artistic exploitation of low-class Negro life. We must leave the real appreciation of what we are doing to the emancipated Negro intelligentsia of the future, while we are sardonically aware now that only the intelligentsia of the "superior race" is developed enough to afford artistic truth.

I am hard at work on a second novel and when I have finished I should like to go to New York towards the end of this year. Again many thanks for your help.

Yours Sincerely
Claude McKay

JWJP TLS

1. Lady Nicotine was a pseudonym for society columnist Gerri Major, who published the column "Between Puffs with Lady Nicotine" in the New York–based *Inter-State Tattler.*

2. William H. Ferris, "Ferris Scores Obscenity in Our Literature," *Pittsburgh Courier,* 31 March 1928, sec. 2, p. 8.

To Harold Jackman

9 May 1928

Marseille, France

My dear Harold,

When I was working on the railroad, I went one night with an ex-jockey and a white European to a cabaret in Harlem. The white admired the colored girls and said, quite naturally, that when he was in some part of the South he used to go with a beautiful mulatto girl. The jockey resented this and he spoke about the fine white girl he had when he was in Canada—a girl that was well-bred and well off too—and he produced a photograph of her from his pocket-book. She was a beautiful girl and the white fellow admired her, asking my friend if he wasn't crazy about her. The white, as I said, was European and did not have the peculiar sex-and-color prejudice of white Americans, but the colored jockey was seething with racial antagonism and resented the white man with his having had a mulatto girl and boasting about it. To the white's question he answered: "No I fucked the bitch when I was in Canada and she wanted me to marry her, but what was I going to do with a white bitch?" You can imagine how the white man felt? I am sure the jockey did not hate that girl but it was his objective hatred for white men that brought out the hatred in him.

Have you read many sex books? Freud, [Havelock] Ellis, [John Addington] Symonds, Jung, another German I can't remember, and any works on the sex life of Ancient Greece and Rome? If you haven't you ought to before you make a sweeping indictment of the sexual attitude of the Negro male. You don't mention the female, but I think that the case you bring up is stronger against her than the male, judging from the obvious issue of it in the West Indies, Africa, and the United States. . . . .

Then sexual life is motivated by conflicting emotions[.] One man may be agitated to the sexual act through a feeling of hate, contempt and perversity as much as another may be through natural love and tenderness. . . . . The duality you find in the Negro is not puzzling to me. All men have it, my dear Harold. The best and the worst of crackers like their nigger wench, but they do not make legitimate society wives of them for obvious reasons! So do the European gentlemen like to bed with their servant wenches, but do not marry them either. If the Negro shows an illogical preference for the white woman and is prone to marry her, when he can, while the cracker would not marry the colored woman, it is simply because the skin of the white woman proclaims to the Negro, denatured by Civilization, that she belongs to the race that bosses the world today. At least that is my opinion. Sex is a primitive, natural, unlawful thing. Marriage is a legal affair regulated by the economic conditions of human beings.

It is quite plain to me why Negroes should "hate white people and want white woman [*sic*]." This hate for white people is an objective and social feeling, the patent result of oppression by slavery and suppression after emancipation of the Negro's social aspirations by the dominant race. It doesn't have anything to do with the black man feeling a stiff urge when he sees an attractive white woman anymore than with the cracker getting the same thing for a juicy black gal. On the other hand there is much to say for this: Crackers may run after black and mulatto wenches because they have a contempt for sexuality and feel that they might just as well get a burdensome dirty thing off on the colored animals. Just as respectable men go with prostitutes whom they hate![1] I know that a great body of white people, especially Nordic males, are neurotic about sex! And Negroes who "make" white women feel, I am sure, that they have achieved something wonderful by getting even with the race that holds them down and calls itself superior—just as a vain-thinking man of any race feels that he can revenge himself on another that he holds a grievance against by seducing his wife! The white man knows this too, even if it is unconscious in his mind and not thought out clearly, and that is why you find the white race everywhere, covertly or overtly objecting to colored men having white women, until it develops into lynching in the Southern states, where the contact and competition between the two races are more acute than anywhere else in the world, except, perhaps, South Africa. For there can be no doubt that many of the lynchings have their roots in sex complications.

To cite comparisons, you know the Irish hating the English did not prevent mixed mating between the two peoples. And many of the Indian nationalists have English wives. And some of these English wives of Indians are the most bitter haters of England and British rule in India. The same thing holds in Egypt. You seem lacking in perception to me when you confuse a very objective and logical attitude with the most primitive and illogical of human emotions. I think too that there may be in this sex business some pre-historic fundamental antagonism of races. The thing that produced in the beginning of their making the different races and their sub-divisions..[*sic*] It is probable that the outstanding differences (physical) between races are not merely the result of climate and great natural barriers that some liberal anthropoligists [*sic*] premise. Natural selection must have played a big part in it, but as there have always been freaks of nature, it seems to me that the off-springs of both, sex attraction and sex antagonism between the races, will last as long as human life.

Now that I have defended the average Negro, whose inferiority complex like that of the average white, is quite understandable to me, (because the organisation of modern society draws its life-breath from inferiority complexes and without them there would be no rank and frantic climbing) I will say that the average Negro should be helped by his more gifted and clear-thinking brother to overcome his white obsession and become consciously strong and superior in himself and in his race. And so it is the task of Negro artists who can apprehend fine distinctions to give back to the Negro race its heritage, by revealing to it the beauty and wonder and glory, the warmth and color and passion, rhythm and music inherent in itself. The fact in America today is, that whatever hidden yearnings the colored man has, he does marry, live[,] have children and is happy with his woman. An artist who feels the rhythm and tragedy of his race can use the life of the Negro as it is with great effect and leave the suppressed yearnings to the psychologist. The Negro artist can help the the [*sic*] race, corrupted by civilization, to see that it has something finer than the thing it hankers after in itself. That is one way of salvation, I believe, for the Negro race in the modern civilized world.

Oh yes, without any exaggeration, I feel the primitive carnal rhythm in me very strongly and distinct from the rhythm that white people communicate to me. Good dancing always gets me in an ecstasy that I would call religious, because I never have any practical sex feeling when I am dancing, but many Negroes tell me that they are sexually aroused—and many whites too. What I feel most when dancing is the desire for a perfect unity of movement with my partner. If you have never been intoxicated by music I am sorry for you. Maybe it is due to the infusion of cold Nordic blood. However, so many white people feel the same intoxication. I had a Jewish friend who could swoon away under syncopated music just as he could under a composition of Chopin. If white people didn't have it too, they could not appreciate it in Negroes. I think, however that white people are having so much of natural rhythm lifted out of them by highly civilized ways of living that they turn to Negroes, who they feel, quite rightly, have more of primitive rhythm than they.

Tell [Wallace] Thurman I am hoping he will answer my letter. The first one was a real pleasure. If the producers set his play back, perhaps they have done it for reasons that might be remuneratively beneficial to him. I was worrying about my novel too because it did not come out last fall. But Harper[']s were holding it for the most auspicious time. They were right I think. The white man knows the business end of any artistic work better than the Negro artist who is just breaking in, so if I were you, I would advise Thurman, if he will listen, to be patient and diplomatic.

Say, you mustn't write me another letter that calls for so much to answer until after I have finished my book! But I want you to write often all the same and give me all the news! That will either make you mad or smile.

Were there no other notices in the Negro papers? What about the Age and News and Baltimore American and Chicago Defender? Did they have anything? Those you sent me were amusing. But the Amsterdam News thing was remarkably good.[2] The analysis of the characters is the best of any review. [Joel Augustus] Rogers came to see me at Antibes when he was going to Paris last year. I have never liked him. He is a mulatto bounder, dull, heavy, and overinformed like the encyclopedical [*sic*] Hubert Harrison and having the same nasty, shitty attitude towards sex. I sent him a copy of my book. He had always tried to get intimate with me from my Liberator days. And I shall always remember his saying at a meeting (that is to me privately) that all a radical woman wanted was a stiff dick. . . . However, he sent me thirteen dollars in '26 when I was broke, for which I was grateful, without liking him any better.

I sent that cablegram because you have been such a disinterested fine friend and correspondent that I hated the thought of causing you the slightest disappointment. A letter would have taken too long. The cable did not cost much—just a dollar. Yours is the only copy of the book I have sent back to America. There is a white woman who gave me five hundred dollars once and I merely asked Saxton to send her a copy. I am so busy with my new book, but it is a pleasure to stop and talk with you nevertheless. Many of my old correspondents who dropped me when I was in eclipse are coming back again. But I am a busy dog that never goes back to his vomit.

Oh thanks for the Benin stuff. And won't you thank Mrs Latimer[3] for me? Add anything you think best will do in[4] place of my writing. If you tell me how to go about the scholarships you mention, I am willing to try.

Sincerely Ever,
Claude

[Upper margin:] About my return to the U.S.A. you, of which you ask, I know of no real obstacle, except what is commonly known—that I am not a citizen + I left before the new immigration laws were passed + to return I must do so by the British quota which is filled up for years ahead I think. I don't know. I am not worrying about these things. Let the Harlem gossips worry for me! Nothing else I know of except my revolutionary ideas and my trip to Russia could class me as undesirable!

[Lower margin:] Why don't you think Thurman will get his book published? Is it obscene in the conventional sense? Tell him I have asked Harper to send him a copy of "Home To Harlem." I didn't know him before to put him on the original list. Also I have asked Harcourt to send you + [Countee] Cullen a copy each of "Harlem Shadows[.]" I will sign it when I see you—CMcK

CMP TLS

1. This sentence is a handwritten insertion.

2. Aubrey Bowser, "Dirt for Art's Sake," *Amsterdam News,* 21 March 1928, 20.

3. Possibly Louise Latimer (1890–1963), artist involved with the founding of the Harlem branch of the New York Public Library.

4. Beginning with "in," the remainder of the letter is handwritten.

To William A. Bradley

14 May 1928

Marseille, France

Dear Bradley

Thanks for your letter and cheque for the usual amount. Will you oblige me by putting through the enclosed for fifteen dollars? It's a little royalty from Harcourt and I wouldn't mind having it in dollars if that is possible.

I hope you received allright the pages I sent to you. I am now forging ahead on the third and last lap. When I did not hear from you right away, I guessed you were not coming! The beach is getting interesting again with some new men, but it is nothing like before, when the franc was cheap and food and wine were cheaper[.] And I don't see much of them, as I am so busy working, except at night sometimes at the Senegalese Bar. I was a little worried about your coming because my suit is in bad shape now, not fit for any but low-class wear.

As this is the last cheque I hope you will ask Mr [Eugene] Saxton about letting me have some money, so that I won't be in a pickle when it is gone. I hope to finish Banjo by the end of this month, and then I want to leave here immediately for some other place and atmosphere, possibly Spain, to read over and emendate before turning the ms. over to Harper[']s. And so, I should like to have back <u>as soon as possible</u> the first part that you sent to Saxton, because I have things in it that are not in the duplicates.

The only way to get Louise [Bryant] is to hold her[,] hammering at her all the time. She is always in a state of emotional predilection for something and if she can sweep your interest into that, she will do lots for you, but if you miss her at high tide I rather think you won't ever get anything out of her. That was my experience with her. She is ill too now and rather worried, seeing so many specialists and taking cures.

Nearly all the reviews of "Home To Harlem" are splendid. Burton Rascoe gave me two pages in the "Bookman."[1] But the Negro Press is hitting me as hard as it can. They say in much stronger Aframericanisms than I used in my book, that my style derives from the barroom and buffet flat. The book that they like and are boosting is [John W.] Vandercock's "Black Majesty."[2] I haven't read it, but I suppose it is grandiloquently romantic. Countee Cullen has been inspired to write a poem about it that might interest you. . . . I don't know if there are any people in the world who have lived such an interesting double group life (compelled to, of course) as American Negroes. But the reality of their lives that they escape from in an orgy of ecstacy, they don't want to see in print. And so they prefer to find artistic refuge in any romantic Nigger Heaven rather than face the amusing reality of a nigger in the woodpile.

I want to get back to freshen my rusty notes for my third book—and get a better background of Washington and New York. And then I'll settle down to do the "nice Negroes" that the Negro intelligentsia berates me for not writing about. And when I get it out I suppose they'll either murder me or make me a monument.

Best regards, Yours Sincerely
Claude McKay

WABLAR TLS

1. Burton Rascoe, "The Seamy Side," *Bookman,* April 1928, 183–84.
2. John W. Vandercock's *Black Majesty* (1928) was a historical novel about the Haitian Revolution.

To James Ivy

20 May 1928

Marseille, France

My dear Ivy,

Oh yes I remember you all right and thanks for your letter. Naturally, I expected the colored brethren to cuss me out and themselves crazy in their rhetorical darky way after they got through licking their fat lips over *Home to Harlem.* But their craziness does not move me in any way. I am an artist interested in imaginative portrayals of life and artistic truth. The average Aframerican is so thin-skinned, he cannot stand up like a man before the artistic presentation of any phase of Negro life. He is afraid of [the] white man's ridicule and mockery. He sees Negro life falsely as a propagandist, and a very unintelligent propagandist at that, and he wants only to see in art a what-will-look-good-to-the-white-public side of it. The sincere Negro artist cannot take any stock of the criticism of black Babbittry because it is ignorant. I don't think a sincere artistic presentation of Negro life in America, no matter whether it is high, low or middle, will ever please the black Babbitts because what they want is not a picture but [a] whitewash or veneer.

Poor hopeless lost souls in the hot desert of [the] white man's prejudice, I understand perfectly their attitude, but I cannot side with nor pity them, as I do not believe in human pity. I believe in human intellect and understanding and Babbitts, black or white, do not have intellect and understanding. They are lost souls and I am finding myself through instinct, intellect and understanding by digging down in the roots of my race and getting in warm contact with it and seeing it, in spite of all the black-and-white raging and clamor, as one great part of the whole of life. . . . So let the howling go on. The noisier the merrier. I've given the old colored beans something to chew on. I have seen only the criticisms in the *Pittsburgh Courier* anyway. I suppose it hurt the editors' patriotism the way I treated the Smoky City.

Of course, I had monies from many friends. [Eric] Walrond and [Harold] Jackman have helped and somebody, I don't remember who, did send me a contribution of money from a number of Harlemites among whom were Mrs. [Lucille Campbell Green] Randolph and Hubert Harrison and Grace Campbell. I was grateful and happy, especially in realization of the fact that Negroes are poor and cannot give away money with the careless gesture of white people unless someone is insensitive enough to take it out of them with [Marcus] Garvey graft, and buncombe. But since I have been over here I have gotten plenty of money from white admirers of myself and my poetry—sums ranging from hundred, five hundred, thousand francs through to two hundred dollars that I had at different times. I have worked very little—surely not more than a year in all at different intervals. Of course I have lived roughly and very cheaply, but with my sensual love of life I have had a tolerably good time. Preacher [William H.] Ferris writes out of the acrimony of his disappointed and frustrated spirit. He is a bad writer with two books to his credit and he lives under the delusion of thinking himself a writer and thinker. The man is just as badly botched in his whole make-up as the nigger newspaper for which he writes.

I am glad you are on the *Messenger.* It is a good magazine. Do [Chandler] Owen and [A. Philip] Randolph still have it? Under them it was a splendid magazine during and right after the War. It had the *Crisis* licked miles and miles, it was so well-edited and strong in its opinion. It was on the same level with the New York *Nation* which I think is the best American magazine from a journalistic point of view. But afterwards the tone of the *Messenger* went down a great deal in my opinion. I don't know why and how, one cannot always tell how decay begins, the same thing happened to the *Liberator.* I haven't seen the *Messenger* however since I left America in '22. You might let me see a copy with your stuff.

The reviews in the big-boss press are great, all of them, and the book is selling in spite of its stark realism. I am working hard on the second one, which is about the life of Negro boys on the beach here, as I have seen and lived it myself. I want to finish this month. Then I am going to travel and may look in on America again. I hope we meet again some day. Are you teaching in a college? How is your French? Couldn't you get a job up North? Let me hear from you again and good luck to you.

Yours sincerely,
Claude McKay

PCM

To William A. Bradley

25 May 1928

Marseille, France

Dear Bradley

Of course I want to meet [Eugene] Saxton when he comes, but I'll have to come from anywhere I may be, because I can't stay another month here and do any work. And I want to get done with it and rest awhile. I am very tired.

The only pleasure I could get out of the town during these last months was in my writing. I have been here for so long a stretch, it has been a great strain holding on to get the local atmosphere in the major part of "Banjo." And now that I have all that done, I must get out and away from this atmosphere that has become depressing to read the stuff over and make it better in perspective.

I couldn't quite make up my mind where to go. I am not in the mood nor in pocket for Paris and I didn't want to go down the coast again, although I have been invited by some friends at Beaulieu. I had Genoa particularly in view, for I have a good short story off Malty that I must see the port again to do real well. But all the fellows say it is no good now. I found it troublesome myself the last time I was in Italy. They held me up at Vintimille a whole night just for spite. That was three years ago and I hear things are worse now. Africa is the most interesting place just now, but I don't think I'd care for North Africa and I mustn't think of farther down until I am all through with "Banjo," so I have hit on Barcelona as the best for the moment.

I will leave here as soon as you send me next month's payment. I badly needed some things, but as there is no prospect of a little extra money just now, I shall still be happy to get away with the ms. only. . . . . Thank you for cashing the cheque. If you did make me my payments through Cook's as I think I begged you some time back, they would get to know me there and I could always cash little checks with them. But as I don't do any financial business with them, they won[']t handle a little cheque when it comes along.

No, I haven't seen the "Anthologie Negre"+ either in French or English, but I have read some reviews of it. In Jamaica we have a Treasure-trove of folk tales, all African, that the natives call "Anancy Stories." My father and mother knew wonderful ones. And they used to tell them to us on moonlight nights while we sat around them on the barbecue. We had many tunes to the verses. An Englishman collected many of them which he published in a book called Jamaica Song and Story.[1] It was while he was collecting them that he met me and became interested in some dialect ditties that I had written. He introduced me to the Governor down there, now Lord [Sidney] Olivier (he was a friend of [George Bernard] Shaw and quite literary)[,] and they helped me to publish some verses in the city daily and later a little book. I have forgotten nearly all the stories but I should like to go there some day and do a book about the present-day life of the peasants and bring in the stories, they telling them, as a kind of link between their present life and old Africa.

Yes, I should like to have the two parts of "Banjo" back so soon as you can get them. I[2] need them for complete revision as I have made additions to them that are not on the duplicate.

Oh and I wish you would let me know the precise flaws you thought were too long. I had a feeling about that myself in the conversation between Ray and the white fellow. I've got to change their character a little. That is one glaring fault in my handling of them that spoils the reality and as they are real persons, I've got to take the fault out which is my own fantasy. Thanks for writing + hoping to hear from you soon again so I can get over [?][.]

Sincerely Claude

+ Have you sent free [?] copy!

WABLAR TLS

1. Walter Jekyll and Alice Warner, *Jamaica Song and Story: Annancy Stories, Digging Sings, Ring Tunes and Dancing Tunes* (1904).

2. Beginning here, the remainder of the letter is handwritten.

To William A. Bradley

3 June 1928

Marseille, France

Dear Bradley

I am sending a letter from [Eugene] Saxton in which he criticizes "Banjo" as I asked him to do. Evidently he wrote it before getting the second section, but I don't suppose that would have made him change his opinion as there is no greater development of plot in that either.

Of course, I know that "Banjo" is not a novel in the conventional manner. It is obviously episodic and, knowing that, I have concentrated all my energy on the various scenes to make them real, vital and absorbing enough to carry the characters and my readers forward by their sheer interest.

Nevertheless the thread of the story is there, running through all of, and uniting them. . . . Banjo coming to Marseille, finding Latnah after losing the other girl. His neglect of Latnah, her yearning for him, her jealousy when she learns that he has spent so much money and continues to spend whenever he has some, on the white girl, the fight between the two women, followed by the breaking up of the beach-boys' group, Banjo's being ill in hospital getting better and obtaining by a ruse a sum of money to leave Marseille. . . . . . It is a plot allright, but not a complicated one that thickens as the story progresses, but a slight one thinly carried along by the episodes.

I might have made it a real triangle thing as you once suggested, but from the practical point of view I thought it better not to overstress Banjo's relations with the white girl for <u>our</u> public! I think that much of the success of "Home To Harlem," and what has saved it from censorship in spite of its undressed passages, is Jake's genuine feeling for the little brown of his own race. For that reason, I have made the sex relations between the beach-boys and the girls of the Ditch implicit throughout the text and not emphasizing it too much when it has to be more explicit. That is I treat it in the way it exists in America. The literate public knows that it exists (like homosexuality) but it does not want to see too much of the naked reality. I had to find a way to win my public in spite of that taboo and Latnah is a very handy and useful creature. There were other difficulties. I couldn't make much of a triangle story with a type like Banjo and two women obviously unmoral in an atmosphere so unsentimental as the Ditch. And a triangle story involving conflict between white and black would have to be highly intellectualised to reach the reading public and win sympathy—like Leonard Merrick's "Queer Companions."[1]

I thought of all the things I shouldn't do in doing this Marseille book. It couldn't be a regular love story because it is primarily a beach-boys' story with Banjo as the chief. And the time covers only one hectic summer of their lives in Marseille[.] The story moves forward slowly and in blocks. And that was exactly what I wanted to convey. The characters are sometimes almost lost in the vivid, crowded scene. . . . The low life of the port going round and round in the same vicious circle of cruelty and pleasure . . . the seamen coming here and, falling into its rhythm and going round with it for a short while until they fall out. That is the impression I want to convey and if I haven't done it, then the book is a failure and I'll have to put it away and do something else, before I can turn to casting it in another form.

The book is almost finished except for the last two chapters, about thirty or forty pages which I want to leave here to do, and am just waiting until you send me this month's cheque. I have been reading a novel of [H. G.] Wells' and [Sinclair] Lewis' "Arrowsmith" and I have remarked their way of carrying forward the tale by piling up a pyramid of incidents on a page or two and telling you that the chief characters have lived them without showing you. I think I could make my episodes go forward obviously by making use of "some days or weeks or months later."

But I should not want to begin with No. 6 as Saxton suggests. That would bring Ray into prominence right off at the beginning and as he is an outstanding intellectual character, it would have the effect of making Banjo too secondary, making the story subjective and spoiling most of the humor that the reviewing "boys" like and that I like myself. The scenes would lose much in gusto and free amorality. But by holding Ray back I think I give just enough of the modern touch of sophistication to the writing and achieve a kind of objective-subjective fusion—a mosaic that puzzles and yet intrigues and holds the reader. As you must know I planned all the scenes carefully out of the first writing that I scrapped and forming them one after the other to make a parade. But it seems that Saxton has been unable to see the formative design or I must not have made it real enough.

Anyway I will not write to him again until I hear from you and you return this letter. After all the book may be called anything else beside a novel. Marseille scenes or episodes or a novel without a plot. My feeling is that the episodes are all so real that reading one will carry the reader clear through them all to the end. The stuff is so much more varied than "Home To Harlem." But if I am wrong something ought to be done to make the scenes more interesting.

Yours Sincerely
Claude McKay

Since writing I have read the pages again from one to 250 and they show me a very clear sequence of events with Banjo standing out good natural, sensual + vacillating on all of them + that leaves me rather bewildered about Saxton's reaction[.]

CMcK

WABLAR TLS

1. McKay misremembers the title of English novelist Leonard Merrick's *The Quaint Companions* (1903), a novel about interracial marriage.

To Langston Hughes

13 June 1928

Barcelona, Spain

[On Letterhead: Au Lion d'Or, Barcelona]

Dear Langston,

I came down here from Marseille on the first and my first effort to write is this letter to you. This is the kind of city that you sleep and dream and dance and play and do anything except work in unless you're bound to. Certainly it is the most subtly fascinating place I've struck yet in Europe. It has all the substantial solidity of London, but it is colorful and not forbidding gray as London is. And there are no nasty slums. It's a great spread of avenidas and boulevards, and queer, narrow, crooked streets all bright and clean—not the rather overdone cleanliness you feel about Holland and nothing of the filth and stench of little French streets. And there is a langour about it that seems so strange when you realize that it is a hard-working and intensely industrial city. But that, it appears to me, is just why it is so charming.

I came down here to see Marseille in perspective while I am going over my book. I thought it would be better to get out of French atmosphere altogether. And there could be no better perspective, I think, than from here, for it is Mediterranean near to the scene of the book, yet with none of its color and character.

I wonder where you are now and are you thinking of coming over this summer? I should love to meet you face to face. [Countee] Cullen writes that he is coming over with Harold [Jackman] (he did not mention his wife) and that they will come to Marseille to see me, but I won't be there! Harold writes to me all the time and he is a very lovable character from his writing. I told him that you wanted to come over + I hope he would come too and let us all three get together, but he never replied about that + the only intimation I had of his coming was Cullen's mentioning it in two notes. I think I had you identified in the bridegroom's party but I am not sure. I thought you would have finished Lincoln [University] by now, judging from the time you put in at Columbia + Howard, only I don't know how long that was. At any rate they ought to give you your diploma. Your being at Lincoln is a feather in its cap + it would be stupid of them to let you quit without your diploma + then have to give you an honorary one some day. The unique thing about it all to me is that you did have the self-discipline to stick through the regular course after achieving fame and success as a poet. I haven't your last letter here and so this letter is not exactly an answer to it.

I see [W. E. B.] Du Bois has given me hell in the "Crisis."[1] If he had praised me it would have been a greater surprise. He is a good writer when he is bitter and combative, but he certainly knows nothing about real life and (judging from his writings) I don't think he understands what art is about and those two great defects prevent him from being a first-rate propagandist. However, I never thought he was dishonest + I feel that now by his printing my poem in the same issue in which he roasts me. There is a history to that poem. I sent it with three others to the "Crisis" towards the end of 1925 when I was ill and broke on the Riviera. At the same time I sent verses to three other N.Y. magazines, The Nation, Bookman, Century, telling the editors I was ill + broke and would be happy if they bought a poem from me. The Bookman ([John] Farrar) took two and paid me a dollar a line. The Nation paid me promptly for one. [Carl] Van Doren in the "Century" did not reply but he was kind enough to return the verses to [Eric] Walrond, although I had not enclosed stamps. The only magazine that did not reply was the "Crisis"! I know they are not rich by any means, but they might have replied. I thought they had not received the poems that they had gone astray in the mails. Then 2 years after, when I had my contract with Harper[']s, I saw 2 of the poems in the "Crisis." I immediately wrote to Du Bois about it. He sent me 10 dollars + said Jessie Fauset was in charge of the office when the verses arrived + neglected to reply. I told him then that those verses had been sent for a special purpose + that I did not care to see them in print now + I asked him to return the others. He never did + the next hint I had of them is in this number of the June "Crisis." I am sending him a letter now that will be good for him. It won't be the first time we have locked horns. But you know I don't give a damn. I love a fight, when I feel I am in the right. This is a bad pen so please forgive the formation of my letters.

Send me a card if you should be too busy to do a letter.

Ever Claude

The envelopes of the cafe were so ugly, I came to the forum to find an uglier one which I have [indecipherable] as I packed mine away in a basket [?] at Marseille by mistake.

LHP ALS

1. W. E. B. Du Bois, "The Browsing Reader," *Crisis,* June 1928, 202.

To W. E. B. Du Bois

18 June 1928

Barcelona, Spain

Dear Mr. DuBois,

I think I beseeched you over a year ago <u>not</u> to publish those poems I sent to the "Crisis" towards the end of 1925.

I must remind you again that those poems were sent to the "Crisis" for a special purpose. I was ill. I had no money. I wrote to a number of New York publications, including the "Crisis," frankly stating my situation and asking them to help me by buying a poem or more. I received prompt replies and help from some of the publications. Others that did not accept had the courtesy, with one exception, to return my poems. The exception was the "Crisis" (the only Negro publication I wrote to) which neither replied nor returned the poems. About a year and a half later, when I saw two of the poems in the "Crisis" I was surprised, because, as I said then in a letter to you (the duplicate unfortunately is in Paris) I thought the poems had gone astray in the mails. You replied with a cheque for the published ones stating thet [*sic*] Miss [Jessie] Fauset was in charge when I wrote and she, I suppose, had no time to waste on a non-influential and down-and-out fellow-writer!

I had expected you, after receiving my letter, to return and not make use of the remaining poems. I wrote to my agent in New York to call in all the prose and verse that I had sent out to various magazines. These were all returned and if I did not list the "Crisis" it was because I had already written to the Editor and I took it as a matter of course that a Negro publication of a recognised high standard would not fail to conform to the common rules of journalistic ethics.

My reasons for not wanting any of the things I sent out long ago published now are private and tactical, and I particularly resent the publication of my poem in the same number of the "Crisis" in which, in criticising my novel, the Editor steps outside the limits of criticism to become personal. I should think that a publication so holy-clean and righteous-pure as the "Crisis" should hesitate about printing anything from the pen of a writer who wallows so much in "dirt," "filth," "drunken[n]ess," "fighting," and "lascivious sexual promiscuity."

But I have no objection to the quoted phrases as criticism, if you did not also choose (to employ the Coolidgism) to question my motive in writing my book and bring it down to the level of the fish market. Now this is personal and you have been an editor long enough to know that it has nothing to do with criticism. And so I will reply personally to you Mr. DuBois by retorting that nowhere in your writings do you reveal any comprehension of esthetics and therefore you are not competent nor qualified to pass judgement upon any work of art.

My motive for writing is simply that I began in my boyhood to be an artist in words and I have stuck to that in spite of the contrary forces and colors of life that I have had to contend against through various adventures, mistakes, successes, strength and weakness of body that the artist-soul, more or less, has to pass through. Certainly I sympathise with and even pity you for not understanding my motive, because you have been forced from a normal career to enter a special field of racial propaganda and, honorable though that field may be, it has precluded you from contact with real life, for propaganda is fundamentally but a one-sided idea of life. Therefore I should not be surprised when you mistake the art of life for nonsense and try to pass off propaganda as life in art!

Finally, deep-sunk in depravity though he may be, the author of "Home To Harlem" prefers to remain unrepentant and unregenerate and he "distinctly" is not grateful for any free baptism of grace in the cleansing pages of the "Crisis."

Yours for more "utter absence of restraint"[1]

Claude McKay

WEBDP TLS

1. In Du Bois's review of *Home to Harlem*, he writes of McKay, "He has used every art and emphasis to paint drunkenness, fighting, lascivious sexual promiscuity and utter absence of restraint in as bold and as bright colors as he can." W. E. B. Du Bois, "The Browsing Reader," *Crisis*, June 1928, 202.

To James Weldon Johnson

6 July 1928

Barcelona, Spain

Dear Johnson

I am not sure if I replied to your last letter and th[anked][1] you for the clippings. I put a pile of letters together to answer when I got here and forgot the bundle at Marseille.

I have been here since the beginning of June. I wanted to see Marseille from a distance while re-writing my book and this place gives me just about the right perspective.

I have heard from Max [Eastman] yesterday and am glad you hooked him to approach Nancy Markhoff for me. I haven't got that letter yet, but the immigration authorities at Charleston wrote me that they have forwarded my papers to the Consul at Marseille and I hope I shall have all the documents necessary when I get back there. I should like to have the matter straightened out now so that I may know just what is my status at any time I may want to return. I really don't know when yet.

Perhaps you know Barcelona—a beautiful city and it is a happy change after France and more to my fancy, but I am working so hard I haven't had a chance to enjoy anything yet.

With kind regards
Sincerely Yours
Claude McKay

JWJP TLS

1. The letter is torn, obscuring this word.

To William A. Bradley

10 July [1928]

Barcelona, Spain

Dear Bradley

Your letter of the 5th crossed mine which it anticipated. I am relieved to hear about the money arrangement, but I suppose it was better and just as well that I should send you that long letter explaining everything. I knew it was no fault of yours as I said nor even of the firm that I was always in a pickle, but rather the result of my own unfavorable situation. [T. F.] Tracy used to have the same trouble before his wife brought him a little money and when he was getting a little pension from the Government. It was always late.

I thought that if [Eugene] Saxton really wanted to see me I could get to Marseille to meet him, but what I wanted to see him particularly about was the money arrangement, which he has already so considerately and promptly attended to. And he would want to talk over the book I suppose. I understand what is lacking. I got it at once from his letter. But I would much prefer that you both see the whole thing complete before making any further criticism. For the third and last part is as different from the second as the second was from the first. Yet they are all coordinated. It is really after the manner of "Home To Harlem." I am working on the very last chapter now and that is the hardest for I have a gang of people to dispose of. I wish I could finish it before Saxton goes back. I will by the end of this month. Then he could read it and I would like to meet him for a talk after that. All the same I will go to Marseille to meet him if he wants to. I have to anyway sometime this month to see Countee Cullen and a friend of mine travelling together from New York.

I wish you could send the money to Cook[']s or the American Express either in pounds or dollars so I can have British or American money orders when I am travelling. I leave it to you however to do it the best way you can. Lloyd's bank is also a good agency. . . . . I think I'll just stick it out here until the book is finished. It is good for a change. It's a great city. Sentimental music in all the little and big cafes but it is player[1] piano. There are bands however playing the Catalan dances at night + they are [some] of the most beautiful things I have ever seen anywhere around[.]

Claude McKay

It is hot however + that gives the people something of the easy laziness of Negroes, but they are hardworking. I think you would like them if you came[.]

WABLAR TLS

1. Beginning with this word, the remainder of the letter is handwritten.

To Harold Jackman

26 July 1928

Marseille, France

Evidently we have bungled trying to meet each other. I didn't quite understand your last card—your asking in Marseille my private address when you knew I was in Barcelona! Anyway I replied and they said at the Amer. Ex. that you had my letter on Monday. I left Barcelona Monday afternoon, arriving here at 7 a.m. Tuesday morning. I lost two weeks rent, paid in advance + worth a month in Marseille, just to get here. I had asked you expressly in my letter to leave a message at any of these three places: Cook's, Am. Ex, or Hotel Nautique. You did neither so if you had not even left on Monday I did not know where to find you! I felt, naturally, that you were really less keen about seeing me than you made me think by your letters! I turned down exactly four invitations, 3 to go to the Cote d'Azur, 1 to Paris from white friends (enthusiastic over "Home To Harlem")[,] fare + expenses guaranteed. But I felt no interest nor enthusiasm and went off alone to Barcelona. I came back here simply because I was eager to see you, because you have shown such friendly interest in me + at a time when I needed real friendship + hadn't much of that! I wanted to show you the scenes here that I am writing about. And to take you to Barcelona for a trip if you could go. Such a beautiful town! I did not finish my chapter, but I brought my machine along + will stay here + work for about 2 weeks before returning to Spain.

Sorry, Claude

CMP APS

To William A. Bradley

24 August 1928

Barcelona, Spain

Dear Bradley

At last I have finished "Banjo," three hundred and seventy odd pages, and I am fagged out. I am revising it with a pen and shall have to find someone to fair-type. I'm so tired of the typewriter I can't revise on it. It was hard grilling finishing. For days I could do nothing, it was so hot, and sometimes I couldn't get more than a paragraph done. I ought to finish the revision by the middle of September. Now that I am through with the actual writing I may move on to some other place. It is very expensive here, four times dearer than France. But I have enjoyed Barcelona. I have had lots of fun dancing in the street dances that are held in all parts of the city over the weekend. I like the Spaniards. They are alert and industrious, yet provincial—in a nice sense. I have never been in any big city like this where I felt so little of outside international influence. Yet they say this is the most cosmopolitan of Spanish cities.

I am enclosing a letter from a playmaker. As you have better contact than I with New York, you might find out if he is a good one and worth working with. I wouldn't mind collaborating with a man who can put the thing over. I can't do it by myself for I know nothing of stage technique and have no time to study it right now. But I don't want to stand fooling with anybody who isn't the right sort.

Maybe as you are my representative it would be better for you to handle the matter. I don't remember what the contract said about it whether I have the right or not to go ahead and choose a collaborator.

Did you never hear anything from any of the short stories? I have just seen by the "Nation" that Crystal Eastman is dead. She was one of my best friends and I feel terribly down.

Hoping you are well
Sincerely Yours
Claude McKay

WABLAR ALS

To Langston Hughes

26 August 1928

Barcelona, Spain

I should be happy to hear from you, where you are and what doing [*sic*]. I don't know if you received the letter I sent you on first getting here. I have finished my book, much longer, more varied and compact than the first. Sorry I did not see you this summer. I went back to Marseille for a few days to meet [Harold] Jackman + [Countee] Cullen but I missed them: I think I'll soon be on the move again. Wish you would send a card or something[.]

Claude

LHP APS

To James Weldon Johnson

27 August 1928

Barcelona, Spain

Dear Johnson

Thank you for sending Nancy Markhoff's address. The fact that she is actually in Moscow rather nullifies the chance of her being useful to me at present and so I think I will not trouble to write, but wait until she returns.

I have completed the new book, but I have the job of revision before me. However I feel a little freer and with all the correspondence under my hand I shall take up the matter of returning with the consul. If it proves to be too much work and trouble I shall ask [William A.] Bradley to tackle it as he said he would.

With kindest regard and hoping you are well,

Sincerely Yours
Claude McKay

JWJP TLS

To William A. Bradley

7 September 1928[1]

Marseille, France

Dear Bradley

I was two weeks at Nice and have just got back to find your letter of last Sunday. I am nearly broke but I had a good rest and a good time all the same.

Thank you for the good news about "Home To Harlem." I found a great pile of papers and letters on my return, among them one from the publicity manager of Harper[']s, date March 20, saying "the book is going over something grand."

Yes, it was a hard struggle as you say, but I have never felt personally bitter about life for it, because I realize that most of it is the direct result of my own temperament. I had a number of easy chances which I let slip from temperamental reasons. However if I had not travelled that hard road I could not have come through with "Home To Harlem"! Another thing I think I always got in with the wrong crowd, people who were interesting from the standpoint of ideas, but not really the kind to help me find my creative metier. Max [Eastman] always discouraged me about writing prose, although I knew all along that I had things to say that couldn't find expression in the form of poetry I prefer to write. But Max was always sentimental about poetry, considering it the aristocratic thing compared to prose.

By the way his book fell quite flat.[2] He said Albert Boni managed it badly and it fell between two seasons, and wasn't reviewed, you know Boni was trying to get me to go over to him when he came to see Max at Antibes—after he heard that Harper had taken me on—but I wasn't such a fool to consider it, although what he said was interesting enough, after you putting me over with Harper[']s.

I had a letter from [Eugene] Saxton of March 15th date saying he was sending me on that very date a special leather-bound copy of "Home To Harlem[.]" The letter arrived the 26th according to Cook's stamp but the book hasn't come + I don't know if it is lost in the mails. I found magazines here that were mailed after the 20th.

Could you tell me anything about payment for articles by French sources? "Europe" published my Bad Boy in last month[']s issue, but I haven't heard a word from them about payment! And it would be a handy thing right now. I am in a dilemma, not knowing if they mail you a cheque like American publications or if they are waiting to be reminded!

After my little vacation I feel refreshed to carry on with "Banjo" and I shall have another hundred pages or more ready for you at the end of this month. Not before! But it will be easy work from now on[,] I have the whole thing planned straight through to the very end.

I had another letter from Johnson James Weldon [*sic*] enclosing a memorandum from the assistant Secretary of State (his friend) about the two possibilities of my returning. It sounds rather complicated + I should go to see the Consul here but I haven't gone yet. I dread official bureaus + I hate to be distracted while I am working. I may go after I get through the present chapter of "Banjo." Then I will send you the letter if all doesn[']t go well.—Some of the Negro papers say I have written a dirty rotten book + are calling me all sorts of names!

Thanks again for writing[.]

Sincerely
Claude McKay

WABLAR ALS

1. While McKay clearly dated this letter "Sept 7," internal evidence suggests that the letter is from early April 1928.

2. Likely Eastman's quasi-autobiographical novel *Venture,* published in December 1927.

To William A. Bradley

1 October 1928

Casablanca, Morocco

Dear Bradley

I left Barcelona towards the end of August and visiting Valencia, Sevilla and Tangier, have just arrived here, to find your letter of August 28 and a cargo of correspondence. I might have stayed on longer in Barcelona if I had the least intimation that you were thinking of coming down, especially as I wanted to go to Majorca myself and didn't. If you haven't gone yet and are thinking of going any time this fall or winter a comfortable and not dear place to stay is the Persian Floret right on one of the Ramblas near the Plaza [de] Cataluña.

I took it into my head to come here after meeting again in Barcelona a Martinique navigateur whom I had met in Marseille and who makes his home here among the Arabs. There is a little colony of them here—Negroes who are not Mussulmen—and it has been very interesting to come among them. For the first time in my life I feel really moved to make casual notes about a new place visited. It is very interesting to see how these colored fellows have adapted themselves to the ways of the Arabs, having Arab wives and all living together in a kind of community Arab house in one of the native quarters a long way from the ville European. They live in a simple, primitive way and although the rooms and the charming court that the families share in common are clean, it is indescribably filthy and smelly outside around, for there is no sewage system. It is the same in the old native town abutting the European.

But away from that the life is very stimulating with its rich variety of color. Now that I am among the Arabs among themselves, I feel about them just as I did about the East Indians when I was a boy and have, in a way, always felt. The two peoples resemble very much. I haven't the slightest sympathetic attraction towards them, but there is so much to admire. There are certainly wonderful types among them, majestic men and women and so dignified and aristocratic compared to the Europeans. There are splendid types of Jews too who make me think of the patriarchs. I have never been able to analyze why I don't feel drawn towards Arabs and Indians. Among the Chinese, on the other hand, I feel comfortable just like one of them even though I don't understand their language.

The European life here is very active—quite different from Spain where a lazy languor pervades everything, everywhere. At least so it seemed to me. There are fine new buildings of neo-arabesque architecture and all over the town between the port and the "gare" buildings are going up feverishly. But I have never seen so much dust and sand before and that makes the landscape sad and uninviting. There are no trees—only shrubs, miserable things under the dust. In the new town they are just putting trees in the streets[.]

All I have seen here is spurring me on to go to West Africa. I have been thinking of a trip there for the last ten years and I want to make it now that I have the chance. And the life of the Negroes among the Arabs here make[s] me more than ever curious to go and see the real thing. I think I could do a book of my trip from a new angle that would be worth the experience of going.

I suppose I could do the trip there and back comfortably on a thousand dollars. And if you can get this sum from Harper's for me, I'll leave as soon as it arrives. You might let me know before hand when it is coming, so I may book my passage in advance. The British Bank of West Africa here is the best for International transactions and as I think I shall go to Liberia and British territory in West Africa it will be better if you ask them to make the money payable in dollars or pounds. I[']ll only draw enough with a little over for the passage there and have the rest transferred by the bank for me.

Also if you have any payments for me for September and October I shall be happy to get some as I am about at the end of my resources.

And now to "Banjo." I toted it along with me, rereading[,] emendating, rewriting and retyping and pasting all the time, and it is now almost as I want it. I shall send it off during this week. If you think it is in shape too awful to go to Harper's, Miss Jessie Hyde of 8 bis rue Campagne Première, will type it over for me. I know her well. She has done work for me before and is a good typist.

My travelling about again is doing me good and I am feeling fine and I hope you are too and your family. Tangier is a great place[,] a kind of little Marseille and more interesting than Casablanca from an artistic point of view.—Thank you for that cutting from "Comedia."

Sincerely Yours
Claude McKay

WABLAR ALS

To William A. Bradley

18 October 1928

Casablanca, Morocco

Dear Bradley

I have completed and forwarded to you to-day the m.s. of "Banjo" under two covers. The last chapter was the most difficult and it took me over a month to make it right. Now I am satisfied with the thing as a whole. The third pack is full of what some people may call propaganda, but I think it fits neatly in with the rest of the book as it is not deliberately dragged in from outside, but arrives from my own experiences, thoughts and feelings. It was a real job doing the whole thing again and I feel exhausted. I ought to have made a final reading but I couldn't work up the will.

If you think it is all right and don't [*sic*] need doctoring again then anything that is left undone I must pick up in the proofs when I return from West Africa.

Thanks for the two cheques for September and October. Now that I am free I want to visit Fez and Marrakech before leaving. I shall make arrangements with the shipping company for the West African trip before going, counting on the money coming from New York. And when it comes I wish you will please have it transferred direct to the bank and not through the post office. I think that is the safest way for a large sum of money. They tell me at the British Post Office that it is unsafe to have money sent by letter post. The British Bank of West Africa here is correspondent for the Guaranty Trust so I have no trouble with my cheques.

I don't want to look at the typewriter for months. I'll take notes though for the new book and make it our third + put back the short stories for our fourth. What do you think?

[Eugene] Saxton says I ought to visit America about the time "Banjo" is published. I don't know what to do about my correspondence for the Consul at Marseille (now that I am tied up for the next few months on this Africa voyage) whether I should send them to you or write the Consul and ask him to reply to you as my friend + representative as I am out of France + hard to get at. Anyway before leaving for West Africa I ought to start something about my American trip.

I am sending "Banjo" by boat as that is safer—and cheaper.

Sincerely Yours
Claude McKay

I am sorry you had an accident + were ill and glad to hear you are better.

WABLAR ALS

To William A. Bradley

2 November 1928

Fez, Morocco

Dear Bradley

I came here from Rabat a few days ago and I've been having such a great time in the native town I'll have to quit (because my head can't stand the storm) and go back to Casablanca and to Marrakech, where I hope to spend a week. After, I'll start for West Africa as soon as the money arrives. I should have started for Casablanca today but I am broke and must wait until the bank puts through the October cheque + remits it here.

The native town is a wonder. The Arabs take to me quite as the people of all classes did in Russia and I have visited and been entertained in many homes—every day during my six days here, sometimes 3 homes during the day and I must take cous-cous or tea in each, while I present a bottle of wine or liqueur in return. The "indigines" are not allowed to buy wine and liqueurs—openly. I can buy, of course, although I am not taking any wine at all now. Oh, about my taking a bottle of something—they say the custom is that anyone invited to an Arab home must take some kind of a gift. I have some very amusing stories to tell you when we do meet.

I get to know many things as I am not French—nor white. I've been in many dens where they make the "kiff" [*sic*] and an old medieval house with a wonderful court where young girls—blacks and Arabs—are actually sold—secretly. But it is not the white-slavery traffic, nor the old-time Negro slavery, it is rather a way of getting a domestic servant or a slave-wife. It is a big experience to know the Arabs among themselves. My admiration is greatly increased although I don't feel drawn to them in any way. I don't feel I would want to live among them a long time as I did among the Russians.

Curiously Fez-Medina is very reminiscent of Moscow. The minarets of the many mosques have the same rich jewel colours of the Moscow churches and I have seen Arabs here of the same features of the Tartar type of Russians. And it is those Arab types that I like most. It is very amusing in the Arab homes to watch the women agitating the curtains and peeping at you even showing you a little of the unveiled face that you are not supposed to see. Once I did stare too much at one of the women's quarters and my Arab companion told me I should never look even if the women did <u>accidentally</u> expose their features, for that would be taken as an affront to the men and Arab customs.

I am anxious to hear what you think of the finish of "Banjo." If your opinion is favorable I know [I] won't have to worry about its fate. It is raining here and cold although it is far enough South. But the country here is surrounded by mountains, some of them white with snow. I left both my overcoat + raincoat at Marseille + must make the best of it.

With best wishes Yours Sincerely
Claude McKay

WABLAR ALS

To Langston Hughes

9 November 1928

Fez, Morocco

My dear Langston

It was great to get your gripping letter here at Fez, the great capital of the North African Arabs, where I am staying for a few days. You are surely going to be a great American prose artist. Your letter says so, whatever you may think.

Just now I am reflecting on "the gentle act of making enemies" as Oscar Wilde, [James McNeill] Whistler, or some wit of the eighteen-nineties said. For I have fallen out with Harold Jackman whose friendship I valued so highly. I wanted to hold his friendship but he is a very refined soul as I am very sensitive and I suppose my frank manner of writing to him (after I made the trip specially from Barcelona to meet him in Marseilles on his return from Algiers and arriving found that he had left—faithful to his itinerary—on the very day of the early morning of my arrival) must have been too brutal. I wrote another letter which I really intended to clear the ground for a better understanding between us, but I believe now it was more offensive than the other for Harold did not even acknowledge it!

I hate to lose my friends—especially the friends of my own race. I suppose that with the great white sea of humankind pressing around we are prone to get on edge sharply critical of another—especially when we are over race-conscious and intellectual. Maybe that is why you as well as myself are so fond of and happy with the common rough colored fellows!

I waited and waited in Spain expecting to hear of you from some point in Europe and that we would meet. I was imagining what fun it would be going round the country with you. I was broke for the first month there but [Eugene] Saxton of Harper[']s cabled me 500 and it would have been allright if you were with me—even if you were low in funds. I left Spain because I wanted to come to Africa. I stayed in Casablanca a month and finished the rewriting of my new novel, "Banjo." Then I came on here to Fez, the great Capital of Morocco. The native city is splendid with narrow streets winding uphill and all about and jewel-colored minarets that make me think of Moscow. And many of the Arabs are like the Moscovites. Only difference, where the Russians are warm-hearted + entertainable people the Arabs are curious and eager like keen knife blades. But they have entertained me too in the gorgeous rich oriental style and I have been having so much fun going around in a free native way that I got the French police on to me, but I made one over them. I have been to many marriages—not many—three—and I ate and drank too much for my stomach. Arab music—there was plenty of it at the marriages—is a barbarous thing and with the influence of the Sudanese and Sengalese [*sic*] which is great here, it sometimes becomes wildly savage. My head was way to[o] bursty [?] under it. I don't know if I could stand the Harlem cabarets again as I used to.

I was sorry to miss you but glad you had a fine time in New Orleans and Cuba. You have been running around like me. Do you know I was at Harvard for a few months—as a waiter at Memorial Hall. I had two fine colored boys at my table.

Thank you for all the news. [Wallace] Thurman has not written for a long time. I'm glad he is married to a nice girl. I myself feel like marrying—again. I fell in love with a fine Sengalese [*sic*] girl at Casablanca. Her father said I could have her for 3000 francs! I couldn't afford it! Maybe I may do the crazy thing before I leave old Africa. All that I feel and see here is pushing me to go to tropical Africa.

I read about Paul Robeson's case in London, also that he has been expelled from Equity.[1] By the way, since you have some experience of the stage writing for it—it may be interesting if we could collaborate on something together. Some man in New York wrote that he would like to do "Home To Harlem" into stage form with me. I sent his correspondence on to Saxton and I haven't heard anything further. I couldn't do anything as Saxton—I mean Harper—holds the stage rights.

If I had plenty of money to invest I would put it into a real cabaret for the common-working Negroes such as was the old Palace on Fifth or Madison Avenue, with a balcony for the whites. The Negro managers are all asses. They can never understand that the white patrons flock to the Negro cabarets because they want to see the colored babies turn loose enjoying themselves in their own "decor."

I am sending you some cuttings—one about Robeson. I can[']t locate. Write me again and if ever you see Harold tell him how sorry I am we broke.

I have promised Harper[']s to come back to New York when "Banjo" is published. I don't know if I'll be able to stand coming back. In the meantime—until I hear from you again—my warmest wishes + I hope the short stories are as rich as your poems. I still love the 2nd book more than the first[.] The poems are neck and neck with the best of Paul Green's short plays—

Ever Claude

LHP ALS

1. Paul Robeson was suspended from the Actors' Equity Association in September 1928 after he failed to appear in New York for a revue for which he had signed a contract. At the time he was performing in a wildly successful production of *Show Boat* in London. Robeson did not return to the United States until 1939.

To James Weldon Johnson

10 November 1928

Fez, Morocco

Dear Johnson

Thanks for your letters which followed me here to Fez in Morocco which I am doing for a few weeks with the hope of going a little later to West Africa.

I have completely finished my new book "Banjo" and am taking a holiday and thinking about the third—but no more creative writing for a long spell. "Banjo" has knocked me down and out for the present. Morocco is a great adventure for me—all the races of the world are here, struggling, fighting and living topsy-turvy together. Plenty of color among the Arabs +

Negroes. Here at Fez I have been entertained in the homes of many Arabs—attended a Negro wedding at Casablanca and two Arab weddings here. They were barbarian affairs, dancing that would make a Harlem cabaret look like nothing at all. At the feast we tore the mutton and fowl with our fingers and stuffed our mouths full, but it was a little too much for me when they scooped up the vegetables with their hands and after tasting it threw back what was left in the same common dish.

The Mellahs, the Jewish quarters, are not nearly as interesting as the Medinas, the Arab quarters, but they are interesting when compared with the ghettos of New York. In the dirtiest and smelliest parts of the Mellahs I feel as if I were in the cradle of the American ghettos. Here you find Jews + Arabs, big young men, peddlers, going round in long shirts and often barefooted and obviously worse off than the same class of Negroes in the South and in the West Indies. The hatred between the Arabs and Jews is strong—social, traditional and economic. The Jews under the French regime have certain privileges over the Morrocans [*sic*], such as selling strong drink, and I have noticed in some instances where they take advantage of that privilege to fleece the Arabs. Here everybody is trying to get the best of the other in a gaudy riotous way that tickles. And that is a big relieving [?] difference between the business here from the grim thing it is in Europe and America.

I shall let you hear from me from time to time. Now I am finished with the book I shall have time to [indecipherable] with the Consul[.]

Thanks for writing.

Ever Sincerely
Claude McKay

JWJP ALS

To Charlotte Osgood Mason

1 December 1928

Fez or Marrakesh, Morocco (?)

Dear Mrs Mason

Forgive me for writing through the Literary Digest and so tardily, but I left your address among other things in Marseille and it was only through the card of the Literary Digest following me here to North Africa that I learned, happily, that you had renewed my subscription to that journal and surely also to the Mercury and Books that I have been receiving again.

I have been here in North Africa for about two months and find it very interesting especially from the standpoint of the various races and strange types struggling through their lives here, the primitive and barbaric life of the natives changing under the feverish springing up of European civilization.

I expect to go down to West Africa[,] for the features of interest here whet my desire to go farther and get some fresh material to put with all I have stored to do a book on my wanderings.

Thank you very much for the magazines and I hope you will drop me a note to the above address so that I shall have your address if I should happen to miss Marseille on my return to Europe.

Yours Very Sincerely
Claude McKay

ALP TLS

To William A. Bradley

15 December 1928

Marrakesh, Morocco

Dear Bradley

I received your registered letter and mandat here. Thank you. Probably it crossed mine with the f500 enclosed which I hope you got allright. You might send it back to me at <u>Post Restante, Casablanca</u>. I wish you would write me there too and tell me the news about "Banjo," whether Saxton found it allright or not. And if it is allright when will the first proofs be ready! I still have a few more things to cut out and put in. But if it is being done, I should like to get at the proofs before going on to West Africa. It is so far away down if you wanted to get at me. I am about through Maroc now and I thought I could go to Tangier + finish the proofs—but if "Banjo" is being carried over until next fall that would not be necessary + I would complete my arrangements to go straight to West Africa from Casablanca. Please let me hear what you think. I will write soon and tell you about Marrakesh and my run around over the country.

Ever Sincerely
Claude McKay

PS

Thanks for the Royalty list. I shall look it over in due time and that was surely allright of you to correct the mistake made in my favor against you.

CM

WABLAR ALS

To Langston Hughes

18 December 1928

Marrakesh, Morocco

You must have received my letter from Fez. I am now at the other end of the country[.] I want to go to West Africa + I want very much to go back to Europe + stay some time at Tanger which your fine poem made fascinating + memorable for me[.] You will hear from me whatever I do[.] Christmas + New Years greeting.

Claude

LHP APS

To William A. Bradley

1 January 1929

Rabat, Morocco

[On Letterhead: Central Hotel, Rabat]

Dear Bradley

I am leaving for Tangier today or tomorrow and will send you a new address in a few days. It is essential for the reception of "Banjo" that I should see the proofs. There are three chapters, "Everybody Doing it," "The Blue Cinema" and another that need just a few lines each to make them strong and complete[.] You know yourself how a few careless phrases might spoil a whole book. At Tangier I'll be in easy reach of you and New York and if I don't like it there I shall cross over to Spain or France again.

Just now I think it is more important to have "Banjo" all right than to go on to West Africa. I am thinking of postponing the trip at present. The North African tournée has been very expensive and the idea of the kind of book I want to do looms bigger and bigger, assuming such proportions, when I scan the comparative and relative notes that I have made, that I feel I had better wait until I can afford to do the most important points of British and French West Africa and continue to the Cape, if possible, and then back to Europe by way of Egypt.

That is a big programme and I had better wait to see if it is realizable. I am sure you'll agree. That it isn't worth-while doing a superficial travel book of places and things when I am going over ground that has been so well beaten by others. The most interesting thing then is the human element from an American Negro's point of view (I still consider myself more American in outlook in spite of my British subjectship). In the book I plan to do I want to draw on the souvenirs of all my other travels and use this North Africa as a point of central interest. I am sure I won't strike any other place like it of more interest to American readers from a sociological angle.

In the meantime, beside the short stories (were they returned from New York?) I have in mind the romance of black, yellow and white that I dropped to do "Home To Harlem."[1] But I'll have to go back to the States to develop the background and so I ought to get busy about that.

By the way I have a letter from an American friend, now connected in some way with legal matters and he writes that I should not have been charged the 5% on my advance royalty payments as my status is still that of [a] resident of the United States, if I have done nothing abroad that would cause me to lose it. He also asked me to give him power of attorney to take up the matter for me, but I want to have your opinion and [Eugene] Saxton's first. In that case it shouldn't be so difficult for me to return since I have never actually taken up residence abroad, so I shall write to the Consul at Marseille as soon as possible and see what he has to say.

Thanks for the mandat for 500 dollars wishing you a happy New Year—

Sincerely
Claude McKay

WABLAR ALS

1. McKay refers to an abandoned novel project (ca. 1926–27) that he referred to in letters as "Black Belt."

To William A. Bradley

18 January 1929

Tangier, Morocco

Dear Bradley

I got your letter last night. I have already typed out the few changes I have to make and so soon as either set of the proofs arrives I'll set to work and get it done in a day and express to [Eugene] Saxton. It is precisely the first edition I want to get in on so that the reviewing copies should not go out before I get the proofs to Saxton. That is most important for me, especially as he has made changes, for I am sure there'll be things for me to make right.

I came on here suffering from acute sciatica and slight spinal trouble and I am taking electrical treatment at a clinic. My fingers are shy of the touch of the pen but all the same I shan't let that prevent my going straight through with the proofs.

Am sorry now I did not write you from Casablanca as that might have prevented the proofs going there. I was waiting all along for word of when they would be ready. Miss Dherny[1] dates the copy of Saxton's letter about them November 1. But that evidently must be a mistake for December 1. Otherwise you would have had enough time to notify me long before I wrote to you from Marrakesh, on about that time which was near Christmas, and I should have held myself ready and avoided the ten days less which came from my making a week's visit to Meknes.

I see only one way of getting the book out in time. When I receive the original, if there is nothing of first importance that justifies holding I'll write "go ahead" and leave the additions off. But if there is something to rectify I may as well get everything in on the first proofs[.]

Yours Sincerely
Claude McKay

No I won't give my friend power of attorney[.] Your suggestion is the better way.

WABLAR TLS

1. Bradley's secretary.

To American Consul General in Marseille

18 January 1929

Tangier, Morocco

Sir

About a year ago when I was staying in Marseille and wishing to return to the United States, I asked a friend, Mr James Weldon Johnson of New York, to ascertain what steps were necessary to take.

In reply Mr Johnson sent me a copy of a letter from the Assistant Secretary of State, Mr Wilbur Carr, to himself with a form letter of advice to aliens seeking non-quota visas as returning aliens and he also suggested I should call on you. I did not do so then, not having the proof of my entry into the United States, for which I wrote to the Immigration Department.

But before the reply came stating that the information had been sent to you directly I left Marseille for another part of France and have been travelling about since in Spain and in North Africa where I am now.

As you have the documents, (Mr Johnson informed me that Mr Carr had written to you) I should be very grateful if you would advise me about the matter, for I still wish to return to the States, if possible when my new book is published this Spring.

I give the bare facts about myself: I arrived in the United States from Jamaica in June or July of 1912 to complete my education. After leaving college I decided to stay in the States, first in a business capacity and later working at different jobs. In 1922 I published a book of poems with the firm of Harcourt, Brace & Co. and in the fall of the same year I visited England and Germany. From Germany I had the opportunity of going to Russia to join my friend, Max Eastman. I returned to Europe in the Spring of 1923 and lived for nearly a year in Germany and later in France, where I have been doing my literary work. When I left New York the new immigration laws had not been passed and I had expected to return in six months, as I did not even give up my studio that I subletted from a Mr Perrier of 25 East 14th street, but my absence lengthened into years and there was no incentive strong enough for me to act upon.

I should like to reestablish residence in the United States, because, firstly, after spending all the formative years of my life there I came to regard it as home, secondly, my nearest relative is living there and, thirdly, I make my living by writing and selling my literary production to the American public.

As I may leave here at any time for an unknown destination I should be much obliged if you would reply to me in care of my representative:—MR. W. A. Bradley, 5 Rue Saint-Louis-en-l'Ile, Paris, 4.

I beg to remain
Sir
Yours Sincerely

CMP TLU (copy)

To William A. Bradley

25 January 1929

Tangier, Morocco

Dear Bradley,

I sent the proofs off on Tuesday. I cabled [Eugene] Saxton to wait, thanks for address, and I have also asked him to send the very first copy of "Banjo" available for you to express to me wherever I may be, so that I may make additional corrections, with the aid of the original manuscript for the future editions. It hasn't yet arrived. There were some things awry in the proofs that I could not make right or I did not have the original to consult.

The weather is bad here, no sun, and therefore hard on my sciatica.[1] In my next letter I hope to tell you my definite plans. I am awaiting news so that I can decide just what I will do next. I suppose I ought to go back to America some time this year.

Besides my sciatica treatment I am having my tooth repaired by an American dentist so I shall probably be there about a month.

Did you enjoy Marseille? Whatever I do I shall have to go back there to get my things. With best wishes[.]

Yours Sincerely
Claude McKay

WABLAR ALS

1. Paragraph not indented in original.

To William A. Bradley

30 January 1929

Tangier, Morocco

Dear Bradley

Confirming my telegram I write.[1] I suppose you could not have seen my typed script after it came from Harper. Somebody has outrageously made havoc and hash of the thing by sprinkling it throughout with nice literary phrases.

I cannot understand [Eugene] Saxton allowing such a thing and I am at a loss to know in what light he considers me and my work. I thought he was a man of taste. He allows someone to intersperse a number of Fannie Hurst and Elinor Glyn phrases throughout my work and expects me on top of all that to let him run off the first edition without my seeing proofs.

I could understand if they had taken out phrases that the censor might pick on. But they have chosen to substitute banal phrases for my simple and solid old English words. I may as well be frank and say that if the first edition is run off and sent out to the reviewers I shall not feel myself bound by contract. I have tried to execute my part faithfully but I shall not feel that the firm has done its best by me if the publication is not held up until this awful blunder can be set right and I hope and depend on you to let Saxton know that; also that you will support my position and let Saxton know that they have hurt me at the sorest spot where a writer may be hurt.

Ever Sincerely Yours
Claude McKay

[Left margin:][2] This second set of proofs with m.s. arrived yesterday. I hope you get the first at the Paris post office + that you will please have them forwarded. I enclose a copy of my letter to Saxton and a list of <u>some</u> merely [*sic*] of the rotten phrases. Remember I have not yet received the first half of the script—two hundred and seventy-six pages!

<u>CMcK.</u>

WABLAR TLS

1. This letter follows McKay's telegram of the same day: "PLEASE CABLE SAXTON STOP PUBLICATION WAIT ORIGINAL WRITING MCKAY."

2. This appears as a handwritten marginal note.

To Eugene Saxton

30 January 1929

Tangier, Morocco

Dear Saxton,

I have just received the second half of the proofs and the m.s. of "Banjo" and I cannot set down here the shock, surprise and pain I feel from what has been done to my writing.

In reading the second set of proofs that [William A.] Bradley sent me after I had missed the first sent to Casablanca, I felt all along something unfamiliar and wrong. In some places I pounced on the phrases that had wrought the change, in others I did not, although I felt the queer difference, because when writing is bad you can often feel it without being able precisely to point it out.

I cannot possibly conceal my resentment. I gave you carte blanche as a man of experience in the publishing business to cut out of the text such phrases that in your opinion might start the machinery of censorship working against the book. You acted so handsomely by me with "Home To Harlem" that I cannot believe you are aware that a literary hand has indiscreetly gone through my text and deliberately cut out my own simple words to substitute literary stock phrases in their place.

Because of that whole paragraphs have been mutilated and made flat. I am not a Jim Tully[1] writing roughly and at random without any deep artistic feeling of the value and relationship of words. I am a poet and have always striven conscientiously to find words to say exactly what I see and feel. I took a long time to write "Banjo" in the face of real difficulties, writing and re-writing to find the right words to render the atmosphere and the types that moved in it. There have been times when I worked at sentences and paragraphs on scraps of paper for days before typing them. And then some one ups and wantonly compromises the character of my writing by replacing my personal words with the cheap two- and three-syllabled stock words. This is intolerably discouraging after all these long years struggling to express myself in words.

I prefer to be crude and ungrammatical and achieve a clean and clear expression thereby rather than spill the sap of my thoughts into dead husks of words.

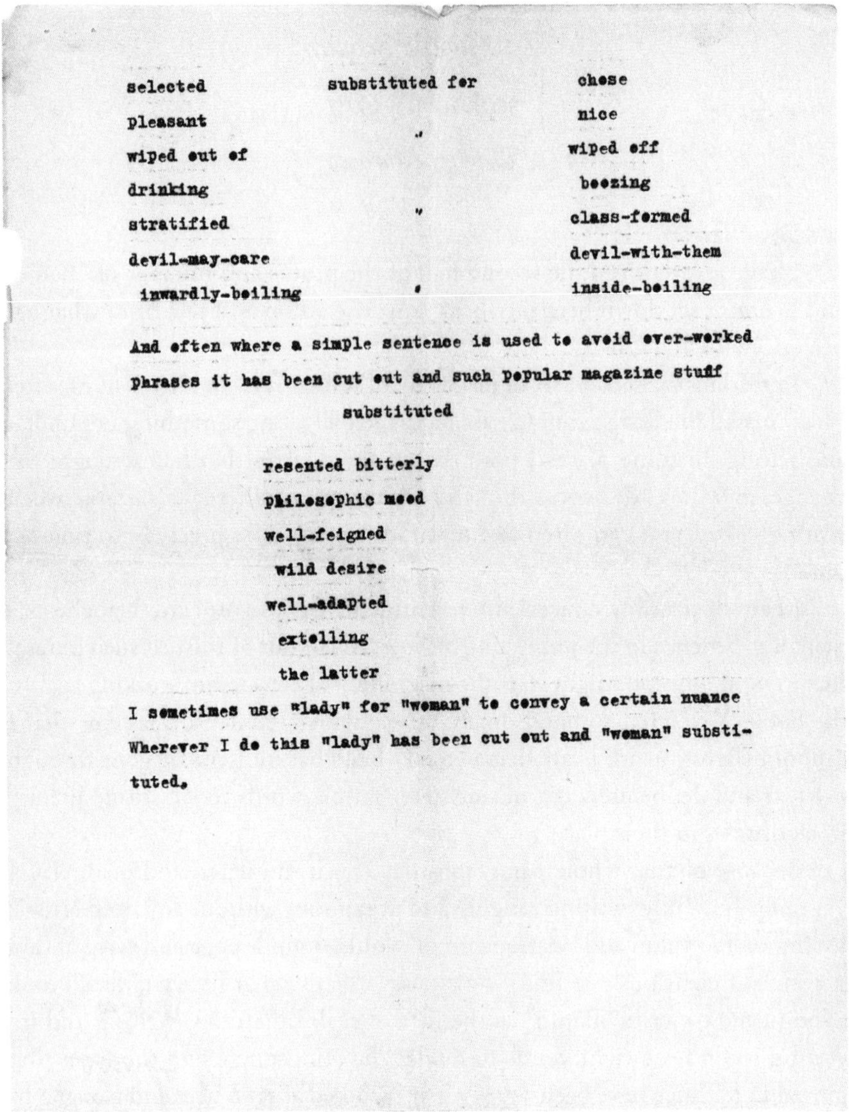

selected	substituted for	chose
pleasant	"	nice
wiped out of		wiped off
drinking		boozing
stratified	"	class-formed
devil-may-care		devil-with-them
inwardly-boiling	"	inside-boiling

And often where a simple sentence is used to avoid over-worked phrases it has been cut out and such popular magazine stuff substituted

resented bitterly
philosophic mood
well-feigned
wild desire
well-adapted
extolling
the latter

I sometimes use "lady" for "woman" to convey a certain nuance Wherever I do this "lady" has been cut out and "woman" substituted.

Fig. 2. McKay's objections to editorial changes to *Banjo,* enclosed with the 30 January 1929 letter to Eugene Saxton. (Harper & Brothers [and Successors] Correspondence, 1923–1954, Franklin D. Roosevelt Presidential Library & Museum)

I cite one example. The value of the last paragraph of chapter 24 is entirely destroyed by the intrusion of this awful Elinor Glyn-moving-picture phrase, "a sudden agonized hush fell, she levelled the revolver." "Agonized hush"? Does that phrase mean anything except in a fake romantic tale of a ladies' club held up by bandits? In the life of Marseille that I know and describe in "Banjo" the bullets bark first and the hush falls after. This dreadful thriller phrase destroys for me the whole value of my book and no real critic, after reading that, would consider me a serious artist in words.

If you think my reaction is exaggerated, you might consult Mr. Glenway Wescott or Mr. [John] Dos Passos or any other serious young writer of these times that you are publishing.

I am enclosing a list of some of the phrases. I have not yet received the first part of the m.s. nor the proofs, but I must beg of you to defer publication until I can put the original manuscript and proofs re-corrected in your hands. If a first edition should be sent out before, I shall feel that I have not been done fairly by and I will never be reconciled to it.

I am very sorry indeed that this trouble should arise. I thought that after the fine, mutual understanding existing between you, Bradley and me in getting out "Home To Harlem," that nothing so exasperating and inexplicable as this could have happened over the second book.

With my best regard
Yours Sincerely
Claude McKay

HBC TLS

1. Jim Tully (1886–1947), American boxer who published several commercially successful autobiographies and novels in the 1920s and 1930s.

To James Weldon Johnson

1 February 1929

Tangier, Morocco

Dear Johnson

I have cabled you today asking you to represent me at the Harmon Award Ceremony. I have learned of the award through a letter from Mr [George Edmund] Haynes that was forwarded by Harper and reforwarded by [William A.] Bradley.

I feel very awkward before this grand array of churches printed on the letter-head especially as I am a pagan and don't think there is anything of Christian morality in my writings. I grew up without Religion, because my eldest brother was a free-thinker and he instructed me. But however awkward I may feel I consider it an honor in the noblest sense of the word that the award should have been won by "Home To Harlem."

The Abbess, Madre Maria, says through Mr Thornton Wilder, "Now learn at last that anywhere you may expect grace" and I might paraphrase a little, "Now learn at last that anywhere you may expect merit to be recognised."[1]

I have written to the Consul at Marseille about my returning to America. I sent him some other important papers that I have received recently. I haven't heard from him yet, But I am hoping to make the trip back some time this year.

My warmest regards to you and Mrs. Johnson,

Yours Sincerely,
Claude McKay

[Upper margin:] I am staying a month here at Tangier, then I shall return through Spain to France. I have postponed the trip to West Africa.

CMcK

JWJP TLS

1. McKay quotes Thornton Wilder's *The Bridge of San Luis Rey* (1927).

To William A. Bradley

5 February 1929

Tangier, Morocco

Dear Bradley

I have just had yesterday's telegram. I cannot locate the first set of proofs with [the] first part of "Banjo." The second arrived safely from Casablanca by way of Paris. I had a notice from the Paris post office notifying me of a packet held. I thought it was perhaps the proofs and m.s. and I mailed you the notice asking you if you would send somebody to get the packet.

I cannot sanction the publication of "Banjo" in its mutilated form and, not knowing whether you did cable [Eugene] Saxton as I asked, I have today cabled him asking him to hold up publication. It is regrettable if that should hurt the success of the book, but as much as that means to me, I prefer that publication be delayed even until the fall rather than that the book should be published with those cheap penny-thriller phrases that Saxton allowed to be inserted in it.

I am sorry you could not find time to reply to my first telegram about it and let me know what you have done. It is an extremely serious matter for me.

I should have gone straight to Paris to see you, but I have been expecting the original m.s. every day for three weeks and have stayed on here because I did not want to miss it again.

Yours Sincerely
Claude McKay

I have written to Casablanca about the packet.

WABLAR ALS

To William A. Bradley

[February 1929]

Tangier, Morocco

Dear Bradley

Here is the other procuration.[1] I had thought that with your name on the packets as sender you could have received them by showing my letter of the 30th ult., but I had reckoned such [?] red tape.

Yes, the mail service between Tanger and Europe is bad. There is a mail boat every day, but when the sea is bad (and that is often) it doesn't arrive. The quickest way is the air mail which I always use.

Of course you must know that I don't object to Harper's censoring the text. He[2] did "Home to Harlem" and I was perfectly satisfied—a few things that I objected to being taken out were put back in. In "Banjo" much more is cut out than in "Home to Harlem," but I don't mind that either. My whole objection is to the improvement tendency and manner of the person who went through the text. He is a mechanical literarious [*sic*] person without the slightest comprehension of the relation of words to thought[,] action and atmosphere. He has sprinkled throughout the text words that are neither right nor wrong—just dead. False romantic words that my brother used to laugh at us for using when we were doing secondary course English under him. And later at college in America they were the kind of words and phrases that were listed as stock things that a beginning writer should never accustom himself to use. The inserted words have not only robbed many of my paragraphs of originality, they have also in many instances given a different shade of meaning than what I intended. In other cases the improver has put in exclamation marks to emphasize subtle points that should quietly make their own emphasis without any such device. I can only conclude that the person who went through the m.s. must have gone off his nut into a state in which he was under the delusion that it was his own work.

There is nothing to do now but wait patiently until the packet arrives. I regret the delay in publication that will result. I did write you from Marrakech before Christmas that I would let you know my new address and suggesting I might go to Tanger. I merely stopped off at Casablanca on my way from Marrakech to have my letters sent back to Paris. I spent the holidays with a Martiniquan family at Rabat + from there I went to Meknes. Maybe you had overlooked the important point of that letter[,] which was that I would send you later an address where you could forward the proofs.

Yours Sincerely
Claude McKay

I am sketching out the plan + chapters of my Moroccan book but I won't start work on it until I get back to France[.] CMcK

WABLAR ALS

1. French "*procuration*" (proxy, power of attorney). McKay's handwriting is difficult to make out in this case. The legal document referred to is dated 12 February.

2. Likely Eugene Saxton or another editor at *Harper's*.

To Langston Hughes[1]

21 February 1929

Tangier, Morocco

My dear Langston

I have been a month here in your nice white town and am leaving tomorrow for Spain. It is charming, a beautiful bay and beach but it is dead as it is almost entirely cut off politically and commercially from the Spanish zone. I visited the other Spanish towns and they were thriving and bustling.—I sent off the proofs of "Banjo" yesterday. It has been delayed nearly two months by being sent to Casablanca after I had left there. It took me seven weeks to get them back!

So I see I have won the Harmon prize. Now that's something for "Home To Harlem" to be indirectly recommended by the Federal Churches of Christ. I shall throw "Banjo" at them soon. Thank you for card and cutting, but I wish you would write when your examinations will let you and tell me more about yourself.

Will write again when I get back to France[.]

—Ever Claude

LHP ALS

1. This letter contains some lines of poetry, written in pencil by Hughes.

To William A. Bradley

[late February or early March 1929]

Tangier, Morocco

Dear Bradley

About the balance of the advance on "Banjo"—I was wondering if it couldn't be put in the bank as was done with the royalties on "Home To Harlem." I suppose that would eliminate the income tax and, as I am investigating the possibility of a refund it might be better not to add anything to the job. Anyway as I am not in any pressing need just now, the $700 balance of the advance could be carried over to the Royalty payment. What do you think?

About "Banjo"—you know I have never been a stickler about technicalities, but in this case it was a matter of ruthless manhandling. I daresay I am at heart more worried than you and [Eugene] Saxton over the delay in publication, but the messing up of the text was too awful for me to permit it without re-correcting. I hope it will never occur again. Such things should never be done. There is no doubt that the person who "improved" my text has a Fannie Hurst or Elinor Glyn idea of literature. Of course, Miss Hurst is a huge success, but I am not in her class. Also I don't reach her public and the introduction of her phrases in my writing would simply ruin me among the discerning critics. And it was a horrible experience for myself to see my text unconscionably mutilated like that.

I need criticism and help in my work of course, I am well aware of that—but not that sort of thing. I have never had any critic as keen and discreet as yourself—except an old English aristocrat, who lived in Jamaica to whom I used to read my dialect verse. With us as you once said in a letter it is more than a mere business affair you are also my advisor and so I hope we shall continue our arrangement even after this first series is finished and I have begun another. That would eliminate the kind of tinkering that messed up "Banjo" this time. Thanks for your letter + the telegrams. I am going to Seville and Grenada [*sic*] and will be in Marseille sometime in March. Will write. I wish to consult you about the next book.

Sincerely
Claude McKay

WABLAR ALS

To William A. Bradley

14 March 1929

Marseille, France

Dear Bradley

I wonder if you have word of Harper[']s getting the proofs and m.s. And whether everything is all straightened out and all right now.

I had a wonderful trip through Spain this time. After Morocco I wanted naturally to see the monuments of the Moorish occupation of Spain[,] and Granada was a new revelation. I was in a strange dreamy state during my three days there, perhaps because the extreme altitude affected my head, but also because the Alhambra is such an exquisite dream. It is as if the builders intended it to be the oversea flowering of their African work. I [have] never seen architecture so dainty yet holding so much permanence. It seemed not to belong to this solid Spanish land. I went to Sevilla, of course, to see the Giralda that legend attributes to the Black Sultan as also the Hassan Tower and the Koutoubia at Marrakesh. I don't know if I told you that I wanted to make the legend the chief interest of my Moroccan book. If I haven't I shall send you an outline of my plan and also take up the matter of the short stories. I don't know yet which book should precede the other.

The more I see of Spain the more I love it. The people are so courteous—simply so—I like them much more than the French. My liking for the French is intellectual and therefore limited, while I like the Spaniards with all the senses. Some people had told me at Barcelona that Madrid was a better city and more Spanish, but to me Barcelona is the more Spanish and charming. Madrid looks bigger and more imposing but it struck me like an imitation of Paris without any character of its own. I did not like it, but I do love Barcelona.

I have changed my mind about that balance on "Banjo" and should like to have it as was promised on publication of the book. I think my accountant-friend is not clear himself about the 5% tax. In another letter from him he hints at some underhand method of my working with him to get the refund and I don't want to be mixed up in that. I don't think it is worth it—especially as he is very vague about what is to be done—

Yours Sincerely
Claude McKay

WABLAR ALS

To William A. Bradley

25 March 1929

Nice, France

My dear Bradley

I can't recall Harper's cable address and as I am worried whether the proofs and m.s. of "Banjo" were finally received, won't you cable for me to find out and charge the cost to me? You might telegraph me here, if necessary, at "Coupon" the cable address of Cook's.

I am here for a few days only[.] I shall go to Paris about the end of next week—first week of next month. Funny we just happen to miss each other in our planning all the time. It happened in Spain + now Morocco. I should love to be in Fez and Marrakech with you. If I could afford it I would make the trip again with you because I love the Moroccan atmosphere. I long for the Arab cafés—the real ones where they smoke kiff [*sic*] and gamble and do all kinds of tricks—not the show places like those at Rabat and Meknes. I'll tell you how to see them, but you must not sit on the matting because of lice. I was lousy all the time I was there, but I got such real enjoyment out of the fondouks that I didn't mind.

How lucky you are to get a free trip. You must go. Morocco is too wonderful to miss. It was a splendid shock to me, the feel of that barbarous medieval life in contact with the modern world. At Marrakesh you'll get a slight idea of what tropical African must be, because it is still semi-savage with the Arabs always coming into the city from the Souss country and slaves from the Soudan and the Senegal bush. But we'll have time to talk about all this.

I read two of [Francis] Carco's books[,] "Jesus la Caille" and another[,] + I don't think he is deep and subtle enough to understand the Spaniards. The Alhambra, the Cathedral at Cordova and all the other Moorish works in Spain seemed more interesting to me <u>after</u> I had been in Morocco and seen the Arabs chez eux. They brought back to me all the significance of two great religions at war against each other. The "spoiling" of the Alhambra, as it seemed to me, is the plastering over of the fine Arabesque roofs and panelling by the fanatic Phillip II (?)[.] Also the renaissance additions that were introduced. Some of this covering up has been removed by restoration and it gives you a shock to see on one side delicate Arab decorative work with the other side covered up by grey forbidding renaissance plaster. But even so there is to me a certain beauty in this vandalism that comes from contemplation when you consider the tremendous struggle that was waged in Spain between cross and crescent and that Arab decorative art in its glorification of the Koran meant antichrist to the Spaniards. I think that that might help to explain why Spain has remained so profoundly religious. I sometimes notice more men than women in the churches. You know Spain is a closed country. You can't get a job there of any consequence if you are not Roman Catholic. I had an Arab friend at Barcelona working for the telephone company as mechanic. He was the only Arab in town and he had to become Roman Catholic before he could have his place. In spite of their narrow nationalism the Spanish attitude towards strangers is quite different from the French. They are romantic about strangers something the way Americans are.

I am quite satisfied about the terms for the Italian translation of "Home To Harlem" and as my representative you might make the necessary agreement with Mr [Jamie] Hamilton. About six months ago a German woman wrote me about a German translation. I sent her letter to [Eugene] Saxton, but evidently he did nothing, for quite recently she wrote about it again. I told her to write directly to Harper[']s. She said she had and had received no reply.

If you go to Morocco I suppose you will return by way of the Spanish zone and Tangier. Ceuta is very interesting. Did I tell you that the British barred me from Gibraltar? I don't know why, but that might explain all the trouble I had with my letters at the British Post Office.—I was about to say that if you return by way of Spain I may meet you there + we could see Barcelona + some bullfights together. But we will talk about that when we meet.

Ever Sincerely
Claude McKay

WABLAR ALS

To Langston Hughes

14 May 1929

Paris, France

My dear Langston,

As usual I was very happy for a letter from you and this is doubly welcome of course bringing your opinion of "Banjo." I like your reaction and your "buddy-teacher" comparison suggests an excellent idea to me while hitting it off. I never thought of "Home . . ." as a buddy but your saying so makes it just that even to me. It is natural because the writing flowed out of a perfect emotional state of embalmed love—the state you fall in in thinking about a good old buddy. "Banjo" grew differently—I admire the chief character but don't love him as I love Jake[,] and while Marseille fascinates, attracts and perpetually interests me I could never love it as Harlem. Briefly, "Banjo" is objective, "Home to Harlem" subjective. Yours is the third letter from America. All three from Negro friends[:] one from New York[,] another from North Carolina and the opinion of each is fundamentally the same.

I saw the scandal of your investigation of Lincoln in a couple of Negro newspapers [Joel Augustus] Rogers showed me.[1] I think it's fine you should have done it and that it got all that publicity. I hope it was also in the National Press. The only way of creating self respect among Negroes as a group is by showing that they have none. I believe in naked exposure of everything, kitchen, backyard and even pig pen. It can never hurt us as a race—rather help.

Do you have any plans after graduation? No thought of coming over? I don't know when I shall get back. Must do another book first and have not yet started. What are you doing? Poetry, stage or novel? I am longing to see you in the flesh just as eagerly as four or five years ago, yet I don't know when that time will be.

Have been here over a month. After Morocco, I had a keen time of it in Spain. Love Spain, but no place like Barcelona, which I did not see this third time. I know you would love it too. Have met a girl here rather a woman but little like a girl, named Anita Thompson.[2] She was bridesmaid for Lelia Walker's daughter. Says she knows you and that she has often visited Lincoln. When I got your letter yesterday she wanted to join me in sending you a card, but we did other things and missed that. She is near-white, more Cuban type, intelligent in a way—has read a lot apparently, fundamentally shallow however. She is the society type that takes up bohemianism because it is smart to do so. She came here with a medical student called Bruce, but they are no longer intimate. She says she was a close chum of Chandler Owen and wanted to marry him but it didn't come off . . . and I remind her somehow of Chandler.

Did you see Wallace Thurman's "Harlem." I have seen and heard that it went way over the top. He owes me a letter. You might remind him if you both meet. And what has become of his magazine "Harlem." I could send him something now. Couldn't when he asked me at first for I had nothing + didn't want to do trash in a hurry.

Hope you will find time to write again soon. My warmest wish for yourself.

Ever Claude

Do you know where Jean Toomer is. I missed Counteé Cullen here. He went to London soon after I arrived. Heard a man named Harvey White sing "Ole Man's [*sic*] River" in "Showboat!" Rotten play but White has a wonderful voice beats [Paul] Robeson. Hope he does big stuff with it when he finishes his present engage—[*sic*]

<u>CMcK</u>

LHP ALS

1. Hughes and other Lincoln University sociology students circulated a questionnaire among the Lincoln student body asking students their opinions on having exclusively white professors at the university. A majority "favored an all-white faculty on the ground that no qualified colored teachers could be found and, secondly, they feared that favoritism would be shown by colored teachers to members of their own college fraternities." The Black press reported on this as a minor scandal. "Lincoln Students Do Not Speak for University," *Baltimore Afro-American*, 13 April 1929, 2.

2. Anita (Thompson) Reynolds wrote about her experience with McKay in the posthumously published memoir *American Cocktail: A "Colored Girl" in the World* (2014).

To Louise Bryant

[early June (?) 1929]

Paris, France

Dear Louise: Florence[1] told me last night you were here. I tried to get you on the 'phone and couldn't. I would have sent you a copy of "Banjo" long ago—I mean since I got my copies about the 15th of May but I did not know your real address. I am here for a little while straightening out some personal difficulties and put up at the Hotel Atlantique 18 rue Jean Jacques Rousseau[.] I hope you are much better from your treatment. What will you do this summer—please tell me when I can see you—Sincerely ever Claude

LBP APS (calling card)

1. Likely Florence (Flossie) Martin, a former dancer and American expatriate who was a celebrated regular at the bars in Montmartre and Montparnasse.

To William A. Bradley

13 June 1929

Paris, France

Dear Bradley

I am back in Paris where I must again stay for some time to straighten out my affairs. There is nothing of confidence (I mean in the sense you referred to it between you and me) involved in these matters. Simply and naturally I have some personal relationship difficulties, rather irritating, that must be adjusted. And as to my health I am taking care of it in the best way and so long as I stay away from parties and people who tease me into taking just one little drink and then—I should not have to worry. I hate parties anyway. You might send me a pneumatique if there is anything important to communicate. I am on the top floor of this hotel for the moment and don't relish going down to the telephone. I am staying for a few weeks this time but I don't think I'll consider being painted by your friend this time—I have not the time—nor the inclination.

Yours Sincerely
Claude McKay

WABLAR ALS

To Louise Bryant

17 June 1929

Paris, France

My dear Louise

After meeting you that first night in the Select I did not get off alone until the following night when we had dinner together. And then I cried nearly all night and couldn't go to sleep until I took four Dial Cibas. I could hardly wake up the next day. Maybe I was foolish to cry, simply because I was disappointed in our meeting like that after I have been looking forward toward our meeting all these years. But I was terribly affected even though I was sitting there laughing and trying to be jolly. You know I have cried only three times in twenty years—when my mother died in 1909, when I was shocked crazy by the abrupt news of Crystal Eastman's death and the other night.

You see I remembered how we first met and you danced with me at the Liberator ball—it was rather romantic—and I remember too the splendid oriental costume you lent Max [Eastman] and my wishing I had one myself. Then I remembered our second brief meeting, when Florence [Deshon] committed suicide and I was trying to take care of Max and my slipping off when you came.[1] The third was our banal meeting at the Dôme when you were with that awfully ugly woman, the journalist, who made me introduce her to some fixture of the café who was always uniquely advertising his good looks.

I left Paris a few days after and I don't know what I would have made of myself if you were not always encouraging me with money and your faith in me and my talent to write in the face of all sorts of discouragements. Even at Marseille, I was so down under the life, that I couldn't see that there was big stuff in it until you made me see in a strong letter about it and myself. This book "Banjo" really grew out of your suggestion. It was after your letter I realized that I was sweating and swilling through a golden mill.

I go over all this old ground because it was so terrible to meet you like that. I know it must have been hell for you in the sanitarium and after the stupid English doctors sentencing you to death. But I am sentenced too and all of us poor human devils are sentenced, excepting that some sentences are short, while others are long and (as I am on the subject) I suppose quite a number of us who went into Russia came out heavily sentenced.

Anyhow, I meant (any place away from that detestable Montparnasse quarter of utterly lost and dead souls) to meet and talk to you quietly about yourself and myself and our work. We were not ourselves those two evenings at the Select—nobody ever is in that atmosphere of poseurs and so-called free people. I shall go by your hotel to leave this letter and whenever you want to see me I am at your pleasure.

Yours ever Sincerely,
Claude

LBP ALS

1. Florence Deshon, Hollywood actress and lover of Max Eastman, committed suicide in 1922.

To William A. Bradley

17 June 1929

Paris, France

My dear Bradley

You know I am always very happy to see and talk to you naturally and quietly and it is a pleasure too to dine quietly with you and Mrs Bradley. But I hate all the artistic teas and parties and that afternoon when I went with you to the lady painter, I should not have gone if I had known it was to be a studio reception. I am just not created to adjust myself to such things and it won[']t be any pleasure attempting to try.

Besides right now, if I must out with it, I am trying to get out of a marriage that I committed over fifteen years ago.[1] I had wind of it from my sister in Jamaica that my royalties, after all these years of struggle, were in a bad way of being tied up by some "pisteur"[2] of a lawyer in New York. And so I quietly got my wife that was to come here and I've been trying all these weeks to find a way out through a divorce that won't raise a stink and take the little I have made out of my pocket. It is no easy job and it makes me irritable and nervous under my calm exterior. Besides I am crazy to get to work and I just cannot. So you'll see I have enough troubles for the moment by my letting you in on just one of them. I cannot describe to you how a crowd of cat-spitting, chattering, people works on my nerves—especially if they are drinking when I must of necessity be out of it. It's different in a café when you're with a friend or a small group. You can ignore the others!—Right now I am in a pickle and no one can help me but myself. And so if my letter gave you the impression that I did not want to see you, it was wrong and if it appeared rude (I did not keep a copy) I want to apologize. My best regards for you + Mrs Bradley[.]

Sincerely Yours
Claude McKay

I met Mrs [Louise Bryant] Bullitt a few nights back!

I will send the receipt for the cheque for 5 dollars—Thanks CMcK

WABLAR ALS

1. McKay married his Jamaican sweetheart, Eulalie Imelda Lewars, in New York on 30 July 1914. They separated six months later, and Eulalie gave birth to their daughter, Rhue Hope McKay, after returning to Jamaica. Between 1914 and 1929, McKay had only seen Eulalie when she came to New York in the summer of 1922. According to biographer Wayne F. Cooper, this visit "sealed his determination to visit the Soviet Union." See Cooper's *Claude McKay: Rebel Sojourner in the Harlem Renaissance* (1987; repr., New York: Schocken, 1990), 168.

2. "*Pisteur*" is a French slang term meaning a tracker or spy.

To William A. Bradley

5 July 1929

Antwerp, Belgium

[On Letterhead: Café Patria, Antwerp]

Dear Bradley

Here is the story for [Edward W.] Titus and please try and get as much as you can for it.[1] He had told me about 500 francs, but I heard later that he was paying much more, about 50 dollars for a good story and mine is good—was good + I have now made it excellent. Besides I did tell Titus you were my representative and that he would have to get the story through you.

I left Paris toward the end of last week. Just had to get away to work on the story. I can't work in Paris, I don't know why—can't even write letters. I feel depressed as I approach the machine and want to run away from it and my thoughts. I was happy having the excuse of the story to get away and I chose Antwerp as I may want to use the Crystal Palace here in my new book. The port is big and impressive and full of shipping. I like it. But I don't get any positive reaction for or against the Belgians as a group. I don't feel them as a real force as I feel the French, the Spaniards, the English or Americans (U.S.A.)[.]

I bought [Francis] Carco's Printemps d'Espagne on the way and I had lots and lots of fun reading it.[2] It is just as I expected, he misses the Spaniards. He sees everything with astounding eyes—but he never gets beyond the surface. I don't know why he reminds me of my friend [Joel Augustus] Rogers (the mulatto I brought to see you) who seems to live in a perpetual state of naive wonder discerning perversities in white people. I chuckled over the guides making a bonehead of him the way they did. I saw the guides myself, but I didn't need them, except to see the Alhambra when the patron of my hotel got me a splendid fellow. In my case, however, I think my great asset in getting by is first my color + second my instinct. Carco was just a white stranger in a white country when I—well the people wouldn't leave me to the guides and I was as finicky as anything choosing the ones I wanted to go with! Even in Morocco, I got on to people, families, without guides + you can hardly do Fez without a guide + the municipality hotels connive to force them on to you.

I don't get a hint in Carco of the essential and natural dignity of the Spaniards of all classes. There is a seriousness about it that borders on sadness and yet the Spaniards seemed to me a people who can realize happiness where the French are merely gay. It's that Spanish dignity that puts the "maricones" in the bordels. You find them in the bordels in Morocco too, extremely beautiful boys ultra raffiné in that barbaric atmosphere having nothing at all in common with the petites tantes[3] of Paris. You know I consider Fez the most Raffiné city I've ever known, yet at first glance, having such an aspect of barbarism and savagery, it makes me think of the cocoanut with the firm husk that you must chop through only to meet the hard shell before you can get the fruit—or the fine drink, which I prefer. I wish you could see the haetera[4] [*sic*] (don't know if the spelling is right) there before it is all spoilt. The country and natural dignity of the girls make you ashamed of the same life in Europe. When you go in their rooms, they offer you tea, sometimes cake, on beautifully polished bronze trays. I remember one incident when a girl said insulting things to one of my companions—a Moulay (noble)[—]and he turned to me and said, she is not Moroccan, but Algerian and it was true. But it is all being spoilt by the members of the Foreign Legion + other French regiments who approach that life in the mean modern spirit. At Casablanca where the French have built a fine modern quarter reservè, it is a hellish business, revolting and uglier than Marseille, where the roughness and cruelty seem to grow naturally, belonging to the rude life of the Vieux Port.

I went a long way off from Spain but then the sex life of Spain and Morocco has a close resemblance, although because of the difference in religion and the right to divorce the Arabs are freer. I can't imagine any Frenchman understanding the Spaniards + their attitude toward sex. The French pretend to take sex lightly and that pretension has become part of the national consciousness. The Spaniards don't pretend; they know that sex is no simple affair and for them it is very complicated by the cult of the virgin before marriage + the presence of the Catholic church. I've never been in any country where I've seen love ripening and filling the eyes and movements of young girls so richly as in Spain. Sex dominates everything, everywhere and the dignity of the male is improved [?] by the female. It isn't the hypocritical reserve you meet among the English, nor the conscious hemanishness of the American. It's a fine native thing and I like the Spaniards for it. I'm sorry I hadn't been able to go to Spain to write "Banjo." It might have been a better book. I am returning to Paris in a few days.

My best regards to you + Mrs. Bradley—

Sincerely
Claude McKay

WABLAR ALS

1. McKay's "Mattie and Her Sweetman" appeared in *This Quarter* 2, no. 2 (October–December 1929), edited by Edward W. Titus.

2. Paragraph not indented in original.

3. Like the Spanish word "*maricones,*" "*tantes*" is a French slur for effeminate gay men.

4. "*Hetairai,*" McKay's preferred Greek euphemism for prostitutes.

To William A. Bradley

"Wednesday" [likely 24 July 1929]

Paris, France

Dear Bradley: Thanks for your pneu.[1] You didn't say but I take it that the party will be for Tuesday after the show. Then you must let me know approximately how many of the "Blackbirds" who are really all yellow except for some of the men, you can accommodate.[2] Then, again if any of your friends have a car, it would be nice if they could call for the two grandes vedettes. Show people are so vain + the colored ones no different from the others! I'll pile the others in taxicabs. I'm having difficulty getting a group together. The sheep don't want to go with the goats, yet the goats are the more interesting. I was with some of them all last night at the music-box[3] and when they got ginned up, I felt just like a mother's boy among them. It was like being Home To Harlem + oh they were so patriotic. Nothing in France or in Europe to please them. My number here if you must call is Louvre 02.10[.] with best regards + hoping Mrs Bradley is getting better[.]

Claude McKay

WABLAR APS (on calling cards)

1. Short for "*carte pneumatique*" (pneumatic telegram).

2. The U.S. musical production *Blackbirds of 1928* opened at the Moulin Rouge on 7 June 1929 and ran for three months.

3. The Music Box was a name used by several clubs in Paris. This may be the short-lived Montmartre club run by Ada "Bricktop" Smith in 1929.

To Louise Bryant

1 August 1929

Paris, France

Dear Louise

I got your address from Flossie[1] and am sending you this letter I wrote after our meeting at the Select. Reading it over I don't see that I want to change it in any way even though it is so sentimental.

Flossie tells me you are going back to N.Y. and I wish I could see you before your going, but I am on the point of leaving Paris myself. I can't stick Montparnasse, there is [*sic*] none of my old friends (those I appreciate about) and I have no new ones that I care for.

I got the Blackbirds to go to a good party that the Blackbirds gave.[2] I only wish you were there. I enjoyed myself immensely. I invited our mutual friend Gwen.[3] I was rather tight—drinking beer—but I had all my wits. When the party was nearly breaking up we were some of us a little off in a group with Gwen among us. Graeme [Taylor] suggested that we should finish the morning at his studio and I said: Yes let's all go and have a nice bi-sexual party.[4] I meant no offence to Gwen (for I suppose there were more people from my side at the party who were that way inclined)[.] But Gwen took it very personally and said to me—"You know, Claude, you have a reputation for being a homo." "Sure" I answered, "I sleep with all the boys, but only the aristocratic ones, and so it's hard to prove anything on me."[5] So she didn't say any more. It was funny because I took Gwen to the theatre party and the party afterwards because I have always liked her, ever since I met her at Cagnes. We went up to Cagnes from Nice—4 boys and some Lesbian girls from St. Paul and had a wild time in Harriet's[6] studio. For my part I have never been with nor at any time liked the he-men crowd who like to "swing on fairies." See Hemingway's book.[7] But I don't like people who wear labels and pose, I don't like he-women any more than I like he-men, nor fairies who scream + play the jeune fille a la Victorian age in this machine age when the best women are the sporty, athletic types. I suppose I am nearer to the ancient Greeks + the Orientals of today who take these things in a natural and dignified manner.

My love to you and the kid.

Sincerely Claude

LBP ALS

1. Likely Florence (Flossie) Martin, a former dancer and American expatriate who was a celebrated regular at the bars in Montmartre and Montparnasse.

2. This appears to be a slip of the pen for "a good party that the Bradleys gave." See the following letter.

3. Probably Gwen Le Gallienne (1897/98–1966?), an artist who had a brief affair with Louise Bryant in the late 1920s.

4. John "Buffy" Glassco, who attended this party (or another like it), wrote about it many years later and remembered the details somewhat differently, though McKay's account, written only a day or so after the event, is likely more accurate. See John Glassco, *Memoirs of Montparnasse* (1970; repr., New York: New York Review of Books, 2007), 191–95.

5. McKay's language echoes blues singer Ma Rainey's queer anthem "Prove It on Me Blues," released September 1928.

6. Harriet (last name unknown) appears, alongside Claude, in Max Eastman's poem "To Waldo Pierce" ("We're all of us becoming movie stars— / Claude dancing ragtime and the Mumbo-Jum / And Harriet the dirge of Rosa's rum"), with a note that sets this scene during McKay's 1926 stint as an extra in Rex Ingram's film *The Magician.* Eastman provides this context: "Harriet, a slim mysterious girl in Cagnes, also claimed to be a dancer, but danced to only one funereal phonograph record, and then only after locking her door and consuming large quantities of rum which she bought at a tiny bistro run by a pear-shaped woman named Rosa." See Max Eastman, *Poems of Five Decades* (New York: Harper & Brothers, 1954), 95–96.

7. McKay references a passage in Hemingway's *The Sun Also Rises* (1926).

To William A. Bradley

"Thursday" [likely 1 August 1929]

Paris, France

Dear Bradley

I had a wonderful time at the party and I think everybody else did. Please tell Mrs Bradley how sorry I was not to be present when she was leaving to thank her for her nice management, but I hope I shall see you both again before I leave Paris to get down to work. I am sorry too I missed thanking Mrs [Stella] Bowen—but I had been drinking with my party—only beer, but it takes just a little to go to my head nowadays—and was in no mood to say an interesting word even with the persons I would have liked to talk to most—like [Blaise] Cendrars. I was only in a mood to enjoy myself, and I did.

I think most of the show crowd enjoyed themselves except Miss [Aida] Ward, perhaps.[1] It was a pain taking her home, she is so over-nice + I'm afraid she can't help being that way. Her mother is a fine person. Snaky Hips and Adelaide Hall,[2] the two that I prefer more than everybody else, were delightful and delighted with everything.

I've got to go to Berlin for a few days, but I'll come back here before I decide definitely about going off. So I hope to see you either before or after Berlin[.]

Sincerely
Cl. McKay

I stayed in bed all day + all night yesterday to recover + am o.k. again!

WABLAR ALS

1. Aida Ward (1900–1984), cast member of *Blackbirds of 1928.*

2. Earl "Snakehips" Tucker (1906–1937) and Adelaide Hall (1901–1993), stars of *Blackbirds of 1928.*

To James Weldon Johnson

5 September 1929

Marseille, France (?)

Dear Johnson

I came down to Marseille to look after some things I had left here and I called at the Consulate and saw the vice-consul, chief of the passport dept, who had replied to my first letter of inquiry.

I told him I would not want to return to America before next year in the fall when I hope to have my new book ready[,] and so I was put on the British quota (non-preference) to be advised by letter when my turn comes. That may be about a year from today, there is a stack of names before mine.

Meanwhile I should appreciate anything you can do higher up to cut the red tape when the time approaches, so I may not find it harder than it is in general to get by. Maybe I could be wangled on to the preference quota. I don't know if I should lose my number if I were called before I was ready. I hear that you have received a study and travelling "bourse" and I congratulate you. Maybe that was what you were referring to when you hinted of coming over here and I shall be happy to see you when you do. I should like to apply for one of those "bourses" myself, but I don't know how to get at it and I suppose I can only do it when I am back on American soil.

I saw Walter White's review of "Banjo" and thought it fundamentally malicious and pretentious.[1] I warrant I know and see very deeply into many phases of Aframerican life[, more] than Walter White does, because I have nosed about on my own much more than he. He's all wrong about the West Indies too and should take a trip down there before rushing into print. He would find the differences between mulattoes + blacks just as artificial as in the States if it were not for European encouragement—precisely as I understand the difference between Eurasians + the natives is stressed + encouraged in Asia. At anyrate [*sic*] I have distant mulatto relatives who pass as white in New York and all my brothers included [*sic*] myself were married to mulatto women. In our village, I grew up on equal terms with white mulatto + black children of a certain clan because my father was a big peasant + "belonged." The difference in the islands is economic + not social.

With my best regards
Yours Sincerely
Claude McKay

[Upper margin:] Someday I hope to be able to sign the copies of the book I have had sent to you or I'll send you find [fine?] photograph that you might put before the fly leaf. CMcK

JWJP ALS

1. Walter White, review of *Banjo,* in *New York World,* 9 June 1929.

To Charlotte Osgood Mason

10 September 1929

Basses-Pyrénées, France

Dear Mrs Osgood Mason

When I left Marseille for Barcelona last year I mislaid, unfortunately, your letters with your address in a basket of things that I stored at Marseille. I wanted to write to you and tried to get your address from Max [Eastman], but he has never answered any of my letters since Crystal [Eastman]'s death until last month.

I got your address from Alain Locke in Paris last month and I am asking Harper's to send you a copy of "Banjo." I am sorry I'm not in a position to write something in it but I am sending you two little photographs which you might just stick on the flyleaf (of both books. I had "Home to Harlem" sent you, too if I remember.) if that seems allright to you.

Let me thank you for having the clippings sent to me all the time. I wrote to the bureau asking that they be sent by letter post, sealed, as the distance is so great; but they won[']t do it + so sometimes I receive envelopes only with nothing in them.

I spent the summer in Paris making a few contacts—some necessary—when one has become an author—but not all very happy. People want one to eat too much and drink all the time and as I suffer from high blood pressure, drinking is hard for me. When a French specialist tells me not to drink it is high time to stop. I want now to conserve my energies for creative work. There is so much to do and I do not feel physically up to the job.

I am in the Basses Pyrénées and want to cross over into Spain again where I find the civilization much more in harmony with my temperament than the French. I loved Morocco, but the French are there with their <u>ouvre civilisatrice</u> which is hellish to me, although much appreciated by the Moroccans in general. Casablanca is a city of brand-new Grands Magazines. I liked the life of the Arabs, but everywhere is the pressure of Administration and I felt that if I must live under the French regime it is better in France where party politics and free criticism help to make it more liberal than in the colonies. I daresay it is about the same with all colonizing nations.

I was so ill in Paris that I paid a medical student to come down here with me during his vacation and treat me for a month. It was expensive for what I earn, but I consider it an investment worth-while since a certain percentage of good health is essential to creative work—and that is all I am doing for now. About the end of the month I am going back to Paris to meet Max, after which I shall go to Spain where I hope to work without interruption until I finish my new book.

The horizontal photograph is as I am unrefined[,] the vertical when the photographer has done his bit trying to make me look sweet. I thought you might be interested in the comparison.

I am happy I shall have a chance of seeing Max again. I was horror-shocked by Crystal's death last year and for days I could not do any work. She had been such a great good friend to me in her big warm way. I hadn't seen her since 1922 when she was very unhappy in London and I was leaving for Russia and I was always hoping we would get together again under happier conditions—but we were both cheated of any such happy chance.

Glancing at the address Alain Locke left me, I notice I have been thinking and talking about you by your second or maiden name, so I must cancel that.

With my warmest regards to you[.]

Yours Sincerely
Claude McKay

ALP ALS

To James Ivy

20 September 1929

Basses-Pyrénées, France, or Bilbao, Spain (?)

My dear Ivy,

I beg you to forgive my long silence, but getting back to Paris in the spring I found myself with plenty of business to go through with my representative, besides a painful intimate affair which lasted for weeks and made me unfit for any kind of work. To get away from myself I dashed about a great deal with old friends, the show people of *Blackbirds* and Aframericans holidaying in Paris. But I was very unhappy all the time and managed to cut loose last month (towards the end) and am here near the frontier working on my next novel,[1] but not yet decided where in Spain I shall settle down to finish it. Barcelona is the most attractive place, but I am sure it must be pretty awful with the exhibition[2] on and the town overcrowded with visitors. However, I'll stay in Spain as I feel more in harmony with its culture than that of France.

It was good to get your last letter and the review of *Banjo.* I really don't think it as good a story as *Home to Harlem* from the esthetic point of view. It doesn't run smoothly enough and is clogged up with "the problem of the Negro." However, I had to get that out of my system. Now I can go on with real creative work. It must be a choice between story telling and essays on the race problem. I don't mind doing an essay now and then, but I don't want that to destroy my creative energies.

Ray is not altogether myself. Most people think so, because he is an intellectual, but I merely use him as a vehicle. There is a little of me in all my chief characters!

Frank Harris was ill at Nice this spring. I was there for Easter but did not try to see him. No, I don't think he is a great writer in spite of your protest. He has one little story about Jesus' resurrection which I think is a masterpiece—it is so well done—a masterpiece as [Ernest] Dowson's "Cynara," but that does not make Dowson a great poet. Harris is efficient, a great journalist, but he lacks the magic, the soul, the stuff of gold or whatever you want to call it that makes a great writer of a man. He is in a class a little higher than [H. L.] Mencken.

I had a wonderful time of it in Africa living among the Arabs and making friends. I did not want to leave if it were not that the French are masters there, and I prefer to live under the French in France where the government is more liberal bossing its own people. They do treat the Arabs badly. I was treated decently because I was a tourist and wore Egyptian clothes. The French are the cleverest propagandists in the world. They hate colored people, yet pretend they are liberal because they have a liberal tradition to live up to. I dislike them because they are the most nationalistic people in the world, and they are never tired of saying they are the nation destined to keep the torch of civilization burning.

My work has been reviewed in one of the leading weeklies of Paris and they have attacked me. I expect more when it is translated, but I shall be prepared for them when I write my travel book.

Don't you make enough to take a trip abroad? So many of the Negro teachers and professors do Europe every summer. [Alain] Locke never misses one and Harold Jackman was here this summer and many Fisk and Atlanta teachers.

[Claude McKay]

PCM

1. Ultimately published as *Romance in Marseille* (2020).

2. The 1929 Barcelona International Exposition, which included the massive renovation of parts of the city, ran from 20 May 1929 through 15 January 1930.

To William A. Bradley

2 October 1929

Madrid, Spain

Dear Bradley

I have to ask you to forgive me many things,—my long silence and my neglect to see or write to you after receiving your message from Miss [Anita] Thompson. I was tied up and confused with so many things at once, that I couldn't make a step to get any one thing done. I couldn't do any work in Paris and I was almost insane wanting to start in on my new book. At last I got away to Marseille, then to Bayonne and over to Bilbao, where I stayed a week. The last place was interesting, but the port is too far away from the town. However I began working there.

The big thing, I mean what mattered for me, was to begin work again and I am going along smoothly. I shall send you soon a few chapters. From Bilbao I came by St. Sebastian and, after a few days there, to Madrid. I don't like Madrid—it is lacking in that pervasive charm that distinguishes Barcelona—the port life—the summer dancing in the streets and the cheap cabarets—but it is a quiet lazy-moving existence here and I can work, being in harmony with it. French life is too nervous and sharp for my temperament. It may be I exaggerate but as soon as I crossed the border I felt as if I had escaped from a swarm of wasps to find myself among a people who can appreciate simple dignity when they meet with it, because dignity is a fundamental of their social life. This is my fourth visit to Spain and each time my liking increases. I am afraid I shall at last grow romantic about some country. Later I may move to Barcelona if my friend there reports that it isn't too crowded because of the exhibition and I can find a cheap place.

You must have seen the N.L. articles about me. I got the first at Marseille, the second at San Sebastian and the third here.[1] Could you tell me who + what is this [André] Levinson? His attitude reminds me of the Aframerican Press which thinks it does certain people a favor when they are mentioned in the news. And some newspapers actually demand payment for that. My objection to Levinson's patter, I won't call it criticism, is sound. He tries to prove that I take my readers to a "Blue Cinema" to show the depravity of the white race and that I make use of a "risque" between white + colored to show that there is no justice for a black in France. And now in reply to my letter he cites the titles of my chapters "White Terror" and "Official Fists" which merely proves my contention that he has no sense of humor. For to those black boys in the Ditch, up against sailors and officers who objected to their presence in cafés and cabarets because of their color and of their race, the terror was as real as "red terror" may be to the bourgeoisie suffering from it or "white terror" to the proletarians under Fascist rule. So were the fists of the police. I have not done more than calling a spade by its name. But Levinson deliberately misrepresents me as I contend. There are the characters. Goosey loves France and wants to stay. Banjo is not in the least disturbed about loving or hating any country. The Senegalese opts for America. Ray is cynical about it all. He is intelligent enough to know that all human beings suffer and enjoy life in varying degrees in every country under the sun, although he is not unaware that the colored man has especial handicaps to meet with under the world-wide domination of occidental civilization. I am sure these points are clearly brought out in the book, and curiously not even the most rabid of the Dixie papers have accused me of propaganda against the white race. Some of them have said that I make my Negro characters finer than the whites. But they were, there in the Ditch, for the black fellows were careless and romantic about the life of the place. They were out on a holiday while the white inhabitants were just rats waiting to do them out of whatever they had. The blacks may be as such to blame themselves for their car[e]less shiftlessness, their ignorance of economic values, that more civilized people must take thought of. All I tried to give was a picture using Ray to give an intelligent philosophical background.

I think I should write Levinson again, but I should like to have your opinion first. Evidently Levinson thinks I should be pleased to have something said in a French revue about me—no matter what is said—but I have lived beyond that peculiar sort of vanity. I have never been in on the Aframerican fad that he mentions. I was never pushed and whenever I was quoted (the Aframerican critics have never liked my independent spirit neither in poetry nor in prose) it was because I was there and they couldn't get around me. I feel the same way about appearing in a foreign language. If I merit it—let me have it. Otherwise I am content now that I have my chance, after struggling all these years on my own, just to carry on expressing in the best way what I have to say. I don't want to be a one hundred percent American, nor a patriotic British subject, nor, (worse [*sic*] fate of all) un ami de France—in literature I want to be myself.

My best regards to you + Mrs Bradley[.]

Sincerely Yours
Claude McKay

WABLAR ALS

1. André Levinson, "Aframérique," *Les nouvelles littéraires,* 31 August 1929, 6; "De Harlem à la Cannebière," *Les nouvelles littéraires,* 14 September 1929, 6; "Cholokhoff et son épopée cosaque: Post-scriptum à Aframérique," *Les nouvelles littéraires,* 28 September 1929, 6.

To Paulette Nardal

2 October 1929

Madrid, Spain

[On Letterhead: Hotel Nacional, Paseo del Prado, Madrid]

My dear Mlle Nardal

I got your card only on Monday. I have been travelling for five weeks without staying long enough in any one place to have my correspondence forwarded.

I am sending you a copy of the letter I sent the N. L. [*Nouvelles littéraires*] after [André] Levinson's 2nd article. I suppose you have seen his reply in his article of the 28th. Can you tell me something about him. Is he a Jew. This defense of Occidental civilization and that "itat d'inferiorite" is very Jewish and amusing you know—page Palestine.

However, I should like to write him another letter either personal or to the N. L., but I should like you to tell me something about him first. I shouldn't mind your reply to him. I wrote a long letter to my representative Mr [William A.] Bradley 24 quai de Bethune about it. You might call him up if you think you will reply to Levinson.

He thinks I should be grateful for being written about in an article that he is paid for and about a subject that is of interest to his readers. What an ass he is! My work must stand or fall on its merit and I do not need to be puffed by a cheap scribbler and panderer like Levinson. You know there is not a single review in America (even in the old slave states) that put the interpretation he did on "Banjo." At any rate I don't mind so much for, to one who knows, French contemporary criticism is too closely allied to party politics to be taken seriously. The one saving thing about America is that the Governments [*sic*] are not intelligent enough to be interested in literature and art.

I sent a photograph with a note to your sister. Is she still in Paris? I am here for the time being and working on my new book but I hope to go to Barcelona + find some congenial place to live in the suburbs. I have asked a friend there to look around. Hoping you enjoyed Germany. I rather liked it, but found the Germans too heavy. Spain I love—it[']s like a bridge between Africa + Europe that I love to rest on. Thanks for writing + Sincerely

Claude McKay

Temporary address {℅ Thomas Cook + Son

Palace Hotel, Madrid

PN ALS

To the Editor of Les nouvelles littéraires

enclosed with 2 October 1929 letter to Paulette Nardal

Monsieur,

In an article in the Nouvelles Litteraires of September 14, M. Andre Levinson in referring to me states that in my book "Banjo" I emphasize the fact that there is no justice in France for a black man and make use of the "cinema clandestin" to show up the depravity of the whites.

The statement is neither critical nor true and I am surprised that a man who aspires to the role of critic as M. Levinson presumably does, should make it.

I drew upon certain scenes and facts about the Vieux Port of Marseille to give a clear picture of the life of a group of black wasters in that part of the town. The characters act and talk for themselves and I arrive at no moral conclusions about them and the life they lead among the other inhabitants of the place. . . . I used the "cinema clandestin" in a chapter simply as a thing in itself that belongs to the life of that quarter and there is nothing to infer that I intended to stress the depravity of the white race nor indict it on account of a secret cinema, which I am certain the great body of respectable people never frequent. I may be among the depraved class myself by going—but that is beside the point . . . there are more important things than a "cinema clandestin" for which the great white race should certainly be indicted, but I do not intend to be trapped and waste myself doing that.

It is rather funny that the intelligent white person will swallow any balderdash that white writers turn out about colored people, but loses his sense of humor as soon as he comes up against anything distasteful that a colored man may write about the whites.

I am much more interested in the character of human being beings [*sic*] under the skin than in the mere color of the skin (although I believe also that color may go a long way towards determining character) and I regard justice and depravity (in relation to to [*sic*] morality) as relative and not absolute things as M. Levinson apparently does.

I remain, Monsieur,
Yours Sincerely
Claude McKay

PN TLU (copy)

To William A. Bradley

21 October 1929

Madrid, Spain

Dear Bradley

Have you any report of the sales of "Banjo" to this month and could you give me the figures? I'm anxious to know how I stand financially as I have new projects in mind. I've now reached that point in my new book, where I need the Genoa background. I've filled it in to the best of my hazy recollection and imagination, so that I could carry on without a break. But that is not enough, however. I want to fix in some definite feature and so I'm planning to go to

Genoa (probably from Barcelona if my soundings there turn out all right) about Christmas, but I should like to know how deep I can plunge.

Miss [Anita] Thompson wrote that you were ill. I hope you are better now and that Mrs Bradley is also.

With my best regards
Sincerely yours
Claude McKay

WABLAR ALS

To William A. Bradley

1 November 1929

Madrid, Spain

Dear Bradley

I know that you are right as you always are in these practical matters but I couldn't hold myself off [André] Levinson. However, I will not write the second letter which would have been worse than the first. It is devilishly comical for me to see this new cavalier riding out of Palestine by way of Russia to defend the "classic" (how he adores the word) European civilization against the attack of the African savage. And I should have certainly said so in my next letter, if you had not written; but since you have a big part in this business of my writing I can't go against your advice. However, I couldn't write Levinson a note of apology even though he may be valuable, because I don't value his writings enough to do that. If it were just a social error I should gladly apologise, but I can't over an intellectual matter in which I am convinced that I am right. He may cherish aspirations of being a French critic but I can't see him any place in the great line.

I feel very [James McNeill] Whistlerish about many of these smart European scribblers and I am proud that my grievance is intellectual. My colored brothers don't understand it. They are very angry in America that I should stress in my book an unforgivable European attitude toward the colored brother, because, they say the Crackers will use it to parrot the old phrase: America, mainly the South, understands the Negro better. But I am interested in facts for the truth and not for one-sided propaganda.

You know when I published a little book of poems in London in 1921 The Spectator reviewed it and said that a white person must feel instinctively hostile to a black man's love poetry; one could not explain why but the feeling is there![1] Of course, I could explain why for The Spectator. A year later, I published much stronger and sensual love poems in Harlem Shadows in America and there was not a reviewer from the meanest section of the South that came anywhere [near] hinting at the Spectator's point of view. All the American reviewers took my poetry as poetry—written by a Negro. People may be crude, brutal and sans tradition in The New World, less profound than the Europeans as a people, not being so deeply rooted, but certainly America is free of the petty intellectual prejudices that hedge the European mind. Of course, I know that the war has had a devastating effect on the European mind as a whole. . . .

Of course, Banjo and his gang do stand head and shoulders above the whites of the Ditch. But they are the "hero" of the book. The Ditch people are not heroes, because every drop of idealism has been drained out of them by the hard cruel existence that is theirs. Some of my friendliest reviewers in America also failed to grasp this distinction. They merely see "Banjo" as a white-and-black novel and think I am deliberately stressing the finer virtues of the blacks. They are not psychologists and fail to see that it is the environment and business of the Ditch that make the whites what they are. The black boys must be better, because they are romantics[,] they are playing while the Ditch is grubbing for a living. Too bad "Banjo" had to be a black-and-white book. All through it are scattered characters, white and black, who react to the environment just as ordinary human beings would. There is Ray's friend, the white chauffeur, for instance, who lives off the girls, white and colored, but would not charge Ray for taking Banjo to the hospital. There is the Negroid girl who robs the very race-conseous [*sic*] Taloufa to give money to her white souteneur,[2] and others—

But I must pay the penalty of being a Negro and therefore even esthetically prejudiced against the whites! Not that I haven't strong prejudices against the general "white" attitude toward life. But I share such prejudices with some of the "best minds" among the whites themselves. But I am not soft-headed about the non-whites, for haven't they also all the faults of humanity in general with some of the virtues? My attitude is one of perpetual wonderment that the minority peoples can be as human (in the finer sense) as they are tumbling over one another like a gang of crabs in a barrel and struggling against the majority-imposed idea that they are inferior.

I will confess to an anti-French feeling in "Banjo," because, frankly, I do not like the French as social animals. I love to read them, from newspaper to classic, [Marcel] Proust, [André] Gide or [Henri] Barbusse; Voltaire[,] [Guy de] Maupassant or Anatole France, however different they may be, they have in common a magnificent malice that I have never met anywhere else in literature. But the French outlook on life seems to me about the narrowest of any people. They don't know the outside world and they don't care because it is not French. And I also think that intellectually they are over-influenced by politics. The French governments know too much about the literary + artistic life. I think it is a good thing for America that politicians know little about literature and art and care less. Only Theodore Roosevelt, if I know enough, tried to dabble in artistic things and he was an awful mess. You remember what he said about Tom Paine.

Thank you for the report your secretary sent me.[3] Now I can make plans about making a short trip to Genoa.

I am working very hard; have entered on the second part of my book. I shall let nothing interfere with me until I have finished. Every and any move I make must be in the interest of the book. It's a great job doing it, now that I am started, but living with it day + night is a great strain on the mind.

Am glad you are better. I am doing much better myself than when I was in Paris. It has suddenly turned cold here and that interferes with my work when the sun turns, for then I can't work. Warm regards for you + Mrs Bradley—

Sincerely
Claude McKay

WABLAR ALS

1. "Two Volumes of Verse," *Spectator,* 23 October 1920, 539–40. The reviewer writes, "His love poetry is clear of the hint which would put our racial instinct against him whether we would or no."

2. "Pimp" (French).

3. Paragraph not indented in original.

To William A. Bradley

13 November 1929

Madrid, Spain

Dear Bradley

If the negotiations for the translation of "Banjo" have not entirely gone through yet, I shouldn't mind if you could hold them up.

I should like to make my first appearance in French by a book that will be less controversial than "Banjo" may be—perhaps the one I am doing now.

I feel about the whole matter this way: There won't be much money in a French edition of "Banjo"—it's [*sic*] real value will be in the critical estimation. And because the "decor" is French and certain parts of it stress the social aspects of life and things[,] the critics may be apt to take it more as a sociological than as a literary or another artistic document.

The truth is the truth and I am not afraid of treating it realistically but I do not care either to stir up any kind of propagandistic controversy. And so I should prefer that "Banjo" should wait and, if it is worth translating, get an ordinary instead of a sensational send off.

I thought of writing directly to Rieder, but it might be better for you to see them. Maybe, on reflection they are less enthusiastic about the translation just as I am myself.

The new book is going splendidly and should be the preferable one, if any, to be translated. It is not a matter of "vanity" but simply because more of my whole self is in it. I heard from [Eugene] Saxton about my bank balance.

With my best regards for you and Madame Bradley[.]

Sincerely yours
Claude McKay

WABLAR ALS

To William A. Bradley

26 November [1929]

Madrid, Spain

Dear Bradley

I sent you a telegram in reply to your first card from Mallarco [*sic*] but I didn't receive the other until this morning!

Since the time was so short you might have telegraphed. However, nothing lost. I have about five more days' work on the book before I shall be ready with the first half—about 100 pages.

But I couldn't let you see it now because there are many essential emendations to be made.[1] I shall post it to you as soon as I get that done. I may think about moving if the creative mood doesn't continue to react as splendidly to this atmosphere as in the past.

I hope you had a beneficial rest and are much improved[.] I am feeling fine—the air is good here although it is very cold.

With my best as always,
Claude McKay

WABLAR ALS

1. Paragraph not indented in original.

To William A. Bradley

"Wednesday" [likely 4 December 1929]

Madrid, Spain

[On Letterhead: Hotel Florida, Madrid]

Dear Bradley

I worked all day yesterday and more than half the night to get the first part of the opus ready for you and brought it along this morning but missed you by half an hour. Sorry, for you could have taken it along on the trip and have an opinion ready for me on your return.

I'll just carry on with the rest, however, until I hear from you about it. I am anxious to get done early in the winter so that I can take a leisurely rest trip round the country.

I'll come down tomorrow afternoon to see you before you go. But I'm leaving the m.s. in case I miss you. I've typed out for you the meaning of folklore as given by my Twentieth Century Dictionary—that was always my idea of what it stands for.

I got some money from my bank this morning and so, if you are short, I can help you.

Faithfully
Claude McKay

WABLAR ALS

To William A. Bradley

"Thursday" [likely 5 December 1929]

Madrid, Spain

Dear Bradley

I shall come to see you this evening as you propose.

Your last card I received only on Monday, I think, and I replied to you at Paris, thinking you were going there directly from Barcelona as you had written you were due back home at the end of the month.

Right now I am engaged on the last chapter of the first half of the book that I expect to show you. But it is very essential to the whole that that chapter should be completed and very important emendations made throughout the text before I submit the stuff to you. The whole half, as I want it to be, will not be ready for about a week at least. As you might guess I am entirely absorbed in it—so much so that I was found a better lodging 2 weeks ago yet cannot take the time and the trouble to move.

Hope you had a nice trip up[.]

With best wishes
Sincerely
Claude McKay

WABLAR ALS

To Paulette Nardal

5 December 1929

Madrid, Spain

Dear Mlle. Nardal

I shall be too glad to correspond with your sister, but is there not a street, beside the address you gave me; or is that sufficient? I would have replied to [André] Levinson again, but my representative in Paris is a very cautious and practical person and thinks it is bad policy to make an enemy of Levinson and, through him, of all French critics! So I decided not to write again. I can use his "post scriptum" some day in a very effective manner, more than I could now, by replying to him again.

My representative has just come to Madrid too on a visit. He has seen Levinson and, as you rightly guessed, he is furious and very hurt. He complained that I sent my letter to the editors of the "Nouvelles Literaires" and not to <u>him</u>! Of course, I knew what I was doing and deliberately sent my letter where it could be most effective.

I have finished the first part of my new book, and expect to have the whole thing done early in the New Year.

I did not get the "Depeche African" with your article. The truth is that although I am a subscriber I have not had a copy of the paper since I came here and do not know whether it has ceased publication or not.

With my best wishes
Yours Sincerely
Claude McKay

PN ALS

To Max Eastman

7 December 1929

Madrid, Spain

My Dear Max,

It was a very sad business to miss you during your stay in Paris. You had promised to write before leaving America and up to the 28th of August when I left Paris I had no word. I was very unwell in Paris during the Spring + Summer and just had to get away with a student doctor the time I did for fear of a serious crisis and breakdown. I also wanted badly to start work on my new book so that I could concentrate my time on that and worry less about my health. And I could not write a line in Paris.

So I went down to St. Sebastian + had my mail forwarded to Biarritz hoping to get some word from you. I told all my friends I was returning to Paris in September to meet you. But when I did not hear up until the last week in September, I felt certain you had postponed your trip.

The student returned to Paris to work and I came to Madrid to settle down to doing my book. Still I had the intention to make the trip to Paris from here. But circumstances connived against our meeting. There are two Cook's offices here. I was staying in a hotel on the Prado and mistook the branch office at the Hotel Palace for the Main. It was two weeks before I found out my mistake when the clerk condescended to inform me that perhaps my mail was at the main office. He did vouchsafe the information after I had grown agitated and a little bit violent from seeing in the Latin quarter column of the Herald that you were in Paris! Then, I rushed to the main office and found your letter from London and telegram with a mountain of mail. I wirelessed you immediately paying 50 francs, but received answer that you had left your hotel without giving any forwarding address. Was that true? The telegram was sent through the Cook agency.

Of course I was very upset. I wanted so much to talk to you about a thousand things—yourself, Ileana, and our old group, politics, prose, poetry. I wanted to talk about your article in Harper's which I liked + your Nation controversy with Mike Gold which I did not like.[1] It was, to my mind, in bad taste and you made that Mike Gold get the better of you. I don't mind his getting the better of Floyd Dell, but I do mind about you who are incomparably his intellectual superior.

But I can't write about all those things, I haven't the time, Max. This writing business is sweet hell when one knuckles down in earnest to it. Writing poetry was just a pastime, but inventive prose is the daughter of a dog.

Wanted too to talk to you about myself intimately—my health. From knowledge + experience you know so much, I am sure a talk with you would have done me lots and lots of good. I'll have to wait until I come "home" next year. I am going just for a few months to get material for a book on that damned thing called nigger society. I am sure I couldn't live there again. I saw enough of Americans white and colored this summer in Paris to know that if I have even nursed the thought of living in America again I was a fool. Still, I want to come back to establish right of residence.

[William A.] Bradley has just come here to see me about my new book. I have done half of it—a straight story about a young colored man who had his legs amputated through an accident [and] got a few thousand dollars for it—a tidy sum and the effect of the amputation and the fortune on his character. I think it is my best thing up to now.

Bradley loved Spain; quant a moi je suis aficionado de ce pays. I wish you could come here with Eliena, You would, I am sure adore, it [*sic*]. There is something of the rich dark Russian quality in the people. I could define it easily in Morocco, but it eludes me here. Travelling + living in hotels are expensive. But once you settle down in a pension or a house of your own I think you would find it cheaper + and more congenial living than any other European country at present.

I see you did not go to Constantinople. What are your plans. I do wish you would write that great critical book + say all you really think without giving a thought to reputations. I think if you did really let yourself go such a book would be a landmark in American criticism.

Unchanging affection for you + Eliena
Claude

MEP ALS

1. Eastman's article in *Harper's* may be "The Cult of Unintelligibility" (April 1929) or "The Tendency toward Pure Poetry" (July 1929). Max Eastman and Michael Gold traded blows over the *New Masses*' rejection of Eastman's articles on Leon Trotsky's expulsion from the Communist Party in letters to the *Nation,* published in the 1 May and 15 May 1929 issues of the magazine.

To Langston Hughes

12 December 1929

Madrid, Spain

My dear Langston

What an amusing young friend you are in anticipating the reactions of this ferocious correspondent on the basis of his reputation among the Aframerican intellectuals! No, mon vieux, I do not intend to meet your anticipations—not if you should again casually mention my bête noire, lettuce,[1] fourscore instead of the four times in your recent letter, or better yet find play time to do it four hundred, four thousand or four million times. My only regret is that the point is not important enough for me to pass on to the publicity department of Harper's, so that it could be used to start a sort of Joan Lowell controversy that might sell another ten thousand copies of "Banjo."[2] If I only knew more about ships and sailors I would try to start something profitable, but alas not! my experience is quite amateurish, despite my publishers' puffs—two or three trips at most. You see, whenever I did menial work it was because I was <u>obliged to</u>. I am too lazy—too much of an esthete ever to have dreamed of doing scavenger work for the love of it or contact and sympathy with the lowest down toilers for copy! . . .

I heard from Mrs [Charlotte Osgood] Mason, thanks. She is rather nice with her white-motherly counsel. Charming person across her letters. Hope to see her when I get back to Gawd's own dear home this next year.

I have sent you a page from the "Nouvelles Litteraires." I got a lot of papers and magazines from many countries, all having something about Negro Renaissance and mentioning the prominent names, but I generally chuck them in the rubbish basket after a look at them. As I am always on the go I only hang on to the very necessary things.

Back to my reputation, I feel sure you may be the kind of person that wouldn't want me to have a different one. But the fact is that I have bawled very few people out in America. I write to so few there. I know I have stopped writing when correspondents bored me, but why should I allow myself to be bored for other people's pleasure. I do think, my dear Langston, that the cultured Negro gossips are just wagging away because I am notorious and the Negro Renaissance is fashionably on and they want to say something about me and they know so very, very little that they make a mountain out of a mole-hill. Of course I have let a couple of Negro editors understand that I didn't care a whoop about being published without being paid and Aframerican editors have not risen high enough in modern journalism to understand why free publicity—why having his name and mug in print!—is not enough for a Negro writer. The only person I really did bawl out and at the very top of my voice (and I am not even through with him yet) was the preeminently elegant Doctor [Alain] Locke for doing what you either would not have swallowed silently—changing the title and consequently the composite sense of an important poem of mine without my permission. Since then (although I called his attention to the wrong when the poem was first printed) he has deliberately and stubbornly refused to correct it!

I am aggressive. I know my faults—if that is a fault. I am not slick and will always call intellectual dishonesty by its proper name. In my up-and-down going and coming I have seen many nice slick and suave persons who made the pace for a little while, thinking they would win through by intellectual trickiness, but they didn't in the long run. Of course, I am thinking of the hard realm of the intellect and not political nor social.

But after all I have never been in with members of the Negro intelligentsia. Maybe they thought I was one of them, an easy one, and if in trying to know me they formed I was a hard case, all they had to do was to drop me hot, as they probably have done.

I know how I am beloved of them. The reception of Home to Harlem was a proof. And the way they all had me fixed. Most of the group drifts back to me from my friends of the enemy race. The Niggerati say that when I published Harlem Shadows I was on the threshold of a grand success! And I committed suicide by going to Russia. All sort of rumors were going around about this fool bastard. I was dead, so when I arose from the dead and came back very much alive with "Home To Harlem" those who had been falsely prophesying turned to hating. Let 'em.

Besides my rep. for aggressive action they say too that I know how to use and exploit people. My me! I never knew the best Negroes were so wealthy and generous and exploitable or I would not have been a life-long parasite on members of the enemy race who must have liked it, since they have not complained! But I suppose my rich and free-handed brethren must know of what they speak. Maybe, like gods, they have helped me in miraculously invisible ways.

Anyway I won't exploit them any more. I'll leave their field to the coming colleagues and hang on to my easy marks of the enemy race who seem to like it. And so right here, Langston, (of course, you know I couldn't dare mention you in the same breath with these people on whom I am now pouring vitriol) I must decline your friendly offer to do little favors for me on the other side. I don't mean to "exploit" you. I love you very much and I don't ever want to make an enemy of you—that gentle art of making enemies! Besides you're a poet like myself and the things (so prosaic) I would want you to do are just what I hate myself anyone asking of me!

But I am allright now. What I have done is to put myself on a business basis. My manager knows many people in New York in a business way and he handles all the little things that I need to have done. It is the best way. Since my manager has an interest in my labor he arranges to run me so as to bring out the maximum of work out of me and is very assiduous in attending to my little wants.

Now I must stop writing up to my reputation. End of this month I shall be four months in Spain. I am altogether aficionado of this insular end of Europe. I admire the life the Spaniards have developed for themselves more than any other in Europe. I like to live my own life and observe theirs without going too far into it. I have never liked going too far into other people's lives. I make a few acquaintances and enjoy the spectacle quietly. I have been here at Madrid all the time, except for a month in the coast towns of the

North. A very modern city this, with rock-solid Spanish-american buildings and magnificent boulevards, too many taxicabs, too much traffic, enormous cafés and luxurious cinema houses given over to all-American films—many atrocious talkies that the Spaniards do not understand—yet they pack the cinema houses, because they are bitten by the bug of American modernism and rather think that all American innovations are <u>the</u> things. I spend much of my night time going to the cheap cinema houses in the working class districts where they often have dancing and singing of Spanish songs.

I can't say I love Madrid as a city but I have been able to work here, which I couldn't do in Paris and the inhabitants are charming enough even though their el Negro muy simpatico becomes a little tiresome to play up to.—I am going to Barcelona for Christmas. When I finish my book I want to make another grand tour of the country.

No, I shouldn't be surprised to hear that you were a member of a country club + playing golf. I don't know the game myself, but I grew up on <u>cricket</u>+ and horse racing and have always loved sports. Wish I had money to indulge in grand style. I have my mind's eye on a roadster—to begin with . . . I thought you would prefer to live in Harlem, you love it so much, but I suppose being near is just as good.

Of course, I am glad to hear of your novel + hope you make money. Making + having real money don't make one a capitalist—wish I had some capitalistic things myself. You might have told me however, in your last letter but one, that you were writing a novel. You must have been well under way when you wrote that you did not feel like writing another line of poetry! Then I should have written you an entirely different kind of letter from my last. If it was a secret for a while I could not, being so far away, let it out. Thus you prevented me from saluting you as a colleague + a recruit to the subtle art of prose in my last letter + now cher confrere I take the opportunity + the pleasure doing it.

—Claude

+ Cricket you know is <u>the</u> game of the British. Supposed to be a big, fair, lofty fine-fellows game. Once you are cricket aficionado you enter the gentleman class symbolically (if you're poor + black + not English) and are supposed to be broadminded + tolerant and all the gentlemanly things, hence the phrase: That is (or is'seh[?]) cricket!

LHP ALS

1. Lettuce: slang expression for money.

2. Silent film actress Joan Lowell (1902–1967) published a 1929 autobiography titled *Cradle of the Deep* that was revealed to be largely fabricated.

To William A. Bradley

21 December 1929

Madrid, Spain

[On Letterhead: Hotel Nacional, Museo del Prado, Madrid]

Dear Bradley

Your letter came the very day I was quitting my pension and if it was a day later I may not have had it. I always use the transient address of hotels and pensions for local purposes only, because I do not consider the proprietors anywhere very intelligent and competent in handling one's mail.

I was very relieved to hear from you at last. I told you (whether you believed it or not) that I wouldn't be able to carry on with the book until I heard from you. It's a congenital state of nervousness, something like your anxiety (and mine too) when you want to take a special train. I spent the interval hospitably reading J. N.[1] Lawrence, [André] Gide + [Jean] Cocteau.

It was really better you didn't spend that extra day here to talk the m.s. over with me. I rather prefer the letter. Instead of the necessarily diplomatic suggestions of conversational criticism, you are in your letter straight, sharp + direct-to-the-point—and that is more to my liking.

I grew up in a hard school of criticism—first my brother was a sharp critic of my infantile attempts at versifying—second the Englishman[2] by whom I was disciplined in poetry. From him I learned to make the most of the simple rugged word. Later when I went to the States and met Max Eastman who was more interested in the polished work I had the background of my earlier training to rest against.

Of course, I'll tackle Taloufa's story in another form. I changed off to the personal because I'm identifying myself more with Malty than any other character in this story and I wanted to make him as objective as possible because I am so much like him. You see there is and won't be any Ray in the tale. I realized that the form was very awkward and that some of my best scenes, the love ones for instance, would be stifled under it.

Of the racial stuff in the story I felt that that came naturally as the talk and thought of the Negroes, like their complexion, giving a peculiar and definite color to the human story. I never thought of it as propaganda nor felt that way in writing, because I know that even the happy-go-lucky Negro does think and feel and talk that way. I haven't read any of the recent problem novels—like Lewisohn's "The Island Within"[3] for example, but I don't see why a good problem novel of Negro life should not be written.

I will admit that perhaps Taloufa's state of mind and my analysis of it do not go with the picaresque story—but if I am to go on as a writer my characters beside acting must think and talk some sense and if those characters are mainly Negroes, there will certainly be in their thinking and talking ideas peculiar to Negroes.[4] After all we read about Americans and Europeans, Russians, Mongolians and Indians for the human interest, but we also look for the little things that mark each out as a different division of the human species. To me the most interesting thing is that all people are fundamentally human under the apparent differences. That will not prevent individuals from thinking and trying to act along tribal, national and racial lines. The fact is that the majority of people do—quite unconsciously and the non-conformists are very few.

Primarily I am not writing a sentimental story about Taloufa. His character is changed by his fortune—but that is also a common human thing. Taloufa excuses himself because he has been amputated but that is also a common human trick.

However, from your criticism I see now where by analyzing his motives I may make him too unsympathetic for the general reader and so I shall try to make him more attractive. He isn't though. It's the girl Zhima who runs away with the story and after her Malty. The climax comes when Taloufa is arrested just when he was about to slip away and Malty + others have to try and get him freed. To make Taloufa extremely acceptable I should have to write a real sob-sister story and that I just cannot do.

I am going to start in afresh on the second part and make a different thing of it. No, I'm not discouraged. I am sure I have a real fine story in hand. The thing is to put it over.

Please send me back the m.s. with your remarks so I can get down to business. 50000 is my goal and I know that to make it is no easy job, so don't bite your tongue in criticism—the harder the better to spur this competitor on. I see now too where I have missed writing the best chapter of the story when Taloufa returns to Marseille.

But—I don't see where I have gone over the old Banjo ground—I especially tried to avoid that—you must show me where—

With my best regards
Sincerely yours
Claude McKay

WABLAR ALS

1. McKay's handwriting is difficult to decipher here; he may mean D. H. Lawrence.

2. He means Walter Jekyll.

3. Ludwig Lewisohn, *The Island Within* (1929). Lewisohn, a successful Jewish-American writer, published a number of books dealing with Jewish-American identity and experience. McKay seems to misspell the name here, but the nature of the misspelling is unclear due to his handwriting.

4. A character—later renamed Lafala—in McKay's posthumously published *Romance in Marseille* (2020).

To Louise Bryant

5 February 1930

Barcelona, Spain

[On Letterhead/crossed out: Hotel Barcelona]

Dear Louise

I don't know if you would like Spain (were you ever there?) but you might try it. The country is just reeking with taboos, conspicuously against women. They don't go to cafés nor cabarets, can't smoke. Yet they appear happier than Frenchwomen. I suppose they just pour all of themselves into sex. Arab life, as I saw it in Morocco, seem[s] freer to me in spite of the veiling of the women. It is based in certain fixed rules and divisions and not just taboos as [with the] Spanish—yet I like Spain. Can't say just why I do so much. Maybe it's the music[,] the civilized indolence—and the taboos! Add to this a native Spanish dignity of every day contact between individuals that seems peculiar to the Spanish. It isn't a formal thing as in France, nor cold as in England just an unobtrusive thing that makes you feel that the people in spite of superficial coarseness + crudity know what is genuine courtesy.

So here I am with a large sunny room (found it this week) on one of the Ramblas, and now hard at work on a real story about Marseille. "Banjo" was just broad daubs of impressionism with notes to them. I was too near the first book and Marseille too to do a real story—the scenes tumbled out in a half-jumbled manner.

Like yourself, I am quite alone—some evenings I visit the bar-fonds for relaxation where there are a couple of Negroes who speak French. And sometimes I meet sailors from the ships there. However, I think it is better to be alone if you can be happy that way than to be worried all the time by uncongenial companions. I didn't enjoy Paris a bit last summer and I felt remote and old-fashioned among the Americans white and black that I tracked along with.

[William A.] Bradley came to see me in Madrid early in December. I came here for Christmas and unexpectedly ran into him again this time with Mrs Bradley. He talked about a book you were doing for him. I have decided to change the form of my book too after talking to him.

I was promised a free house to live in in the native quarter of Fez, but I am afraid I can't go this winter. I want to finish my book and Morocco makes me feel so lazy. I thought I would finish the book so I could go this month, but I can't. Told Buffy [Glassco] + Graeme [Taylor] they could take the house if they cared to but they have written that their finances have gone bad. Glad you are all right and working. I have some magnificent days + some terribly low ones. I want to go to Germany this summer—for the cure!

Please let me hear what you intend doing[.]

Sincerely Claude

LBP ALS

To Charlotte Osgood Mason

13 February 1930

Barcelona, Spain

Dear Mrs Osgood

Hard work on my new story has kept me postponing writing to you right along. The only break was my coming here for Christmas. I went round amusing myself with some friends for two weeks or more and just forgot the job.

Now I am on it again. Plenty of writing and condensing and rewriting. I am doing a "pure" story and it's harder than the other two in which I used so much scenery and color to pull the tale along.

You must have heard that I missed Max [Eastman]. He didn't notify me in time. I was travelling in Northern Spain and when I reached Madrid and received his letter it was too late to go to see him in Paris. I have written to him in New York but maybe he is too busy to reply. If you see him do please remind him of me.

No: no earthly thing could spoil me—it is too late now for that! I am proof against that, like an old preserved skin from which all decaying substances have been removed by the surgeon hand of time. I feel almost as you do toward "Banjo." I was too near the Marseille scene and too much in the midst of what I was writing about. I like penetrating criticism—it is a help I believe to all truly creative people. I was lucky always in having good critics from my early beginning days. What I can't stand is the personal tripe of these times that passes for criticism. There are few critics who can evaluate a work of art for itself. Most of them start ranting about the motives and desires and ideas of the artist. Whatever these may be they should not concern the critic so much. They are rather the concern of the artist's biographer.

The Negro renaissance movement in America seems a hopeless mess to me.—I cannot help being frank.—If I were in touch with any of the young aspiring Negro artists I'd advise them to get as far away as possible from it. I read the writings of the so-called leaders and I got a good drift of the whole thing from some of its members in Paris last summer. They all are no doubt terribly insincere. They have no real idea of what they want to do—what they can get in an artistic form from this life of the Negro. They were much more interested in the opinions of a few white persons of <u>authority</u>—even though these were lacking in the fine esthetic spirit of appreciation.

The people that seemed more real, interesting and sincere to me were some "society" Negroes who were out to work "Negro art and artists" for all they were worth socially. I really prefer them to the Negro intellectuals. They are at least not fake. They know what they want. They are good tinsel.

Spain is wonderful for me, after the formal cut-to-pattern life of France. There is something very American in this civilization. In the architecture[,] in the manners of the people I find things that have subtly influenced and fashioned American (North) civilization—things that I have never noticed in any other European country. But one thing the Spaniards have that we haven't in America + that I fail to find anywhere else in Europe is a deep-rooted courtesy for another human being. Added to this is the dignity of being human. The country is full of taboos—because of the Church and the attitude toward sex and women in particular. The Arabs are a freer people—yet I like the

Spaniards more! There can be no doubt that a great deal of the art forms and the social customs of the people is derived from the Arabs. While I was in Morocco, the Arabs called the best of their songs, Chansons Andaluz. But the Spanish Flamenco is much richer[,] more vivid and vital than the Arab thing. Perhaps it is because the Spaniards could develop the art in the theatre. The Arabs have no theatre (they are just starting in under the French in Morocco) and like the Jews no pictorial art.

I hope you did nothing about the magazines, thanks, because I <u>did</u> renew the ones I needed when I returned to Paris.

My health is much improved, but far from good. I hope to go to Germany to get a thorough overhauling in the Spring or Summer. If only I can finish my book in time.

It (the book I am doing) is about an African youth, a final adventure of his many that crippled him—how he pulled himself together and returns to Africa. It isn't a sentimental story nor propagandist. Just a straight tale that has its basis in a true incident.

Langston Hughes + [Alain] Locke write beautifully about you. I like Langston's work very much. I think he has big stuff in him. Locke is nice. He <u>means</u> well but his judgment is weak + because he is so uncertain about his own opinions and creative art in general his intellectual attitude is rather negative. The negative style is quite a phenomenon in Aframerican. I like it in speech, for it is both amusing and revealing, but I do not like it in writing especially creative writing. It lacks frankness + sincerity[,] two things it seems to me that are necessary to good writing.

Barcelona is charming + I love it. I loved it more before the International Exposition. But I am enjoying it as much as I can while writing. The first week of this month was like spring—but this week brought rain + sleet. With warmest regards

Sincerely yours
Claude McKay

ALP ALS

To William A. Bradley

17 February 1930

Barcelona, Spain

Dear Bradley

I am buried in the book denying myself everything, all indulgences except the absolutely necessary so that I may finish it sometime this spring to take a good spell of rest and play.

That's why I couldn't write to you before and have neglected all my correspondence. Worst of all, I haven't thanked [Eugene] Saxton since he had my letter of credit sent to me just when you came to Madrid. I was waiting to hear from you about the book as I wanted to report to Saxton. And when I got your long letter just before quitting Madrid I forgot everything and everybody in my eagerness for a change of scene and in thinking up places for a new drive in the book. You might drop a word of explanation to Saxton when and if you do write.

Well, I changed lots of things even names (Lafala now for Taloufa) so that I should work clear of the dead weight of "Banjo." Then I picked up Lafala (Taloufa) right on his return to Dreamport and he is very manageable and going pretty good. This I am going to clap right on the first part that brings us up to Lafala's leaving New York. I don't think I will get over 200 pages out of the stuff, but it will be a neat compact little story. I have left out all the long-windedness you picked me up on—some of which was really introduced to spread out and lengthen the tale.

I am now on a chapter that deals with the important climax of Lafala's getting arrested and as soon as that is finished, in about a week or two, you will be able to judge what I have done.

My only worry is that with the change in form and method the story has taken on quite a coating of sentimentality. I can't help it at all, it is in spite of me, that the thing has taken that course. It lacks too the hilarity that Jake and Banjo had, but Lafala is a different type. African and the African appears to me more sombre than the American Negro. However, what Lafala lacks in hilarity he makes up for in emotional loving.

I enclose two letters referring to "Home to Harlem" and "Banjo." Perhaps it would be better you took the matter up with both parties. I did hear from a friend that "Banjo" was being done in German, but I did not know by whom.

I wonder, too, if you could have a box of mine removed from Cook's and put it in a corner of your office? It is not large and won't be in the way. I am enclosing the vouchers and shall pay all the expenses so soon as I know how much[.]

Well, I am happy to hear Mrs Bradley is all well again, my regards to her. The weather here is fine—cold enough but plenty of sunshine—something like late Autumn in New England. For the present I am in a large old-fashioned room on the Rambla [de las] Flores and get the sun from morning until evening.

By the way did Harper's British prize prospect take definite shape? It would be fun to walk away with it from the English.—Had a card from Algiers from Louise Bryant. She thinks she might come to Spain.

Oh, I mustn't forget that I found out it isn't true about that Arab lad having to change his religion to get a job. I happened to run into [a] Swiss here who belongs to an association of strangers working here. There are lots of them of all nationalities—engineers, mechanics + interpreters—clerks in hotels + stores always have a chance. But Spain is a comparatively poor and except for the large cities a very insular country, therefore it isn't easy for an unskilled worker to pick up jobs as one might in the U.S. and perhaps in France.

The Arab is an awful liar. He was brought here during the Riff [*sic*] war by a Capitaini [*sic*] General of Barcelona and he himself (I have heard) expressed his desire to become a Catholic. He isn't a member of an orthodox Mussulman family—but the street Arab type that will say or do anything to get something material even of insignificant value. He is clever though to have worked himself in where he is in the telephone company. I met lots like him in Morocco—very clever at catching on to mechanical things but curiously they seem to act without thinking—they seemed quite rootless compared to the Jews who seemed to be forging ahead + leaving the Arabs behind materially + mentally.

Sincerely Yours
Claude McKay

P.S. Here is a story I rather like. The author is a friend of mine and if you think it worth while you might get in touch with her. I didn't like the last paragraph because we see the lesson, implicit in the tale, without her pointing it out but I like the decor. It is West Indian[,] might have been in Jamaica, if the characters didn't speak French. You might get her to write a book of them—there is a great deal of interest + curiosity in the States about the West Indies. CMcK

WABLAR ALS

To Paulette Nardal

[early March 1930, before 18 March]

Valencia, Spain

[On Letterhead: Regina Hotel, Valencia]

Dear Mlle. Nardal

I have sent your story to my representative asking him, if he likes it, to get in touch with you, because I think you could do a number of such stories to make a nice little book—10 or 12 of them.

It's a fine story and I loved it, except for the last paragraph where you yourself point out the lesson. I think all of us Negroes have the fault of overdoing a piece of creative work. I pointed out too many lessons myself in "Banjo." [René] Maran's preface to "Batouala" should have gone in a book of essays.[1] We are prone to that fault because the white critics (like my friend [André] Levinson) insist upon seeing us not as <u>Negroes who are creative</u> artists just as white Frenchmen might be creative artists, but almost always as <u>Negroes who are different human beings.</u> Our one answer to that must be writing the swine down. Forget them when we write and we shall go so high as to confound them.

When we have something controversial to spit out let's put it in an essay, but try our best to keep our art above the heads of the white mob.

I gave W. A. Bradley, (my representative) 5 Rue St. Louis-en-l'Ile, your address.

I hope you will forgive my long delay but I have been working hard so much so that my head just refused to go on and I had to quit and come to Valencia for a few days['] rest. But I am going back to Barcelona at the end of the week . . . I have just noted your request for the photograph and if it is not too late I shall hunt one up when I go back to Barcelona.

You mustn't mind our pretentious blacks and browns and near-whites who object to realistic art. It's our best road to salvation as a race. We must ignore our <u>trop raffiné</u> members of the race. We are realists and artists because au fond we are more sensitive than they . . . Your story is splendid. I saw something of my own Jamaican background unfolding as I read it. And it is fine that you with your upbringing and education are able to interpret such a phase of life. Is it not much better for you with sympathy + understanding to make such a piece of life breathe and glow in print than for a Paul Morand to go and observe superficially and write about it foolishly?

I think it would be a fine think [*sic*] if you could have a book of short stories translated and published in America first—get a good press there and after publish in French.# I had my first story published in French—in Europe. Or anyway it is done it doesn't matter whilst it is done right. Excuse me saying so much but in spite of my long silence (it was done only to hard work) I am quite wild about your story—it is so good. It makes me ponder on the artistic treasures we have in the race—if we could just end loose—cut loose and away from our own inhibitions—forget the conclusion of our friendly-white enemies—and create—create!

Let those who are not artists do the propaganda. We can help them here by creating pure art—although we cannot convince them of that now.

When you write your sister tell her that I am going to write to her soon—soon. I shall try to get off a card from here.

With my warmest regards
Claude McKay

P.S.
O yes! I do believe in a good black Press! Why not—you mustn't take "Banjo" literally—it is fiction! But my criticism there was of the Aframerican press, which for the exception of the Crisis—Opportunity + one or two others is very bad. They have no standard. . . .

About myself writing—I am too busy now—but if you could send me a questionnaire of exactly what you need it would be easier for me to answer you. Then you could put what I say in an article or in any form you like . . . Sure! I believe in a black Press—only where they live among the whites they should not isolate themselves intellectually but organise to put themselves over—like the Jews who control the Press of New York!

CMcK

Because all Europe is now practically writing for the American market which I consider a bad decadent sign.

PN ALS

1. René Maran's 1921 novel *Batouala* won the French Prix Goncourt. The novel's preface urges Black writers to speak about their experiences of colonialism.

To Louise Bryant

[early March 1930, before 18 March]

Barcelona, Spain

[on postcard of Seville—no postmark]

Dear Louise: Did you get my letter in reply to your card from Alger? I thought you would let me know your plans and whether you would try Spain. What about coming for Holy Week at Seville? This is the time when you might like the country best. The chairs are out on the ramblas, the crowds fill the paseos before the lunch and dinner hour with the girls and young men calling to one another, sea bathing and bull fights (I think you might like the colorful spectacular side of the bull ring) have begun and there's a ferial air everywhere. It is all miraculously different from the heavy masculine atmosphere of the winter. I have just got back from Valencia—a beautiful town + I am feeling much better. My new novel is half done, the rest will not be so bad as was the working out of the plot to the climax which has been reached. Had to rewrite + rewrite. I want to be done by early summer so I may be able to go to Berlin to consult a specialist. Hope you will drop me a line.

With my best + sincerest
Claude McKay

LBP APS

To William A. Bradley

18 March 1930

Barcelona, Spain

Dear Bradley

I am clean knocked out by this latest Royalty Statement with a charge of #150.75 (one hundred and fifty and seventy five dollars) for "making corrections on 2000 copies of Banjo." That seems a stupendous amount to me, especially as there is a change of #51.57 for author's corrections in the statement of June 1929.

I made no page proofs corrections on "Banjo" nor any after the book was published. And according to the contract (art. 3.) I should be charged extra for corrections only on submission of the "final revised copy." The above charge therefore seems unfair and I don't understand it nor the cause of it, unless the Firm had printed off 2000 copies of "Banjo" before I had received and corrected the galley proofs! If it is so I should not be held responsible for the cost of correction. I have written to [Eugene] Saxton and do hope that you will take the matter up with him also for the item has taken all that I should have received in payment this time—money that I have great need of.

Many thanks about the trunk. Please let me know the cost. Thanks also for your letters. That of the 23rd ult. was very encouraging and as a result I finished up the first half with a happy flourish. I feel the story well under my hand now. The love interest is paramount and yet the problem of environment and racial distinctions implicit in the story are being revealed without any obvious philosophical reflections on them as occurred in my first draft. And as you predicted Lafala is standing up strong on his own corks without any special aid from myself and the Arab girl is growing bigger than I ever dreamed and running away with the book and me.

I came up from Valencia in time to see Josephine Baker act here.[1] I had seen her in New York before she became famous, but it was the first time of seeing her since the Folies Bergere debut. All the people I saw in Paris last Summer said she was finished. But after seeing her I don't think so. She's got a wonderful body well-kept with which she can do a thousand things. She's like a wonderful tall monkey and has more real acting in her and more possibilities that [*sic*] any girl that was in "Blackbirds." All she needs is a first-class manager and a company—better a colored one to support her. She doesn't go over all by herself and is positively awful when she dresses up like a mannikin all in the wrong colors and sings sentimental love songs.

It was very sad to hear of D. H. Lawrence's death. Although I have never met him, it was like losing a close friend. Reading his Lady Chatterl[e]y's lover I felt the same sensation that I did when as a boy of 18 I read Shakespeare's Venus and Adonis. What a beautiful love poem. I really felt it was marred by the stock phrases of the underworld that Lawrence introduced in it. Lawrence has lived a long time away from his proletarian environment. Proletarians don't use words like "shit" "piss" and "cunt" in the hearing of their women nor in referring to them. They use such words only among men. Perhaps workingmen are even more reserved about obscene expressions before women than "bourgeois" people. I never heard peasants talk like that nor workingmen white or black in America[,] and I spent over a year in England and met many Welsh miners and other classes of workingmen who I never heard talk to nor about their women as Lawrence's gamekeeper does. However I have heard intellectual bohemians talk like that. But it didn't seem real. I was always under the impression that they were trying over self-consciously to be revolutionary and free.

Take the word "fuck" for example. It's a dead bad word among us. You can't revive it by printing—although one may get a temporary kick from seeing it in print. But workingmen don't use it nor about their women. They use it about a whore only in a nasty sense. If a man goes with a nice girl even for money he never says: "I fucked her," but always: "I had a good time," or "I had a nice piece," or some phrase. Simply because the word "fuck" has a bad meaning among them. It is like a fist in the face and is nearly always used in that sense. When a man says: "Fuck you!" it is a blow stronger than "son of a bitch" and when he uses it about or to a woman it is that he is disgusted with her. Of course I realize that words that are quite dead among working people themselves may seem quite vivid and alive to people of another class, and vice versa. Lawrence doesn't seem to realize this and is all mixed up in his article censorship.

His "Lady Chatterl[e]y's Lover" is a wonderful modern love poem. One wants to shout for it, every literate person to read it. And so one feels that it is too bad that such a book should be censored because of a few banal functional words that are apparently not inevitable to the recital of the poem.

I have carefully planned out the rest of the book to the clear end, I was tied up a long time doping it out. Now that I have it I think the second part will go easier than the first.

Glad to hear that Mrs Bradley is all well again . . . Every thing here is quiet politically. The Spaniards are regionalists and have no nationalistic feeling. Suppose you'd have to get them a few rich colonies to get them thinking that way again. Only the military and students seem to care about politics. Perhaps because they are the classes who benefit directly from it. Life is just too quiet and sometimes I feel as if I could stand a little more excitement.

With best regards
Yours Sincerely
Claude McKay

WABLAR TLS

1. Josephine Baker performed "La Venus de Ébano" on 3 March 1930 in the Principal Palace in Barcelona. See Jordi Pujol Baulenas, *Jazz en Barcelona, 1920–1965* (Barcelona: Almendra Music), 38.

To William A. Bradley

30 March 1930

Barcelona, Spain

Dear Bradley

Just a word before going off to thank you for your letter. I was really anxious to have it, even though I felt I had taken the right turn with the new draft because I do set a high value in your opinion and the occasional hints that I can turn to good account.

I have worked all the Genoa part of the story into half a dozen pages, bringing Malty in under another name and a role in keeping with his character. As the story carries on Lafala's sentimentality explains itself + the sophisticated reader will forgive it—I think. Because it isn't a soft heart sentimentality but the sentimentality of sensuality arising out of his strong sexual appetite and the weakness of the flesh. In the end he gets out of it by his own deliberate action and it is Aslima who suffers—for she is really sincere.

I am glad however, that you feel doubtful about Lafala for it strengthens the suspense of the tale and that is my weak point in storytelling. On the other hand by making Lafala a little sentimental I can work in a lot of the poetry of love, a strong element in my talent which I cannot put into an entirely picaresque character.

I was a little worried thinking there may be a smell of Jake and Felice of "Home To Harlem" in the intimate scenes between Aslima + Lafala, but since you don't scent it they may be alright. Come to think of it there wasn't much intimacy drawn between Jake + Felice + so it leaves me a clear field to work on Aslima + Lafala.

Won[']t you please have made and sent to me one fair typed copy of the m.s. + you may keep the original? The cost may be put to a/c. I don't have an arranged copy + I won't bring myself to think of doing another copy myself.

Am going to rewrite the chapter beginning with Lafala's return to Dreamport + give a clear picture of the two girls + Lafala's relation with them instead of the present wobbly version.[1]

No thanks. I don't need any cash right now. I am working with the hope of getting a thousand when the job is done or nearly and I don't want to be deprived of the stimulation of the spur by getting it before! CMcK

Am going off somewhere with a new acquaintance for the Easter vacation—but will write—Taking the job along, though. Hope Mrs Bradley is keeping well—my best regards to you[.]

Sincerely
Claude McKay

WABLAR ALS

1. Beginning with this sentence, the text is written sideways in the margins. It is unclear if McKay intends to begin a new paragraph here.

To Jenny Serruys Bradley

14 April 1930

Barcelona, Spain

Dear Mrs Bradley

Just returned here from Valencia and Saragosa [*sic*] to meet a friend coming here from Paris for Pâques, and found Mr. [William A.] Bradley's letter. I suppose he is now on his way to America. In the same mail I have a letter from Mr [Eugene] Saxton asking if he may see part or all of the new book so that he could report on it for their book conference that will be held on the 1st of May. But unfortunately I haven't a good duplicate to send. As I was working fast I did not make one of the first 40 or 50 pages more or less which I rewrote. But Mr Bradley promised to give instructions to have a new copy made for me. If this has been done won't you please send me the new copy and the original direct to Mr Saxton? It may reach him by the first and be of some use, although it will not give him an adequate conception of the new book, for I am again making important changes in it.

I may go to Seville for the Samaña Santa if my friend come[s] to-day—but will be back here by the end of the week. I hope I shall finish up work next month and return to France.

With my best wishes for bonnes Pâques[.]

Sincerely yours
Claude McKay

WABLAR ALS

To William A. Bradley

25 June 1930

Berlin, Germany

Dear Bradley: I just have your letter and one from [Eugene] Saxton. I mailed the manuscript to Saxton the last week in May and left Barcelona right after about the time you were preparing to leave New York I dare say. I had hoped it would have reached New York before you left so that you could read the completed version. There was nothing to do but send it to Paris, your not being there.

I came right through from Barcelona to Berlin chiefly to consult a specialist for my head which has been giving me a lot of trouble and was very bad during the last month of working on the book. And I shall probably stay here for treatment this summer, do the proofs and a personal preface or footnote I have in contemplation for the novel. I want to pull myself together this summer and I understood that Berlin was about the best place for competent medical diagnosis and treatment.

Saxton said he was sailing on the 7th inst. for London so he must be there or in Paris now. He also said that they all, like yourself, liked the first part. But I changed it a lot in the new version, making the rivalry clear between La Fleur and Aslima and showing why Lafala preferred the last-named and (toward the end) the emotional secret that dominated him throughout the affair. So the completed tale is perfectly plausible and even throughout and infinitely better than the first draft that you read.

I'm against the 1931 publication date—very, very much. If the book is too late for September, then it might be published in November or December, but I should like it to come out in 1930. I wish you would take the matter up with Saxton. I suppose the completed m.s. did not arrive before he left but he said he would ask his assistant to keep him posted about it. So I wish you would put as much emphasis as you can on this year's publication in your talk with Saxton.

I am running very short of money and as soon as Saxton has his report I should like a thousand advance on the book. I suppose I can ask for that with impunity in spite of the reported slump in the book market and the price-cutting war . . . I should be glad too if you would send me the little amount you owe from the last Harper payment after making your deductions. Any little will be very helpful right now.

Will you please send me the original of the first draft of the m.s.? There were a few lapses in the typed script that Mrs Bradley sent me which I'll need to verify . . . Please give her my regards . . . I'd like to hear too as soon as is possible if Harper received the completed m.s. all right, for I haven't a fair duplicate.

My mail address here is with Thomas Cook & Son, Unter den Linden 22 and tel. add. Reiseunion if you should need it.

I went up to Montserrat in April and it was splendid and back to Valencia for a few days. I was reading [Henry de] Montherlant's article on Montserrat in the Nouvelles Litteraires which incited me to visit the place again.[1]

Hope you enjoyed New York and that your business went well and that the heat isn't so oppressive in Paris as it is here in Berlin.

With kind regards
Yours Sincerely
Claude McKay

WABLAR TLS

1. Henry de Montherlant, "Montserrat," *Les nouvelles littéraires,* 26 April 1930, 5.

To Louise Bryant

27 June 1930

Berlin, Germany

[On Letterhead: Hotel Hermes, Berlin]

Dear Louise

It was good to hear of your finished story and that you are concentrating on your writing. I hope you will do a book—it's a long time due! And you've had a full enough life for a big one when you do do it.

I left Barcelona the last week in May and should have had your letter there according to the date but it wasn't mailed until the 21st, a week later. I heard from an acquaintance you were divorced and felt badly about you not having custody of your child. I suppose you will be allowed to see her, though. I can understand your being ill and down with all the trouble. But you ought to pull yourself to[,] soon again, if you can control the drinking. I have to, as I would no doubt pop off at any time if I didn't; And sometimes the craving is so strong, I have to indulge a little pint to quiet it.

See, I'm here in Berlin. Came straight through because I want to consult a specialist here, they say they are good. (I wonder if you know anybody here could help me find a reasonable one[.]) My "vertige" was very bad during the Spring and I felt I ought to be overhauled. They say the German doctors were better than the French for me chiefly because the German remedies are superior. Max [Eastman] writes that the best doctors are in America—but I am in Europe!

I finished my book in May. I had sent the first part of it to Harper's + have just received a letter from [Eugene] Saxton saying they all like it. But I have improved all of it a great deal, so the completed text is quite different in style and richer in matter.

Saxton is travelling in Europe + I hope I may meet him. Did I tell you he mentioned you in a letter some time back? [William A.] Bradley is back from America.

I am feeling pretty rotten under the "vertige" and sciatica. I am so tired out doing the book it's too bad I am not in good health to enjoy myself. I should like to go off to some mountain place where there was plenty of fruits + water for swimming.

Hope you are out of your bed by now[.]

Always sincerely Claude

LBP ALS

To Max Eastman

27 June 1930

Berlin, Germany

[On Letterhead: Hotel Hermes, Berlin]

My dear Max

Only two things perhaps could prevent me from writing all this time—a long unbroken dream of love or serious devotion to some duty. There has been nothing lengthy or dreamy about my love affairs, so you'll understand that I was really buried deep in my latest devotional exercise to the gods.

The first part of the book that I worked at at Madrid until Christmas was only the outline and after completing it, it was rather hazy. I went to Barcelona + rested and played through the holidays. The [William A.] Bradleys came to see me there (he had previously been to Madrid in November.)[.] After they left I started the real work on "The Jungle and the Bottoms" (the title of the new novel) and while in the midst of it received your long overland-and-sea letter.[1] It had to go with the pile because I could not write you just a note on card in reply. So I kept straight on knuckling down to the job, except for a week-end off to Valencia in March, because of the pressure of "le vertige" on my brain. Valencia was lovely with chubby orange trees full of fruit, fields upon fields of them and pickers and carriers and ships loading and sailing and the town has a fluffy creamy color that is very delicious. I returned to Barcelona feeling much better and finished the book last month.

The scene is the same as "Banjo," but I call the town Dreamport as it might have been any of six European ports, but the book is not "scenic"; it is a real story with something of a plot, involving a West African young man (who had lost his legs stowing away and received good compensation through the efforts of an ambulance-chaser) and a North African Negroid girl. They two represent the "jungle" in the "bottoms" that the girl, who is a whore there, wants to leave to go back to Africa with the man. I sent a first draft to [Eugene] Saxton and have just received a letter saying they all like it. I sent the completed m.s. the last week in May, but I am afraid Saxton did not get it before he left for Europe on the 7th of this month. I was so tired I did not even enclose a letter. I want them to publish this year, but they want to put it off until January. I think this year is the better, I have a feeling for it.

As I couldn't get to America, I came from Barcelona straight through to Berlin to get some real treatment. Everybody says the German treatment is better. In Spain all the doctors use the German method. They say the German chemical products are better, but on account of the commercial rivalry they are not used in France. That's a good subject for an Upton Sinclair tale. I have very little money left so I hope the treatment won't be too expensive. My two last tests were negative, but the heavy dizziness in my head is awful and I am rather a victim of muscular pains that move regularly from one part of the body to the other. And in my case I don't know what is the exact cause as I have had both venereal diseases. I have been here two weeks but haven't seen a specialist yet. Everything is very dear, and doctors are not inexpensive, so I am waiting for information about a reasonable and good one.

I wish you were here to give me counsel! I feel pretty strong and optimistic, but one never can tell. Then I have been told that too much medicine is just as dangerous as too little!

I was glad to hear about your work, that you are making good money and that you still think of your creative work. Did you finish and distribute your Russian film?[2] I suppose there is quite a bit of money in it! Over here everybody is talkie-mad. I can't stand them although I'll admit some talkies are technically fine. I was never a great lover of the movies anyway. I met a man last summer, Montgomery Evans, who knows you and seems to be making money out of the independent films business.

I saw a good article of yours in either the Bookman or Harper[']s and expected others to follow, but have never seen any more.[3] Many people in Paris liked and talked about it and it was quoted in "This Quarter." I think you ought to do your biography up to a certain date. I predict it would be a best seller.

I was glad to hear of Eliena's work; she still has an engagement to do me and I hope that by that time I shall have a more favorable outline under her practical hand; for if you remember the first thing she began of me was rather discouraging. Have you ever seen the professor she did at Antibes? And what has become of Charlotte + Jan Boissevain? And dear old Mrs [Betty] Hare? I had a nice letter from Mike Gold (months ago) and shall soon reply now I have time. Tell him so if you see him. Do you have any circle of friends as in the old days? I was told that there was nothing there I could fall into now, except perhaps in Harlem. The fact is that since the writing of "Home To Harlem" I don't have any real hankering for the States. All of it seems to have gone out of me into that first novel. I would like to return for a tour of the U.S. and the West Indies + South America, but I have no desire to settle down anywhere.

Do you still correspond with Trotsky? I hear that [h]is biography is very good. How sad it must be for him to be confined there in Turkey. I suppose they wouldn't have him in Switzerland nor Spain! Stalin is most certainly a great politician, so great that he is converting intelligent people into believing he is a great statesman. But I suppose he is just the shrewd mediocre mind able to grasp concrete facts that Russia needs as a boss to build herself up economically. I don't know. He seems to have no set policy "zig-zagging" as Trotsky says, but I am afraid Trotsky was not the practical man for the post-revolutionary period. At any rate he gave away all his chances to win leadership quite impractically—he was so lofty. And I've never been able to visualize the practical working of that famous phrase of his: permanent revolution.

Last summer I met two men from Moscow in Paris—a Negro named Patterson + a journalist. They were both trying to get me to visit Russia again.[4] I told them my visit wouldn't be so interesting as I wouldn't be able to meet Trotsky there and they dropped me hot! I heard that Lydia Gibson (all broken and unhappy so the report had it) was there with Bob Minor, who wasn't cutting such a fine figure. I suppose they are back now in New York. Louise Bryant has been divorced with the loss of her child. She writes from Brittany that she is quite ill. I had a card from Ivan Opfer somewhere up there.

Well I wish I could meet you + Ileana + we could eat some good food together with wine (of course I would only taste the wine but I can still enjoy other people drinking) and talk and talk. I am waiting for the report on the new book as I want to ask a thousand advance. I may have to come home for publication but I am not looking forward happily to that. Let me hear so soon as you can (much obliged for the clipping + remembering me that way) + tell Ileana I should like to see her scratch on a card.

With tropical love + yearning for you both
Always Claude

MEP ALS

1. *The Jungle and the Bottoms* was, along with *Savage Loving,* an early title for the manuscript posthumously published as *Romance in Marseille* (2020).

2. Beginning in late 1928, Eastman worked with director Herman Axelbank, providing narrative coherence and narration (and collecting additional footage) for *Tsar to Lenin*, a documentary film about the Russian Revolution. Eastman completed the film in 1931, but it was caught up in legal issues and not released until 1937. For Eastman's version of events, see Max Eastman, *Love and Revolution* (New York: Random House, 1964), 527–32.

3. Likely Max Eastman, "The Cult of Unintelligibility," *Harper's,* April 1929, 632–39. This was mentioned in Edward W. Titus, "Sartor Resartus," *This Quarter* (July–September 1930): 129–41.

4. Possibly Lloyd Patterson, an African American who worked with Langston Hughes and Louise Thompson on the unfinished film *Black and White.*

To William A. Bradley

4 July 1930

Berlin, Germany

Dear Bradley

Thanks for your letter and please forgive my misreading the royalty statement and getting that #69 on my credit side instead of debit. I made the same mistake in writing to you and [Eugene] Saxton when I took up the matter of the amount charged for proof correcting but both of you either overlooked it or thought it was not worthwhile pointing out.

I should like to meet Saxton if he is coming to Berlin and if not I think I could come to Paris especially if I am sure I can get some ready money . . . I have already seen two specialists, one is a professor of the university faculty and is said to be very good. I have also undergone two small but extremely painful operations. The first made me quite ill and I was in bed for two days . . . Tomorrow I shall hear the result of the most delicate of the two which was getting some fluid from my brain (when the needle went in it sounded like a thrust one hears sometimes when a skil[l]ful matador pierces a bull with his sword) and then I shall know how long I shall have to remain here.

I am feeling all broken up in body but that is the result of the operations and they gave me a lot of morphine. I have just enough money for the end of this month and then I should like to have that advance. I suppose the matter should be taken up right now. But I will wait until you see Saxton this week.

With my best wishes
Yours Sincerely
Claude McKay

WABLAR TLS

To William A. Bradley

[received 19 July 1930]

Paris, France

Dear Bradley: I called you up through the hotel office three times, twice at the office and once at home, the office line was busy both times + no one answered the home call.

My head began going bad during my talk with [Eugene] Saxton + I just braced myself up to finish + then get home. I don't know what's the cause of its getting so bad whether it is the noise or the rainy weather. I think I shall go away tomorrow.

Here enclosed is a summary of a book by a young French writer who came to see me this morning. The book will soon be published by La Nouvelle Revue Francaise + I thought you might be interested to see if it was worth while for the American market. I read the part about the lycee + found it very fine reminding me of [André] Gide's Si le grain ne meurt + the first part of [Jean] Cocteau's Enfants—it[']s all quite different of course as different as Tom Brown's Schooldays—it[']s more the feeling of atmosphere that makes it allies to the others—I put his address on.[1]

When I told him about you he thought it had better wait until the book was published in French but I thought you would like to see it in m.s. He thought you might not be interested as he had not a <u>name</u> but I told him that it was the authors without "names" that you were mostly interested in.

Yours Faithfully
Claude McKay

WABLAR ALS

1. McKay references André Gide's autobiography *Si le grain ne meurt* (1924), Jean Cocteau's *Les enfants terribles* (1929), and Thomas Hughes's *Tom Brown's School Days* (1857).

To James Weldon Johnson

29 July 1930

Luxembourg

Dear Johnson

May I impose on your generosity in asking you to try and obtain for me three numbers of the <u>Crisis</u> containing material which I would like to use as reference among other things for an article I am doing on Negro Writers and Criticism?

Unfortunately I do not remember the exact months of publication and you may have to have your secretary do a little research work. The numbers I want are: 1. The <u>Crisis</u> containing W. S. Braithwaite's speech on Negro writers, delivered at the N.A.A.C.P[.] Conference either in 1924 or 1925. 2. That with Dr. [W. E. B.] Dubois's criticism of Carl Van Vechten's "Nigger Heaven" which came out either between October or November of 1926. 3. That with your own article on Negro writers and Negro criticism which appeared in the New York Evening Post either before or after its appearance in the Crisis, I am not sure.

Also, I should like to have a copy of your "American Negro Poetry" and you might present the bill to Mr. [Eugene] Saxton's of Harper['s] with my request that he should pay, since that is about the easiest way for me.

[William A.] Bradley told me that he saw you in New York. . . . I finished my new book in Barcelona and left straight for Berlin to consult a brain specialist about my head which had become so bad with chronic heaviness and dizziness during the last weeks on the book, that I had barely enough will to finish. I had two good specialists and underwent two very painful little operations, the taking of liquids from my brain and spine to test them. Fortunately the result of the examination was good. The doctors said there was no sign of danger. I had been overtreated for my illness when I came out of Russia and especially that attack of facial paralysis in '24. And of course I have been drinking too much. That I must now stop altogether and I was advised also to take a little vacation from writing. So I am here in little Luxembourg, where it is quiet, for the summer.[1]

It was after I returned from Berlin that I saw Bradley. I might have stayed the summer in Germany, but I had to go to Paris because I wanted to meet Saxton. He is a very nice man and it was a pleasure to know him. . . . I thought you would have come to Europe from Japan with Mrs. Johnson and I was hoping to meet you both again for dinner or something and a talk. I've always remembered with pleasure that evening spent at your house with some of the influential literati before I came away to Europe. If ever you come to Europe soon, you must be sure to visit Spain. I am sure that both you and Mrs. Johnson will be charmed by it. It is the only European country that touches me emotionally.

I hope that you both had a delightful time in Japan. Thanks for the card and my best regards to you both.

Yours Sincerely
Claude McKay

[Handwritten:] Am trying a new signature now after just a little trouble with the old!

CMcK
JWJP TLS

1. McKay received an 18 July 1930 letter from John "Buffy" Glassco inviting him to stay with Glassco and his partner, Graeme Taylor, in Luxembourg.

To William A. Bradley

8 August 1930 [postmarked 13 August 1930]

Heidelberg, Germany

Started off on the 1st to do the Rhineland by way of Metz-Nancy + Strassbourg [*sic*]. I stay longest in the small + quiet places. Metz was really the best + I am sorry I did not go there to rest instead of Luxembourg (but I did not know of it[)]. It[']s charming + quiet. The old canal town of Strassbourg [*sic*] is unique. I'm going to take the boat to Coblence—from Mayence. Hope to get back to Luxembourg about the end of the week or the first of next. Did you hear from [Eugene] Saxton? I hope also that you got the m.s. I sent you by [indecipherable] before leaving Paris. My head is doing better. A new development better than the old. Will write letter[.]

Sincerely
Claude McKay

WABLAR APS

To William A. Bradley

28 August 1930

Luxembourg (?)

Dear Bradley

I had just written off to [Eugene] Saxton about the balance of the advance which we had forgotten to discuss and so I must thank you for cabling and for your letter and the statement under another cover. I was worrying a little over the money more than the report on the new book, because after my two weeks' trip, my pocket went considerably flat.

I felt Saxton would take some time before reporting on the book from the fact that he was so cautious in Paris. It is really very different in style and need from the preceeding [*sic*] ones, the character studies are now fully realized and the conflict between Aslima, Titin and Lafala is a serious thing. But

I have been worried myself about the minor characters of Big Blonde and the page and wondering if the chances would not be better if I changed them a little! If Saxton also thinks so in his letter, I should not mind having back the m.s. to rewrite the two chapters in which they play an important part. As the book is a more serious attempt than the others and will set the tone for future work I should like to make it as perfect as I can.

I thought I had sent you a post card of the Beethovenhaus from Bonn. I went from Heidelburg [*sic*] to Frankfort which I liked very much. I went reluctantly with an acquaintance to visit the Goethehaus and when I got there I found it very exciting. The history of the family and the entire atmosphere are preserved in the rooms, family paintings, pictures, furniture, musical instruments and souvenirs; and everything is most uncannily vividly alive. I get the impression of a very agre[e]ably and comfortably arranged middle class family. And I could picture Goethe growing out of it, spreading and ascending to the peaks of placid meditation. I felt a greater understanding and admiration of the master after seeing there the different paintings and sketches of him and how much in harmony he seemed, in all the different aspects, with his surroundings. Tolstoy's face couldn't give that impression under any circumstances, nor Beethoven's.

I didn't care much for the Beethovenhaus except for curiosity. It is more of a museum, a show place which is what it is. The attic room where he was born is so small, poor and sad and one feels that a child couldn't have been happy up there. When I got there it was full of tourists, many of them coming from the Passion Play and they were all lined up to sign the visitor's book that is kept there and which is one of the most interesting things. I could not look around very well so I left and returned early the next morning, but I didn't like having to pay twice.

I enjoyed the trip immensely. I took the nine o'clock boat from Mayence to Coblence and it was very quiet, being too early in the morning for the regular tourists. Of all the towns I prefer Frankfort and Bonn. They're all romantically laid out and in harmony with the splendour of the Rhine. But I don't think I'd want to live in any of them. They're too sweet. I don't like garden cities and the Germans plant the trees so thickly they obscure the view! After seeing the Rhine towns I could better understand Berlin. It was as if the town planners were trying to bring some of the romantic beauty of the Rhineland into that city, but that it didn't seem to harmonize with the massive industrial works and energy of that city.

I finished up at Cologne. I must confess that I didn't feel moved within by the famous cathedral. It is surely a marvel of elaborate ornamentation from the outside from base to pinnacle. But it was too overwhelmingly elaborate for me, there was no place to rest the eye. I didn't care much for the town either. I liked the bridges, I went to a museum there and saw three marvellous Frans Hals[es], an old man, an old woman and a child all perfectly placed in a group. In the same museum I saw the loveliest [Maurice] Utrille [*sic*] I've ever seen anywhere. Just a building with a foreground of trees, but the most delicious tracery and delicate tints.

If the money came I wish you would hold it until I get back to Paris. I may be there about the middle of next month. I want to spend a little time in Belgium after leaving here, the length depending on how long the francs hold out. It has finally turned hot at last this week and I spend the afternoons in the valley and up in the forest—or rather woods. Strangely my head isn't doing so well now with the change in the weather, but I hope it will soon adjust itself to it.

With best wishes
Yours Sincerely
Claude McKay

WABLAR TLS

To William A. Bradley

[received 18 September 1930]

Paris, France

Dear Bradley: Won[']t you please send me also your duplicate of "The Jungle + the Bottoms," since I may have to leave here without having the other. I got home to find an express letter from my Moroccan friend who will arrive at Marseille on Saturday + I very much want to see him, so I shall leave here at least on Friday.

I think I shall decide to substitute the short stories for the new novel which must go on the shelf for a time while I am determined to make a big effort to put over a real piece of good + sincere work[.]

CMcK

WABLAR AGS (pneumatic)

To William A. Bradley

[received 19 September 1930]

Paris, France

Dear Bradley

It has just occurred to me that the stories may be in that box you have so kindly kept for me and I wish you would let this man take it for me. I am sorry we can't have another talk, but I am so busy getting round and arranging little affairs with some old friends before starting that I am rather flustered and couldn't talk intelligently about my book right now, but I shall of course let you know where I am as soon as I have settled down. Kind regards[.]

Yours Sincerely
Claude McKay

WABLAR ALS

To William A. Bradley

[received 23 September 1930]

Paris, France

Dear Bradley or Mrs Bradley

Since the m.s. From Harper[']s has not arrived, will you send me the other duplicate (The Jungle + The Bottoms) so that I may be able to use both in working again on the book? For both versions are not the same. I had no luck with the stories; they were not in the box, but I hope I shall find duplicates in my trunk at Marseille. I have not been able to get everything done + got away yet.

With best yours
Sincerely
Claude McKay

WABLAR ALS

To James Weldon Johnson

29 September 1930

Marseille, France

[On Letterhead: Grand Café Glacier, Marseille]

Dear Weldon Johnson,

It was extremely kind of you to send me the books which I appreciate very much. About new poetry, there is "Desolate" that appeared in [Countee] Cullen's anthology, but I have written no poetry for five years. I have some among my papers in my trunk here and I shall see if there is any good enough to send you.

I will write you later about living in Spain: this is merely an acknowledgement of your letter and the books. Briefly however, living in hotels in Spain is dear, but in a family pension or your own "piso" it is cheap. I lived extremely comfortable [*sic*], like a middle class pensionaire [*sic*] on 50 dollars a month with the peseta at 7 to the dollar.

Raw food + vegetables extremely cheap—clothing dear.

[William A.] Bradley spoke about you + is enthusiastic about "Black Manhattan"—the get-up of which is very pleasing (I haven't dipped into it yet)[.][1] He is getting Langston Hughes' novel translated I think.[2]

I shall send you later all the new material you need + some interesting old one that I have half-concealed up to now.

Again thanking you and my respectful regards to Mrs Weldon Johnson.

Sincerely Yours
Claude McKay

JWJP ALS

1. Paragraph not indented in original.

2. Langston Hughes's first novel, *Not without Laughter* (1930), did not appear in French translation until 1934.

To William A. Bradley

29 September 1930

Marseille, France

[On Letterhead: Grand Café Glacier, Marseille]

Dear Bradley

I remember the last time at your office I saw, I believed, two copies of "The Jungle" etc[.] and as no copy is the same I wanted to compare them in making revisions, as the m.s. from Harpers' [*sic*] has not turned up.[1] But according to this letter enclosed from Mrs Bradley the office could only account for one copy. I don't know if you remember there were two copies beside the Banjo manuscript. One, I believe, was incomplete belonging to the first draft. I sent you the second before leaving for Luxembourg + had none for myself. Maybe you might find out something about it + if the m.s from Harper turns up please send it on here[.]

Yours Sincerely
Claude McKay

WABLAR ALS

1. The history of the manuscript eventually published as *Romance in Marseille* (2020) is complex, and evidence suggests that at least one of these versions of the manuscript is not extant.

To Max Eastman

1 December 1930

Tangier, Morocco

My dear Max

It's a great treat to hear from you again and to read your poem, The Swallow, which is very simple and very beautiful. How happy you and Eliena have been! I must confess that I feel a jealous pain not being there to share your happiness, especially as I know that we could all be happy together again as we have been before. And I have not been any so happy since I left Spain. My happiest time since you left Antibes was the summer of last year in Paris when I was with the Blackbirds' bunch—the same summer I missed you.

In Berlin I was examined by two good specialists. The operating one is a professor of the University Faculty. He took liqiud [*sic*] from my spine and brain and examined it, also my blood, of course. He found nothing wrong and after studying the chart of my treatment, he came to the conclusion that I have been over-medicined! He thinks that my continued head trouble—dizziness, heaviness or even lightness if you will—is due to that.

I was very happy and left Berlin to spend a month in Luxembourg. From there I visited the Rhineland, going down to Strassbourg [*sic*] and to Baden, Heidelberg, Frankfort, Mayence, Coblency [*sic*][,] Bonn, Treves, Cologne. The boat trips were fine. I liked especially Frankfort and Bonn. I could live in Frankfort, but I couldn't live again in Berlin. Berlin has spread wonderfully and is much more modern than Paris with all those modern comforts and improvements that one associates with American life. Maybe it would be delightful if the atmosphere was jazzy but it is all heavily methodically cut and patterned and where it is not, like in the pretty garden dancing halls, it is too saccharine for the appetite. One can stand that on the Rhineland, for the whole atmosphere makes for that, but not in Berlin. There is no doubt that the Germans love their great city though. Why not? It is of their making. And there is no longing among them for Paris. When they look over the horizon it is toward New York and America. God, they are a strong and forward-marching-together people though, worthy of all admiration.

I went from Berlin to meet [Eugene] Saxton in Paris and talk the new novel over with him. It was a new departure—a low-life love story between a young West African and an Arab girl. I had sent the m.s. to New York after Saxton's departure for Europe + he had not seen the second half. And when he returned he wrote suggesting changes in the last few chapters. Saxton's letter was not so enthusiastic, so I went through the novel again more critically and decided that the whole second half could be rearranged for the better. And as my contract called for <u>two</u> novels and a volume of short stories I suggested that it would just do to publish in between the short stories I have done (you know them) with a few more thrown in to make a fat lot.[1] The sales would be less, but I would be holding my ground, which would be better for my future than publishing a novel that none of us thought satisfactory. But [William A.] Bradley was not pleased at all, (thinking no doubt of his commission) and wanted me to start work immediately and make a few changes in the book and prepare it for publication . . . I quit France in September for Morocco + he doesn't know where I am yet! I had really arranged (I must hastily add) to return here however, because I love the country. And I felt that more actual experience would help me make my novel better—later. Only, with the eagerness to get away from Paris + Bradley's many rendezvous and practical suggestions my voyage was precipitated.

I had been promised a native house to live in free of cost at Fez. But no sooner had I arrived there (travelling by way of Marseille-Oran) in October that the French police got after me, said that the British Secret Service had me listed as a propagandist and asked me to quit the French zone during the Presidential visit. Unhappily my arrival coincided with the President's visit of which I knew nothing + I suppose the police thought I was going to throw a bomb. From one trouble into the other! The British Consul gave me no help + so I came here and have written to London to have the matter finally settled so that I won[']t be bothered. They did bother me the last time, prevented me from visiting Gibraltar + having my mail delayed. But I expect to go as far as I can on my passport. I guess "Banjo" has a great deal to do with it. They know I'm no political propagandist but they are afraid of what I may write next! Well Tanger is lovely + if they don't continue to boot me out I shall take a house here, where I shall be near to Spain + be able to visit easily all Morocco. And when you come next year with Elieana you must come and live with me.

I am hoping to have a little brown Moslem yet, even if I must go Moslem for that. I need to settle down and no place has satisfied me since I left home as much as Morocco. There are many things in the life of the natives, their customs and superstitions, reminiscent of Jamaica.

I have finished a short story that you would shout for even more than you did for "Home To Harlem" if you remember when you said the m.s. felt like a [*sic*] 1000 dollars in your pocket. I wish I could read it to you. I want to have the short stories published because they will show that I am a writer of many moods and open the way for any book on any theme I may choose to write instead of my being taken solely as a writer of picaresque stories. Give my love to Mrs [Betty] Hare + Miss [Charlotte Osgood] Mason and the [Boardman] Robinsons. Some one wrote that you were living in a very prosperous way + nobody understood how you could do it! I am glad you are living comfortably.

I hope I shall soon see your book—although the title sounds so literarious [*sic*].[2] Did you have anything to say in the humanist battle. What a lot of prigs on both sides! And not one strong and certain voice above it all. The best I heard was Rebecca West's. And I wondered if America couldn't show better than hers!

With my love for you and Elieana
As Ever
Claude

[Upper margin:] I see our mutual friend Raine of Riviera-Palace (Nice) is writing for the "Nation."[3] I felt he wanted to go high-brow. I get exasperated by the tone of the Nation. It is more crudely journalistic than ever, like an old woman forever warning in the same pitch of voice without humor + without real political intelligence. It's good to get it though + know what's going on!

[Lower margin:] I hear that in spite of the general depression in the literary market there is a great deal of money being given out in advance with new contracts and many authors are being signed up. I wish you could do some scouting for me! I could stand a few thousands in advance! And with new offers I could make a better deal with my present publishers. CMcK

MEP ALS

1. This collection would appear in 1932 as *Gingertown.*

2. Likely *The Literary Mind: Its Place in an Age of Science* (1931). There is very light indention beginning with this sentence; it could be a continuation of the same paragraph, but probably not.

3. Likely William MacLeod Raine (1871–1954), a British-American writer of western novels and stories for pulp magazines. His "Costigan of Colorado" appeared in the *Nation*'s 29 October 1930 issue.

To William A. Bradley

10 December 1930

Rabat, Morocco

Dear Bradley,

I have just these last days received your letters and telegrams. I was in a fix and could not receive nor reply to them before. I don't know if I mentioned to you that the police bothered me when I was in Morocco the last time, meddling with my mail and shadowing me. This time they have done worse. When I decided to scrap the novel for the time being and publish the stories I thought I would return here and dig down deeper with the native life and get much material that would help to make the novel a first-class one when I turned to it, besides taking into account the cheapness of living here (if one knows how) and the congenial atmosphere of the native life.

I had a Moorish friend at the Mosque who had promised to get me a home to live in rent free. I happened to arrive at Fez during the Presidential visit and no sooner had I arrived than the Police were down on me. This time they were definite: said they had information from the British authorities that I was a propagandist and that I would have to quit the French zone during the Presidential visit, according to the order of the Diplomatic Cabinet. I protested, the British Consul said he did not know of the British information but he did not help me. So I came on here to Tanger accompanied by policemen. I have written to the Resident General, the British Consul and the British Foreign Office, but received no replies.

I wonder if you could write to the Residence that you know me personally and that I am not a propagandist. It might be effective, they might reply to you, and you might ask if there is any official bar against me in French Morocco. I remember you told me that you had been offered free tickets to make a trip here, so they evidently hold you in high esteem—perhaps because of your work. Technically I can travel (I skipped away from Tanger down here to Rabat to see my Martinique friend but I was harassed by the police + my hotel watched) because my passport is good, but I should like to have the police bar lifted because it is embar[r]assing.

Maybe "Banjo" has something to do with it! They (at least the British officials) know that I am no propagandist, but they have perhaps listed me as an undesirable writer! If I was invested in propaganda or documentary writing I could have done all I wanted during my first seven months here in 1928. I told the police that I was only interested in simple native life. Maybe that is just what they are against! The police have treated me in such a way as to make [me] see the French cock-eyed through a police veil. But I have not lost my sense of humor. I was glad they sent me to Tanger. I like it much better than the last time—more than Rabat where I had intended to stay after visiting Fez. Fez is interesting as a large native city, but there is something stifling about it, I couldn't live long there. But I could in Tanger + from there visit other parts of Morocco. Then I intend to learn Arab [*sic*] because some time in the future I want to visit the closed country beyond Agadir. I am in touch with some shop-keepers in Tetuan and Tangier who are from that Souss country + visit it periodically.

I got [Eugene] Saxton's letter with yours + have sent him two new stories. One is called Nigger Lover + is better than Home to Harlem (the short story)[.] I shall make it the title of the new book. It is the best short story I have done + I shall let you see it. On account of the trouble I have not done as much as I thought I would with the stories. But I am keeping steadily ahead. It took me a long time to get my mail. Since the police gave me so much trouble the last time, with my letters, I took the precaution on this occasion not to have them just carelessly forwarded—but waited until I reached Tanger where I took a box in the Spanish post office. Of course it took a considerable time for me to get my correspondence. I am sorry about the m.s. of The "Jungle," but I am not thinking about it now. Only I don't know exactly what was [*sic*] Saxton's technical criticisms.

You might send me the cheque to the above address. I thought Saxton would have waited for the new contracts until I had finished the present volume. However you might send them to me or they may wait for my next visit to Paris.

I have an old friend in London[,] an M.P.[,] and I am writing him to see if anything can be done there.

With my best regards
Yours sincerely,
Claude McKay

WABLAR ALS

To William A. Bradley

14 December 1930

Tangier, Morocco

Dear Bradley

I am back here [Touring Hotel] and will you please write to me at this address instead of the other and register and even seal the letter if it is important. Also, if any letters should come through you to me, especially from London, will you not have them put into another envelope and sent to me registered?

Before leaving the French zone, I went to see the Chief of the Moroccan Police at Rabat and was given to understand that it was the British authorities who were really at the bottom of the whole thing.

I was very politely received both by the head of the diplomatic cabinet and the secretary of the police. He wanted to know about my funds and I showed him my letter of credit, from the Guaranty Trust. In your letter to the Residence, I wish you would explain that my novels sold well and that the firm of Harper[']s is an old reliable one and made me periodical payments in advance. I think they were in doubt about how I was financed, their thoughts on red funds perhaps. . . . .

Funny that all this should come eight years after I was associated with any radical work at this time and in a place like Morocco where I feel entirely removed from any sort of political atmosphere. Strangely too I seem to like and understand the French here even better than in France. Except by that one police officer at Fez I have never met with any discourteous treatment neither during my first prolonged stay in Morocco in '28 nor this time. I have been well treated without people knowing that I am a poet and that is the real test of true courtesy, for people to meet one another humanely without knowing who each may be. I felt that thing very strongly in Spain, the poorest person standing simply on his dignity as a human being. In France I always felt the atmosphere more formal, that how one is treated may depend entirely on how one has been introduced. But here it is different. I have a theory that the soil, the natural formation of a country, has more than anything to do in the moulding of people.

My Moorish friends say I am treated so well because I wear good European clothes. But my Martinique friend insists that it is because I am "distingue et sympathique" (when I want to, I suppose).

I am working on a new story called "The Agricultural Show."[1] It is a quaint thing about the first thing of its kind that was organised among a section of the Jamaican peasantry and the naive fresh manner in which they reacted to it. I also have a splendid Moorish story that I want to get into the series, the crudest mixture of superstition and sex. I shall have to make a trip among the Arabs in the mountains to get the right "decor" for it. It will be about an Arab who could not tear himself away from the love of a girl for she had given him a love potion to keep him forever. But he was of noble family while the girl was common and his parents were determined to separate them. But before the parents succe[e]ded the girl slow-poisoned the lover with the broth of a "langue de borico" (an ass's tongue). He went crazy and was chained to a Marabout's tomb for five years out in the open in the sun and the rain, after which the spirit of the Marabout interceded with Allah for him and he was cured and became a saint.

I got the story from an Arab boy who wanted to work for me, when I was negotiating to take a little native house and an arab girl as a "bonich," (argot marseillais). The boy said it would be dangerous for me to have a native girl, for she might do things to me if she got to like me. Then he told me the story and said it would be safer for me to take a boy. I asked him if it wouldn't be just as dangerous and he said no saying that a man would eat with me according to Arab custom and so would not poison the food that he had to eat himself. But the girl would not eat with me and might do anything to the food. I didn't have to make any decision for I didn't get the house I wanted and am still in a nice little room giving on the terrace of the hotel with a fine view of the sea.

But please don't tell this story to anyone as I should hate to have it raped.

With my best regards to you and Mrs
Bradley
Yours Sincerely
Claude McKay

WABLAR TLS

1. This story appeared in *Gingertown* (1932).

To William A. Bradley

25 December 1930

Tangier, Morocco

Dear Bradley

I have received the cheque and am much obliged to you for it, your good letter to Monsieur [Eirik] Labonne and the others your secretary has kindly forwarded to me by registered mail.

I enclose receipt and a letter (copy) from the secretary of a labor M. P. whom I knew slightly in London ten years ago. It was as I thought the British Intelligence Service using the French police to do its dirty work. The explanation is simple. I was blacklisted as a propagandist when I visited Russia with Max Eastman in 1922. I remember somebody sending me a cutting from the London Times in which I was referred to as Negro propagandist in Russia, also another reference that was read into the senate record by Senator [Henry Cabot] Lodge. But since I did not accept any active propaganda service, the

Secret Service men lost track of me when I came out of Russia, but picked it up again when "Home To Harlem" was published with the ensuing publicity. They would no doubt like to provoke me back into the propaganda rut to justify their stupid attitude, or to show that their job is worthwhile, but I am too far on the literary road for anything to turn me back. You know one of the things that maddened me about [André] Levinson's article was his saying that I could not return to the States for I was barred by the American authorities. Since the statement was not exact I was suspicious and wondered where he got his information. Now I don't know if the lost m.s. of my novel did not fall into the hands of the British Secret Service—yet I wonder how it could!

Anyway I am going to hang on here if I can. Water must find its level and I must find mine if I am to do any real artistic work. I can't help my temperament, I must make the best of it. I have never had any desire to visit any British territory.

I haven't done any work since I returned from Rabat. It is cold in my room even although [*sic*] there is sun and I am arranging to instal[l] myself in a little Arab house a couple of miles out of the town by the end of the month. The cheque came at the right moment to help. I will have a kind of pot stove that the Arabs use. It gives lots of heat.

I had intended to go to Rabat for Reveillon[1] with my Martinique friends, but the police stopped me at the gare. However I had a nice dinner with a Senegalese-Arab family. I hope some good will come of your letter to Monsieur Labonne. And if every thing turns out well and I get fixed here I hope you and Mrs Bradley will make a trip over next winter. With my best wishes to you both for a bright New Year[.]

Yours Sincerely
Claude McKay

P.S. As I shall be moving I think it is better to use the post office address.

WABLAR TLS

1. Réveillon is a traditional Christmas Eve meal in French-speaking countries.

To William A. Bradley

25 January 1931

Tangier, Morocco

Dear Bradley

Herewith is the story "Nigger Lover."[1] The other is not in good shape to send. I have not heard from [Eugene] Saxton whether he received those I sent to him.

I am now comfortably installed in my new place but it is unusually cold compared to what it was two years ago. There is plenty of sun but indoors it is too chilly to work well.

About this new contract. Since the "Jungle" novel is definitely off for the moment, don't you think it would be better to have a new one altogether for future work when the old is completed with the publication of the stories? I note what you say about the stories. But you know it is necessary that I should have a success d'estime[2]—for "Banjo" was a falling off from "Home To Harlem" and the "Jungle" did not seem up to the standard of "Banjo"—at least on first appearance. I think it would be very bad for my reputation to come out with my third book, third rate. That was my reason for deciding on the short stories and in the meantime I would be working out the big Jamaica book.[3] I had kind of written myself out on the picaresque stuff—the Jamaica book will be of a primitive pattern. With the short stories I shall be on safe ground—I want just enough out of them to keep me going while writing the Jamaica book. And besides, they will also help prepare the ground for that book as I am including two or three stories of Jamaican life.

All I need is a little time and a comfortable position and I am well-fixed here where living and loving are cheap and my surroundings are genial. I spent all of this month fixing up my little house in the native village—a little out of the town. It is rather orientally filthy getting by into it, but once inside it is fine. It is a Hassani house[4] with three little rooms and a terrace with [a] view on the sea. I have a Fatma looking after me. She did not show up this morning and I have missed a hundred francs from the drawer, but I am not going to worry with the police. She served me well for ten days. I shall find another.

I heard nothing from the Residence although I wrote myself to M. [Eirik] Labonne. I shan't worry. I don't think the Spaniards will tar me + when I want a change I can visit their zone or Andalusia. I love Spain, Tangier is Arab-

Spanish + it is nice to be so near to the Spanish ward. I feel more contented here than ever in ten years. This is the fasting month of the Muslims, the mosques are crowded during the day and I am getting a bornous[5] + Fez to enter myself.

When you read "Nigger Lover" you might let me know whether you think it good for a novel. It seems to me rather complete, but you might see something there that I haven't as you did in "Home To Harlem[.]"

The "best seller" will be the Jamaica book—dealing with the religious customs and social of the peasants. I am ripe for it as I am also feeling very religious now among the Moslems. Let me know definitely what you want done about the contracts. I think they ought to be for the Jamaica book and the others that will follow. After my experience here the "Jungle" seems rather thin + cheap. I was right in coming back here to feel that.

Did you read the new Goncourt Prix book and if so is it worth getting?[6] I read a review by Rene Maran which sounds quite interesting from the viewpoint of my own work.

You must excuse my penmanship but I am again suffering from sciatica and my fingers take poorly to the pen also the typewriter.

With kindest regards
Yours Sincerely
Claude McKay

WABLAR ALS

1. This story appeared in *Gingertown* (1932).

2. A "*succès d'estime*" is a critical, but not popular, success.

3. *Banana Bottom* (1933).

4. A traditional Arab dwelling; McKay's rendering of Hassaniya, a Maghrebi Arabic dialect.

5. McKay's rendering of "burnoose," a traditional hooded cloak worn by Arab men in North Africa.

6. Likely Henri Fauconnier's *Malaisie* (1930), which won the 1930 Prix Goncourt and was translated into English in 1931 as *The Soul of Malaya.*

To William A. Bradley

16 February 1931

Tangier, Morocco

Dear Bradley

I had to delay replying to you a little to send the only convincing reply, perhaps, to your letter of the first—this new story that I have just now finished. I have about three more with the same country background to do to complete the series.

All that you say is technically right—only you missed one point. That is that the third book, The Jungle + the Bottoms would perhaps not have been either a "success d'estime ni d'argent"! You yourself thought + said it was not as good as "Banjo" + perhaps that was [Eugene] Saxton's opinion also. And I could not then just get on the job + make it mechanically a first-rater. I felt I had about written myself out on the picaresque stuff was tired out + just had to turn to something fresh. I think the Jamaica book that I am starting right after I get off the stories will have that poetic freshness and charm that was in "Home To Harlem," even to a greater degree + which was lacking in "Banjo[.]"

The action will take place in one of the villages of this Agricultural Show. I will work on it all this summer + it won[']t be so far behind the short stories which are really bringing + shaping up old memories + sharpening me for the real book.

I am also sending today a copy to Saxton[.]

With best wishes
Yours Sincerely
Claude McKay

I think we had better leave "The Jungle" where it is on the shelf until I can see it with fresh eyes + tackle it with new vigor. Especially as I may have some fresh experiences out of my present life to vivify it[.] CMcK

WABLAR ALS

To Max Eastman

5 March 1931

Tangier, Morocco

My Dear Max

I wonder how you and Eliena are! I know you must be working and well because periodically I see you booked in the Nation for a lecture. I am well settled in my little house, which is just about the size of yours at Antibes and I am working pretty steadily. Hope to have my new book in the hands of the publishers by the end of this month.

The weather has been extremely variable and naturally affecting my health, rheumatic pains in dangerous areas, the last one, still with me, having an awful grip over my heart and I can't think of any remedy but aspirine. I don't know if I should consult a doctor again.

Did you publish your new book and those poems? I haven't seen any reviews. I had read about Trotsky's place being burnt down in Prinkipo. Do you still correspond with him and other important people in Europe? And to [Lucien] Monods?[1]

I have never heard from Mike Gold since I wrote asking him for a copy of his book![2] I didn't think that was too audacious as I had had both mine sent to him. But maybe it was. I see him very frequently mentioned.

My love to you and Eliena and hoping that you will be able to get away from there and over here on that vacation. I would love to entertain you in my little native home and gossip over my low and high adventures and police troubles which seem to be apparently settled now.

As Ever
Claude

MEP ALS

1. Lucien Monod (1867–1957), French painter and friend of the Eastmans when they lived on the Mediterranean.

2. Mike Gold's *Jews without Money* was published in 1930.

To William A. Bradley

10 March 1931

Tangier, Morocco

Dear Bradley

I am now on the sixth and last tale and will finish in a few days and would like you to ask [Eugene] Saxton to send me the originals of the three I sent him so that I may have them in time for the assembling. I want to have that done by the end of this month. Four of the stories are Jamaican and helped to make the outline clearer for the novel. Did you get the last one I sent you?

I think only about six of the old ones are good enough to publish and so we will have about 12 in all.

I am typing to you from bed where I have been for over a week gripped by sciatica and a damnable dull pain in the region of my chest. I suppose I am under because the weather has been so dreadfully fickle. I haven't tried a doctor yet this time. Started taking aspirines but, although they do relieve the pain a little, they make me constipated and therefore nervous and irritable, which is worse.

With my best regards
Yours Sincerely
Claude McKay

P.S. I have on the first copies sent to Saxton important emendations that are not in your version nor mine.[1]

C.McK

WABLAR TLS

1. The postscript is handwritten.

To William A. Bradley

17 April 1931

Tangier, Morocco

Dear Bradley: I am sending off today the completed m.s. of the short stories[1] (if when I go to town I find the stories from you at the post office. I have just received a notice for a registered letter.)[.] There are six new ones and six old, thoroughly revised. I had sixteen in all but weeded out four that were not up to the standard.

I have changed "Wit[h]in The Belt" to "Near-White" and the text also a great deal and would prefer your giving Rieder a copy of it for publication if that is possible. I was all in trying to finish the m.s. before Easter and could not make a duplicate of the revised stories.

About that biographical note I have nothing much new (over what Max Eastman wrote in the preface to "Harlem Shadows") of which you are not aware. But in case you have lost your copy here is an outline:

Born in Jamaica 1890. Educated by my brother who was a schoolmaster. Won a gov. trade scholarship at 17, but did not follow the trade. Published a little book of poetry in the Jamaica dialect in 1912. Same year went to the Negro institute at Tuskegee. Six months there and then to the Kansas State College where I studied until 1914. Went to New York. Ran a restaurant and cabaret and went broke. After that worked at many handy jobs, the most interesting as a railroad waiter from 1917–1919. In 1919 visited Belgium, Holland and England. Stayed over a year in London and published a volume of poetry there, "Spring in New Hampshire," in 1920. Returned to New York in 1921. Became assistant to Max Eastman on the "Liberator." Published "Harlem Shadows" in 1922. Visited Russia in the fall of that year, stayed six months. Left for Germany in 1923. Stayed six months. Paris in 1924. Work at odd jobs and writing chiefly for Aframerican publications. Published "Home to Harlem" in 1927 [*sic*] etc. . . .

Now I shall rest up a few weeks before starting work on the Jamaica book. I am writing to [Eugene] Saxton about that. I should take a little holiday in Spain but cannot afford it. I wish I was there during these eventful days.[2] I had interesting letters from friends at Madrid and Barcelona foreshadowing them and inviting me over. Even here at Tanger it has been very lively for the Spanish colony is the largest European.

Sorry I didn't get to this Rieder thing before. Just noticed now in writing to you that you said, <u>at once</u>! I was all <u>bouleversé</u> finishing up the job. It was as difficult as doing a full-length novel and took quite as much time. However I feel satisfied with the ensemble. Technically it is the best I have done yet in prose.

With my best regards
Yours Sincerely
Claude McKay

P.S. Thanks for your telegram. Apartado 26, Tangier is enough for telegraphic address as that is my box at the Correo Español. McK[3]

WABLAR TLS

1. *Gingertown* (1932).

2. McKay refers to the beginning of the left-leaning Second Spanish Republic, cemented in the elections of 12 April 1931.

3. The postscript is handwritten.

To William A. Bradley

15 May 1931

Tangier, Morocco

Dear Bradley

It was a relief to hear at last that the manuscript of the short stories was received all right and I thank you for your letter and telegram.

Just now I am resting up a little before starting to plan the new work. I have a ton of correspondence that I must get at. I had to let most of it go while I was working at the stories. However, when I get down to it, I don't think that Jamaica book need[s] to be autobiographical. I think I will use all the familiar material and background to write an objective novel after the manner of one of the Jamaica short stories. Autobiographically I fear I may become too self-conscious.

I envy your trip to Madrid right in the midst of great events. Both of my friends in Barcelona and Madrid have turned out to be staunch Republicans although they never hinted of politics when I was there. I did meet some students at Barcelona who were quite outspoken, however.

Tanger was very lively with the Republicans flying the new flag, parading the streets and throwing down the Royal arms and portraits. But everything went off smoothly. It seems to me it is the French here who fear the Republican enthusiasm most and its reaction on the Moors and maybe the feeling is even more social, if one is permitted to make such a distinction these days, than political. In the Spanish Zone I have noticed a much more fraternal and easy-going spirit between the average Spaniards and the Moors than in the French Zone. The Spaniards seem more careless and inclined to laissez-faire. But business in general is very much more prosperous under the French. And so the Moorish commercants prefer the French Zone. When I was in the Spanish

Zone recently I saw many Arabs celebrating the Republican victory with liquor. But right after my return there was trouble at Tetuan[.]

They said that communist agents had been at work among the natives and a delegation of them had gone to the High Commissioner and demanded the same pay as Europeans for the same work, and that all Spanish working men should be sent back to Spain, while their [*sic*] were natives out of work. That hardly sounds communist, at least the second part, and I have heard some people say that the agents were really agent-provocateurs. At any rate the natives staged a demonstration in the Square at Tetuan and it seems a couple of them were killed by the guards and many were wounded.

I am very pleased myself the way the Republic was put over and I admire the sanity and clear realism of the Spaniards and am more firmly convinced than ever that they are the first people of Europe and the most interesting.

Oh yes, Anita Thompson is here. She wrote from Paris that she was doing a book for you and wanted to come down here if she could have a room of her own and leisure to write, because she had no freedom in Paris. But since she came she has been doing nothing but talking marriage, says she is thirty and would like to marry to please her parents. Of course I couldn't help her there. In spite of the fact that I have been vagabonding away from my first marriage all my life, I have always felt yoked to something and nothing in the world could induce me to be twice-yoked—unless it was after the easy manner of the Moslems! Miss Thompson has finally decided to send for M. [Kristians] Ton[n]y and marry him and I hope she does do it, so she may become a tolerable person. As she is she is impossible and full of a thousand vain old tricks to compass that goal.

There is a little something I should like you to correct for me and I think it might be easily set right. I should prefer to talk to you about it, but then that is impossible. I hear that it is being said that I wrote you an "insulting letter" and it sounds very bad, you know, especially as you are my representative.

I think it grew out of that Stella Bowen's studio reception of which I was quite unaware until I walked into it. You remember you said you were taking me to see her about painting my portrait and I thought I was going to see a person at work in her studio and had not the slightest idea that it was a cocktail party. I explained to you in a letter that I couldn't stand those drinking parties since my illness of seven years standing now. That is no joke at all. My illness is something terribly real. And for seven years past I have been living radically different from my old way of existence, almost solitary, so that I could conserve myself for a little creative work. My appearance may deceive, but one doesn't go shouting one is ill to all one's acquaintances all the time. It wouldn't do any good anyway. My letter might have been irritable a bit and not so carefully worded (I think I was suffering severely then from head trouble) but I thought we had talked it over and that that was settled and forgotten. And so many things have happened between us in the friendliest way since then it seems absurd that such a rumor should be afloat. I don't think it is fair to either of us that it should be.

It is summer here now, beautifully hot. I would enjoy it more were it not for the swarms of flies which are terrible out here where I live in an unsanitary native village. On my return from the Spanish Zone I caught a cold in my right shoulder and my right arm went quite dead. I am just getting to use it again now after two weeks. I hope that you are quite well again. I was sorry to worry you while you were ill, but then I didn't know and I am always worried about mss mailed until I know they have reached their destination, especially when there is only one fair copy as in the case of the stories—and the loss of the ms of "The Jungle" is still fresh in my mind.

Here is a receipt that I found this week among my papers.

With my best regards
Yours Sincerely
Claude McKay

WABLAR TLS

To Langston Hughes

23 May 1931

Tangier, Morocco

Dear Langston

I don't know what you must be thinking of me now. I did receive your letter here in the midst of lots of trouble with my own work and the French police who were making it hot for me in the French Protectorate aided and abetted by the British authorities. I couldn't write you or anybody real friendly letters during that period so I just attended to business and work and kept friendship waiting for happier days.

I was hard put to by my own work last fall, whether I should change the latter half of my third novel or write a series of short stories as was specified by my contract. At last I decided to put the novel away for fermentation and do the stories and it was no easy job getting them done with my poor health and the police and secret agents baiting me as a Bolshevik and Undesirable.

But I dug myself in in your "I Thought It Was Tangier" and hope to stay in this pretty green-and-white part of North Africa a long time yet.[1] The book is off my hands at last and I am now waiting for the proofs.

I left Spain in May last year and thought you knew. All summer I was in Germany and just stopped in Paris for a few weeks in the Fall before coming to North Africa. Your novel that you said you sent, probably to Madrid, I never got. In fact I left Madrid in December 1929 for Barcelona, which is my preferred city of Spain. I should love to meet you there some time.

However I read two good notices of your book in the "Nation" and the Herald-Tribune "Books" and although they gave me no inkling of the style, I had an idea what it was all about. And I must, of course, congratulate you and I hope you made a little money thereby. I saw also that amusing review you wrote of Mrs Robeson's "Life" of Paul.[2] I suppose you have almost finished a second novel.

Oh I don't care so much myself what the Niggerati say—I've got a sharp enough retaliating tongue myself, but I do care when they lie. Frankly, I am really romantic about artistic folk trying to make good. I want them to make all the money they can, even though they may be rotten imposters like Eric Waldrond [*sic*]. Blasé though I am I can still get a kick out of literary and artistic success. I only wish the Negroid aspirants would quit wrangling about what should and what should not be done and do some work like the white folks. . . . I'm doing an interesting preface, by the way, for the new book.

I don't know where I should send this letter, you have probably left Jersey, so I shall try your publisher. You may even be in Cuba or God knows where now.—Oh I also saw some good reviews of [George S.] Schuyler's book[3] and I hear it was a great success kidding all the Negro uplifters; also that he is somewhere in Europe on a special mission for his publisher—somebody said so in a letter. "Banjo" is coming out in Paris next month and the same publishers are doing your book, I think.

Right now I am full of the idea of becoming a Moslem. I have fallen under the spell of the primitive medievalism of Mohammedanism and have no fundamental reasons against embracing the faith. And the social side of it is more to my taste and temperament than that of the Christian world. I feel at home and at peace among the Moslems although I don't know their language and their civilization is so radically different and centuries separated from that I was brought up in. But then I have always been very conscious of a lacuna in my life! I hope this won't set you to thinking for you told me once you were too lazy to think.

Oh by the way our mutual friend, Anita Thompson, is down here on a visit. She is writing a book and was staying with me in my little native house. (I took a little one six months ago in an Arab village about a mile out of the town, a little dirty and unkempt outside but nice and comfortable inside, three little rooms[,] a tiny kitchen and primitive little W.C. and a terrace looking out on a little curve of the bay.) But after a little while Anita sent for a painter boy she has been living for over two years with in Paris and to avoid complications I asked her to go to a hotel. I thought that was better than creating a situation for an inevitable mess. The night before she left she said she had really come to Tanger with the intention of marrying me. Well, if ever I do that respectable thing again it will be for a respectable lot of money, or it would have to be a matter of realistic understanding and cooperation with some woman, for I don't think I could fall into sentimental love again.

With my best always and ever
Claude McKay

LHP TLS

1. Langston Hughes, "I Thought It Was Tangiers I Wanted," *Opportunity*, December 1927, 368.

2. Hughes reviewed Eslanda Goode Robeson's *Paul Robeson, Negro* (1930) in the article "Ambassador to the World," *New York Herald Tribune*, 29 June 1930.

3. George S. Schuyler, *Black No More* (1931).

To James Weldon Johnson

25 May 1931

Tangier, Morocco

Dear Weldon Johnson

Now that summer is near at hand you may be thinking about that trip to Spain and so I want to give you as much as I know of the information you asked for. The cost of living in such places as St Sebastian, Madrid and Barcelona is about the same.

In good second class hotels the pension, everything included, is from 12–16 pesetas a day. Good unfurnished flats cost from 50–100 pesetas a month and furnished flats and small villas about 100–200. I found the hotels in Sevilla, Grenada [*sic*] and Malaga a little dearer than the rest because I suppose they are the real tourist towns. The peseta is now worth just about half in dollars as when I was last in Spain and a friend writes from Barcelona that the cost of living has not increased. It seemed to me that living on the whole was really cheaper than in France. Foodstuffs in the market were cheaper and servants are poorly paid.

Barcelona was to me the most inviting town and it has lovely suburbs. And all along the Cataluñian [*sic*] coast down to Valencia are the most beautiful port towns and villages of brown-gray and soft creamy color that I have ever seen anywhere. . . . I had a card from Nella [Larsen] Imes who it seems was wintering in Mallarco [*sic*]. I replied there but she may not have had it. She was leaving for France when she wrote.

It was very kind of you to send me "Black Manhattan" and the elegant and amusing "St. Peter etc." You certainly get a lot of literary work done in spite of your duties. I congratulate you. I cannot go very fast although I work steadily—as much as my health permits. My new book is finally finished, however, and in the hands of the publishers, and I hope it comes out in the Fall. It will include that critique I wrote to you about as a kind of preface. And now my original contract with Harper[']s is ended and I am on the point of negotiating another. This time I want to shelve [William A.] Bradley and that is a delicate task, for he has been trying to sign me up again. He did have a new contract drawn up sometime ago but I evaded signing on some technical point. My feeling is that if I should have an agent again, he should be in New York where he could be actually on the job. "Banjo" will be published in Paris next month.

I have taken a little house, a Dar Hassani, here in Tangier out in a native village about a mile from the town. It is quiet and has a terrace with a small view of the bay. The little town is very worldly and cosmopolitan, but the real native life is far removed from it. The mentality of the natives is medieval and an American needs an historical background to understand and appreciate them. I am trying to pick up a little Arab, but it is difficult absorbed as I am in my writing. However, I am seriously contemplating becoming a Moslem. The social side of the life that is blind to racial and color prejudices appeals to me greatly and as the religion is mostly great poetry, I can conscientiously subscribe to it, as a poet.

For my next book I am going to Jamaica, the West indies for my material and characters. With my best always as ever[.]

Claude McKay

JWJP TLS

To William A. Bradley

14 July 1931

Tangier, Morocco

Dear Bradley

First I must thank you for the cuttings about "Banjo," letters etc. and the magazine "Europe" containing my story that you had sent to me.

I have been very worried not being able to write to you before, especially as I wanted to take up the matter of the new contract, but right after finishing the short stories I started on a preface to go with them. Then Anita Thompson came along and I had to break off and when I started again I was ill all the time doing it with my head and stomach trouble. I always suffer from the last in the spring + summer and became so weak sometimes that for days on a stretch I couldn't type a line. At last I got the thing done[,] re-wrote it, nearly 40 pages, and have just sent it off to [Eugene] Saxton. I don't know if he will like it for the book. It is a kind of review of criticism and semi-biography.

Well it was a funny affair between me and your "protogée" [*sic*] (I must say that since you put it in her head that she could write and she insists she is writing a book for you).

I tried to accommodate her in the best way I could even to the point of making love without feeling much of an urge any more, but she was many women and I am only one man. Even now I am not sure what she wanted—if I had accommodated her with marriage (God save me!) it would have made little difference. The only passion I can find in her is hate under all her fine airs—hate of herself, of the fact of herself and to make others unhappy because she is.

No, she hasn't left! She is still here (I suppose it is a siege) with her [Kristians] Tonny. But we hardly see one another and don't take any notice when we do. I couldn't help but put her out of my little house, because I had no desire to have her and Tonny together and to go in for those Montparnasse "partous"[1] and such things that I left behind me long ago. The last I had of her was her breaking into the house one day when the Fatma was here alone and leaving a note in high Victorian style: "Villain if you say things about me reflecting on my character as a lady I shall make things uncomfortable for you"!

The only thing I regret is that you did take her into your confidence and relate my affair with the British authorities and police. She is blabbing about it and I would have preferred that it remained until I wrote the full account of it myself.

What you write about the Russians is true enough but I have almost forgotten they were Europeans. Curiously I always think of Russia as being more Asiatic, semi-oriental than European.

I haven't been back to the Spanish Zone since April. I was even thinking of going to settle down somewhere between Tetuan and Centa, where I saw some of the loveliest villages, but I won't make any change until things have quieted down. I think that is the wiser way for me in my position, since I am none so sure about my status. Still I have a great craving to get away from the sea somewhere up in the mountains where there is a river. I haven't heard yet of any suitable place with a modicum of comfort. But even if I do I can't make a move until I get some money. Besides I have a little house here and a Fatma, rather capricious, to whom I am getting decidedly attached. I should like to take her along with me if I did go to the mountains, but she says she won't go.

I'll have to get this money matter straightened out soon and as no doubt it depends on the new book and the new contract I shall send you in a day or so another letter dealing with that subject.

Yes, it would be a good thing if it were possible for us to meet. A trip to Tanger wouldn't be such a bad thing! Or if I could afford it we could meet in Spain. Granada they say is cool in summer. My friend at Barcelona has invited me to go to one of the Isles off the coast but I haven't been able to give any definite reply. Anyway you will want to straighten out the matter of the new contract with me before you decide on anything. I should like to have some changes made and as no doubt you will have to refer the whole matter to Saxton I shall write a formal letter about it instead of going into details here.

I have received a couple of copies of "Banjo"—a rather thick book. Too bad I couldn't have gotten the short stories with <u>my</u> preface out before.

I went to see a good doctor here and was put on a diet. With nothing to drink and little to eat I shall be passing from austerity to asceticism!

With my regards to you + Mrs Bradley
Sincerely Claude McKay

WABLAR ALS

1. McKay's rendering of "*partouse,*" French slang for an orgy or group sex.

To William A. Bradley

16 July 1931

Tangier, Morocco

Dear Bradley

Regarding what I said in the other letter, that I desired to write to you before but was held up trying to complete a preface to the short stories—what I wanted to take up was the matter of the contract with Harper[']s.

As you will remember I did not sign the last one that was sent to me here, chiefly because I had decided to put aside the novel on which the contract was based and also because I could not make up my mind whether I wanted to subscribe to it in its original form or not.

After deliberating over the matter I came to the conclusion (but with much hesitation mainly because of our always amicable relationship in working out important points and getting things done) that now that the old contract is filled with the completion of the short stories, I should like a little change in the making of the new.

The chief thing is I should like you to continue as my European representative if you will have no objection to that, and agree to the termination of the arrangement of your acting as my representative in New York. My reason for this action is simply that now that I am known a little on the other side, I feel that if I should have a representative over there, it should be someone right on the spot in New York, who was in contact with magazine editors and managers and could be always looking out for me in trying to sell an article or short story or poem—anything that could bring me a little extra remuneration while I was engaged on a major work.

Needless to say this does not mean that I haven't the highest appreciation of the splendid work you have accomplished for me on both sides of the water, but since you may continue to act for me in Europe, happily we should still be working together almost as before.

I am sending a copy of this letter to [Eugene] Saxton so that he may be aware of the situation. I am also writing to him and shall send you a copy of my letter.

With sincere regards
Yours Faithfully
Claude McKay

WABLAR TLS

To Eugene Saxton

16 July 1931

Tangier, Morocco

Dear Saxton

As you must be aware I did not sign the last contract that was forwarded to me through [William A.] Bradley, chiefly because I had decided to hold over the novel on which it was based and also because I wanted to be finished with the last and turn the situation over in my mind.

I came to the conclusion finally that I should prefer to have an American agent right there in New York, one who could handle the job of marketing stories and articles etc. for me, while asking Bradley to continue as my European representative. This last I have done and I am sending a copy of this letter to Bradley and enclosing a duplicate of the one I wrote to him.

I have been unduly tardy getting down to this, chiefly because I started work on the preface I sent you right after finishing the short stories and, besides being a little tired, my health was much below par all during the writing of it. But now that the matter is cleared up I wish you would send me the new contract on the best possible terms you have to offer.

Regards to you
Yours Sincerely
(signed) Claude McKay

WABLAR TLS (copy)

To Max Eastman

19 July 1931

Tangier, Morocco

Dear Max

I must share a great deal, if not all the blame, for any delay and doubt in [Eugene] Saxton's reply to you. I did not do in time the two important things—send him an outline of the Jamaica book and write [William A.] Bradley about the contract. All because I was busy doing a preface for my new book—started it right after sending off the short stories and as my health was not good (head and stomach trouble) it took me longer than I reckoned to get done. However, it is now done and has been sent off to Saxton[.] (I think I did a good job—rewriting it about three times. You might ask Saxton to let you see it. There is a little mention of you in it.) Ask Saxton to show it to you.

Well as soon as I got the preface off my hands, I was free to think up those letters to Bradley and Saxton. I have written them and enclose copies so you may see what I have done.

I still believe it would be a good thing to have a representative there in New York. Not just a mere literary agent, but someone with social and artistic contacts, who besides the economic interest had a real flair for literature and would always be talking about and getting things done for me. The thing is to find such a person as I chanced to find Bradley! I don't mind giving the rake off at all so long as I am getting the benefit of it. Bradley was excellent in his "young" days, but since we knew him he has become quite a business man with a large office and well-staffed and he travels all the time, + gives less time to individual matters.

The Emancipation Centennial is the hundred-year anniversary for the first great and general liberation of Negro slaves which took place in August 1833. The general abolition did not really occur until 1838—but it was in 1833 that the first Abolition Act was passed suppressing slavery in British colonies. So if we make enough money we must pay that long-promised visit to Jamaica for the Celebrations—if the British Authorities will permit me to return to the island where I was born.

About Eugen [Boissevain] and Edna St. Vincent [Millay], it's all right—I feel a little guilty towards them myself so we might cancel out the feeling. I remember the m.s. but it wasn't a very good story and I wouldn't have used it in the present collection any way even if I had the original. It was one of my first attempts at a Jamaica story—I shall use the pictorial part of it, which was the only good part, in the novel.

I did tell Saxton I was asking you to take up the matter of the contract—in two letters. And when I sent him the preface I wrote just as you did that I was disappointed that he did not say anything definite about the advance. I feel sure that the short stories will more than cover what they have already advanced, because they are good stories and I already have enough of a name that will help to sell them. The whole misunderstanding started with the novel I held up. It wasn't good enough and I didn't want to go the way of—say Floyd Dell. I had about written myself dry on the picaresque stuff—the novel began in the picaresque style but ended on a melancholy and serious note. Bradley wanted me to botch it up to make a good sale and I am sure that would have ruined me as a novelist. That was why I came here where I could live cheap to do those short stories and prepare myself for the Jamaica book.

Well, as soon as I decided to substitute the short stories for the novel as was called for in the contract—Bradley seemed to have been alarmed, I don't know why. However, he got me 500 dollars advance that I had not even asked for (for I had a thousand bucks) and sent me a new contract tying me up for another term of four books. But as the book that the contract was based on was the one I had decided to hold up I had an excuse for not signing. All the time both Bradley and Saxton have been harping that short stories do not sell—but I am not a machine-writer who can turn out a novel every year. I should rest a little sometime, change to a poem, a short story or article or nothing. Bradley I am sure feels that I want to get rid of him but Saxton has no cause to think that—although I heard that the Cosmopolitan Co raped Harper[']s of some of their best writers!

Anyway that is the story and when you see Harper[']s (Saxton) again you might lead up to the subject and let him know that there was nothing obscure behind my decision. I couldn't patch the novel and I couldn't write another. Happily I had the short stories on hand and on my mind and since the contract called for them, they were just right. Give them a chance, they may do much better than Saxton imagines. The six Harlem stories go much deeper into the life of the Harlem Negroes than "Home To Harlem" ever did.

Well, I shall surely be happy to see you here. Maybe I could go to meet you both in Spain and we could do the country together. I feel like settling here for good. I am a good Moslem now, wearing the tarbosh and burnous sometimes. I have a little house (exactly like yours at Antibes) for 100 francs a month out of the town in an Arab village, but I want to change to a place up in the hills. Living is cheap, you get the best meat for 8–10 francs a kilo, which is a little over two pounds.

A colored wench that I had liked a little in Paris about 2 years ago (when I got back from Morocco) came down to see me this Spring—said she was tired of Paris and felt a "need for Africa." But she wasn't here a month before a white fellow followed her here. I turned her loose of course and now I have a nice little Fatma taking care of me. She is dumb and can't pretend to be intellectual and that is best.

I shall write you at length about my health. I finished a series of piqures in the fat of the butt—white bismuth—and that did me a lot of good. I suppose it is not the same as the spinal cord. The doctor put it in alternately in both sides of the rump. My head is much better—most of the trouble now is in my stomach and I am dieting—I had an awful attack of indigestion. The doctors do eat up all my extra money. I tell you I am living more frugally (from the point of view of health conservation) than ever. I have a few Arabs who come in sometime and sing and play music and I give them a little drink, but I never touch the stuff myself myself—except for a little beer once in a while.

"Banjo" is out in French[1]—a fat thing and that story of mine you liked so much—the one about the octoroon girl—appeared in Europe—I shall send you a copy—you are mentioned by Romain Rolland in the same number.[2] Also [Georges] Friedman[n] wrote the introduction to "Banjo" and describes his meeting me at your place at Antibes. Shall send you a copy also . . . Much obliged for all you've done—I have enough money for the end of this month—I suppose it will be all right[.] My best to Eliena as ever[.]

Claude.

MEP ALS

1. Published in French translation by Rieder, *Banjo* was popular with writers and critics in the Négritude movement, as Brent Hayes Edwards has documented in *The Practice of Diaspora* (2003).

2. A French translation of McKay's story "Near-White" appeared as "Presque Blanche" in *Europe*, 15 June 1931, 207–26. Eastman and the *Masses* are mentioned in Romain Rolland's essay "Adieu au passé," *Europe*, 15 June 1931, 161–202. This issue also featured a translation of Alain Locke's essay "The New Negro."

To Max Eastman

1 September 1931

Xauen, Morocco

My dear Max

It was a unique pleasure to have your selected collection of poetry and again go over the familiar ones and read the new. Of the recent ones I like the, "We have been happy etc" best.[1] The reading of all as a whole emphasizes the feeling that your poetry is the exquisite utterance of a highly civilized and a very cultivated human being. It evokes images of the paintings of [Antoine] Watteau of which I saw some excellent examples in the Prado at Madrid the year before the last. It is carefully selected and executed, every word and phrase and beat, and if it seems to lack anything it is a sort of primitive wildness of passion that sometimes takes one unawares in poetry and kind of gives the impression that the poet himself was surprised by his own words. But a discriminate [*sic*] mind would not look for that in your poetry nor cavil. For you are Greek in spirit and I always think of you more in the spirit of Plato (who perhaps is the only great Greek who is more than a name to me and who represents for me the perfect flower of the exquisite scholar and great man). It would be absurd to look for the spirit of Plato in Shakespeare or vice versa, but who wants to? I prefer the giants of culture without many points of resemblance.

I was suffering so much from head trouble that I left the coast for this high little mountain town as soon as I got the money (on the 21st Aug. it arrived). I drink nothing but the pure water which pours out of a rock in the mountain and with the rare air I feel much better already. What I love about these Moorish towns is their living medievalism and that they are not mere shells of the past like in Europe, for the thought [*sic*] of way of life of the inhabitants are still medieval. I suppose for me the feeling is also spiritual, since we were taken out of a primitive tribal life and set down into the most modern without having passed through the feudal tribal stage. It may be that my attachment to the native life here is a sort of spiritual looking backwards. This town has a different aspect from all the others I have seen because the roofs are not flat terraced after the Arab style but are tiled oblong-shaped (can't remember just now our name for this style of roof). It was founded in the 15th century by an Arab chief who was expelled from Spain and they say the style of building is Spanish Andalusian. But it reminds me also of some of those old towns in Provence, mostly in the Var.

I have brought all the notes for my new book and want to get them into shape to start work right away when I get back back [*sic*]. I wish you were here to talk it over with me! I do hope you can make the trip in the Spring. I have taken a little house right on the sea for 50 francs a month. I paid down a year in advance. I shall have to put in about 500 francs [for] repairs but it is cheap even at that. It is about 2 miles from the town. There is another next to me for about the same price that I could get for you. Both have gardens like your old place at Antibes. And living here is cheap. Fresh meat at 8–10 francs a kilo (not pound)—we can live on 10 francs a day.

[Eugene] Saxton liked the preface, but said he couldn't put it in the book. He says he will try and place it with "The Bookman." I wish you could do something with it for me. If it wasn't for your own work I wouldn't want a better representative than you over there. For you could talk about me to editors. I should like you to read the preface (Saxton will willingly show it to you if you tell him I want it) and suggest something. It is short[,] about 35 pages. But maybe I could elaborate it into a little book and find another publisher. That would not be infringing on my contract with Harper[']s, since it is not fiction.

What about your prose work on poetry? Also the movie you were going to make of Russian scenes? I hear that for a time Russian films were the rage in New York and were the only ones to hold their own against the talkies. Charlie Chaplin has a wonderful press over here, but the French don't seem to like him so well, perhaps because he visited Berlin from London before coming to Paris! He was in Algeria and it was announced he was coming to Morocco and I thought I'd have the chance to see him. But I suppose it would be impossible—I don't know if personal letters get through to him. Are you still good friends and have you seen him since your return to America?

I am sending this letter to Croton for I have forgotten your other address. Love to you and Eliena.

As ever
Claude

MEP ALS

1. Max Eastman's *Kinds of Love, Poems* (1931) featured new and collected poems, including the 1930 verse "We Have Been Happy."

To Max Eastman

1 December 1931

Tangier, Morocco

Dear Max

Of course, it might be some fun and a good thing to collaborate with your lady to make a piece out of "Banjo" or any other stuff of mine.[+] I always felt I could do a bit for the theater if I had somebody to help me with the technical and practical side of it. Especially as I usually have my people right under my eye in scene and action as I write. I see you are doing real "representative" stuff for me. I hope you will be coming over soon. I have taken a little house in over an acre of land about two miles from the town. It was a dilapidated old barn without doors and leaky all over but I started in repairing it after my return from Xauen and now it is very habitable, but I spent the best part of my assets making it so. However, I have faith in the place and myself. One half the land is good truck garden soil and I have planted two sacks of potatoes and a little peas and carrots and turnips, so if the international crisis should get worse and the elements are not unfavorable to the garden I might in time be able to feed off of my own place. As soon as I can manage I shall get a milking goat. The house is right on a river which divides it from the sea and at high tide when the sea rides up the river the water washes the foundation. It is deep enough for good bathing especially when the sea is high, with a little stretch of sandy beach, and next summer I want to build a runway right into the water. The house is just about the size of yours at Antibes and planned almost the same way. It commands a most lovely view of the sea, the town of Tangier and Spain on one side and on the other the mountains of the Spanish Zone.

I didn't answer your letter right away because I was so busy fixing it up after coming back here. Because of that too I haven't even got under way yet with my new book (but please don't unwittingly let the boss know anything of this if you should be talking at any time to him). Now I am all set with a girl to cook for me and a boy on a bike to run errands and I am planning with a will to crowd three months['] work into one. It won't be so hard as I have the plan of the new book all worked out.

And I hope you will be coming in the Spring or even earlier. There are two vacant houses next to me with nice gardens, one of which I may be able to rent for you. Living is cheap here if one doesn't try to keep up the standard of the European and tourist. My first little Hassani house in the Arab village cost me between one hundred and one hundred and twenty-five francs a month according to the change (I was paying in Spanish money). And this new one is six hundred francs a year. I paid one year in advance and am exempt one because I did the reparations, but it must have cost me around 3000 francs. Everybody said the rainy season would make me sick of it out here (they never quite believe that I was born and raised in the backwoods and loved it) but so far there has been more sun than rain and I am equipped with a stout pair of tramping boots and the road is fine. The weather has been lovely too and so if it is chillying [*sic*] there and you have a mind to follow the swallows and can just make it, you couldn't do worse than here. I can live on ten francs a day buying the best market food. And good help costs from fifty to a hundred francs a month.

As Ever[1]
Claude

[Left and right margins:] [+] I don't see why both propositions couldn't be tackled. Do "Banjo" first and after the musical thing. I think I could do some popular Negro lyrics for a comedy if I had a good composer for the music. You know in my first book of Jamaican poetry there were some six lyrics with music which I had composed myself and sang for my friend who wrote down the music. I supposed if Mrs Marmel [?] should really decide to come her[e] I'll have to make arrangements for her! CMcK

[Upper margin:] [Indecipherable] the proofs of my new book was [*sic*] held up waiting on the house but they are off at last. I am crazy to see your "Literary Mind"[2] and hope it is as grand and lasting to bring you sound success as "Enjoyment of Poetry." I've seen ads. of it in the American magazines.

Love to you and Eliena[.]

CMcK

MEP TLS

1. The remainder of the letter is handwritten.
2. Max Eastman, *The Literary Mind: Its Place in an Age of Science* (1931).

To Nancy Cunard

1 December 1931

Tangier, Morocco

Dear Miss Cunard

Please forgive my not being able to write before, because for three months with my work and letters heaped up waiting for space and time, I have been engaged repairing a little old house that I rented outside of Tangier—a troublesome job as I was working with native labor only and do not speak Arab [*sic*].

I will do you an article for your book just as soon as I have done a certain amount of a contracted work (I am three months behind) to show my boss. Poems—I haven't written any new ones since 1925. But I'll go through my papers and if I find any worth while among them you may have your choice.

My thanks for sending the "Crisis" which I had not seen for some time and was therefore a reminder to send in a subscription. I was with you in the same room once in Paris at Nina Hamnet's studio where I was posing, but we didn't "meet." Since then I heard of you several times in Paris and Nice when I was in those places and once I was asked to the "Falstaff"[1] to meet you but we missed each other somehow.

I think I will stay here in Morocco for quite a long time. I found the little house I am staying in dirt cheap for 600 francs a year and engaged it for two. I was here three years ago and liked it so much I had to return. It was a choice between Morocco and Spain—if I were compelled to live in Europe—and I chose Morocco because I feel closer to the Moors and have a profound empathy for certain features of their social life.

Maybe you would have found Spain sympathetic with Mr [Henry] Crowder—if you haven't been there. I found it the most interesting of European countries—something like a bridge between Europe and the orient and an introduction to Morocco. There may be something wistful or sad about the people in general—but they also have their big moments of spontaneous joy that I've never noticed among any other people excepting Negroes. The night-time street dancing in Catalañia [*sic*] in the summer for instance is the most beautiful I have ever seen.

I am sending two little photographs that are not good but I'm out of stock now after sending all I had to the Paris publisher of "Banjo" and to New York for my forthcoming book. I have one which you might have liked but I have no duplicate nor plate and I think it would be too much trouble to send and ask you to return it after the cut was made. However, I think the one you got from Berinice [*sic*] [Abbott] will compensate for all the bad little ones.

And now in a couple of days—this very week—I hope to fish out my papers and see what poems I have. New ones I cannot write because I haven't been poetry-minded for a long time, though I hope to get into that state again.

Yours Sincerely
Claude McKay

P.S. I feel very excited about your book, of course, because I think from your attitude and angle of approach, if I surmise rightly, you will produce a fresh and artistically stimulating contribution. We poor Negroes, it seems to me are literally smothered under reams of stale, hackneyed, repetitious stuff done by our friends, our moral champions and ourselves that never strikes people piercing [?] anywhere. We most of us live in fear of the fact of ourselves. And can hardly afford to render even the artistic truth of our own lives as we know and feel it, but it is unimaginable that you could be handicapped or allow yourself to be by the social-racial reactions that hamper us sometimes unconsciously even. And so I hope the stuff you are going to put out will be a revelation and important to us[.]

CMcK.

NCC ALS

1. The Falstaff Bar, a Montparnasse establishment frequented by American expatriates.

To Nancy Cunard

26 February 1932

Tangier, Morocco

Dear Miss Cunard

At last I am finishing the first pressing part of my work and I am going to give next month to the contribution for your book. I am still not yet sure just what it will be, I have notes on three or four subjects and shall make outlines of them and then choose the one that would seem to be the best to fit in your collection.

I don't know if you have heard about the story of the Black Sultan of Morocco and if it would interest you. I first heard about it in Barcelona in 1928 from a young Moor, when I was invited by a Martinique seaman living in Casa to visit Morocco. The sultan was one of the greatest rulers of Morocco and a great deal of legend has grown up around him and it isn't even certain whether he reigned in the twelvth [*sic*] or fourteenth century. The popular tale says it was he who built the three great Moorish monuments, the Koutoubia at Marrakesh, the Hassan Tower of Rabat and the Giralda of Seville. But the date of these monuments antedates by two centuries that that is given on the tomb of the Black Sultan at Shellah, Rabat.

He is mentioned in the guide books and there is a reference to him by Leo, the African. This sultan was married to an Englishwoman and it is said that it was she who induced the sultan to make Marrakesh again the southern cap—[*sic*] of Morocco and embellish it. The city had been abandoned by the Merinides dynasty and when she saw it in the midst of a vast tropical plain at the foot of the great snow-covered Atlas she was so captivated that she said she would become the wife of the sultan only on condition that he made it his capital.

The Moors called her the Morning Sun and the long panegyric on her tomb calls her the "free, the pure, the pious." The tomb is a sanctuary for Moorish women and once a year is held there the festival named after her: Lalla Shellah.

Here is a chance I think for someone with the intellectual equipment and inclination for research work to dig down and separate legend from fact.

In your second letter you had some mention about my returning to America and the different opinions you heard about that. Most of the unfavorable talk and even writings about that have originated among Aframericans themselves. The Aframerican intelligentsia and racial leaders as a group are carefully conservative and unreceptive of any bold ideas outside of racial action. They have a naive belief in political promises and plums and that they will achieve social rights through the goodwill of the governing classes. And of course, I was regarded as a very impractical fool for identifying myself with a group of people of impossible ideas and with no influence nor money, when I might have turned my talent to better account. When I wrote, "If We Must Die," the leading Negro literati said I was "arrogant" and "vituperative" and suchlike and when I wrote "Home To Harlem" (which I like better than "Banjo") dealing with the lower level of Harlem life I was[1]

NCC TLU

1. Letter survives in incomplete form; it breaks off here.

To Nancy Cunard

29 March 1932

Tangier, Morocco

Dear Miss Cunard

Jamaica is the most important of the British West Indies—the largest of the group and I think the oldest British colony—and ought to be interesting for you. The people there are divided into three clearly defined groups: black, colored (brown to yellow) and white and there are Chinese, East Indians and an old colony of Spanish Jews.

You'll find color there an entirely different thing from what it is in America—economic rather than sociological—and compared to the states the island is a paradise for the "colored" people which make the middle and upper middle class.

If your friend is brown enough as I presume to make the colored group I think you'll have an enjoyable visit without the slightest annoyance. If he is dark-brown, he may be told there are no rooms at certain hotels although there are. But the discrimination would come from the colored proprietors themselves. But I can't imagine any annoyance arising from you both being together. When I was there there was quite a number of black men lawyers, doctors and preachers who had white wives + all English! The wealthy mulattoes as a group keep pretty well intact rarely marrying black nor white—the latter due no doubt to the fact that from the standpoint of education and culture in general the members of their group are of a better quality than the whites that would be available.

Then there are colonies of whites (poor) of German origin in several parishes and they get mixed up with the blacks naturally in time. To get in touch with the highly interesting exclusive mulatto classes in Jamaica (I think you might find something very valuable there for your book) you might communicate with H. G. DeLisser (a mulatto) editor of the "Daily Gleaner," Kingston. He is a cultured man, has been in London several times and writes books himself, published broadly. I don't know him personally but he knows about me and is quite a friend of my eldest brother, whose address and name are U. Theo. McKay, Frankfield. He is right out of the black peasantry and can give you any information you want about them and how to see something of their life from the inside. Frankfield is far away in the interior of the island but a branch railway line goes up there and my brother has a place near Kingston I think, so if you drop him a line he could call to see you. I will send you two notes one for him and the other for DeLisser if you tell me where to write to. Another friend is MacDermot, T[homas]. H[enry].[,] a poet who is also editor of the "Jamaican Times," Kingston but I don't know if he is still there or where. DeLisser might be able to put you in touch. I think, if your friend is dark, you might have some difficulty seeing the mulatto smart set in their homes with him. (I remember when I achieved real fame as a poet at one house where I was asked the light-colored servants didn't want to wait on me.) But the social and material prestige of your name may cow them.

I feel sure you will enjoy the West Indies with your friend (any social trouble would come from American influence which is spreading at an alarming rate) and I envy you the trip. The book I am doing now is a full-length novel about the native life in Jamaica.[1]

In New York I hope you find time to meet my friend Max Eastman whose address is Croton-on-The-Hudson (if you have never met). I collaborated with him on the Liberator magazine. Maybe you heard a little of the old magazine "The Masses" when he was editing it during the war. Then there is a young woman you may find interesting Gladys Wilson of the Lincoln Hospital, The Bronx. She is intelligent but not with any of the movements and you may find her interesting as a type of Aframerican girl that just manages to keep out of the menial class.

When you get to America this time I hope you'll ask someone to introduce you to the Negroid society of Washington. I know it myself only from hearsay. Only it seems so much like an imitation of the West Indian thing but pathetic as it lacks the economic means + cultural background to hold it up.

I don't mind at all your letting people know where I am, didn't mean to give you that impression by my last. Just wanted to show you what a tragic thing the color problem was even among ourselves. All these movements and class struggles and national strife are horrible things working havoc on the purely intellectual mind often lumping together people who have nothing in common intellectually and emotionally + keeping those who do have apart. And just that is one chief reason I suppose why intellectuals are attracted to them and to fight. . . . .

I am sending you a report of another kind of Southern atrocity than the usual (hope you're not going to risk the life of your friend below the line) also an article out of the American Mercury on the Caribbean if you have not seen it.

Will write more if you tell me where to—This must go off now to catch the aeroplane. It was a great pleasure to hear what you have to say about Gingertown and I am happy you enjoyed it.

bon voyage Sincerely
Claude McKay

It is McKay not Mac ay[.]

NCC ALS

1. *Banana Bottom* (1933).

To Max Eastman

25 April 1932

Tangier, Morocco

My dear Max

I made some notes on your book to write to you about three months now at least, but I couldn't, because all my time was taken trying to get a part of my new work off to [Eugene] Saxton (you know why) and I wanted to write you a long full letter.

I read the book twice and thought it your most brilliant prose work since the "Enjoyment of Poetry."[1] I hope it sold well, which it deserves, and netted you a neat sum. It makes me think more again of something that has always puzzled me and that is why a first-rate critic of poetry like you has never been offered a permanent place as poetry critic on one of the first-rate American reviews instead of having to drudge your life out lecturing awful stuff? It can't be your radicalism, you couldn't be too radical in poetry criticism for the New Republic, The Nation or The Forum. So it may be because you are too conservative! And that your competence as a critic of poetry was overshadowed by the modernist movement that has so skillfully and with the aid of the advanced intellectuals taken, held and dominated the field of poetry in America for the last twenty years.

Well, I was tickled to death by your forthright attack and demolition of the ultra modernists in poetry and prose and their praiseful critics. Personally, I believe that a good many of the unintelligible poets and prosateurs really lack that high mental equipment that makes for clarity of expression of a high order. I say this because often when I take the time to go through the odd punctuation and trick phrasing and get down to the bone of their stuff I find it as banal as Eddie Guest's or (in the case of T. S. Elliot [*sic*] for example) as pedantic and commonplace as Martin Tupper. I except a few who I regard as crusading revolutionists against the dead weight of formal respectability under which modern literature is buried. Like James Joyce who I consider a Don Quixote of contemporary literature, but that is the James Joyce of Ulysses.

As for the younger generation of new humanists, I think they are battling for their existence. Some of them sound too intelligent, from the stuff I've read, to be altogether with the older humanists, so I have a hunch they are also in revolt against the movement, proletarian as well as bourgeois, (see [H. L.] Mencken) that would make literature a thing of mass expression or popular ballyho[o] instead of a skilled and arduous profession.

However, although I found the book exhilarating and enjoyed your tilts at and decapitation of the literary pontiffs, I can't for the life of me work up any enthusiasm over the thesis, which, fundamentally, is the conflict between science and literature. Because I can't see why there should be any conflict except for morons, even though such morons happen to be seated in the authoritative places of academic literature. I could understand better a conflict between religion and science since religion is supernatural and had to surrender the major part of its premises when Science turned its light upon them.

I mention religion because it seems to me the best analogy of illustrating what I feel about the matter of Science and Literature. The great literature and music and painting and architecture that grew out of the periods when the elite of humanity believed in gods and God are still wonderful works of art to us who do not believe—and in spite of their scientific errors! Dante's hell has a magical power over me even though I don't believe in hell and I can adore the presence of the gods and the angels and the saints in Homer and Milton and the great renaissance painters even as I do the Koran in Mohammendan architecture.

So I believe that when a real artist has something to say or sing or sculpt or paint about human life he'll do it forthright, without in the least imagining that he was handicapped or limited by the progress of science. And if his intelligence and comprehension are of a high order he cannot but feel that his work is facilitated by the discoveries of science, even though Science should lay its operating hand upon him body and soul and lay bare the why and wherefore of his creative energy and of the material by which he works. For instance, if science could prove what <u>is</u> the literary mind then it would be so much better for the future generations of litterateurs.

Also it would be easier to determine real from fake literary excellence, just as the science of photography has chased a lot of cheap painters to cover and out of business, which I believe is responsible for (if one dare not say the Cult of Intelligibility) the Cult of Bunk in modern art and the confusion of real masters like Cezanne and Monet with the gang of geometrical tricksters. And while I am on it I must say that I was a little surprised you did not mention modernist painting too for there can be no doubt that it is correlative to the modernist literary movement. And more, my idea is that both are a kind of bourgeois attitudinizing of the social revolutionary ferment. I thought of that when I was in Moscow and used to frequent [Vsevolod] Meyerhold's theatre. I noticed that the audience was mostly members of the old intelligentsia and whenever I met a proletarian he was an intellectual. And when I talked to Meyerhold he seemed like a lost person who did not know what the new social order was all about, but thought that a revolutionary art form in the theatre was necessary to interpret the revolution. Meanwhile all the proletarians who could get or buy tickets were crowding the Bolshoi theatre to see the ballet.

I agree with your statement that poetry is a communication of experience, but so are painting and music in varying degrees. So I think poetry could stand a more definite definition, but that is difficult since it overflows into other art forms just as as [*sic*] music does into poetry.

I can't see any fundamental conflict between science and literature so long as literature has the vast province of social manners to disport itself, even the field of science also which has great need of the literary hand to interpret it. I remember your saying once that many scientific treatises were impossible because their authors did not know how to write. I think the poet or story-teller can make effective use of scientific discoveries by allusions without usurping the role of the specialists. The danger is that he may bore the general reader.

Aldous Huxley knows a huge lot about science but when he puts the technical knowledge of the making of a phonograph and the recording of a disc in his novel, he becomes tiresome unless you are technically interested. For that one would prefer to go to a straight populariser. You know the popular science book that tells us all about the nature of electricity and photography and so on. Tennyson too becomes thin and dated with his Darwinian references in "In Memoriam."

But this doesn't seem to me to imply science encroaching upon and limiting the sphere of literature, but rather literature remaining upon its own unassailable ground. Rather it shows that these pious souls who want to make "literary truth" take the place of "scientific fact" are foolish and wrong just as were their spiritual forbears before them who accepted "literary truth" as revealed religion. Today you and I smile at the supernatural pretensions of "literary truth," but that "truth" remains great literature for us all the same and we don't care a damn that it was created in an unscientific atmosphere.

I can't imagine any intellectual of these times who keep[s] abreast of the thought currents of this age accepting a "literary truth" as against a "scientific fact." I could understand one accepting a "religious truth" but then that lies outside the pale of reason. The intellectual fogeys who want "literary truth" to be scientific or to function today as it did in the time of the Hebrew prophets or the Greeks or even up until the eighteenth century ought to get themselves transferred from this earth to some other planet. But I think that if the intellectual idea of "literary truth" were analysed it would prove at bottom to be nothing more than a "wise saying" or a "beautiful phrase" delivered in an unique and startling matter—an addition to the sum of the universal wisdom of mankind.

Such a wisdom exists telling of the passions, the folly and sagacity, success and failure, pain and joy of living life. It existed long before modern science and I believe it will continue to exist as vigorous and independent as ever as long as humanity retains the faculties of feeling, thinking—the inexhaustible source from which great and authentic literature springs, whether it be cerebral or sentimental, realistic or romantic.

A Jamaica slave sang: Rock stone a ribber-bottom no
feel sun-hot

when he wanted to say that his master sitting all day in the shade did not know what hard toil in the sun meant. And that saying has become a classic in the folk language of the peasants.

And when Lady Macbeth cries, "Not all the perfumes of Arabia can sweeten this little hand," all those who have set their hand to any deed that they regretted will recognise that as universal poetry.[2]

I cite and accept these with enthusiasm as <u>literary</u> truths and I don't think your citation from [Blaise] Pascal was a particular[l]y pregnant and happy one. And I couldn't agree with you at all when you state on page 241 that "Science has withdrawn intellect from literature." That may hold true for those who lack a comprehensive intellect and the futurists ought to take comfort from such a statement and go on being unintelligible. If science has rid literature from its false pretensions, then so much the better it seems to me for the future of literature which will have to stand on its own intrinsic merit, and although our age may not be very favorable to the creation of great literature I am convinced that intellect and a real one is absolutely necessary for the making of a literary masterpiece.

Therefore I believe M. [Julien] Benda rests upon sound ground when he demands that artists make "an attempt to comprehend life."[3] They should and only so far as they do comprehend life in its universal aspects will their work have more than a contemporary interest and take rank to stand the test of time. . . .

I hope you will be coming over this summer. I haven't heard from you since your card from Bermuda and don't know where you are and what doing since. You would love it here for a change, I think. The garden has sprung full of wild flowers with lovely poppies of various kinds and daisies.

I suppose you are doing a new book. You never wrote any more about the woman who was going to do the play. I struggled through revising the first part of my new stuff and have sent it to Saxton, asking him at the same time for money, for I have enough just for a couple of weeks more. I am afraid to look at the summer in the distance with my work half done before me.

I hear that in spite of the slump the authors are doing pretty well and that many of the newer men have a permanent contract and draw a monthly allowance. And of course I wish I was in on that too.

I have just met an American here who knew you by sight, has seen you at parties in New York. And he spoke most flatteringly of you and Eleana together. Well, I hope I see you both this summer.

With my best as ever
Claude

MEP TLS

1. Max Eastman, *The Literary Mind: Its Place in an Age of Science* (1931).

2. McKay paraphrases Shakespeare's *Macbeth* V.i.50–51.

3. Julien Benda, *La trahison des clercs* (1927), translated as *The Treason of the Intellectuals* (1928).

To Nancy Cunard

30 April 1932

Tangier, Morocco

Dear Miss Cunard

I have written directly to my brother about you (you have the address) and here is a letter for H. G. Delisser [*sic*], who is the editor of the "Daily Gleaner," Kingston. It is rather formal for he is not a personal friend, but I think it will do.

I wish I had seen the "Afroamerican's" mention of your booklet and it would be interesting too to read the reaction of the Negro press in general.[1] Maybe you don't know that many of the Negro weeklies are subsidized by either the Republican or Northern Democratic local machine. And so like the press everywhere (only perhaps a little more) the Negro press is ultra conservative and regular in anything that concerns morals and politics. It would be a hopeful sign if it could show a break from tradition in your case. It is allright to have shouting headlines against lynching and race prejudice (all the Northern politicians who need the Negro vote are against that as well as liberals). But it's quite another thing to be confronted with prejudice mixed up with a person like you who are frankly unconventional and don't care about social and traditional standards. Besides the bugaboo of miscegenation is so real in America, all the politicians, black as much as white, are scared of it, no matter what their performance might be in private. The cracker is always roaring (and frightening even the radicals + revolutionists): Social Equality means Miscegenation. The Negro politician of the [W. E. B.] DuBois's [*sic*] type replies: We want social and political equality to defend our rights and <u>live our own lives</u>. I don't think there is any other group of people that is living so strenuously hard to prove that it respects all the conventions (even those that imprison it) as the better class of American Negro . . . So I think you'll understand and sympathize and feel even a little amused in your anger if the Negro press should misrepresent your booklet—even as I did when it came down on me when I published: "Home To Harlem[.]"

It is possible that your Ashanti friend has met persons in London who knew me. I was there all of 1920 until March I think of 1921, and I spent most of my evenings at the International Club in East Road, and for a time lived in a little street off Great Portland in the house of the Frenchwoman who used to serve in the club. Also I used to go, but less frequently, to a club in Drury Lane, or near the Drury Lane theatre, for colored men chiefly demobilized soldiers. And it was a very interesting conglomeration of West Indian and American + African Negroes and Mulattoes, Egyptians and Arabs and a few Indians. I wrote an article about it for the "Negro World" in New York, whose London agent used to leave copies of the paper in the club.[2] The club was managed by the wife of an Indian army officer of lower rank + I didn't like her—the oleaginous way she talked about her Negro boys as if they were all a lot of silly children. And when she saw the article I wrote she was furious—so I stopped going there. But at The International Club we had a nice little group that stuck together: myself, a painter named Budgen[3] (with whom I still correspond)[,] a Belgian Jewess to whom he is now married, a mulatto from Trinidad who had been a student at Oxford, a Jewish seamstress and a Jewish fur dealer who was very stupid, but who always put up the money for the parties in Limehouse and at an Italian restaurant in Soho. So although I could say I lived in London it was altogether in a foreign milieu—chiefly Russian-Jewish—except for the little time I worked with a Miss Smythe[4] on Sylvia Pankhurst's "Worker's Dreadnought." And that was very uncongenial.

I could not like the English as a people and nothing about them could stir me with a feeling of that objective admiration that the French inspire as a whole with their special characteristics. In London I felt I was in a cold citadel of Respectability which frowned down on everyone who did not have the qualities or the means to make him respectable. And there were unforgettable incidents arising from the Problem—things that could not have happened in America because there were no hypocrisy and cant there where the race problem was concerned. At last I was glad to escape from that atmosphere to the black belts and the scrambling rough and tumble of America. All the same I think Europe, the Continent, an infinitely more congenial place for the American Negro, who can afford living there, than any part of the U.S. There isn't enough and never will be enough of them, I believe, to bring about a race problem. But if the social conditions were favorable to the growth of Negro colonies I hardly think they would fare as well as the Jew. I try to see things whole and in an historical perspective and I have always regarded North America as an outpost of European civilization. And the attitude of white America towards black America can be compared interestingly with that of Europe towards native Africa.

Oh yes, you might do something for me in Jamaica and that is to send me a copy of "Gardner's History of Jamaica" if you can.[5] I should like to have it for some facts for the Jamaica novel I am writing now. Also, if by chance you can pick up a copy of my first published work, "Songs of Jamaica"—not the sheet music of six songs title[d]: "Songs from Jamaica" of which I have a copy, but the book of poems with my photograph as a constable. I haven't a single copy + have tried without success to get one for it has long been out of print.

Being a cop, even though it was for a short time, was one of the few things that I ever did that I profoundly regretted. However, the experience was interesting though I loathed it and I have expiated by frankly writing the story. And then too it provided the opportunity of studying the type of mind that exists solely to make trouble for others because it fattened on that. And also it served me well to estimate and understand the same type among different people. I hope you are enjoying your trip and that America proves more congenial this time than the last.

Sincerely
Claude McKay

NCC ALS

1. Likely "Nancy Cunard's Black Man and White Ladyship Pamphlet Shocked London," *Baltimore Afro-American,* 16 January 1932, 3.

2. This letter appeared in the *Negro World,* 13 March 1920. See Winston James, "Letters from London in Black and Red: Claude McKay, Marcus Garvey and the *Negro World,*" *History Workshop Journal* 85 (2018): 281–93.

3. Likely Frank Budgen (1882–1971), English painter, writer, and socialist.

4. He is referring to photographer Norah Lyle-Smyth (1874–1963).

5. W. J. Gardner, *A History of Jamaica* (1873).

To Max Eastman

18 June 1932

Tangier, Morocco

Dear Max

You can't imagine what a wonderful tonic your letter was and how powerfully it pulled me up in spirit for I have never yet felt so far away[,] out of depths and down at the bottom as this spring. After finishing the new book and sending it off to [John] Trounstine[1] I made outlines of exactly three short stories, but I just couldn't write them. I was frantic and afraid with my head swelled out big like a balloon and turning round with a drum beating inside worse than when I fell ill last November. But this time I was determined not to, knowing that it would be all over if I did and so I started writing poetry—loose free-running things very different from the old classic designs. I have roughly done ten of them already and my head has vastly come back down from the clouds.

Your letter was mailed the very day the m.s. was sent off to Trounstine . . . About the Guggenheim Foundation Louis Untermeyer was always well-disposed towards me. Also I think I could count on Heywood Broun, Lewis Gannett[,][2] John Farrar (if he still has any influence). Also Arthur [Arturo Alfonso] Schomburg of the Division of Negro Literature, 135th St. Branch N. Y. P. Library has just written that Carl Van Vechten has much influence with the

Guggenheim people. Maybe he (Van Vechten) would do something if you approached him. I'm positive he adores you for your composite physical and intellectual personality. I've heard that in Paris from several persons who spoke about it in a funny way—hope you understand and don't take offence. I know him very slightly myself and don't think we impressed each other favorably. Met him one summer night in 1929. I had gone to the Cafe de la Paix to meet a friend from Harlem after the opera. And when I arrived Van Vechten was with him. My head was in a terrible way then (from my illness you know) and I couldn't afford to drink and then go insane. Van Vechten was tight. And when he asked me to take something I ordered a soft drink! I could see the surprise on his face and a little later he excused himself and went to the toilet and never came back. So I paid the bill and left! If you should see him, you might tell him about it.

I know Joel Spingarn slightly but don't know if he is still alive literarily and would let me use his name—also in the same way Waldo Frank and Frida [*sic*] Kirchwey. The news about America sound[s] so discouraging in the French papers and even the American ones you have sent that I have been in great doubt whether you can get people to think of you as an individual, when you are not on the spot, on account of the general panic.

If the application blanks should arrive before I hear from you again, I will delay filling them out until you pass on the literary people.

I am praying day and night and haunting the post office for favorable news from you or Trounstine about the book. As I write to you now I have only 35 francs and a few stamps. Whenever I put my typewriter in pawn I always feel very miserable as if my one means of production has been taken away from me. Certainly I should be glad to change to U.S. citizenship if I can. I am of the "New World" anyway and although I could exist anywhere there is food and water to get. I've never felt I was legitimately British which I am not after all. Those few islands in the New World belonging to European nations are certainly a bastard forsaken lot. Many times I thought of taking out papers when I was in America, but always put it off—and now I am sorry.

I've read your introduction to Marx and Lenin's splendid note, thanking you for the book![3] It was necessary a very long time ago for an American intellectual who was a Marxist student to make a sound and convincing statement about Marxian economics—theory and doctrine—and I am glad at last you have publicly crossed the Rubicon. I don't know if your theory about the cultural disparity between the Anglo-Saxon peoples and the German-Russian peoples is the real cause of the different attitude towards Marxian science. The

French people as a whole are by far more intellectually sceptical than the Anglo-American peoples and Marxian socialism is a great power in France. The French, however, have not developed along scientific industrial lines as the Anglo-Saxons + Americans, but the Germans did outstrip the English and were much more highly organized industrially than the Americans though not on so large a scale. Seems to me the leading European (continental) peoples have been more receptive in applying advanced social ideas to modern social and industrial developments[,] while the Anglo-Americans taking the first place and leading in the modern industrial world have a rooted confidence in laissez-faire and "rugged individualism" and have been more reactionary and hostile to experimenting with progressive social theories in modern life than the Continentals. E.g. In 1914 the German and Scandinavian states were much more advanced politically in social services for the working people than England and America. Maybe it was the very amazing material success of the British and Americans troubled so little by social upheavals during the big period of their development that made them so politically contemptuous towards theories of a general social betterment.

But this is merely by way of critical points that may be raised but which can by no means count against your exposure of the theological side of Marxism and the tendency of the orthodox Marxians to develop and stress it in social science.

I think now you might make it possible for the eclectic intellectual, the Voltarian type, to accept Marx as a great social scientist and teacher without the dogma and the infallibility, and thus doing a service for the advancement of the American social revolutionary movement, the extent of which will not be realized for many years. Marx will certainly have to take his place in history alongside other social thinkers and stand above them by his actual achievement. For myself I am unable to understand the doctrinal attitude of Marxian intellectuals and attribute it to a "relic of a religious attitude" as you say. And for the same reason while I admire the social scientists in their particular field as I do—say the astronomists in theirs[—]I think the eclectic rationalist intellectuals altogether superior. Why do people give up a pope and a god in religion to accept a pope and god in science? It seems to me it is because of intellectual weakness and mental fear, an unconscious religious desire for infallibility at the price of Truth or Scientific Fact.

Marx's "historic necessity" will have to go as much as the idea that God created men equal or good for the true intellectual hasn't need of such false truths to convince him that man should be just towards his fellow man. Trotsky seems to me an eclectic type of intellectual and should be one of the first to salute your attempt to divest Marxism of dogma for he has suffered so much from that very thing! Because of his wise independent revolutionary attitude! Because he was not just a tame old Bolshevik he has been made the victim of another doctrine—Leninism.—

You know I have been discovering that in the golden age of Mohammedanism when Europe was in Christian darkness and Science was kept alive by the Moslems, there were some very distinguished Mohammadan free thinkers! But the magic men of the religion smothered them under dogma just as they tried to do later in Europe. And as they did to Christianity it seems to me the same thing might happen to Marxism, because of men's instinctive craving for churches, creeds + a capacity of going backwards often [indecipherable] by [?] striding forward.

Claude

[Left margin:] Have just received the Guggenheim application forms. Tell me should I write Mr [Henry Allen] Moe asking if I can apply although not an American citizen? Also what should I do about questions whether I am married and have children since I do have a wife and a child somewhere. I'd rather leave out. But can I honestly? Won't fill out forms till you advise me. They say the fellowships are open in exceptional cases to permanent residents who are not citizens[.] But I haven't been a permanent [resident] for ten years!

MEP ALS

1. John Trounstine, who became McKay's agent after McKay left William A. Bradley in July 1931 over contractual disagreements following the publication of *Gingertown.*

2. Lewis Gannett (1891–1966), American author and journalist who wrote for the *Nation* and reviewed books for the *New York Herald Tribune.*

3. Eastman edited and wrote the introduction to a 1932 Modern Library edition of writings by Marx and Lenin titled *Capital, The Communist Manifesto, and Other Writings.*

To Nancy Cunard

20 August 1932

Tangier, Morocco

Dear Miss Cunard

Your letters and the newspapers from Jamaica make me nostalgic . . . Before they came to hand (rather late even from far Jamaica to distant Tangier)

I was informed of your movements by the newspapers. First the "scandal" of the Grampion appeared in the French-Moroccan newspapers and the New York Herald (Paris) carried as straight unsensational news your leaving Harlem and arriving in Jamaica.[1] Also [James] Ivy wrote me about his afternoon with you + big [Arturo Alfonso] Schomburg.

I was vexed about all that vile notoriety—and especially it coming before you had collected all your material and launched your book. I can't understand the treatment you received in Cuba—it seems more than the Press under that and I have a conviction (in spite of everything I haven't developed the persecution complex) that it might be the work of the nefarious British Secret Service. Anyway I think you had better be on the lookout for them in your work and in your travels as they might endeavor to embarrass you and defeat your work. Your "Black Man and White Ladyship" must have infuriated the higher-ups who are engaged in a grim struggle to uphold Anglo-Saxon prestige and British Imperialism . . . The last time I saw Frank Harris in 1927, he told me he was barred from re-entering England and that British agents were trying to have him driven out of France as an undesirable because of his "Confessions." I suppose you are aware too of the high-handed action of the British Postal authorities about D. H. Lawrence's poems . . . Another case. When I was in England right after the signing of the Armistice I had a German-English friend who was assistant editor and cartoonist on a little anarchist paper called "The Spur." There was an old English assistant living in Italy who used to give the paper money and articles. I used to see some of his letters—quite harmless—a kind of anarchist idealist. But after the Fascist coup d'Etat he left Italy, travelling to Mexico, Japan, and other countries. And he wrote to my friend that wherever he went he was being spied upon by secret police. . . . All indications seem to show that the International Police have a fixed policy of making things embarrassing and difficult even for mere Communist sympathizers. Sometime ago Panaite [*sic*] Istrati was barred from Egypt + recently Henri Barbusse from entering England.

In getting interested in that group of humanity which General [Jan] Smuts[2] brilliantly described as "patient asses," I think you'll find yourself up against real opposition and intrigue if your programme go[es] beyond the artistic. Since it represents the last docile mass of the exploited, the exploiting powers must want to keep it in that state perpetually, resenting any influence that may nourish a spirit that is difficult from that of "patient asses."

Your American visit sounds like the rottenest thing. It seems you missed doing most of what you'd planned to—trip South—trip to Washington among the Blue-Veins. Maybe it would have been better if you had gotten on to the Carl Van Vechten crowd. Do you know him? He may be passé. I don't hear much about him now. I didn't attempt to give you any N.Y. names, since you were there already, had written for the "Crisis" and must know the crowd there and had an Aframerican friend. James Weldon Johnson (formerly Secretary of the N.A.A.C.P.) is a really fine man—quite different from [W. E. B.] DuBois and Walter White and I am sure he would have understood + helped you. Moreover he is in touch with the right people in Haiti and Cuba—too bad you did not get a chance to do these two islands. But you must know James Weldon Johnson and his very nice wife.

I feel badly about this New York debacle. Because I am convinced that in spite of all its drawbacks and the snob spirit of the Harlemites any distinctive group movement, artistic or political, of Negroes will have to be nurtured in New York. The West Indies haven't the kick although it seems to me they have a great deal to contribute because of their social background. And as your Book is so different in spirit and plan from anything that has been done before (since, happily, you stand outside of all of the groups interested in the Negro) I thought it might become when it was published the rallying-point for a strong new expression. It is because I think so much of the work that I am vexed about these newspaper scares and scandals which may depress and discourage you and perhaps diminish its chances among the critics and artistic people who count.

I am glad you enjoyed Jamaica, sorry Cuba was a flop (Langston Hughes had a fine time in Havana among the Cuban Negroids) and that you couldn't do Trinidad and Haiti especially. I've had a hearty laugh over the reception and those "martyr" speeches (remind me of the way I was corral[l]ed in Russia) but the sight of [Marcus] Garvey[+] with his smug smile and "God save the King" programmes makes me sad and resentful. Evidently he is quite content to be a little Jamaican after making mistake after mistake in spite of helpful warnings and advice and throwing away his opportunity to be a big world leader. Those who were at the trial said that in his overweening conceitedness and ignorance as "Provisional President of Africa" surrounded by his knights, lords, ladies and dukes created from Liberty Hall, he practically took his case out of his lawyer's hands and railroaded himself to jail. It is an unkind after thought [*sic*] but maybe he was glad to be put away, conscious that the thing he had created was too big for him. The British Government have him just where they want—out of America upon a little island, where he may yet reach the highest honor—Member of the Legislative Council.

The thousands of dollars he collected all wasted when they might have provided good theater, hotel or social center for Negroes. And it was the Aframericans who lost most for they are the real dreamers who pursue the chimera of a political utopia for Negroes and they were the ones who bought the fake stocks while the West Indians did the shouting. Because of Garvey the difference between the American + West Indian groups of Negroes in the U.S. is greater than ever. It is so stupid and idiotic—the jealousies, rivalries and discords between [the] West Indian and American Negro. Garvey increased it. He always tried to emphasize that difference between black Negroes + the brown-yellows which is more real in the West Indies (because of its class basis) than in the states. The American Negroes may play the blue-vein game of shades, but as it is not recognized by the Government and the whites as it is in the West Indies and South Africa it has no social influence. The Aframericans black and light-colored make one political and social block. I can't go at length into this in a letter.

Both Americans and West Indians are to be blamed for existing conditions between them. The West Indian, because he has had a greater social freedom at home[,] is often absurdly overbearing to the American, especially the British West Indians[.] I've often heard him mouthing stupidities about the fine quality of British Justice towards natives—merely from his small West Indian knowledge of it. On the other hand the American Negro makes fun of the crudeness of the average West Indian immigrant, his clothes, his accent and his Britishness when he is British.

In America I have always preferred the American Negroes to the West Indians who on all occasions display too much "class" spirit for my liking and when I was there I lived with American in preference to West Indian families. Of course I had a good break from the start. I landed in the South on my first trip to America and after six months at Tuskegee went to the Middle West where I stayed two years before going to New York. In the south and the West the West Indians are liked by the Aframericans much more than in the East. Also I was a student, but when I did go to work as a menial I formed excellent comrades—strangely nearly all my fights were with West Indians. The West Indian Negroes are solid and seem more reliable as a rule than the American, but I like the flair, the good-time "party" spirit of the Americans.

Thank you very much for the books. I wonder after all if you did get the right poems the first published book "Songs of Jamaica." That is the one with my photograph as a Constab and not the "Constab Ballads" which is not nearly so good. The first contained my early dialect poems and I am afraid that the advertisement with "Constab" in brackets might have brought you the second Jamaica book "Constab Ballads." Those poems were not so fresh as the first—sort of made up and written for a second publication but the first ones had some real spontaneous singing things about the Clarendon hills, the peasants, cultivating and marketing. But thanks for all the trouble you took and for remembering in spite of all the worries and the many things you had to think about. I am very happy you got the history.

My new book deals at length with Obeah. It was and I think still is rampant in Jamaica. When I was in Clarendon the peasant family that did not believe or deal in the thing was a rare one. In our village there were three exempt. And in the towns and in Kingston the thing thrives. Those who don't visit the common Obeahman consult the clairvoyants. Funny my brother did not supply the information about it. I remember as a kid he used to lecture against it and try to convince his friends among the well-off peasants that Obeah was a fake. But I am sure he had no success.

How fat he is! He was always huge but never so paunchy. That comes from my mother and I am fighting all the time against that dead fat form. Our father (I hope you saw him) is as lean as a greyhound and none of his brothers were fat. He is over ninety.

Well, I am sorry my contribution is not ready yet, but I promise you to send it in time. I told you I would do it so soon as I got that first half of my book finished and off to the editor. I thought that would have brought me another advance and given me a chance to rest + do your stuff in the interval, because I have been suffering from high blood pressure for some years and can concentrate on one thing only at a time.

But, alas! "Gingertown" was an alarming flop. Only 1100 copies sold—not enough to cover a quarter of the advances made to me—and the publishers refused to give anymore. They made me angry too neglecting to answer my letters until I had to waste needed money on a cablegram. There was nothing for me to do but just keep on grinding, and worst of all my friend, Max Eastman, who usually acts for me in New York[,] is somewhere in Constantinople visiting Trotsky. I had no one to make personal contact with the publishers.

I finished and sent them three parts of the book. I am still on the fourth and hope to finish it by the end of this month. But in the meantime I wrote a man in New York asking him to try and sell me to another publisher—in spite of the contract with Harper's. Some publisher who would be willing to pay enough over an advance that would enable me to repay Harper's. I don't know yet if the letter reached the individual and if the thing can be done—

the book trade, they say, is so bad. In the meantime I have asked Rieder my Paris publisher to buy the m.s. outright for serial publication in their magazine and I am waiting for a reply. That would not infringe the American rights and if it did I could demand that it be waived under the circumstances.

I am now doing the final chapter and as soon as it is done and this matter is settled either way I shall start my brain to work on your article.

What is this Excelsior House? A hotel? When I was there there was not even a hotel at Chapelton and the May Pen's lodging house was very poor and so tourists hardly ever ventured up the Rio Minho valley. I suppose the railroad and banana trade have given Frankfield a little boost. My book is about all that country and a part of the neighboring parish, St Ann, which is called, "the garden of Jamaica." So you will be able to judge whether my composite rendering of the scenes and atmosphere as I remember them is good. Yes, the country people <u>are</u> wonderful. They just have <u>no idea</u> of the hard and fast moral standards of Europe and America. Any really fine-minded person could live among them in <u>any way</u> he pleases[.] Only the monotony would get him in the end. I am showing this by the leading white character in the book—the only one lifted from real life—the English "squire" who sent me to the States. I remember when my first poems came out, the market women stopped me by the roadside and asked me to read to them. Those were the happiest readings I ever gave[,] I dislike audiences.

I'm sending you some cuttings. I remember you told me about an article on boxing. This Sparrow Robertson is the oldest sports writer living—I think very fair to Negro boxers—has known the best of them and might do you an article on these as a group in his unique style.

Also there is a Martinique woman Paulette Nardal, <u>7 rue Hébert Clamart</u> près Paris, editor "Revue du Monde Noir." I wrote her about you. Might be of use. Don't know if I should add it might be better if you didn't talk "left" politics with her.

Sincerely Claude McKay

+ Of course, I won't deny it is good Garvey is doing <u>something</u> in Jamaica—but so insignificant compared to the chances lost in U.S. Since you missed Haiti—if you are not in touch with anyone there, you might get good information from William Seabrook, author "Magic Island." Thanks for photographs. Sorry you did not get one of Father. Been asking my brother to get one for three years.

NCC ALS

1. Cunard was hounded by the New York press about her interracial romances after checking in to the Grampion Hotel in Harlem in early May 1932.

2. Jan Smuts (1870–1950), South African general and political figure who described Africans in 1930 as "docile animals, the most patient of animals, next to the ass."

To Nancy Cunard

31 August 1932

Tangier, Morocco

Dear Miss Cunard

I wrote to you about 10 days ago right after receiving your letter and the newspapers mailed from Havre. And although it was a long letter I was planning to write another as so many important points had been left untouched:—"Communism and the Aframerican," "The Negro in Morocco," "Strivers' Row," "Bernice" etc and I also wanted to invite you here if you were not too tired out after your trans atlantic randonnée.

But a series of coincidences have terribly upset me. The very day (last Friday) I stayed in town jotting down notes in a café, I came home to find my little house broken into and my French carte d'identité and British passport enclosing 300 francs stolen. I am at a loss whether the burglars are just common marauders or if it was a police trick to deprive me of my papers and turn me against the Moslems. There is so much petty political intrigue here.

When I came here towards the end of 1930 I was so harassed by the police that I became convinced their objective was to deprive me of my passport. And so I kept it all the time at home.

But since my finances turned bad I have been seriously considering leaving here for my old place and I wrote to a friend in Paris about the matter. They say the correspondence of suspected persons is read here. I asked my friend to ask my French publishers (Rieder) to buy my new book for serial publication in their magazine "Europe." He was just leaving for Russia and had time only to write to the publishers and send me 500 francs himself. I took my passport as identity to get the money (Thursday) and it was 300 of it that was taken on Friday just as I had left it in the passport.

I called in the International police to take a look at the job and I reported it, of course, to the British Consulate. There I was told that it would take about 3 months to make inquiries and get me another passport and as I am on the blacklist of the British Authorities[.] I don't know what the outcome will be.

I don't know what to say of the robbery. The little house is off by itself upon a river and it was fine before they stuck up the tunny factory near it. I liked it because of the site and the bathing. I am not much of a swimmer but very fond of floating in deep water and at high tide the sea drives up the river which is always calm and excellent for bathing when the sea is often rough because of the strait and Levant winds. On the hill above there is a village of about 500 people and a few friends always come down from there and over from the town to visit me. Strangely enough my European clothes and shoes were not touched. Only Moorish things were taken—a brass tray and candlesticks[,] four little rugs and three woolen blankets. All of very little value. I bought the rugs at a native bargain sale because they were bright and pretty-patterned. The blankets were the best of the lot. I've never worried about thieves because I felt that all I had worth stealing was in my head. The room in which I do my writing was not entered.

The worst of it is that I was engaged upon the last chapter of my book which is a description of a Negro peasant wedding and was doing it with gusto as if I were making a home run and now, with the interruption and consequent upset I have lost the verve to finish it.

If you are near Paris you might drop in on my French publishers Rieder (Editor-in-chief [Jacques] Robertfrance) and find out what they think of my proposal to publish the new book serially. Since my friend has left for Russia I have no one to make a personal contact which is so much better and especially as my french is poor for writing purposes. I did write Robertfrance but have not heard from him directly. If I knew that they were favorable to it I could forget the irritating worries and make the final effort to finish the book and then start to lick the whole thing into shape for immediate publication.

Yours Sincerely
Claude McKay

I have received the book of verses. Thanks, although after all the trouble it is the wrong one. Yes, you may surely use the poem you like. I never could stand this book because for one thing it was dedicated to the Inspector General whom we all (constabs) disliked. But the Englishman who sponsored the publication thought it was "good taste" to give the Inspector General the dedication especially as he was trying to get my discharge from the service. I wanted the dedication to go solely to Inspector [W. E.] Clark[1] whom we all liked. And many of the verses are just "made up" as compared to the fresh singing "Songs of Jamaica" ones. The History not to hand yet. But I shall need it only in revising to get a few dates right.

CMcK

NCC ALS

1. McKay's *Constab Ballads* includes a dedication to two Jamaican police officials, Lieutenant-Colonel A. E. Kershaw, the inspector general of the Constabulary, and Inspector W. E. Clark.

To Nancy Cunard

18 September 1932

Tangier, Morocco

Dear Miss Cunard

Hope I don't bore you to death asking favors but this stupid cheque drawn on N.Y. will take 25–30 days before I can cash it there (the first time sent like this) and I need the money now. My bank here will not cash it spot [*sic*] because I have no funds left—will collect only which will take an even longer time. So will you put it through yours for me and send the equivalent in Francs—preferably <u>mandat</u> which is the safest? Since both my friends who could do this are out of France you're about the quickest person I know who can fix me up.

I have finished the chapter! Now typeing [*sic*] all I hand-wrote when machine was in pawn—100 pages nearly. After that revision and ought to have <u>all</u> done by the middle of next month.

And please <u>don't</u> worry about my contribution. It will be a real relief and joy to turn to something else after a year's hard work on my peasant saga. Since you won't have fiction I am going to do an authentic bit of personal history—a travelogue and perhaps a poem and you can choose the most fitting.

I am very buoyant about my three months more lease of life—I am sending you [Eugene] Saxton's letter—also Rieder's so that when you go to Paris you will have all the necessary details in approaching him. I don't expect a whole lot from them—the French pay so little for writing—last year I got 200 francs for a short story—but whatever they give will help eke out Harper's.

No, I dislike Eric Walrond. And he does me too. Think he is very pretentious light-weight. Knew him when I was on the Liberator with Max

Eastman+he on the Negro World with [Marcus] Garvey, 1922. Garvey had given me hell and more in his paper (he held a grudge about me for showing up the preposterous side of his movement in the Liberator) because the police had broken up a Liberator affair and beaten some guests on account of my dancing with a white woman—Crystal Eastman[—]+ the N.Y. papers had made quite a scandal of it. Eric came to see me and give some inside dope on Garvey's character for me to make a comeback attack—the crassest moral stuff+besides he was working for the man. . . . . Next time I heard from him was 1925 in France he wrote asking me to send stories for a competition in the Negro magazine "Opportunity" for which he was assistant editor+offered to place some stuff for me. I was glad to do it for I was quite broke. The stories and poems I sent in did not take the prizes but because I was known a little the magazine proceeded to print them without paying me. And so I put my agent on them to collect. The Negro magazines and papers are almost all pirates paying no attention to the ordinary journalistic procedure such as recognizing the source of reprinted stuff and payment. In fact most of them have a way of making people pay for "write-ups" and their mug on the page. . . .

But my ultimate success with "Home To Harlem" after years of struggling brought all the black venom out against me. I was told that Walrond said "I knew how to exploit people." Although I have never yet been clever enough to have a chance of exploiting any of "my own people." And my friends of the "enemy race" whom I have shamelessly exploited have never to my knowledge complained. I was called every damned thing. [Arturo Alfonso] Schomburg# who I always counted a close friend called me (in a review) a buzzard a hog and what not?[1] Walrond (in a widely reprinted article) said I had been invited to Russia by the Soviet Government and the impression was that I had become a bolshevik agent.[2] A lie. I had to peddle autographed copies of poems, bum my friends+work as a fireman from N.Y. to Liverpool to get to Russia. And although the bolsheviks tried to make me represent the Negro race, I let them know that I was a free spirit, a poet although politically my sympathies were communist.

What maddened the American spades was my making money out of my novel. Because the whole intelligentsia crowd have a wards-of-charity mentality—a helpless looking to the powerful philanthropists for awards and scholarships. I told Walrond he ought to have used his scholarship to try and achieve liberty of mind+freedom of expression. I have gone carefully through his stories and stripped of their futuristic verbiage they reveal nothing but the average white man's point of view towards Negroes. The "Palm Booth"—the best one—is just a "White Cargo" written by a black man.[3]

Of the Negro writers today I think Langston Hughes is the real thing—also Wallace Thurman once he finds his stride. Rudolph Fisher a nice humorist. [Alain] Locke a kindly professor.

I am not sentimental about my race. I hate oppression of subject races and peoples. Because it either emasculates the oppressed or diverts the energy they should pour into artistic and cultural channels into political propaganda and struggle for independence. This, changed a little, could also sum up my attitude towards the class struggle and revolution. The spirit wants free contact with individuals of all peoples and social groups everywhere upon this damned earth conspire to keep one shut off in a narrow cadre.

Yours Sincerely
Claude McKay

Schomburg especially amazed me. Because he was always a funny old dog full of naughty tales. Couldn't imagine him setting well with [W. E. B.] DuBois. But I suppose he slated me to curry favor with the Aframericans, being West Indian. Moreover, when I was broke in Marseille, he wrote me asking that I should copy my book of verse by hand for which he would pay 50 dollars. I put my novel (Home To Harlem) aside + started the job just to have the ready cash + after I had begun it he said he didn't want it—had changed his mind.

NCC ALS

1. Although Schomburg did not use these exact phrases, he published a scathing review of *Home to Harlem.* See Arthur A. Schomburg, review of *Home to Harlem, Philadelphia Tribune,* 15 March 1928, 15.

2. In a July 1929 review of McKay's *Banjo,* titled "The Negro Renaissance," Eric Walrond wrote, "He was invited to visit Russia as a guest of the Soviet Government and he set forth, sundering all ties with America." This originally appeared in the London socialist weekly the *Clarion* and was reprinted in Louis J. Parascandola and Carl A. Wade, eds., *In Search of Asylum: The Later Writings of Eric Walrond* (Gainesville: University Press of Florida, 2011), 9–11.

3. McKay misremembers the title of Walrond's story "The Palm Porch."

To Nancy Cunard

29 September 1932

Tangier, Morocco

Dear Nancy Cunard

Mille Mercis for the mandat which I finally cashed today after some delay. By some mistake in the French post office I received instead of the usual slip of notification the entire mandat and when I presented it the fonctionnaires from the controleur to facteur were not interested in paying the money but in knowing how I got it. I got the money after three days' delay the fonctionnaires trying to blame the perfectly innocent Spanish Post Office for their own carelessness.

Now that you have suggested to me what you want for your book and something that suits me exactly I have been already outlining the outstanding notes under three major headings, viz.: Jamaica, America, Europe. . . . Also I want to give you a new poem. And I hope I shall be able to compose it in time. I haven't written a line for about ten years and since I have always felt a desire to work in more elastic frames than those in which I have set my earlier poetry.

Max Eastman thinks I should try. He arrived here last Wednesday on a short visit with his Russian wife. They came from Istanboul [*sic*] (and Palestine) where they had gone to see Trotsky. Lovely people and I still love them even more than ever. He was my first American-white friend and has remained the most faithful—since 1918. Last time I saw him was in the Spring of 1927 when he left Southern France to return to America. He wrote the preface to my American Book of poems "Harlem Shadows" published 1922. Did you ever see it? If not I shall send you my only copy if you let me have it back some time—no hurry. It is out of print.

He is very sorry he did not meet you when you went to America last Spring. He sailed from N.Y. the first of June. I am so sure that if you had stayed for a couple or more of days with them at Croton (about one hour's rail from N.Y.) you would have been in one congenial atmosphere at least in America. I lived all over America, South, West (Middle) and East and it was the only place I ever felt really happy—as I used to be sometimes in Jamaica. I went to live in his little house with black friends, white friends and a Chinese friend. The people who frequented it were of all kinds: communists, socialists, liberals, artists—nearly all free large spirits. And there may have been little prejudices lurking among them (where are they not found?)[.] But the atmosphere was too rare for them to flourish. It was too bad Eastman had to give up the magazine and the group was scattered. It was the <u>only</u> thing of its kind in all of that mammouth [*sic*] vast America. And it was not really understood even by the people who appreciated it. They characterized Eastman as a hedonist and simply because he was not doctrinaire nor moral of attitude about the difficult art of living.

And I have found Socialists, Communists too and Negroes fighting for social equality more bigoted than some of the bourgeois in their intellectual and moral outlook. Of course I subscribe to the Communist economic programme, but man does not live by bread alone. My main objection to the Communists is their attitude towards art and artists. I don't believe in proletarian art nor bourgeois art nor all the other loose social definitions of art. To me authentic art is just there, whatever its origin, racial, national or any kind of social, transcending its cadre and becoming a possession of all humanity and I don't give a hoot for the pedantic divisions and names except as means of identification. The Communists rant about proletarian art and artists. True art is too rare a thing to be dictated to by politics. For Communism is politics like Socialism, Republicanism, Monarchism—the science of governing people and regulating their social and economic life. The artist who is Communist in politics should be at least as free to express himself in a Communist society as his confrere in a bourgeois society who is Republican or Monarchist in politics. I think the Communist theory of proletarian art is wrong. It means really propaganda art while I believe in organized political propaganda I don't in organized propaganda art. About art I am romantic. I salute it everywhere. I don't expect artists to be angels full of brotherly and universal love, even though I rate them so much the higher <u>if</u> they possess such qualities.

This brings me to your mention of literary animosities. Happily I am free of that. I am so romantic about creative art that I really get a kick out of an artist's success—a live one. That kind of success thrills me more than any. But I loathe insincerity in art and pretentious artists. And there are so many of them—the fake ones who make the most noise and do their damndest to spoil and cheapen the genuine.

I was thinking of a short article (I think your original limit was 260 words) but now I will be able to let myself go. The thing right now is to finish the book and knuckle down to your stuff. Max Eastman has a car here and wants to carry me off to Seville. Thinks I need a vacation and it is lonely here a little and the fish factory. But I wish he had come the end of October instead. It is imperative I should finish. And the loneliness is good for working. After that I hope we meet and spend some days talking a little about everything. I am going to tell Max and Eliena to go to see you in Paris. They are shocked to death over what happened to you in America and Cuba. Eliena likes America—but in the same way you do and also myself—the eye something to look at—and the energy. Only she likes the picture enough to live with it and for me it is one to admire but not to live with. I was never happy in Harlem, but I was always excited, restless, and enjoyed the excitement.

Must stop now. Thanks again for the cheque put through.

Sincerely
Claude McKay

NCC TLS

To Nancy Cunard

15 October 1932

Tangier, Morocco

Dear Nancy Cunard

I have finished the new book and am wondering, if you haven't yet seen Rieder, my French publisher, whether it would not be better to send the duplicate m.s. to you. That would serve as an introduction to him and you could find out at once if he intends to take it and how much he will pay and when. Please let me know if this plan sounds all right to you.

About your article. Will the first of December be all right to get it in? Also if you have a copy of Katherine Mayo's "Mother India," could you lend it to me?[1] I want it for a single reference only in the article—but a very important one.

In my last letter I omitted to state some of my strong convictions about Communism as a political theory, thinking as a layman and not as an artist.

I have faith in organized labor and its purposes and I consider Socialism a great weapon for the workers to use in their struggle for economic power and freedom and Communism a yet better and sharper weapon . . . I have and still consider myself a Communist, but I have never been one in the general orthodox sense. In Russia I was referred to as non-partisan and that made some of the tovarishes a little cold. Yet I wasn't really very non-partisan, I was a member of the Workers' Party of America.

But I have a very independent attitude that unfits me for strict and stupid discipline and to make belief that propaganda is truth and that half-truths are truths. Modern life and modern thought are full of confusion and for the integrity of my own mind I want to examine problems carefully before I plunge headlong into them. I accept Communism as a political theory of economics, by which the world may arrive at a fairer social system, but not blindly as a religion as so many people seem to do nowadays. Happily I grew up without religion and have never felt any need of it and it seems to me that Communism is often propagated in a sense as if it were a substitute for religion.

There is only one thing I could accept religiously and that is scientific truth—I mean the things proved by scientific experiment and experience to be true according to natural laws. Socialists and Communists speak of Marxian science as theologians do of Biblical truth. But there is as much theory as fact in Marx. I consider Marx the greatest of economists, but he is not an infallible being to me as he is to the Marxists.

While politically I prefer to be a Communist than anything else, I am not certain and nobody is, that it is the system that will be the salvation of man in the machine age. There are many points in the Communist programme that conflict with my idea of freedom. I will take a cardinal point: the idea of equal wages for all. I don't believe it is a good solution of the wage problem. [George] Bernard Shaw cites the Army, Navy and Police to show that man can get along well with the equal wage. But those are branches of service that call for strict discipline and obedience and little initiative and invention. The fact is that some of us may not want to work as hard as others and may be satisfied with less to live on and I don't see why all the proletariat should have to dance to the same tune for the same number of hours.

I think there is too much regimentation of the world under the machine system and Communism, by its implications, is committed to an even greater expansion of the machine system than we have. I do believe there is a great deal too much bureaucratic regulation of human life. Here in North Africa it is easy to discern a large and "loose" feeling about life even under the Oriental callousness and neglect that I suppose would make the Occidental uplifter wild. I get the same feeling in Spain. But already here you can see the occidental mind at work producing that hectic atmosphere that reigns everywhere in the occident world.

In spite of all this I am on the side of Communism. Economics is the life breath of man and nothing can be accomplished without economic means, yet society has organized and laid down great plans for the professions and sciences and is scared to death of dealing frankly with the basis of all—the economic organization of society. And so when Marx and Lenin come along with a plan to put order into the economic anarchy I rise to salute them.

But I keep my head, and I don't look to Communism as a cure-all for all the various ills of humanity. I have hopes that Communism might work an economic miracle. But for more knowledge and understanding and tolerance in human relations I prefer to put my faith in scientific illumination.

The Communist comrade with his slogan of international fraternity I have found very often to be just as bigoted and impossible as the Christian brother with his pious talk of brotherly love. Finally, Communism after all is just a revolutionary system of governing people and administering their affairs better than in the past. And personally I have no love for any kind of government. I am not an anarchist, I have no reason for believing that human animals are capable of living without government. But I am not an enthusiast of any system of governing people.

Sincerely
Claude McKay

You did not say if you have my U.S. book of verse + if not if you want.[2]
CM

NCC TLS

1. Katherine Mayo's *Mother India* (1927) was a study of gender and patriarchy in Hindu culture.

2. The postscript is handwritten.

To Nancy Cunard

28 November 1932

Tangier, Morocco

Dear Nancy Cunard

I went through a siege. Three weeks in bed and now in the fourth I am barely able to shuffle outside and sit in the sun. At first I had thought it was an attack of the chronic head-and-face trouble from what I have suffered ever since I returned from Russia in '23, but I was soon aware it was a real breakdown from overwork[,] overstrain and anxiety. I made a complete flop and even now that I'm a little better it is hard to do any thinking because of the continuous noises in my head.

And for the first two weeks I was penniless. After I received your note with the bank's memo that you sent just before starting for London I had to send my typewriter to the Mont de Pieté for a 100 francs. About the same I received ten dollars from [Max] Eastman and so I could have the doctor come to see me. That money was wired to the Banque Algerienne here on the 3rd and I was never notified by either bank. It was only after waiting and waiting I wrote to the Banker's Trust and received a telegram from them indicating where the money had been sent, and then on the 16th I was notified by the local bank. I could lay it on the system—but when I was in Toulon in '24 + the Garner [*sic*] Writers' Fund[1] was giving me a small sum for six months, the Amalgamated Labor Bank of New York, which handled the money, forgot to send the duplicate draft to the local bank at Toulon and I just had a hell of a time one month.

And now about Banana Bottom—you've done a right quick job but I am afraid we haven't yet got the thing we want to give me the immediate help I need.

All my novels have been published in London by my American publisher who is one of the oldest of New York publishers (Harper's). But the London branch is a small thing with a poor distributing agency and if I could find an established English firm to take my book Harper (my American publisher) would make the necessary arrangements to publish through such a firm.

But the duplicate I sent you was for Rieder, the French firm. They are expecting it, had asked me to send as soon as possible (remember letters from then I sent you) and I was banking upon an advance from them to carry me over the winter—until the book was published in N.Y. (Even if an English publisher accepts it I couldn't get any kind of money out of him—the English publisher would have to submit to arrangements made by my American publisher and the book could be published in London only after it was published in N.Y.)

So I am in a quandary. I ought to get the m.s. in Rieder's hands. So much depends upon that! If Mr [Otto] Theis (I am writing to him) found a publisher, the best plan would be to send him a set of the proofs of Banana Bottom as soon as I received them from N.Y.

Yes, I shall have that article done in spite of everything. In searching through some papers to find items for it I found there two old Liberators, May, 1922, p. 24 with my article when I was insulted at the theater—June, 1922 p. 9—article by one of the Liberator staff when the dancing hall was closed because I had danced with Crystal Eastman + other white girls. Take these Liberators back. Also these songs (my only copy) may interest you—from my first book of dialect verses: Songs of Jamaica. Sending also Harlem Shadows. My American book of verse—And now I finish wondering how well [*sic*] manage about the m.s. for Rieder.

Sincerely Claude McKay

[Left margin:] I stick here because I suppose it's the only place where I can live on 1000 francs a month—+ as there are many mulattoes and Negroes, I don't feel so awfully strange and different as I do in Europe. Those are the two main things that hold one in North Africa. C.M.

NCC ALS

1. McKay means the Garland Fund.

To Nancy Cunard

[mid to late December 1932][1]

Tangier, Morocco

Dear Nancy

This letter from Mr [Otto] Theis gives me some worry. See, he has gone and given the m.s. to the representative of my American firm in London, the same man who published my other novels in London through the Harper branch. He certainly won't want to give up his right (if he really has any) on "Banana Bottom" since it is a much better book than the previous ones.

I had been hoping so much to get for "Banana Bottom" a good English publisher who had distributing connections with the dominions such as the Harper Branch in London has not. That was why when you went to London I was willing to let you try the manuscript on Hogarth and have Rieder wait a few weeks even though I was so very hard up and expecting some cash from Rieder if they had decided to translate right away.

When I saw the head of my American firm in Paris two years ago he told me that it was allright for me to scout for an English publisher and never mentioned any "first option" of his English representative. I am writing to him to get that point clear. If there is a "first option" I don't think there is any way for me to get around it as I am bound by my contract with the American firm, unless Mr [Jamie] Hamilton is willing to waive his right and let an established London publisher handle me. So now the whole matter of "Banana Bottom" in England rests there.

I have asked Mr Theis to send the manuscript back direct to me when he has finished and not to Pierre Vogein. I am very put out that P. V. did write to you at first without asking if he should. It complicated matters and caused needless worry and letter-writing. I gave [Georges] Friedman[n] (my Rieder go-between) your address telling him that you were communist or pro-Communist and he being just out of Russia you both might have found it interesting to talk to each other. I met him five years ago when he was pro-Communist also and was publishing a monthly review called "Esprit" with a group of the same persuasion. He had money then for his father had been a banker and had recently died and left him plenty. He never told me about the incident but I heard he gave a million francs to the group to run the magazine along Communist lines. Somehow they pushed him out of the organization and hogged the money away from him and wasted it on themselves. One of them I understood gambled away a hundred thousand at Monte Carlo. Since then Friedman[n] went to teach in a lycée (he is a graduate of the Ecole Normale Supérieure) and has become a Communist.

I had just sent off my letter about the "Banana Bottom" business when I received your nice one. The Moor I asked to take it to the post office said it cost five francs air mail and I was vexed and told him he might have had enough commonsense to send it by ordinary. For a week I haven't gone out, it has been raining continually for three weeks and I am bound by mud and water with my little house leaking all over and my condition still unsatisfactory.

But I have finished your stuff, doing most of it on my back. Tomorrow I start typing it. Maybe my brother is too worried by the banana business to write about it. He wrote me last year that it was very, very bad. I haven't written to him or any of my relatives since you were there. I was so busy with the book and right after your article. I have a pile of letters from relatives and friends months old to answer when I get through.

Shall be glad to see Mr [Tony] Butts if I am still here. Yes, I met Mary Butts[2] at Villefranche 1927 when I went there from Antibes with the Eastmans to visit Paul and Essie Robeson. She was staying I think with Glenway

Westcott and his friend and interested me stating[3] her grandfather was the patron of William Blake, one of my favorite English poets. I quote one of his poems in "Banana Bottom." Yes, you may keep "Harlem Shadows" a long while yet. It is out of print but I have another copy in a basket in Marseille; don[']t know that I'll ever recover it. The music of the songs is my own. I wrote nearly all my dialect poems to popular tunes and some made up by myself. My family was musical, <u>every member</u> reading music + playing some instrument, eight of us. But I never could read music nor learn to play anything, but I wrote verses. My English friend (Squire Gensir in "Banana Bottom[,]" dead now) thought those tunes you have particularly good, so I sent them to him + he wrote the music to them + had the accompaniment done in London. He collected Jamaican tunes + stories (peasant) + had a book published in London—Sincerely Claude

NCC TLS

1. Response to a 10 December 1932 letter from Cunard.

2. Mary Butts (1890–1937), English modernist writer. Anthony Butts (1901–1941), an aspiring but less successful writer, was her brother.

3. Beginning with this word, the remainder of the letter is handwritten.

To Nancy Cunard

16 December 1932

Tangier, Morocco

Dear Nancy Cunard

Pierre Vogein has forwarded your letters to me at the same time apologising for having 'meddled' and I am sorry indeed he did write to you <u>first</u> and then inform me of it <u>afterwards</u>. Vogein is a mutual friend of myself and [Georges] Friedman[n], the young novelist who first put me in touch with the firm of Rieder and to whom I wrote upon his return from Russia recently giving all the details about "Banana Bottom," which I did because he has interested himself in it and me and was dealing with Rieder about it up to the moment of his leaving for Russia last summer. I am now waiting to hear from him why he did ask Vogein to approach you instead of doing so himself.+

When I asked you to see Rieder it was not with the idea the [*sic*] you should 'influence' him from the standpoint of publishing. You had generously said in one of your early letters that if there were anything I wanted done that you could do I should ask you. And since I was in a difficult pecuniary situation I thought I'd ask you to take the m.s. to Rieder (the firm was already favorably disposed towards it through Friedman[n]'s efforts and my own letters) and get a definite offer from them, because personal contact and the spoken word in such cases are so much better than letters. That seemed to me a better plan than sending the manuscript direct by post.

I made this unusual proposal to you because I was in a very difficult situation, caught in a jam as thousands of others much more favored and shrewder than I have been in these times. I had spent nearly a year working on my book of short stories which, contrary to the expectations of my publisher and myself, brought me in not a penny.

I did explain to you that I had a contract with a N.Y. publisher and that any English firm publishing me would have to negotiate with him—but also that I had the right to scout for an English publisher. Thus if any English firm had accepted the book they would probably not publish from the manuscript but from the plates of the original in New York. That is often the procedure adopted between English and American publishers.

But it is all very complicated and I realize now that I was altogether over exigent, you being as busy with your book as I was buried from necessity in mine.

I received a letter from Mr [Otto] Theis just before I sent mine, so I added a postscript giving complete details but I have heard nothing yet from him about the m.s.. I regret the mix up. It was an annoying business your being pestered with letters from different sides and I hope such a thing will never happen again.

Yours Sincerely
Claude McKay

+ Nor did I tell Friedman[n] to ask you for the manuscript then because I had received your letter telling me that you had left it in London.

NCC TLS

To Nancy Cunard

12 January 1933

Tangier, Morocco

Dear Nancy

I could not get the article off until the tenth. I had finished it in pencil before Christmas and hoped to type it off by the end of December as promised, but an aggravation of spinal trouble hindered my sitting up for any length of time so I had to do it at little intervals. It's a little long, but the original was twice as much with some most important things left out even before I cut it by half.

You are free to cut it some more if you have no space (I have been wondering why you must have the French and English texts in one volume which might be a little incommodious to the eye of the reader when I think, perhaps wrongly, the kind of book you are publishing will not only be in immediate demand in America but also in France where a translation will be asked for) only I hope I shall be able to see a proof to give it a final overhauling.

And now that I am finished I want to know if you pay for articles and if so when? before or after publication? for living as precariously as I do I cannot afford to write for nothing, even for a special kind of anthology as yours. You didn't mention in your announcement whether the articles were to be paid for or not.

My literary stock is at its lowest now. Your Mr [Otto] Theis seems to be more worried about my American publisher's rights, which are in no way endangered, than in placing my manuscript. I asked him to send it back to me, but in a recent letter he said he would like to keep it a little longer as there were two publishers interested. When he wrote asking at first if he should send the m.s. to M. [Pierre] Vogein he thought it necessary to add that he thought my publisher owned the rights of my book in France. I answered that I was quite aware of that. And that I didn't want Mr. [Jamie] Hamilton[,] my publisher's English agent[,] to place the book abroad as he had suggested. On the other two books that were published in Italy and Spain, commissions had to be deducted for my own agent, Harper's agent in London (Mr Hamilton) and the the [*sic*] English firm that carried on the negotiations for the translations. C'etait un peu trop!

On this new book I want to get all that I can for my hard labor by a little elimination of the middle man.

Kindest Regards
Yours Sincerely
Claude

NCC TLS

To Nancy Cunard

25 January 1933

Tangier, Morocco

Dear Nancy

Frankly truthfully I wrote that article with payment in mind. I am sure you had no realization of my exact position and if I had thought there would be no remuneration, I would have been bound because of my illness and pecuniary troubles to postpone writing the article indefinitely and do instead the short story that my agent in N.Y. had asked for. You see I started writing for you right after my partial recovery from my sharp illness of last November and had no time in the interval to do anything else and you were so exigent.

All other anthologists have paid me for the inclusion of my work—even old stuff—and I had no idea nor intimation that your work was not being done on a remunerative basis.

For the past six years I have been existing by my writings solely and everything I have written has been done for pecuniary consideration. I could never afford to write for nothing—I have never had the itching vanity to appear in print just because it is a lovely thing and I have refused many little magazines and Negro newspapers, feeling that my creative work should not be exploited shamelessly as my common labor had been because of the necessity of daily living.

I am going to leave this matter to your good judgement. I told you once in a letter that I was "romantic" about artists and creative work but my romanticism is different from those nice people's [*sic*] who ask and expect artists to write, sing, act and perform in other ways freely and charitably for a Cause while they would not dream of asking the carpenter and caterer and others who do the manual tasks to work for nothing. I look upon the artistic work as more important but I do not say this thinking for a moment that you could have the slightest trait in common with such people.

I received a last payment of forty-six dollars from my publishers in November and that's all the means I have had to live upon until now.

Yours Sincerely
Claude

Thanks for the books. Will give my opinion later. Have not time yet to look at them.

C

NCC TLS

To Max Eastman

27 January 1933

Tangier, Morocco

Dear Max

Glad you have written and that you saw and approve of [John] Trounstine. He sent me a contract which I did not sign but made some changes and returned to him because I thought it was too stiff. You may be interested to see the duplicate with the changes I have made and so I enclose it. I am doubtful too about the last paragraph although I did not make any alterations, but I am afraid that it may mean that I may be charged for telegraph and cable expenses to other people "regarding my work" even though the result of the expenses was nil. I shall be much obliged if you can find time to send me your opinion.

I finished correcting and returned the proofs to Harper's before your letter came, but I shall put in that note and also I have still to compile a glossary.

Nancy Cunard seems to belong to the class of those unbalanced bitches always hot about something. When I told her you would be in Paris she made no great effort to get acquainted, but after reading your preface to my poems and that article by Charlie Wood about the breaking-up of the Liberator ball (I sent them to her) and realizing that there were a very few healthy-spirited Yankees who were free from race prejudice, she wanted very much to meet you—when you were back in America.[1] "Where was I when they came to Paris?," she says, "London, I suppose." I worked like hell on that article for her doing most of it ill on my back and after turning it in and asking her what she was going to pay, she replied that she was not paying for contributions. I answered her saying I could not write for nothing.

Well, the doctor said that my illness may have been the result of my getting wet. I was returning from Tetouan with Eliena and I suppose I was chilled a little riding so much without a wind shield. However the original sin they say (and scientifically too) is responsible for all sorts of complications. A few weeks after I got out of bed, he prescribed me a series of a new kind of bismuth. I took the first but must let the second wait until I can find some money somewhere. One disquieting symptom was a severe spinal pain right over the small across to the hip bones, which began with the first series and remains with me still. Otherwise I am not so bad.

If "Banana Bottom" makes any showing at all I want to go "home" for a trip this year. . . . Harper's have used "English" spelling throughout. I don't know why for I wrote American . . . I guess I'll need help for that homecoming as my being an alien and my Russian trip may be on record against me.

Thank you for writing to the editor of Europe. I shall send him the second set of proofs as soon as I get through with the glossary (I didn't get the duplicate m.s. back from London yet). I am jotting down notes for some Moorish pot-boilers for Trounstine and hope I'll get the first done in time to make two ends meet.

Is it true Louise Bryant died? If not give her my greetings should you see her and Eliena my love. Sorry she could not get my portrait. I have given up hopes of ever being done really by any painter. I should like to send a copy of the new book to Mrs [Betty] Hare if you will send me her address also Charlie Wood and Mike Robinson[2] and please if you have a servant round have her do up some N.Y.[3] magazines to send me. I couldn't renew any of my subscriptions and feel very badly being entirely cut off from American contemporary literature. Wish you lucky the New Year + love to you + Eliena[.] Ever Claude.

If you can find + spare time you might telephone Trounstine for a talk. Certainly I have no intention of paying him a commission on books that he doesn't handle esp. my present contract of novels with Harper's and I think I ought to reserve the right of personal negotiation.

C

MEP TLS

1. Charles W. Wood, "An Open Letter from Charles W. Wood to Hon. Richard Enright and Hon. John F. Hylan on the breakup of the *Liberator* Ball," *Liberator,* June 1922, 9–10.

2. A nickname for Boardman Robinson.

3. Beginning here, the remainder of the letter is handwritten in the margins.

To Nancy Cunard

[ca. February 1933][1]

Tangier, Morocco

My dear Nancy Cunard: This your latest letter irritates me to no end in manner and matter and I most emphatically refuse permission for my article to be mutilated and quoted from before published in its entirety. I am astounded that you, yourself an artist, should calmly announce that you're abbreviating and quoting from a writer's work before first consulting him about it. That doesn't come anywhere within the rules of the writing game and my commercial publishers have never yet attempted to take any liberties with my work without first obtaining my authorization.

If your letters are or were not <u>exigent</u> I will quote from them for your edification if you want me to.

But the point is this: Writing is my means of livelihood. I wrote the article Up To Date for payment. You are not paying for articles, you say. Well, the very obvious way out is to <u>leave my article altogether out of your anthology</u>. That seems to me the most satisfactory manner of settling the matter. I have not the slightest wish now to appear in your anthology and I hope you will respect that wish.

As to the other points of your letter: Since your anthology is not literary, I would be out of place in it for my writing is literary. Also if you want me to pack your letters up and send to you I will so that you may find yourself that precious word "voluntary." In your first letter suggesting a biographical piece you said 5,000 words (I showed it to Max Eastman and we thought it was about the length of a good Liberator article). I can't find that letter, but I am sending you a part of one you wrote a little later asking if the article could be done in 4,000 words. So much for your insistence on a capital NOT more than 3,000 words. And as to your very smart, This happens often!, when I say I have been paid by other anthologists, you have merely to write to the publishers of my poems, Harcourt, Brace & Co., New York, to verify the fact. I have appeared in perhaps a dozen anthologies in America. Your reference to an anthology in a foreign language is begging the question. I would say to any enquirer that I have been decently paid for my work by all my publishers, in spite of the fact that for two novels translated in Russian I and my publishers have not received a penny, because I would be having in mind my publishers in the original English.

The old "Masses," "The Liberator" and the "New Masses" in the beginning (I don't know what the policy is now) always paid their contributors. Of course, not nearly as much as the ordinary periodicals, but our group believed that radical aggressive and independent work should also be remunerated and I remember on the "Liberator" we often used the only money in hand to pay the poor writers and artists and asked our printer to wait!

I consider the matter of the article as now settled between us and that it will not appear in your anthology neither as a whole or in part. And while feeling obliged for the handsome-looking volumes you have sent me, I am willing (not caring to receive presents under false pretenses) to return them if you had sent the lot to me as to a "voluntary" contributor to your anthology.

Yours Very Sincerely
Claude

NCC TLS

1. Responding to Cunard's letter dated 28 January 1933.

To Max Eastman

[ca. early April 1933]

Tangier, Morocco

Dear Max

I am in a fix down in a hole and wondering if you can help pull me out. Just heard from [John] Trounstine that "Banana Bottom" is a flop. Published at the very worst time possible, but all the same there must be something lacking. Evidently my readers prefer my realism of rough slum life than of rural life. If so I can supply the need. The Jamaica book was [Eugene] Saxton's own suggestion and everybody who read it in m.s. and all the Harper staff liked it.

The news from Trounstine was like a knock-out blow, but I haven't taken the count though. I still have assets. Since January I have been remaking my novel of low-down past life, "Savage Loving,"[1] but I haven't changed the unhappy ending as Saxton desired because it is classic—not sad and sentimental but just in keeping with the spirit of the tale. I have had to rewrite whole pages because [William A.] Bradley lost the original and there are many missing.

The problem is this: Will Saxton permit another publisher to chance it as he did turn it down and I wrote "Banana Bottom" as a substitute? If so that may be a means of saving me, for another publisher might advance me $500 on it. If not it seems I am lost for I still have the Harper debt of $1000 on my back, both "Ginger Town" and "Banana Bottom" being failures. I rewrote it[,] "Savage Loving[,]" by hand, but I am now typing, for I took my machine out of pawn this week when I received f1000 from Rieder for the rights of "Banana Bottom." They like it too very much.

I am jammed and damned here and can't budge. Don't know where to [go] with British agents after me. It's no persecution mania—I'm not that type as you know, but I knew they were following me—probably my house was broken into and my original passport taken by them. Because I got the new one through an acting Consul. But the Consul who was away returned and found that out when I went to Centa with you and they were looking all over Tangier for me thinking I had departed with you. As soon as I returned they took back the passport and took off the British Empire saying they had orders against my visiting Empire territory. I don't doubt they were perhaps responsible for your arrest in Madrid. Those dogs never come out in the open you know, but set others on to you.

The only place I can think of now is America. I could make a living lecturing to Negro audiences. But I am an <u>alien</u> and I am sure they won't let me in with my Russian record without special intervention. I think I could easily get in on the six months visa, but I should have to be invited by some responsible person and have funds which I haven't.

Don't you know of anyone who could help me? Are they all dead or busted? I will mortgage my future—but mortgages are no good now and there's the nightmare of the Harper debt over me.

Do you think the Guggenheim Foundation would give me a scholarship? I wrote to Trounstine about it. We could say, to be specific: make a study of the Negro in Moroccan civilization. James Weldon Johnson who likes me and you too would be a good reference on the Negro side. And you could see about the white side. I suppose "Banana Bottom" is not so impalatable for nice foundation people, so that it couldn't be a recommendation.

I tried a reportage for "Voila" but they said it was too literary. I just can't get the knack of journalese. It takes a special mind. My best stuff won't do for journalism and when you take that out there's nothing left. Unless I had somebody to guide my hand. And then it's impossible to do articles when you're buried in a book.

I thought you had given me up as a hopeless case—Trounstine said you never mention me—but I received those magazines yesterday and was very happy that you remembered me. I fell on them at once. It was like being among a roomful of New York intellectuals and I didn't feel so terribly lonely anymore. For I am all alone since I recovered from my illness. Couldn't afford to keep anybody. I wish I was living in town instead. However when I am finished working I take long walks over those hills. And I have been swimming in the river since last month. For two weeks I had nothing but some potatoes I planted in my garden when I got well—and unsweetened tea. I didn't plant very much for I had no money to buy and they are all gone now. I don't think about my health at all—better <u>not</u> to in my state + so I am physically fit so to speak.

Have you read Trotsky's letter in M. Monthly and reference to you, wondering what is the full context.[2] If it means that you reject Marxism as an infallible religion but accept its logical tenets as a revolutionary weapon, I salute you! Trotsky is a wonderful historian but his history demonstrates to me quite clearly that Marxism is not an <u>exact</u> science as some Marxists seem to imagine. To me Proletarian Revolution isn't inevitable + will only triumph under the direction of great intellectual engineers. I wonder if Trotsky is aware that if Trotsky + Lenin had not arrived in Russia in 1917, that country might have been now where Germany is today. Otherwise he has an unconscious belief in God!

<u>Do write me</u>: Claude

MEP ALS

1. Along with *The Jungle and the Bottoms, Savage Loving* was another working title for the novel posthumously published as *Romance in Marseille* (2020).

2. Leon Trotsky, "A Note on Max Eastman," *The Militant,* 28 January 1933, 4.

To Max Eastman

21 April 1933

Tangier, Morocco

My dear Max

I cannot thank you enough for these three gorgeously bound volumes of the "Russian Revolution" that you have had sent to me. They dwarf everything else in my room and give it an air of importance.

You haven't answered the letter I wrote replying to yours from Chicago, but I suppose you had nothing encouraging to say and preferred not to write—or you were busy. Myself, I have not had much courage and pleasure to write to friends, having been so much down in the depths of distress and still there. All the same I am working and have begun the new book—by hand for for [*sic*] weeks my typewriter has been at the Mont de Piété. I am still keeping to the West Indian scene in the new book. I think it is better. Hope you got your copy of "Banana Bottom." Both [Eugene] Saxton and [John] Trounstine write that things are very bad in America with the book trade and more now on account of the acuteness of the financial crisis. But I am hoping all the same to make something—enough to give me a holiday of which I am badly in need.

It is hot here now. My flowers are gorgeous and I have already started bathing. Again thanks for the book and love to you and Eliena[.]

Claude

MEP ALS

To Arturo Alfonso Schomburg

7 May 1933

Tangier, Morocco

Dear Schomburg

Maybe you have thought that I have not responded to your letter because I have hard feelings against you. But that isn't the case. I have literally been buried under work ever since I came to Morocco, trying to write all I can to get from under the Depression without any real success.

It wasn't necessary to apologize for your bad criticism of my best prose work up to date. I don't mind criticism, hostile criticism. But I do object to the uncritical yawps of Negro writers who pass as critics. They ought to take a leaf from the white press—learn what criticism is—one doesn't call a man a hog and a vulture in criticism—although that may be implied by saying that the man's work leaves one with the feeling of a hog-pen or a vulture swooping down—it[']s all a matter of knowing how to write criticism and avoid calling one nasty names which is not criticism—a classic example was the reaction of the Indians to Mother India.[1] But the Indians know how to criticise. I am not saying that Negroes should not resent my writings if they feel resentment— It's just a matter of how they express such resentment—if they make pretentions [*sic*] of being critics—then they ought to follow the rules.

Yes: Nancy Cunard did mention you in her letters. She went to Jamaica and stayed with my brother. I am not contributing to her Anthology because she wanted me to write for nothing and under these terrible hard times I could not afford it. I think she's a somewhat hysterical and unstable female.

I should like to go to America if I could to look over the ground to do a full-length novel about the West Indian contribution to Aframerica. It ought to be done. But I am an alien and have no funds. I wonder if the Guggenheim folk would put up the money? Do you know anything about them?

I had a letter from Langston [Hughes] somewhere from Siberia months ago just like yours but I haven't yet answered. Too much work and no pay to speak of. Did you get a copy of "Banana Bottom." You were on the list I sent in a couple years ago, but my friend says that the publishers were cutting down on complimentary copies. They have even refused me six extra copies. I owe them money + books are not selling. This last hasn't sold any.+ I suppose people want all they can get to buy bread and books are so dear. Many use the circulating library[.] I have picked up a few words of your beautiful native language and so if ever we do meet I shall be able to ask como usted?

Do you know the whereabouts of James Weldon Johnson?[2] With my best to you[.][3] I've had no news of Aframerica—no newspapers—nothing for 3 years and know nothing of people and things.

My best wishes and no rancour
Sincerely Claude McKay

+ I am told most people are making use of the circulating libraries—

AASP ALS

1. Katherine Mayo, *Mother India* (1927).
2. This final paragraph appears in the margins, with no indentation.
3. This appears to be a closing, but McKay added an additional sentence.

To Langston Hughes

10 May 1933

Tangier, Morocco

My dear Langston

I wanted to write long ago but I was very hard at work trying to get from under the accursed Depression with no success. Your letter was written and reached me (exactly six weeks later) when I was very ill. I came down with a bad attack of head trouble with my whole body run down just after completing my novel "Banana Bottom," and I was down for two months. I have never quite recovered.

I envied your being away off there in Soviet Asia and wished I were there too. Saw in the newspaper that you were in Russia and that the film was postponed—they say for political reasons . . . [1] Well in America we have no Negro films . . . for social reasons.

I hope we are going to meet sometime somewhere. I am sure we have lots to talk about. I was hoping to go to America this year but don't see how I can. They tell me books are not selling at all and my book was published at the very worst time—during the banking panic. I have no hopes of a sale. The short stories did not sell at all. I hope you got a copy of "Banana Bottom." You were on the old list. But [Eugene] Saxton said they were cutting down on free copies for economy. And my credit isn't even good enough to get an extra six!

Your work in Russia sounds interesting and I hope you publish it in English as you say. Are you writing any poetry? Somebody sent me a pamphlet or magazine about Negro workers which had two poems of yours I liked. Maybe you don't get to write as much as you want to—the trouble with us all.

May! This is the month you say you're leaving Russia. I picked your letter out among the many to be answered + decided it shouldn't wait longer than this month after waiting so long. But I must address you through Knopf's for I don't know where you may be. I am working on a new novel—port life—

but not like "Banjo" or "Home To . . ." Don't know if you will like the tone—if it gets published.

My warmest thoughts
Sincerely Claude McKay

LHP ALS

1. Hughes was involved—along with Louise Thompson—in efforts to make a film in the USSR titled *Black and White,* and produced by Meshrabpom Film Company.

To Max Eastman

24 May 1933

Tangier, Morocco

Dear Max

Yesterday I sent off the manuscript of the new book to [John] Trounstine entirely rewritten. I worked in fury like a nigger—typing out all that I had written and connected by hand. It's real low-down stuff of mediterranean port life but I haven't named any special port. It's the story of a colored boy who stowed away after a colored girl had jilted him and was locked up in a w.c. on the ship and so frozen that his legs had to be chopped off. In N.Y. an ambulance chaser got on to the story and got him compensation of thousands of dollars. The story goes on to relate his return to the port and taking up again with the same old girl and what happened to them.

It is a short book—no padding—no picture painting—a straight story. I hope you get in touch with Trounstine for me, Max. I'm in a terrible way. I kept working with my head expanding and a fire in it as if it were going to blaze up—but I kept on afraid and yet determined to finish. And just before I had finished a colored woman came here sailing yesterday from Gibraltar on an Italian ship and I gave her the m.s. for Trounstine, so he should get it as soon as possible. Maybe it was a foolish thing I think now. But she seems to be a reliable person. I was in a groggy state like and she offered to take it. I even forgot to take her address in N.Y.

Hope you are trying to do something for me. Now that I have the book off I am thinking of writing short stories and poems—but I want some good news first. I can't do anything anyway for a week. I am groggy with work and anxiety. I hope you're trying to help me about that Guggenheim Fund. I tell you brother, it has been and still is some ordeal. I didn't think "Banana Bottom" would sell like "Home To Harlem" because of the crisis, but I never guessed it would be a total failure—after two years['] steady working. The woman who passed through said I ought to get a scholarship for I am the only Negro steadily working at creative work. "Ought to" is one thing but get it is the other. They are all so jealous. If I could only get something to hold on to some place to anchor. Wonder if there is no magazine would run the new book—It's awful rough stuff but genuine. Think there is any magazine to dare.

Hoping on you
Claude

MEP ALS

To Arturo Alfonso Schomburg

15 June 1933

Tangier, Morocco

Dear Schomburg

It was James Weldon Johnson who was trying to get me back and had asked the assistant Sec. of State Mr [Wilbur John] Carr to do something on my behalf. I did sign all the papers that the Consul at Marseille told me to and, as I was to return on the British quota, he promised to notify me when my turn came, but I never received any notification. When I returned to Morocco in 1931 I sent my new address to the Marseille Consul so that he could notify me. But as you know the Crisis was very severe (I mean the World Crisis) and President Hoover had notified the consulates to clamp down upon immigrants!

I never had any correspondence with Walter White upon the subject. I must say to you in private that we are not good friends. He does not like me—whatever he may say as a matter of form to mutual friends—white and colored. And I shouldn't expect a great deal from him, for I have no idea what is his particular attitude. However as Secretary of the N.A.A.C.P. he may be useful and indispensable in this matter.

You know I have another novel done, now in the hands of my agent in N.Y. It's a short story and I am trying to get some money on it if I can come to term[s] with Harper's for I owe them over a thousand dollars advance which has not been realized on the last book. If I am returning to N.Y. it should be just about the time that new book was published. To tell you the truth I look with horror upon the idea of returning indefinitely. I am very sure I won't like Harlem and I have a chronic head trouble which makes any large city an inferno for me to live in. But there is no choice. I may have to become an American citizen if I can. I wrote to Max Eastman also about returning. Naturally I am very left in political ideas but I have never been active in any politics since I left Russia. And don't think I want to again. My new book now being planned is about Americans abroad but the main characters are colored of the Smart Set—very different in scope and execution from "Banjo."[1] Wish you would tell me more of Nancy Cunard in N.Y. And that man [A. A.] Colebrooke.[2] Details if possible. Nancy wrote me she had to leave Colebrooke in Jamaica because of his father's illness but I was under the impression he was to join her in France. He said as much in a note to me sent in one of Nancy's letters. But now my brother has written that Colebrook[e] is still in Kingston trying to sell automobile polish and my brother has a very poor opinion of him. He had been front-paged and written up in Jamaica (photographed together with Nancy) as her Secretary and what not! And the big reception [Marcus] Garvey gave them!

Personally I think Miss Cunard a very unreliable person and lacking intellectual purpose and balance, mixing up as she does her love affairs with the Negro problem. I am not sorry I did not collaborate on the book and I doubt if she (as editor) can make a good thing of it.

Oh no! I had very much less than half of the sum you mentioned for "Home To Harlem." And I had received over a thousand dollars a year before publication. I did have a wonderful time with seraphs and cherubs when I visited Morocco for the first time in 1928. But when I returned in 1931 it was to work and that I have been doing ever since! Two books, some poems and a third planned. I myself received only six copies of "Banana Bottom" not enough and when I asked for more Harper refused! Said they were in too much of a hole on the book.

I know [Carl] Van Vechten but slightly. He was drunk one night at the Café de la Paix when I met him with Harold Jackman—I was ill with my head and not drinking—he left us for the lavatory and never returned! You may tell him about it. I remember it as a funny joke. But if he will let me I should use his name for the Guggenheim thing. Will you ask him?

Will take your advice and make the Negro a going proposition in my next. We were all very funny in Paris and abroad during the inflation years. Thanks for writing promptly + I reply as you ask.

Sincerely Claude-McKay

[Left margin:] Will ask about the Moorish writer + when I get more money take a trip to Tetuan to see! There m[ay] be many many Negroes in Arab art and literature (There was the great legist Ahmed Baba[3] a Sulten [*sic*] burgur [*sic*] from Timboutoo [*sic*]) but since there is no color + social distinction in Islam—the Arabs speak only of Moslem writers + interests. There is a black painter here—very good—a brown poet, etc etc—

AASP ALS

1. McKay never completed this project, and no material from it is known to survive.

2. A. A. Colebrooke was a black Bostonian who traveled with shipping heiress Nancy Cunard.

3. Ahmad Baba al-Timbukti (1556–1627), Sanhaja Berber writer.

To Max Eastman

20 June 1933

Tangier, Morocco

Dear Max

Just look at this letter from [John] Trounstine. I sent him "Savage Loving" by an American colored woman who came to see me here in Tanger the very day I finished it. Maybe I was wrong. But I did it to save time—6 days from here to N.Y. Italian boat "Rex." Damned yaller nigger woman knew I was broke and promised to deliver it right away—waited late into the night until I finished—with the result that Trounstine hasn't received the m.s. a week after her landing.

Anyway Trounstine located the woman and instead of finding out before writing to me whether the m.s. is safe he writes that he is going to get in touch with her. That makes me frantic in my present perilous state and you know how bad my head is. And I'll have to live through days + weeks of anxiety now until I am certain whether the m.s. is safe or lost.

What incompetence on Trounstine's part—a very neurotic and fussy sissy Jew and I think it would be better if we were rid of him. [William A.] Bradley, shrewd level-headed yankee[,] would never have pulled such a boner.

I am very very unhappy Max. To get to sleep tonight I have drunk half a litre of red wine which is bad for my head + I could have put the 1 franc to better use—still I can't sleep. Tell Eliena I thank her for praising the book, but I hate to look at my single copy ([Eugene] Saxton refused to send me extra ones because of my debt to the firm). I can't work up any enthusiasm over a book that cannot bring me in as much to buy a loaf of bread and soap to wash my black skin after one years' [*sic*] hard labor. Say: The application blank has this: "Have you any constitutional disorder or physical disability?" What shall I say?

Also: I notice that awards (Guggenheim Scho.) are also made for research work. If I say for a "Study of the Negro in Morocco" would it not be better then [*sic*] "a novel about the Negro in Morocco"? There are some very interesting things about [the] Negro in Morocco. I wrote a paper for Trounstine but he did not dispose of it. It was a brief treatment of the influence of the Sudanese in Morocco including the famous Black Guard of the Sultans and the legendary Black Sultan.

Claude

MEP ALS

To Max Eastman

21 June [1933]

Tangier, Morocco

Max: Wonder if you can find anyone to cable 10 dollars when you get this? Just to keep the blood circulating until there's definite news about the book.

Couldn't think of going to Paris now as you suggest. My French friend has no job, old [Charles] Rappaport lost his Russian correspondent job. All the expatriates were seeking cheaper havens than Paris before the fall of the dollar and now it is worse I hear. And they say the French are hard on them. Better if the chance comes to go direct to America from here if I can get enough to keep me alive until that time comes.

Am terribly upset by that hysterical [John] Trounstine's letter. No sleep or peace of mind. We should get rid of him for a cool-headed Yankee. Fancy writing like a castrated tomcat screaming and spitting all over the place.

Claude

MEP ALS

To Max Eastman

28 June 1933

Tangier, Morocco

Dear Max

[James] Weldon Johnson's letter sounds as if I were the Coolishest of the Coolish virgins. But in fact I did do everything that the consul of Marseille required of me. Then I had to wait for my turn and when I came here to Tanger I sent him my address, but I never heard again from him.

I have just heard from [John] Trounstine that he received the manuscript the very day he wrote me that alarming letter. He waited a week before writing, leaving me worrying in hell for two weeks because of my stupid action. He writes that he was discussing the title of the book with Countee Cullen who thought it sounded obscene. Can't understand why he should consider the opinion of that little prig important and also give out the titles of my book in Harlem before it has found a publisher. Next thing he will be showing them the manuscript up there. Think we made a mistake about him. Don't think he has one per cent of [William A.] Bradley's efficiency. Writes me the most pathetically discouraging letters that if I didn't still retain a little faith I'd jump into the river.

About starting story writing. I was planning another novel. To cover the field of my experiences of the period centering around the time we met when you returned from Russia. It is fermenting in me as "Home To Harlem" was five years ago. The leading characters will be the Aframericans abroad and our antics. I will send you the first chapter, which is a kind of short story as soon as completed. And you can tell me what you think. The only trouble about it is that I don't know how much I can let myself go about that class of Negroes. They are all so touchy. And if I go back "home" I'll have to live among them. I don't want to do anything more than assemble the facts and get down to the truth, but that is just what those people cannot stand. I don't mean to libel them for I like them as a group, but all they like to see is pretty painting.

Fact is I am afraid of the idea of returning for good. For now I can't live like in the days before the "Liberator." I'll have to find myself among the "Niggerati" as I hear they call themselves in Harlem. And I think it will be more losing that finding. However I think it would do me good to get back for a time and the right moment should be just when the new book is coming out. By then I ought to have the manuscript of the next completed.

I wish I was neurotic and didn't know what was wrong with me. But the trouble is I do know. I ought to be closely attached to somebody, woman or even man, instead of being off at loose ends living lone-wolfishly. But I never can feel a sentimental attachment for the persons that attract me intellectually. And the types that stir up passion in me are are [*sic*] no good for intimate attachment . . . I can't get my mind and my emotions in harmony together and concentrated upon someone. That's my whole tragedy. I need somebody to look after me. But generally I appear so strong to people as if I don't need looking after. Last time I was in Paris Fanny Rappaport told me that I looked in every way as if I were sufficient unto myself. So there I am. And whenever I try to get away from myself I choose the wrong person as I did with that girl that was here with me.

Don't be fed up with all this. That fool Trounstine has just sent me a letter in which he spoke about my "writing like my old self again." Made me feel as if I were a has-been. But[1] will leave you to judge when I send the chapter mentioned. Love to you + Eliena[.]

Sincerely Claude

[Left margin:] Thanks for the five bucks I got 18 francs [to] the dollar. The changers don't even want to take the dollar bills anymore. A little before I received a draft of $25 from the American Express. Don't know who sent it. CMcK

MEP TLS

1. Beginning with this word, the remainder of the letter is handwritten.

To Max Eastman

5 July 1933

Tangier, Morocco

Dear Max: Another appeal and please don't get weary! Just had another note from [John] Trounstine and it occurs to me that you yourself might have more influence and chance in disposing of the new novel before he has exhausted all the publishers and made acceptance extremely difficult.

From Trounstine's letters I don't think he has any real influence among publishers such as [William A.] Bradley had, but is rather the type of person who is quick to get on to something that is already safely doing well and ride on its momentum. So far he has tried only the publishers I suggested to him and I've been too long away from America to know what publisher would be most favorable. The other point is that according to his letters he has been talking to publishers about the book over the telephone. And it seems to me that the chances of the book being accepted depends on personal presence and diplomacy. He would have to be very tactful to explain and convince the new publisher why we were leaving Harper and I don't know how well Trounstine can do this.

I know you are busy with your own troubles but please try what you can do. I think I can do something substantially fine yet if I only get another chance and everything don't [*sic*] go smash. I'm in an awful vexing fret. My lease of the house runs out next month and I don't know what the next step should be. I was thinking after your last letter that I could stay here a few more months to finish the new book and bring it to New York, but I was counting upon the acceptance of "Savage Loving" and an advance to go through, and hoping to get back just at the time of publication and grab a few lectures among our nice Negroes.

But the terrible uncertainty weighs me down and retards the writing of the story. And I want so much to get that first chapter done and send it to you, so you can tell me whether it's aiming straight for the bull's eye. But I need something—a little lifting of the spirit to harden and encourage me to bring my writing up to standard and in tune to the mood of five years ago.

Sincerely
Claude

MEP TLS

To Henri Cartier-Bresson

6 July 1933

Tangier, Morocco

Dear Bresson

My pen wouldn't work and I took it to the Jewish agent here for reparation and he broke the point in half and insisted I brought it to him that way and so I must type.

First I must apologise to you and Miss Mitchell[1] for my own fault and for getting in a panic about it. And please understand I don't mean to be ironical in any way. Would you believe that on the very day my agent wrote to me in that frightening tone about the manuscript, he received it from the hands of Miss Mitchell and yet kept me worried without adequate sleep for nearly two weeks before another letter reached me to say that the manuscript was safe? And since he had located Miss Mitchell before writing all he had to do was to telephone or see her first and then write afterwards. So much trouble and bad feeling over two unnecessary blunders. Again I must apologise . . .

Now if I had been a good Frenchman like you with a heritage of the finest tradition in the world (to my mind) of understanding and meeting women on their own level I should have been less harsh in my strictures upon Miss Mitchell, but my background has been different and my personal experience so bitterly unfortunate that I will readily admit that I am unusually prejudiced. . . . So let us forget all that.

Thanks about the article, but I don't think I shall write to [Florent] Fels. It's a long time since I saw the Barrio and a good reportage means writing with a fresh photographic eye. I would have to see your pictures to know what to write about and I cannot get to Barcelona now of which I am very sorry.

And I am busy planning a new novel with Paris as background during the inflation years but it will not be atmospheric. The characters will be mainly Aframericans on holiday and Paris is the scene because it was there we all went to spend our holiday.

I got my Rimbaud back and the author is Jean Marie Carre.[2] Hope you are enjoying beautiful Barcelona. I have a friend there named Jose Roger who works in the Banco Uriugo Catalan (not sure that's the way it's spelt) speaks French and English. Many in the Barrio, but don't have their names.

Did you ever read [Francis] Carco's Printemps en Espagne? Very bad. I like better [Henry de] Montherlant, although his outlook is sentimental and the Spanish are not a sentimental people.[3] I like Montherlant and think he has a close affinity with D. H. Lawrence.

I feel bad thinking about Barcelona for it makes me sad being away from it for such a long time. Hope you'll enjoy celebrating the Quatorze there!

My very best to you
Sincerely
Claude McKay

HCBA TLS

1. Willa Olivia Mitchell (1902–1979), African American stenographer and friend of Langston Hughes; she was regularly mentioned in the Harlem society columns. Mitchell made several trips abroad in the 1930s, studying interior design in France. Her name appears on the list of passengers returning to the United States from Gibraltar on 1 June 1933 on the Italian ship the *Rex.*

2. Jean-Marie Carré, *La vie aventureuse de Jean Arthur Rimbaud* (1926), translated as *A Season in Hell: The Life of Rimbaud* (1931).

3. Henry de Montherlant's *Les bestaires* (1926) takes place in Spain.

To Max Eastman

23 July 1933

Tangier, Morocco

Dear Max: I've been hoping for a letter from you since I received the Guaranty Trust's cheque for 144.50, but you've evidently not been able to get round to writing with all the other things you've been doing for me and so flung the life-belt over the water instead. I am very, very relieved and thankful to you and only wish I could be happy, but I feel myself in such a frightening precarious position and although I believe I could get out of it if I took the right step, I am not sure which step would be the right one. Then, I'm wondering if I'm not bothering you too much now I'm down in the hole, for the fact is that getting down again has shaken my confidence, not in my mental equipment, but in trying to live practically.

I've finished that story—I mean the prelude to the nineteen t[w]enties experience novel. I will send it to you in a few days as soon as it is all typed out, for I won't be able to carry on with a sure hand until I hear from you or some other good critic that I am on the right track.

Am enclosing a copy of a letter from the Guggenheim foundation. I want to do the thing that will give me the best possible chance, but I think everything depends on the right references. I have [Louis] Untermeyer, [James] Weldon Johnson, and You. I think two more would be good, another critic and a novelist such as Joel Spingarn and Sinclair Lewis or [Carl] Van Vechten, but perhaps I should sound out these last and I don't know their addresses, not even their publishers.

[Arturo Alfonso] Schomburg of the Negro Division of the 135th Street Library thinks that America has lost interest in books about Negroes and advises that I should write about whites or do an historical adventure novel, but

I think I have a better chance writing about things I've had experience of and am interested in. Anyway it's about time I send in the Gugg. application, but I'd like to hear from you first. I was very much tempted to take a chance of Paris when I got this money, but I thought it might be better to stay a few months more and do most of the new book, going to France when it is finished for a few factual points.

So much obliged for the magazines. I wish I was back in America, but I hope I will [go] this year. Contemporary literature (periodical) is lively and interesting again for the first time since the war and early peace years and fine to look at after the blatant smug years of the "American Mercury." You are terribly hard on Hemingway.[1] I didn't read his latest, but evidently, like most American writers and celebrities, he has to live up to one record. I heard a story here that at a party in Paris he was knocked down by a fairy. Don't know how much truth in it. Anyway the bull may be a stupid animal, but he is also a madly vicious one. When I was a boy in the backwoods I saw one gore a poor helpless woman to death and injure two men and a donkey. Did you in Spain see the bulls in the corrals the evening before the fight when they were brought in from the wilds. There are cows in the corrals to tame and keep them quiet. Twice I was taken to see them and each time I saw a great bull who just kept jabbing his horn into the behind of a fine cow until he killed her. Then he jabbed another and another until tired of just jabbing he made friends at last with one. The Spanish sporting audience is the most wonderful I've ever seen and I've also seen it at football and boxing. It wants its money's worth and the best antagonist to win. I saw the Catalans go wild in Barcelona over a Senagalese [*sic*] Negro walloping a Spaniard nearly twice his size and who had built up an artificial reputation knocking down sticks. With the bull and the man the audience is fifty-fifty. It knows that the bull cannot get away from being killed for that is the classical point of the show, but it wants a good savage bull that can put up a stiff fight against a trained matador. I've seen audiences rage and throw chairs and sticks i[n]to the arena at a poor matador who murdered a bull badly—and also give an ovation to the matador who is a neat killer. I saw the only Catalan who is a good bull-fighter kill six bulls skil[l]fully one afternoon and the very last bull gored him just after he had given the fatal thrust. You should have seen that audience divided between admiration for the matador and the bull.

I think the animal is despatched [*sic*] much finer than I have seen native butchers at home and here do their killing. What touches me is the injury done to the horses who are led into the ring blindfolded. And the picadors are nearly all so fat and bad. But the show in itself has for me the picturesqueness of the Russian ballet. I always think of it that way especially the lesser "novillados" that are given at night, when there are no horses used. But to the real Spanish "aficionado" the "corrida" without horses is like an orchestra without 'cellos. For after all the whole thing is like an operatic piece limited to a certain time with every part complementing the whole, the poor bull being the living body upon which the thing is built. Terribly hard as you are on Hemingway I think your diagnosis of him perfect, but I think too that if he allowed himself to be doctored, he would be ruined as a writer precisely because he is all a very special kind of emotion and no intellect. Perfect what you say about the matadors too, but they are mere actors and like nearly all members of that class, skillful but not intellectual. But one is content to admire them for their skill and they are the only butchers I have ever been able to admire for their combined skill and elegance . . . In Catalunia where the Spaniards are more highly civilized than elsewhere it seems to me, the "corrida de toros" is not so popular and there was only one good Catalan matador, Juan the Catalan, among all the bull-fighters when I was there. Nearly all the good matadors are Andalusians. In Madrid student friends told me that [Sidney] Franklin was not such a good matador, but popular among the women especially because he had "cojones"—that is he was regarded as a kind of Don Juan. The remarkable thing about the Spaniards is their freedom from blood-thirstyness as compared to other European peoples. When [Miguel] Primo [de] Rivera gave up the dictatorship he said: "Mi manos son limpia." He had not caused anybody to be executed and it is said the popular feeling turned definitely against King Alfonso after he executed the two officers of the democratic uprising. Perhaps Hemingway had to feel as he wrote to write a great book about bull-fighting, but if itas [*sic*] you describe it he will only get a laugh from the Spanish critics when it is translated in Spanish, just as the audiences in Madrid and Barcelona laughed at the film of "The Bridge of San Luis Rey," which was even less romantic sentimental than the book and other romantic American versions of Spanish life.

With my best, such as it is, to you and Eliena[.]

Sincerely

Claude

MEP TLS

1. Eastman's distaste for Hemingway resulted, four years later, in a notorious fight in the office of Max Perkins at Scribner's.

To James Weldon Johnson

23 July 1933

Tangier, Morocco

Dear J. W. Johnson

Many thanks for your letter to Max Eastman about me. About your intervention on my behalf to go home about five years ago, the fact is that I did go to see the Consul at Marseille, twice or more times. I filled out the forms that he gave me under the British quota and when I came here to Tanger I sent in my new address but I never heard from him again, whether my number came or not. The consul told me I would be notified and I have never had any notification. I don't know what happened except that the neglect might be attributed to the crisis and the fact that new immigrants were being officially discouraged from entering the States. My own plan was to come in under the six months provision, if my latest book had had any success but unfortunately it didn't.

Since I haven't the means to come in as a tourist, I think I might be invited by some organization. I could do some kind of lecturing for awhile and I have also started another book, which I may get done or not, all depending on when I am able to go.

I have always felt I should return, at least to take notes for one other book about New York, but the fact is that my plans, both literary and financial[,] went wrong in 1930 and I was waiting for a better turn which never came. For over a year I had been working under the extremest difficulties and when the last book proved a financial failure putting me in debt I thought the only hope and possible way out was getting back to America and find[ing] something to do while I was writing another. Again thank you with kind regards[.]

Sincerely
Claude McKay

JWJP TLS

To Max Eastman

19 August [1933]

Tangier, Morocco

Dear Max

I am sending you the script of the prelude to the work I mentioned to you. I could develop a lot more using the three principles: Lady Mandylee, Prince Gamin and Lake.[1] All depends on whether I have the right stuff. I shall be anxiously waiting your opinion.

I was thinking of a trip to Paris to go over the ground, but I haven[']t the money and on thinking it over, the trip might spoil the mood—if it is a good one.

Have copied two of the poems for you. The others are not ship-shape. I guess I could do poetry still if I were not bound by prose to make a living.

Terribly hot and most difficult to work. I try to work naked but the flies from the factory! [John] Trounstine sent me a copy of his note to you. Am moving into town next week + giving up the lovely place. Love to Eliena[.]

Sincerely
Claude

MEP ALS

1. Characters in an abandoned novel project.

To Henri Cartier-Bresson

24 August 1933

Tangier, Morocco

Mon Cher Bresson

Milles Mercis pour le Rimbaud. I like it for the new facts and the writer's enthusiasm, which, however is not convincing. I have always loved and marvelled about Rimbaud. When I was a lad in Jamaica I read an article about him in T. P's Weekly (the same number I think in which I had won a prize for a poem: it's a London magazine. I was about twenty.) with a translation of "Bateau Ivre" and a photograph of Rimbaud as a youth. It was such an interesting photograph of the purely child-vagabond type and made such an impression upon me that I cut it out with the poem[,] carried it with me to America and had it for years. It was years later that I read a few more translations of his better known poems and a brief account of his relationship with Verlaine, which said of course that he was the evil genius of Verlaine. Then I read Verlaine and liked him too for the lyrical simplicity (what I must call a kind of Anglo-Saxon and Germanic quality) of his poetry.

Rimbaud for me remains a most marvellous personality and a flaming poet. And a realist if ever a poet was one. Nothing of the mystic about him for me. He was poor and hated his bourgeois environment and wanted to write great poetry and live like a poet. But experience soon made him aware that poets must have material means to live. Those he knew were satisfied to versify in the contentment of a little bourgeois comfort. He hadn't even a little, since his people did not understand him. It was a question of poetry or money or Death. And he turned away from poetry and poets and went in search of the means of living.

Only a poet without money and "pull," a sensitive mind who has to give up his talent and turn to purely material things to work for a living, knowing by experience how destructive such a life is to the spiritual wells of poetry can understand the full tragedy of Rimbaud. And Rimbaud's genius was such a delicate flame, albeit so wonderful. There wasn't in him the stuff of Reconciliation and Compromise as there was in Verlaine. He was pure poetry and couldn't find the way of Compromise between pure poetry and prosaic means of making a living perhaps to write then less than pure poetry. And so he just flamed forth wonderfully and finished. . . . I like to think that he might have returned to poetry again after making money and returning home. And I always like to speculate what his poetry after the many barren years might have been! Vain speculation.

Any way to me Rimbaud is far from being a Voyant in the general sense of the word. He has plenty of Magic like every great poet, but that's a different thing. In brief to me Rimbaud is in poetry a supreme Magician and in life a supreme Realist. Poets must always admire him for he is so pure and strong and the great majority of us are weak.

I just bought a copy of VOILA seeing some pretty black girls on the cover Aug. 19. And I was surprised to find an article on the Barrio Chino of Barcelona by Jacques Roberti. I know him by letters, we have been corresponding for over two years, but never met. He sent me his book A la Belle de Nuit which I liked. He [text smudged] I think. Don't like his article. Good when he reports, but awful when he comments. Didn't think he was so sentimental, bourgeois sentiment too! All the old bourgeois tricks and cliches and hypocrisy about prostitution and perversion. And of all languages French seems to me the most impossible for excessive sentimentality. . . . What I like about Barcelona, the Parello [*sic*] and even the Barrio is a spontaneous, joie de vivre au dessus[,] the sordidness so different from Marseille where all is sordidness. More anon. Je crois que c'est a vous cette photo signé[.] CM!

Claude McKay

[Left margin:] If you have would thank you for sending me the other two preceding issues of <u>Voila</u> with Roberti's articles—can't get them here. CMcK

HCBA TLS

To Max Eastman

7 September 1933

Tangier, Morocco

Dear Max

I have moved into town and used up nearly all of my "capital" doing so and getting fixed in a new place, which may best be described as a cage.

However, I feel better for the change. There is plenty of movement and noise around me and the oppressive feeling of loneliness which descended upon me during the past few months has somewhat lifted.

Thank you for making a new typed script of the m.s. but I feel rather discouraged about it. I think if there was a chance for it I would have heard from you before now. I wish I didn't feel dependent upon it as the means of enabling me to go on working. If I could get even a $250 advance I could make it carry me up to March when I might get the fellowship or finish the new book. I want to do a good thing, a comeback, to surprise everybody and madden some and consolidate my position so that I may never be pushed back again but the atmosphere of anxiety in which I work is almost paralysing. I really thought Knopf was going to take the m.s. [John] Trounstine said they were thinking of me favorably as an author for their list and it was a real disappointment when he wrote that they had rejected the story.

I can count on your old colleague [Joel] Spingarn as a reference. I had a nice note in which he wished me good luck (wished he had slipped a bank note with it) and added ". . . but I must tell you that the professors who constitute the committee on selection have paid little attention to some of my recommendations in recent years . . ." Made me smile. Same old grouch.

Had another funny note from another person referring to you. Can't tell you what now . . . until some day when we meet again.

I suppose you are back in Croton by now or going. And brown as a deer. I have that photograph of you and Eliena on my little table and all the Arabs think it is obscene and ask if that is civilized. They are a strange people the Moors. The most sensual and sex-crazy people I know with very reactionary and fixed ideas of outward form. I feel so sorry for the women wrapped up in yards and yards of cotton and flannel. Last summer a few girls of the street went to the beach with bathing suits and bathed and they were arrested and imprisoned by the Moslem authorities. However a couple of them came down to my place this Spring with an acquaintance and we all went bathing in the river. I have been bathing since May going across the river to the sea as the water was polluted by the drainage from the fish factory. Guess it was the stench that made me sick at the stomach all the time. Apart from that I have been fine all spring and summer, but for the last two weeks I[']ve been having some terribly penetrating jabs of sciatica.

I wrote to Jo Bennett right away but she hasn't replied[.] I told her I was broke and disappointed and wanted a change of scene. I have enough francs to last me just until the end of this month. Then I am hoping that some miracle will happen before and save me for "art's" sake! I sent you a short m.s. unregistered for it was too late to do it. Hope you got it all right. Love to you and Eliena.

Claude

Thanks for the Lenin [?] + Charlotte notes but I don't know <u>who is Charlotte</u>?[1]

MEP TLS

1. The postscript is handwritten. Charlotte Kuh (1892–1985), member of the Greenbaum banking family in Chicago, teacher, activist in support of children's welfare, and author of children's books, sent money to Eastman to support McKay's return to the United States.

To Max Eastman

21 September 1933

Tangier, Morocco

Dear Max

I have done seventy[-]five pages of the new work and I am somehow at a standstill with fear and trembling not having had any opinion at all of it. Don't know if you can imagine my state.

In fear and trembling too over my financial state and my isolation. Not a single letter from any source for over a month. I keep at work, working all the time that I may not crack to pieces. I've been having a strange experience. For the last month after making my breakfast I couldn't work. I felt sluggish and went to sleep mechanically over the machine. One whole week like that—but in the evening I could work only the light hurt my eyes. So I gave up breakfast—drank only a glass of water on getting up and went straight to work until midday. With the change my head worked excellently, but there is a certain feebleness of body. I don't know if it is the heat or anemia.

[Arturo Alfonso] Schomburg sent me a note from Walter White last month. Said Asst. Secy. of State [Wilbur John] Carr told him I could come "home" <u>if I had the necessary funds</u>. I wrote back that I hadn't and the best way would be for some organization to invite me over to lecture.

I wish you would send me some more old magazines. Have had nothing since May and don't know what's going on in the world. French papers all political opinion and propaganda—no news.

Tell me is business picking up over there with the dollar off gold. And is the Roosevelt plan going successfully? The papers say that [Henry] Ford and other big industrialists and financiers are in opposition. Difficult to know what is really happening—the French are so mad at America, the papers won't tell the truth. A funny situation—Like Russia after the Revolution . . . I suppose my m.s. is dead and we must bury it—I am prepared for the worst and won't shed any tears now.

Sincerely
Claude

Have sent in the Guggenheim application.[1]

MEP ALS

1. This postscript is written around the closing.

To Max Eastman

5 October 1933

Tangier, Morocco

Dear Max

Maybe you're having a hard hell of a time yourself but I hope not as much for you as also for myself! But I wish I could hear from you. [John] Trounstine wrote (Sept 13) that you had just taken the m.s. to Simon and Schuster.

I haven't a sou and since I moved into town I have been selling my few sticks of furniture in the native market. The new house was too small to take my European furniture excepting one chair for writing and so it was a help in a way leaving me something to sell. It is twice as dear as the old, because it's in the town. I have just heard from Jo Bennett writing from Hartford returned in June. A nice letter but she didn't send me anything although I told her I was "disappointed, ill and broke."

Nobody has sent me a penny but <u>you</u>! [James Weldon] Johnson never replied—[Arturo Alfonso] Schomburg writes and suggests all kinds of schemes but not a cent—and others! I wonder Johnson didn't try to raise some money the way he told you. But he couldn't I suppose among Negroes, <u>they love me so much</u>.

Did you get the new m.s.? I don't know where I shall be when you receive this—if I don't hear from you before. It is hell to work under present conditions, but it is still the only safeguard.

You know if I get the Gug. award I should like to come home and take a short trip to Jamaica.[1] I supposed that will be alright. I want to see it again and get the romantic memories out of my system. Maybe you and Eliena could go too for a midwinter trip. But I don't want to mention it much so as not to have any trouble with the British before I get in. I want to do it quietly. (Of course, even if they tried to stop me I could get in it being my birth place—but I prefer not to have the trouble.)

If I can keep working I should have the new book finished about January and bring it along. I am trying to make a good thing—not heavy + problematic, but sharp, vibrant etching. I have a few white characters but <u>all</u> subsidiary to give wings to the colored ones. There is no real plot—just the doings of a group of colored persons on a vacation abroad.

The cold wave has come and gone for the present (for it[']s warm again) and I haven't a piece of winter underwear—no winter clothing—all worn to rags—Everything wrong with me at this awful time—Do please write[.] I feel so lost—Love for you + Eliena[.]

Claude

MEP ALS

1. This is a paragraph break, but not indented, on a new page.

To Max Eastman

20 October [1933]

Tangier, Morocco

Dear Max

I am writing instead of cabling for the money hasn't come yet and the Consul (I went to him the morning after receiving your letter on the 19th) must write to Marseille for information and the correspondence between Asst. Secy. of State [Wilbur John] Carr and the Consul there. That'll take from ten to fifteen days[,] about the same time that this letter will to reach you.

The #80 you're sending will just about take me from Cadiz to New York third class—maybe I could get a cheap tramp boat from Barcelona—I'll find out what it will cost to get to Barcelona by train and if it would be worth while paying it. I won't have to spend much before leaving here—beside paying for my typewriter. Seven francs a day can do for the time being—before I used to keep in the margin of 10—and I'll recover what I spend by selling the few remaining things before leaving. So all I'll need is #10 for visa+[,] 60 to show on landing at N.Y. + #10 for incidentals between here and Cadiz—about 70 dollars more.

I wanted to get back to America this year and had written "Banana Bottom" with that expectation. Sorry I didn't make the move right away when you sent that #140. I also want to get back to Jamaica for a visit by hook or crook. I felt convinced that I should return after the publication of "Gingertown" last year. As soon as I got your letter I stopped writing the new story. I had done exactly 114 pages. I will send you under separate cover two or three of the ensuing chapters which are a little better than the first. It was difficult to start anything in the state that I was in. I couldn't think of a short story there that would go over with the New Republique [*sic*]—because my kind of writing when it is good really belongs to the popular magazines—what I lack is the genteel sophisticated touch . . . But I thought it was absolutely necessary to get something done during that oppressive heat to show you that I was working.

But it was too much! To keep on writing like that one book after another! No creative writer can do it and the moment I stopped I felt better as if a great weight was lifted from me. And I feel better all over with the idea of a voyage and going "home." Oh God, I haven't been out of this little international wasps' nest since you took me to Centa and it was beginning to get worse than a Black Belt.

Of course—Don't know I'll get visa! [Donald Fairchild] Bigelow who was so charming has left for Geneva and the new man is a typical American—a shrewd type like our [William A.] Bradley. Knows of you + Jack Reed. Although I didn't show him your letter. But he seemed to know about me beforehand. I told him the Liberator crowd was radical but nobody went actually communist but Jack! And he said he could understand that none of us was so crazy even though radical, as to want in America the kind of regime that exists in Russia! I said I was convinced that whatever changes do come in America there will be little if any resemblance to the Russian social form—even if we called it Soviet. I showed him [James Weldon] Johnson's letter received the same time as yours and urging me to come + that they'll try and get me a lecture tour. Oh I forgot—he was Consul at Odessa during the Bolshevik revolution—Told me about a Negro who had the most fashionable restaurant in Moscow + was a millionaire and that the Bol. kicked him out. Funny I never heard of him. Ask Eliena. Wonder if it was he that went to Constantinople! Heard of a Negro there with one of the smartest + most sinister establishments—after the war—+ Russian princesses as waitresses.

Well—I feel that I have stretched our friendship to the limit and worried you so that you may have been even unhappy about me. That is just how I feel and I don't like to think I've made you unhappy. It was a terrible jog after writing to so many people to find that among them all you were the only practical friend[1] in time of need. I have three or four sketches about Moroccan life that I may be able to sell when I get over there—with a little publicity—simple individual sketches of certain types. And say can I come up to Croton for the time being when I arrive? Am waiting for the money so that I can mail this letter. If it had come with your letter I would have made 100 F more[,] for the dollar went up 2 points after Hitler scared Geneva. Can't understand delay. Your letter was mailed the 5th + I received one mailed the 8th a day before.

Funny a man's life seems to work out going round in cycles.[2] The situation now is exactly as in 1926 when you invited me down to Antibes. The same kind of feeling. Only I don't feel so depressed now. When you receive this you might cable the amount you can for I'm giving notice to leave the house [at] the end of the month. Have you any address in N.Y. City? Will try if I can get a chance to work across, but am afraid there are too many experienced men on the beach for any success.

I don't know if the <u>money to show</u> at N.Y. would not be better sent in dollars registered + sealed[.]

\+ Don't know if there has been any change. Will ask.

MEP ALU

1. Beginning here, the remainder of the letter is written in the margins.
2. Marginal writing continues here on a different page. The paragraph break is speculative.

To James Weldon Johnson

30 October 1933

Tangier, Morocco

Dear J. W. J.

I was so glad to get your good letter. I went straight to the consulate with it the following morning, taking the quota slip that the Consul at Marseille had given me in 1929 or '30.—(The first time I went to the Consul at Marseille with the duplicate of Mr [Wilbur John] Carr's letter that you had sent me he was extremely nice. I had to go through certain formalities—one of which was getting from the Immigration office the date of my first entering the U.S. The immigration official replied that they had sent the necessary documents directly to the Consul at Marseille. But when I went to see him again, he was not as nice as before, telling me shortly that he would notify me when my turn came. I told him I was going to travel and he took the duplicate of Mr Carr's letter (I'm not sure if it was the first or second time) and told me that wherever I was I should ask the American consul to communicate with the Consulate at Marseille if I wanted to go to America.)—

The Consul here (a Mr [Hooker Austin] Doolittle) was very nice. He had been in Russia before and after the revolution. I told him I had been there too and even here in Morocco I was being shadowed by British + French agents because of it. He wrote to Marseille about me. That was ten days ago. And when I called upon him today to find out the result, he showed me a copy of a letter from the American Immigration office dated—1923 saying that they had had information that the Negro Communist Claude McKay had left Russia for Copenhagen with a large sum of money for propaganda in America. This explains why the Consul at Marseille was so changed when I went to him a second time! Because during the interval he had received the secret information against me.

The Consul here is a clean cut typical American—individualist + therefore very anti-bolshevik, but extremely fair, well-informed many-sided—<u>frank and plain</u>. He knows all about the Negro movement and is willing to help me. He had a letter from Max Eastman to Mr [Donald Fairchild] Bigelow the former consul here, who recently left for Geneva—a nice letter praising me—but he remarked: Max Eastman is no recommendation to help you get back to America—and he laughed.

The only trouble I must wait here many weeks more for I must get "two copies of birth certificate" from Jamaica. Absolutely necessary. I had been hoping to get back for thanksgiving—I had enough money from Eastman to pay the fare. I shall be very happy to return but I am existing in fear and trembling + even if I do get the visa, I won't feel safe until I get by the immigration authorities at New York.

Mr Doolittle told me about a Negro who had the first restaurant in Moscow before the Revolution—Afterwards he went to Constantinople, but didn't seem to do so well there. Said I ought to get his story and do a novel of him! Strangely I never heard a word about him while I was in Moscow.

I sent in your name as a reference to the Guggenheim Foundation + hope it's alright.[1] <u>I would like very much to get back before the awards were made</u>. I may stand a better chance then, since I am not a citizen. I have been having a horrible time since last year. I know my bad luck is mostly my fault—<u>There is a tide</u> . . . and I don't always make the best of a <u>practical</u> opportunity—but I blame no person or system but myself—

Warmest thanks again for your good letter—Claude

JWJP ALS

1. This paragraph begins in the margins, with no indentation.

To Max Eastman

30 October 1933

Tangier, Morocco

Dear Max

It's terrible to ask more after all you've done, but you'll have to try and make the amount a little more than I said if I'm to get across—about $150. For I wanted to sail about Nov. 15, but I can't now. I've got to have "two copies of birth certificate" from Jamaica and I've just written them today. They'll take about 2 months to get here.

I went to the Consul today (a Mr [Hooker Austin] Doolittle) and he had heard from Marseille and showed me a circular from the American Immigration Department dated 1923 saying that they had received information that I had left Russia for Copenhagen with a large sum of money for propaganda in America! Now I know why the Consul at Marseille was so changed + cold when I went to him a second time after I had written to the I. O. in 1929 asking for data concerning my first entry in the U.S. The Imm. officials replied that the documents were sent to the Consul at Marseille. When I did come to Tanger, I gave him—The Consul at M.—my address, but was never notified about my quota number. I suppose the information just turned him against me as it did the French authority at Rabat + Fez. And all because of those dirty British bastards working respectably in the dark. I wish the Consul at Marseille had showed me the letter. Would you believe I was shadowed in Berlin in 1920? Letters sent to friends in Paris were missent to London + there was a silly forged letter over my signature in the London Times headed: ["]A Subtle Propagandist!"[1]

Anyway the Consul here has been very nice and willing to give me a chance. He showed me your letter to [Donald Fairchild] Bigelow and laughing said that though it was splendid you were no recommendation to get me back to America. He knows all about you. Hates [Grigory Yevseyevich] Zinoviev—likes Trotsky (as a man of action). It's really nice to talk to him—he is better than I thought at first, well-informed[,] knows Russian perfectly and about six other languages—typical American who likes people who "start in a from a scratch and succeed." But I'll remain pessimistic until I get that visa and land in N.Y. For I know that a cat plays with the mouse before he kills it.

In the meantime—I'll be working on the Moroccan sketches—which may find a market when I land with a little publicity. Simple sketches of the common people. Don't need any concentration—just like writing poetry . . . "Home To Harlem" + "Banjo" were written without plan. [Clifton] Fadiman[2] thinks "Savage Loving" not "thought out" when it is really my first straight planned story—It was written before "Banana Bottom." Conclusion!

Thanks for Everything. Don't be mad about my note to Eliena. I was in such a case. I must hurry to get the mail boat.

Claude

MEP ALS

1. This letter, written by another, Australian Claude McKay, was about the reception of the Australian cricket team. "Cricketers All: 'A Subtle Propagandist,'" *Times,* 1 May 1920, 12.

2. Clifton Fadiman, a reader for Simon & Schuster, read the manuscript at the request of Eastman and dismissed McKay's novel manuscript as "sex hash," and the text (later published as *Romance in Marseille*) went unpublished until 2020.

To Langston Hughes

12 December [1933]

Tangier, Morocco

Dear Langston:

Just got your circular letter last night. I have none of my original mms. in hand. Home To Harlem is somewhere in one of my boxes in France and the others I destroyed because they were too much extra baggage to cart around. I could write out a poem and sign it, but I suppose you want something looking originally ancient. But it is to[o] late now! I didn't see any references to the boys in the newspapers, but I don['']t read regularly.

Got your letter from Siberia, was it? Answered through Knopf, Read of your being expelled from Japon.

I am plumb broke, my last book had no sale at all, and I am trying to get back to America. Difficult, as I am on the black list as Communist propagandist and not a citizen. What does it matter though I insist I have never been a paid propagandist and out of touch with the whole Communist movement for the last ten years! The slimy international secret agents have to have victims to justify their pay and existence. Guess they want to make me repent my visit to Russia, but that adventure was worth . . . The Trouble.

I have been too worried the last months to work and have only done a couple of Moorish tales which I hope to bring along if I can get my visa. In spite of the industrial stagnation, the U.S.A. seems more interesting than ever to visit since I left.

Was that Negro film ever made in Russia? And what are you doing? Greetings and Happy Holidays.

Sincerely
Claude

Found a batch of poems in the pocket of an old valise and am sending a little one, was written ten years ago.[1]

CMcK

LHP TLS

1. The postscript is handwritten.

To James Weldon Johnson

8 February 1934

Croton-on-Hudson, New York

Dear JWJ: Finally was able to obtain all the papers required and the American consul graciously gave me the visa. I went to Spain and skipped from Cadiz, arriving here on the 2nd.

I must thank you very sincerely for all you did to bring me over again. Maybe it was the best thing that I did settle down for a stay in Tangier, for I might never had had otherwise that police document that was required.

An American woman in Tangier showed a notice of your just published "Autobiography" of which I wish to congratulate you.

Of my plans I can say nothing yet. I am broke and it was by the kindness of well-wishers only that I was able to come over. As soon as I am rested up and get my bearings (everything is so enormously strange) I shall see what chances there are of getting a little living in some way.

My regards to Mrs Johnson and thanking you again[.]

Yours Faithfully
Claude McKay

JWJP TLS

CHRONOLOGY OF MCKAY'S PUBLISHED WORKS

1912 *Songs of Jamaica* (poems) and *Constab Ballads* (poems)

1920 *Spring in New Hampshire* (poems)

1922 *Harlem Shadows* (poems)

1923 *The Negroes in America* (essay) and *Trial by Lynching* (stories) published in Russian translation in the Soviet Union

1928 *Home to Harlem* (novel)

1929 *Banjo, A Story without a Plot* (novel)

1932 *Gingertown* (stories)

1933 *Banana Bottom* (novel)

1937 *A Long Way from Home* (travel book/memoir)

1940 *Harlem: Negro Metropolis* (nonfiction)

1979 *My Green Hills of Jamaica and Five Jamaican Short Stories* (memoir and stories), published posthumously

1990 *Harlem Glory: A Fragment of Aframerican Life* (novel), published posthumously

2017 *Amiable with Big Teeth: A Novel of the Love Affair between the Communists and the Poor Black Sheep of Harlem* (novel), written ca. 1940–41, published posthumously

2020 *Romance in Marseille* (novel), written ca. 1929–33, published posthumously

GLOSSARY OF NAMES

Correspondents are listed in ***bold.***

Abbott, Berenice (1898–1991)—American photographer who photographed literary and artistic luminaries in 1920s Paris

Allen, Ruth (1895–1975)—American friend of McKay and Josephine Herbst; former director of the Cincinnati Art Theater, she attempted to found the Negro Art Theater in Paris

Anderson, Sherwood (1876–1941)—American writer of *Winesburg, Ohio* (1919) and *Dark Laughter* (1925)

Arens, Egmont (1887–1966)—American editor of the *New Masses* and co-owner of the Washington Square Bookshop

Arlen, Michael (Dikran Sarkis Kouyoumdjian, 1895–1956)—Armenian-British author

Ashleigh, Charles (1888–1974)—English communist and labor activist who was an organizer for the Industrial Workers of the World; he was romantically linked to McKay

Barbusse, Henri (1873–1935)—French author and political activist

Beach, Sylvia (1887–1962)—American expatriate owner of the Paris bookstore Shakespeare & Company and publisher of the first edition of Joyce's *Ulysses* (1922)

Bell, William Service (1886–1980)—African American veteran of World War I, NAACP official, singer, and actor (as "Service Bell," he appeared in Orson Welles's Harlem production of *Macbeth*)

Bennett, Gwendolyn (1902–1981)—African American artist and writer, she contributed the "Ebony Flute" column to the Harlem Renaissance journal *Opportunity*

Bennett, Josephine "Jo" (1880–1960)—American feminist activist and patron of American artists in Paris, including Harold Stearns; she was the wife of M. Tuscan Bennett, the executive secretary of Brookwood Labor College

Bernhard, Andrew (1895?–1982)—American editor who worked on the Paris edition of the *Chicago Tribune* in the 1920s

Bigelow, Donald Fairchild (1896–1979)—U.S. Consul, Tangier, in 1932

Block, Harry C.—American editor at Alfred A. Knopf who rejected McKay's *Color Scheme*

Boissevain, Charlotte Ives (née Danziger, 1886–1976)—American thespian; sister-in-law of Eugen Boissevain

Boissevain, Eugen Jan (1880–1949)—Dutch businessman; husband of Edna St. Vincent Millay

Boni, Albert (1892–1981)—American cofounder of the publishers Boni & Liveright and Albert & Charles Boni

Boni, Charles (1894–1969)—American cofounder of the publisher Albert & Charles Boni

Booth, William (1829–1912)—English founder of the Salvation Army

Bowen, Stella (Esther Gwendolyn Bowen, 1893–1947)—Australian artist who lived in Montparnasse during the 1920s

Bradley ("Mrs. Bradley"), Jenny Serruys (1886–1983)—Belgian literary agent; wife of William A. Bradley

Bradley, William A. (1878–1939)—American, Paris-based literary agent for many modernist writers; he was McKay's agent from 1927 to 1931

Braithwaite, William Stanley (1878–1962)—African American poet and critic, he was a literary columnist and reviewer for the *Boston Evening Transcript*

Braley, Berton (1882–1966)—American poet

Broun, Heywood (1888–1939)—American journalist and member of the Algonquin Round Table

Bruce, Roscoe Conkling (1879–1950)—African American educator and follower of Booker T. Washington

Bryant, Louise (1885–1936)—American feminist, political activist, and journalist who covered the Russian Revolution. She was married to John Reed until his death in 1920, and later married to William C. Bullitt, Jr.

Bullitt, Louise—*see* Bryant, Louise

Bullitt, William C., Jr. (1891–1967)—American diplomat and journalist, he was the first U.S. ambassador to the USSR; husband of Louise Bryant

Campbell, Grace (1883–1943)—African American activist and communist, she was the first African American woman to run for office in the state of New York

Carco, Francis (François Carcopino-Tusoli, 1886–1958)—French novelist of urban life, including the memoir *De Montmartre au Quartier latin* (1927), called the "*romancier des apaches*"

Carr, Wilbur John (1870–1942)—United States Assistant Secretary of State from 1924 to 1937

Cartier-Bresson, Henri (1908–2004)—French photographer who was influenced by the Surrealist movement and a pioneer of street photography

Cendrars, Blaise (Frédéric-Louis Sauser, 1887–1961)—Swiss-French modernist novelist and poet

Chaplin, Charlie (1889–1977)—English filmmaker and celebrated Hollywood comedian

Chukowsky, Korney (1882–1969)—Russian poet of children's verse

Coalfleet, Pierre (pseudonym of Frank Cyril Shaw Davidson, 1893–1960)—Canadian-British author who eventually served as co-editor of the *Forum;* he had a romantic relationship with American artist Marsden Hartley

Cocteau, Jean (1889–1963)—French author, set designer, filmmaker, visual artist, and critic

Conradi, Maurice (1896–1947)—Russian-born Swiss partisan of the White Army who assassinated a Soviet diplomat in 1923

Crowder, Henry (1890–1955)—African American jazz musician known for his relationship with shipping heiress Nancy Cunard

Cullen, Countee (1903–1946)—African American Harlem Renaissance poet and editor

Cunard, Nancy (1896–1965)—British shipping heiress and activist involved in modernist circles, she edited and published *Negro: An Anthology* in 1934

Davis, Anna Norwood (1873–1943)—American leftist activist and secretary of the Garland Fund

Dede (or Dédé), Nelson Simeon (dates unknown)—Nigerian merchant sailor who, due to mistreatment while confined for stowing away on a steamer bound for New York City, became a double amputee and the source of two of McKay's fictional characters: Taloufa in *Banjo* and Lafala in *Romance in Marseille*

DeLisser, H. G. (1878–1944)—Jamaican journalist and author

Dell, Floyd (1887–1969)—American writer and co-editor of the *Masses* and the *Liberator*

Dill, Augustus Granville (1882–1956)—African American business manager for the *Crisis*

Dixon, Thomas (1864–1946)—American author of the racist novels *The Leopard's Spots* (1902) and *The Clansman* (1905), which were inspirations for the film *Birth of a Nation* (1915)

Doolittle, Hooker Austin (1889–1966)—American diplomat and secretary of the U.S. Legation in Tangier in 1933

Dos Passos, John (1896–1970)—American novelist who wrote *Manhattan Transfer* (1925), an inspiration for *Home to Harlem*

Douglass, George Norman (1868–1952)—British author

Dowson, Ernest (1867–1900)—English author of the Decadent movement

Du Bois, W. E. B. (1868–1963)—African American writer and sociologist, founder of the NAACP, and editor of the *Crisis*

Dunbar, Paul Laurence (1872–1906)—African American poet and novelist, known for dialect poetry

Eastman, Crystal (1881–1928)—American cofounder of the *Liberator* and ACLU; sister of Max Eastman

Eastman, Eliena Krylenko—*see* Krylenko, Eliena

Eastman, Max (1883–1969)—American writer and activist, he was the co-editor of the *Masses* and the *Liberator*

Edward, Eli—one of Claude McKay's pen names

Engdahl, J. Louis (1884–1932)—American socialist journalist

Evans, Montgomery (1901–1954)—American son of a wealthy Pennsylvania banker, he was involved—as a writer and editor—with a number of modernist figures and horror writers like Arthur Machen and Lord Dunsany

Farrar, John (1896–1974)—American editor of the *Bookman,* he was the founder of the publishing companies Farrar & Rinehart and Farrar, Straus & Giroux

Fauset, Jessie (1882–1961)—African American novelist and literary editor of the *Crisis* during the 1920s

Fels, Florent (1891–1977)—French journalist and photographer

Ferris, William H. (1874–1941)—African American author, minister, and scholar

Fisher, Rudolph (1897–1934)—African American physician and writer

Ford, Ford Madox (Joseph Leopold Ford Hermann Madox Hueffer, 1873–1939)—English author and editor of the *Transatlantic Review*

Frank, Waldo (1889–1967)—American author and radical activist

Franklin, Sidney (1903–1976)—Jewish-American bullfighter

Freeman, Joseph (1897–1965)—American writer and editorial staff member of the *Liberator*

Friedmann, Georges (1902–1977)—French communist, novelist, philosopher, and sociologist, he wrote the introduction to the French translation of *Banjo*

Frost, Wesley (1884–1968)—American consul general in Marseille from 1924 to 1928

Fuller, Walter (1881–1927)—English editor and peace activist; husband of Crystal Eastman

Garvey, Marcus (1887–1940)—Jamaican activist and founder of the Universal Negro Improvement Association

Gibbon, Edward (1737–1794)—English historian

Gibson, Lydia (1891–1964)—American leftist illustrator associated with the *Masses*

Gilpin, Charles (1878–1930)—African American actor famous for starring in the premiere of Eugene O'Neill's *The Emperor Jones* in 1920

Glassco, John "Buffy" (1909–1981)—Canadian expatriate, partner of Graeme Taylor, and author of *Memoirs of Montparnasse* (1970), which identifies McKay as a short-term lover

Glyn, Elinor (1864–1943)—British novelist and scriptwriter

Gold, Michael (1894–1967)—Jewish-American communist activist, writer, co-editor of the *Liberator*, and founding editor of the *New Masses*

Grainger, Percy (1882–1961)—Australian composer, he was a champion of "Nordic" music and culture

Green, Paul Eliot (1894–1981)—American playwright

Grosz, George (1893–1959)—German Dadaist and New Objectivist artist

Guest, Edgar A. (1862–1939)—British-American poet

Hale, Ruth (1887–1934)—American journalist and feminist activist; wife of Heywood Broun

Hamilton, Jamie (1900–1988)—Scotch-American Harper & Brothers representative in London, he was later founder of the British publishing house Hamish Hamilton

Hamnett, Nina (1890–1956)—Welsh artist and writer known as the Queen of Bohemia

Hare, Betty (1898–1981)—Welsh thespian

Harris, Frank (1855–1931)—Irish-American writer and editor of the U.S. edition of *Pearson's Magazine*

Harrison, Hubert H. (1883–1927)—West Indian-American writer and activist, he was the editor of Marcus Garvey's *Negro World*

Hartley, Marsden (1877–1943)—American modernist painter

Haynes, George Edmund (1880–1960)—African American sociology scholar and civil servant

Heartfield, John (Helmut Herzfeld, 1891–1968)—German visual artist known for anti-fascist book jackets

Hemingway, Ernest (1899–1961)—American novelist and short story writer, he wrote *The Sun Also Rises*, an inspiration for *Home to Harlem*

Henderson, Francis Riddell (1860–1931)—Scotch owner of The Bomb Shop, a radical bookstore in the West End of London

Herbst, Josephine (1892–1967)—American journalist and author of proletarian novels

Herrmann, John (1900–1959)—American author; husband of Josephine Herbst from 1926 to 1940

Hope, Rhonda—one of Claude McKay's pen names

Howe, Marie Jenney (1870–1934)—American feminist

Hughes, Langston (1901–1967)—African American poet, dramatist, and journalist

Hurst, Fanny (1889–1968)—American novelist and progressive

Hyde, Jessie (dates unknown)—professional typist in Paris

Ingram, Rex (1892–1950)—Irish-born Hollywood film director, whose film *The Four Horsemen of the Apocalypse* (1921) made Rudolph Valentino a star. Ingram relocated his production company to the South of France, where he filmed *Mare Nostrum* (1926), *The Magician* (1926), and *The Garden of Allah* (1927).

Istrati, Panait (1884–1935)—Romanian author

Ivy, James (1901–1974)—African American educator and journalist and contributor to the *Crisis*

Jackman, Harold (1901–1961)—African American, London-born queer Black educator and member of Harlem Renaissance circles

Jekyll, Walter (1849–1929)—English collector of Jamaican songs and stories

Johnson, Charles S. (1893–1956)—African American editor-in-chief of *Opportunity* magazine

Johnson, James Weldon (1871–1938)—African American writer, civil rights activist, and NAACP leader

Katayama, Sen (1859–1933)—Japanese communist and original member of the American Communist Party

Kirchwey, Mary Frederika "Freda" (1893–1976)—American journalist, editor, and publisher

Knopf, Alfred A. (1892–1984)—American publisher of major American and European authors

Krylenko, Eliena (1895–1956)—Russian American painter, dancer, and poet; wife of Max Eastman

Labonne, Eirik (1888–1971)—French diplomat who served in Mexico, Spain, and Morocco

Lachman, Harry (1886–1975)—American painter who became a production manager for Rex Ingram's film studio in the South of France

Larsen Imes, Nella (1891–1964)—African American novelist and author of Harlem Renaissance classics *Quicksand* (1928) and *Passing* (1929)

Levinson, André (1887–1933)—Russian-born French literature and dance critic

Lewis, Sinclair (1885–1951)—American author of novels like *Main Street* (1920) and *Babbitt* (1922)

Lindsay, Vachel (1879–1931)—American poet, he wrote "The Congo," published in *Poetry* magazine in 1914

Liveright, Horace (1884–1933)—American cofounder of the publishing company Boni & Liveright

Locke, Alain (1885–1954)—African American writer, philosopher, educator, and editor of *The New Negro* (1925)

Lodge, Henry Cabot (1850–1924)—American Republican politician

Louverture, Toussaint (1743–1803)—Haitian leader of a slave insurrection from 1791 to 1804

Loving, [Edward] Pierre (1893–1950)—American playwright, actor, journalist, editor, and translator

MacDermot, Thomas Henry (1870–1933)—Jamaican poet, novelist, and editor

Malone, Dudley Field (1882–1950)—American politician, liberal activist, and actor

Maran, René (1887–1960)—Martinican-French poet and novelist, author of *Bataoula: A True Black Novel* (1921)

Markoff, Nancy (dates unknown)—American author and clerical worker for the *Liberator* and *Daily Worker*

Marshak, Samuil Yakovlevich (1887–1964)—Soviet Belarusian-Jewish translator and poet

Mason, Charlotte Osgood (1854–1946)—American socialite and patron of the Harlem Renaissance

Mason, Walt (1862–1939)—Canadian-American journalist

McKenna, Pamela Jekyll (1889–1943)—English peer and poet; niece of Walter Jekyll; married to banker and liberal politician Reginald McKenna

Mencken, H. L. (1880–1956)—American critic and tastemaker, he was editor of the *Smart Set* and the *American Mercury*

Meyerhold, Vesvolod (1874–1940)—Soviet theater director, producer, and actor

Millay, Edna St. Vincent (1892–1950)—American poet, she won the 1923 Pulitzer Prize for Poetry

Mills, Florence (1896–1927)—African American singer and dancer, she was part of the original cast of *Shuffle Along* (1921)

Minor, Robert "Bob" (1884–1952)—American leftist illustrator associated with the *Masses*

Moe, Henry Allen (1894–1975)—American philanthropist, he administered the Guggenheim Awards from 1924 to 1967

Montherlant, Henry Marie Joseph Frédéric Expedite Millon de (1895–1972)—French author and reactionary

Moore, Richard B. (1893–1978)—Afro-Caribbean, Barbados-born activist and socialist in Harlem

Moore, Thomas Sturge (1870–1944)—British poet, author, and artist

Morand, Paul (1888–1976)—French author, translated by Ezra Pound

Naidu, Sarojini (1879–1949)—Indian political activist and poet

Nardal, Paulette (1896–1985)—Martinican writer and early figure in the Négritude movement

Ogden, C. K. (1889–1957)—English linguist and philosopher, he edited the *Cambridge Magazine*

Okhremenko, P. F. (dates unknown)—Russian translator of McKay's work

Olivier, Daphne (1889–1950)—daughter of Sidney Olivier, in the orbit of the Bloomsbury Group, she worked for C. K. Ogden on the *Cambridge Magazine*

Olivier, Sidney (1859–1943)—British Fabianist governor of Jamaica

Opfer, Ivan (1897–1980)—Danish illustrator, he was a contributor to the *Liberator* and friend of Montgomery Evans

Oppenheim, James (1882–1932)—American poet, he was the founder and editor of the literary magazine the *Seven Arts*

Ovington, Mary White (1865–1961)—American suffragist and journalist, she cofounded the NAACP

Owen, Chandler (1889–1967)—African American socialist, writer, and cofounder of the *Messenger*

Pankhurst, Estelle Sylvia (1882–1960)—British feminist and socialist activist, writer, and publisher

Petroff, Peter (1884–1947)—Russian activist and journalist

Pickens, William (1881–1954)—African American writer, journalist, and prominent member of the NAACP

Primo de Rivera y Orbaneja, Miguel (1870–1930)—Spanish dictator, in office from 1923 to 1930

Randolph, A. Philip (1889–1979)—African American labor leader and cofounder of the *Messenger*

Randolph ("Mrs. Randolph"), Lucille Campbell Green (1883–1963)—African American businesswoman and activist; wife of A. Philip Randolph

Rappaport, Charles (probably "old Rappaport," 1865–1941)—Jewish Russian-French communist politician, journalist, and writer

Rappaport, Fanny (dates unknown)—French physician and communist; daughter of Charles Rappaport and wife of Pierre Vogein

Ray, Man (Emmanuel Radnitzky, 1890–1976)—American, Paris-based Dadaist and Surrealist artist known principally for avant-garde photography

Reed, John "Jack" Silas (1887–1920)—American journalist and communist activist, he was the inspiration for the radical, independent John Reed Clubs (1929–35); second husband of Louise Bryant

Reiss, Winold (1886–1953)—German-born American artist and illustrator for *Survey Graphic* and *New Negro*

Richards, Grant (1872–1948)—British publisher and author

Richards, I. A. (1893–1979)—English literary critic and poet

Rieder, Frédéric (1873–1933)—French publisher (Éditions Rieder) of *Home to Harlem, Banjo,* and *Banana Bottom* in translation

Roberti, Jacques (dates unknown)—French author of *À la belle de nuit* (1932), translated by Samuel Putnam as *Without Sin* (1932)

Robeson ("Mrs. Robeson"), Eslanda (1895–1965)—African American anthropologist and activist; wife of Paul Robeson

Robeson, Paul (1898–1976)—African American singer, actor, and prominent communist activist

Robinson, Boardman (1876–1952)—Canadian-born American illustrator for the *Masses* and co-editor of the *Liberator*

Rodney, George Brydges (1718–1792)—British admiral and baron, he was commander-in-chief of the Jamaica Station in 1771

Roger, José (dates unknown)—Spanish banker

Rogers, Joel Augustus (1880–1966)—Jamaican-American journalist and historian

Rolland, Romain (1866–1944)—French dramatist, novelist, essayist, and mystic

Rose, Pauline (dates unknown)—American communist, journalist, and translator

Saxton, Eugene (1884–1943)—American editor and publisher at Harper & Brothers

Schomburg, Arturo Alfonso (1874–1938)—Puerto Rican–born Black historian and bibliophile

Seabrook, William Buehler (1884–1945)—American author and explorer

Sinclair, Upton Beall, Jr. (1878–1968)—American novelist and muckraker

Souvarine, Boris (1895–1984)—French communist, he was an opponent of Stalin and editor of the *Bulletin communiste*

Spingarn, Joel E. (1875–1939)—Jewish-American educator, critic, and civil rights activist

Sterne, Maurice (1877/78–1957)—Latvian-born, Jewish-American sculptor

Stoddard, Lothrop (1883–1950)—American racial pseudo-scientist, white supremacist, and author of *The Rising Tide of Color against White World-Supremacy* (1920)

Sumner, John S. (1876–1971)—American head of the New York Society for the Suppression of Vice

Swope, Herbert Bayard (1882–1958)—American editor of the *New York World*

Taggard, Genevieve (1894–1948)—American poet and contributor to the *Liberator*

Tannenbaum, S. A. (1874–1948)—American psychoanalyst and literary scholar

Taylor, Graeme (1907–1957)—Canadian expatriate; partner of John "Buffy" Glassco

Theis, Otto (1881–1966)—American writer, editor, and literary agent; connected to Nancy Cunard

Thompson, Anita (1901–1980)—African American model, dancer, and actress

Thurman, Wallace (1902–1934)—African American novelist and editor

Titus, Edward W. (1870–1952)—Polish-born American art collector and editor of the modernist magazine *This Quarter*

Tonny, Kristians (1907–1977)—Dutch Surrealist painter

Toomer, Jean (1894–1967)—African American author of *Cane* (1923)

Tracy, T(homas) F(rancis) (1899–1980)—American expatriate writer and World War I veteran who published in the modernist little magazines *New Review* and *Pagany* and later wrote for pulp magazines

Trotsky, Leon (Lev Davidovich Bronstein, 1879–1940)—Jewish-Russian Bolshevik revolutionary, Marxist-Leninist theorist, and Soviet Russia's People's Commissar for Military and Naval Affairs from 1918 to 1925; advocating Lenin's 1917 "oppressed nation" thesis, which identified "Negroes" and "Mulattoes" as potentially a critical popular front, Trotsky's vision of inclusive internationalism appealed to McKay during the early to mid-1920s

Trounstine, John (later John B. Turner, 1904–1964?)—American editor and McKay's literary agent after William A. Bradley

Tupper, Martin Farquhar (1810–1889)—English poet and novelist

Untermeyer, Louis (1885–1977)—American poet and critic

Van Doren, Carl (1885–1950)—American writer, critic, and literary editor of the *Century* magazine from 1922 to 1925

Van Vechten, Carl (1880–1964)—American writer, photographer, and patron of Harlem Renaissance figures; his controversial novel *Nigger Heaven* (1926) was a flashpoint for Black critics

Vogein, Pierre (dates unknown)—French communist, engineer, and husband of Fanny Rappaport

Walker, A'Lelia (Lelia McWilliams, 1885–1931)—African American businesswoman

Walrond, Eric (1898–1966)—Afro-Caribbean author and editor

Washington, Booker T. (1856–1915)—African American educator, author, and orator

Watts, John Hunter (1853–1923)—British socialist

Wells, Thomas Bucklin (1875–1944)—American editor of *Harper's* magazine from 1919 to 1931

Welti, Franz (1879–1934)—Swiss politician, he was one of the men who prosecuted Maurice Conradi

Wescott, Glenway (1901–1987)—American poet, novelist, and essayist

West, Rebecca (Cicily Isabel Fairfield, 1892–1983)—British novelist, journalist, and literary critic

White, Walter F. (1893–1955)—African American novelist, activist, and leader of the NAACP

Wilder, Thornton (1897–1975)—American playwright and novelist

Williams, Albert Rhys (1883–1962)—American memoirist of the Russian 1917 October Revolution

Wood, Charles W.—American contributor to the *Liberator*

Wood, James—English writer, he was the co-author (with C. K. Ogden and I. A. Richards) of *The Foundations of Aesthetics* (1922) and a contributor to Ogden's *Cambridge Quarterly*

Zinoviev, Grigory Yevseyevich (1883–1936)—Russian chairman of the Comintern from 1919 to 1926

ACKNOWLEDGMENTS

Letters in Exile took some ten years to conceive, compile, transcribe, edit, annotate, and get into print. Assembling and preparing nearly three hundred letters from over two dozen archives is a massive undertaking and would have been impossible without substantial help from friends and colleagues in many far-flung places. McKay was never afraid to ask friends for assistance (usually financial, but sometimes in the form of research); inspired by McKay's example, neither were we. As a result, we have many people to acknowledge.

We are grateful for the support of the Literary Estate for the Works of Claude McKay on this project. Letters that previously appeared in print appear here by the permission of the estate. Diana Lachatanere and Faith Childs were supportive of this collection from its earliest stages. Much thanks to our literary agent, Don Fehr, for helping us find the perfect home. On that subject, we thank Yale University Press, in particular Jessie Kindig, Senior Editor, Humanities, for the willingness to take on this project and accommodate our wishes.

The number of archivists and librarians who provided assistance along the way are too numerous to list, but—especially during the Covid lockdown—librarians at all the archives housing McKay's correspondence were exceedingly generous with their time and expertise in locating and digitizing material for our use. The staff at Yale's Beinecke Rare Book and Manuscript Library, which holds the largest collection of McKay material, was patient with repeated requests and re-requests. Melissa Barton at the Beinecke answered several minute queries along the way. We thank Emily Grover of Lilly Library, Indiana University, for going out of her way to make extensive pdfs. Head of Collections Cheryl Beredo, Schomburg Center for Research in Black Culture, was also very helpful, making the Claude McKay Letters and Manuscripts collection available for one final pass.

We found other McKay scholars, though unquestionably enormously busy, to be willing to share material and advice on the project. Brent Hayes Edwards provided copies of rare correspondence, including letters to Paulette Nardal and Henri-Cartier Bresson. Olga Panova provided transcriptions of McKay letters held in Russian archives. We traded notes with McKay biographer Ernest Mitchell and other McKay scholars, including Kate Baldwin and Anne Reynes-Delobel. Martha Patterson and Brett Seekford helped run down additional information on McKay's contacts.

We also would like to thank William J. Maxwell and Yvette Grant for their advice on developing the project.

Support for some of the archival travel was provided by an Edna Shaeffer Humanist Award from James Madison University. The College of Arts and Sciences, Ohio University, also provided funding to support research travel that helped complete this book.

Initial, rough transcriptions of McKay's correspondence were produced by James Madison University undergraduate students working as research assistants under Brooks Hefner. Nico Penaranda and Reilly Flynn spent two terms, and Corinna Ensley, Sydney Moon, Kara Myers, Jessica Park, and Jordan Zapp each spent one semester working on this project. We would like to extend a special thanks to these committed students!

Finally, we'd like to thank our respective partners, Bethany Hurley and Kim Holcomb, who graciously accompanied us on trips to McKay sites and patiently listened to innumerable stories of Claude's associates and misadventures.

INDEX